Bedard, Tony.
Green Lantern, new guardians.
Volume 1, The ring bearer

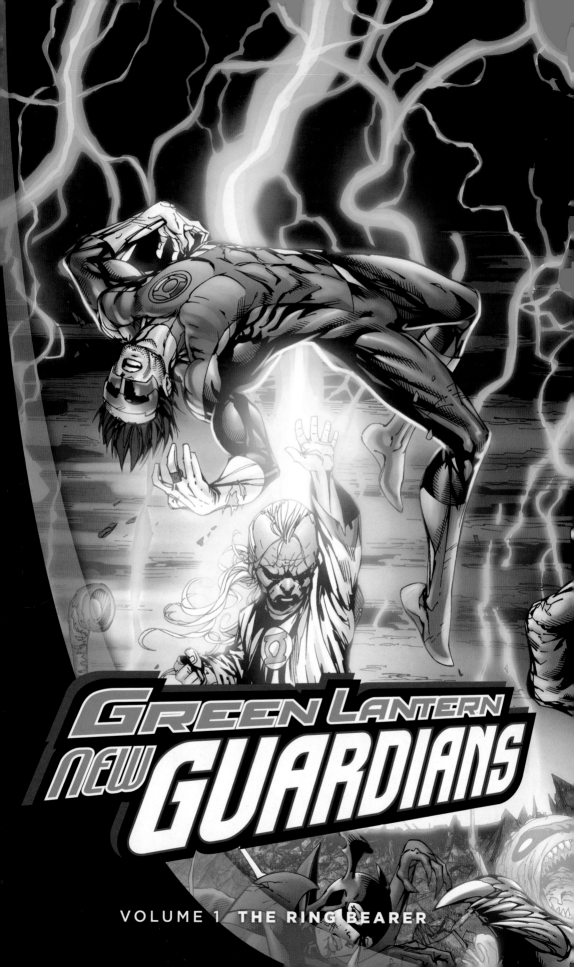

GREEN LANTERN NEW GUARDIANS

VOLUME 1 THE RING BEARER

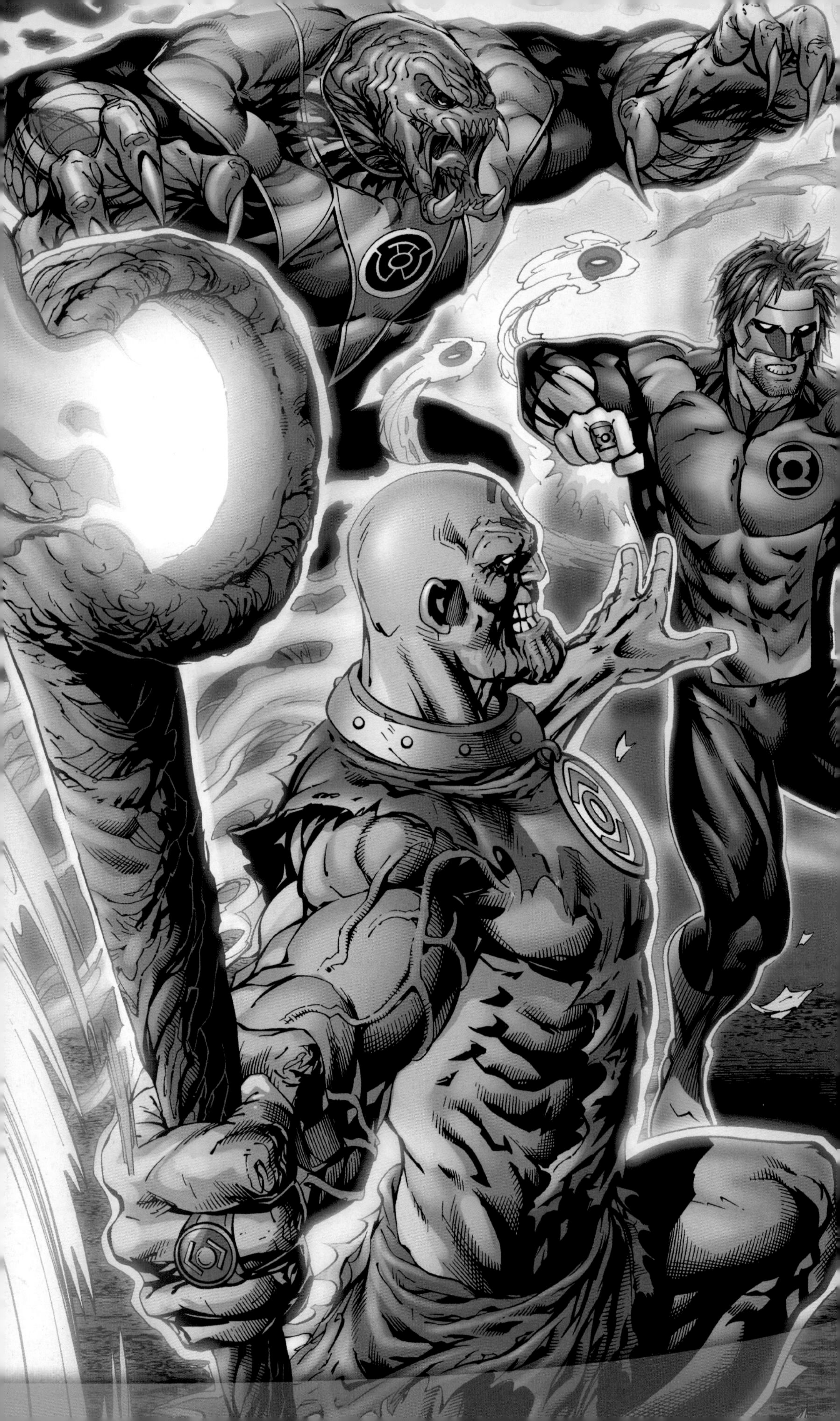

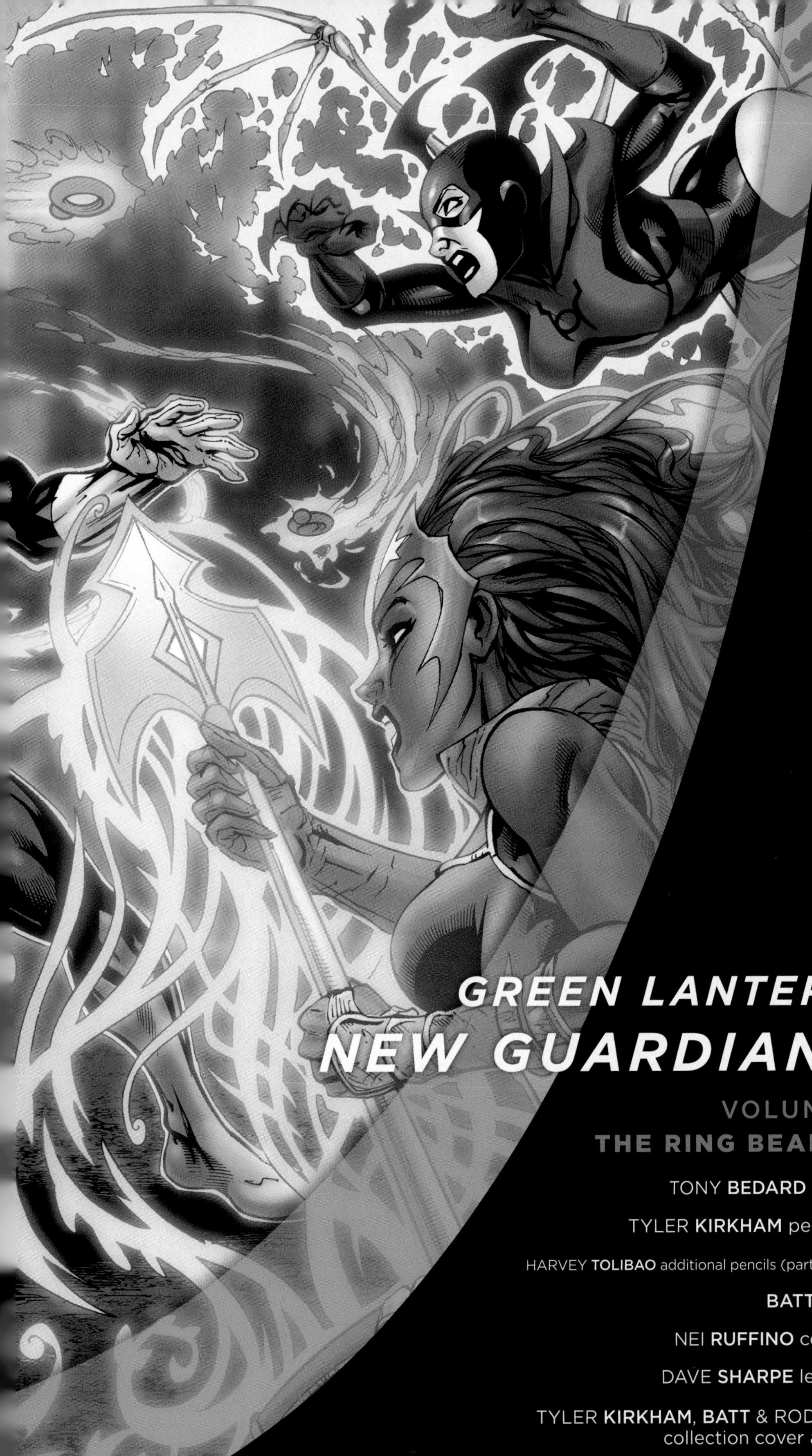

GREEN LANTERN
NEW GUARDIANS

VOLUME 1
THE RING BEARER

TONY **BEDARD** writer

TYLER **KIRKHAM** penciller

HARVEY **TOLIBAO** additional pencils (parts 2 & 3)

BATT inker

NEI **RUFFINO** colorist

DAVE **SHARPE** letterer

TYLER **KIRKHAM**, **BATT** & ROD **REIS**
collection cover artists

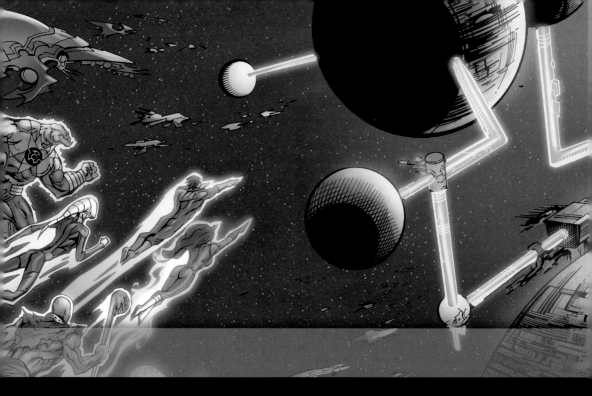

PAT McCALLUM Editor – Original Series SEAN MACKIEWICZ Assistant Editor – Original Series
PETER HAMBOUSSI Editor ROBBIN BROSTERMAN Design Director – Books
ROBBIE BIEDERMAN Publication Design

BOB HARRAS VP – Editor-in-Chief

DIANE NELSON President DAN DIDIO and JIM LEE Co-Publishers
GEOFF JOHNS Chief Creative Officer
JOHN ROOD Executive VP – Sales, Marketing and Business Development
AMY GENKINS Senior VP – Business and Legal Affairs NAIRI GARDINER Senior VP – Finance
JEFF BOISON VP – Publishing Operations MARK CHIARELLO VP – Art Direction and Design
JOHN CUNNINGHAM VP – Marketing TERRI CUNNINGHAM VP – Talent Relations and Services
ALISON GILL Senior VP – Manufacturing and Operations HANK KANALZ Senior VP – Digital
JAY KOGAN VP – Business and Legal Affairs, Publishing JACK MAHAN VP – Business Affairs, Talent
NICK NAPOLITANO VP – Manufacturing Administration SUE POHJA VP – Book Sales
COURTNEY SIMMONS Senior VP – Publicity BOB WAYNE Senior VP – Sales

DC Comics, 1700 Broadway, New York, NY 10019
A Warner Bros. Entertainment Company.
Printed by RR Donnelley, Salem, VA, USA. 9/14/12. First Printing.

HC ISBN: 978-1-4012-3707-3
SC ISBN: 978-1-4012-3708-0

SUSTAINABLE FORESTRY INITIATIVE

Certified Chain of Custody
At Least 25% Certified Forest Content
www.sfiprogram.org
SFI-01042
APPLIES TO TEXT STOCK ONLY

Library of Congress Cataloging-in-Publication Data

Bedard, Tony.
Green Lantern, new guardians. Volume 1, The ring bearer / Tony Bedard, Tyler Kirkham.
p. cm.
"Originally published in single magazine form in Green Lantern: New Guardians 1-7."
ISBN 978-1-4012-3707-3
1. Graphic novels. I. Kirkham, Tyler. II. Title. III. Title: New guardians. Volume 1. IV. Title: Ring bearer.
PN6728.G74B33 2012
741.5'973—dc23
2012022427

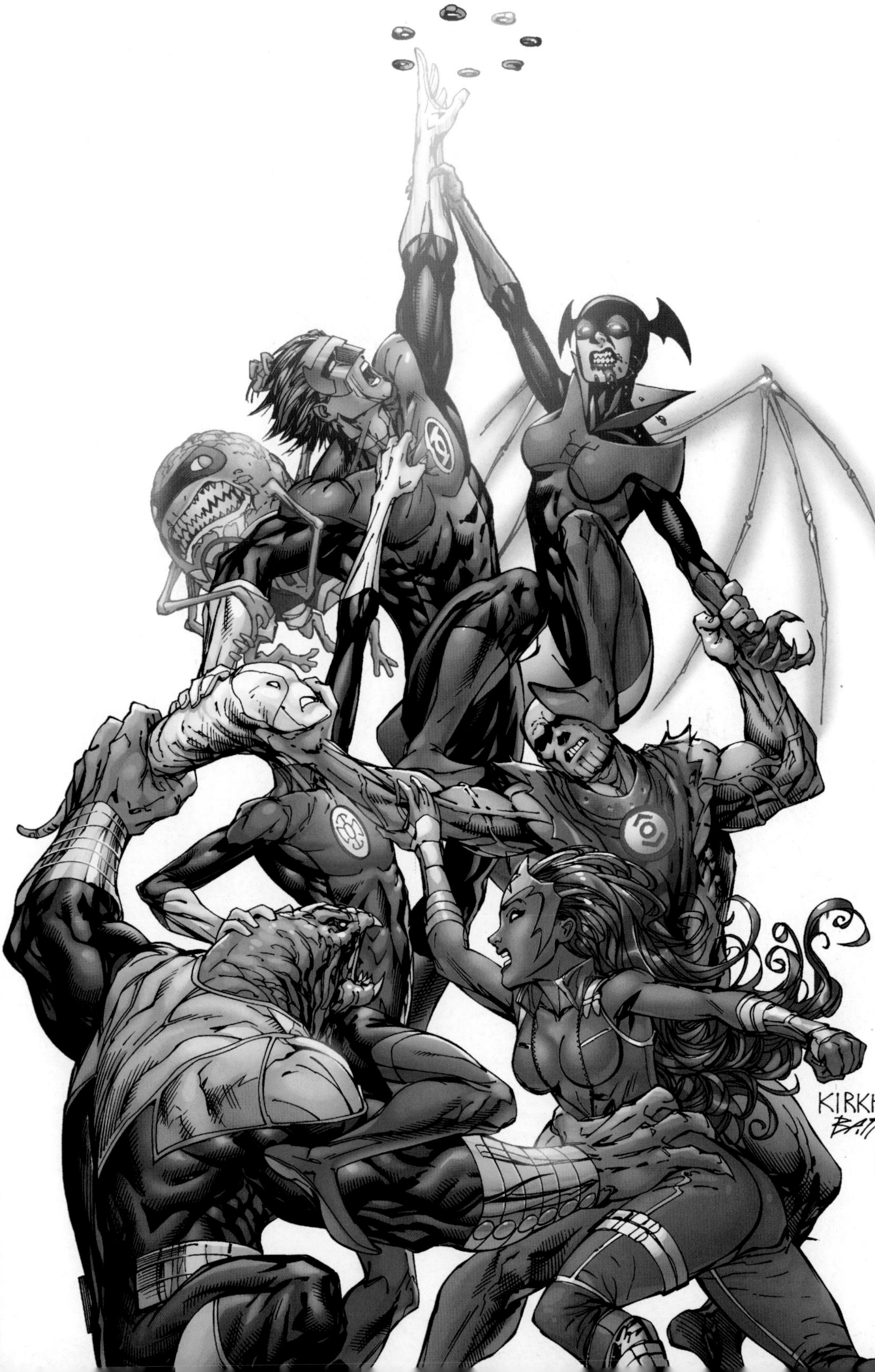
KIRKHAM
ROD REIS

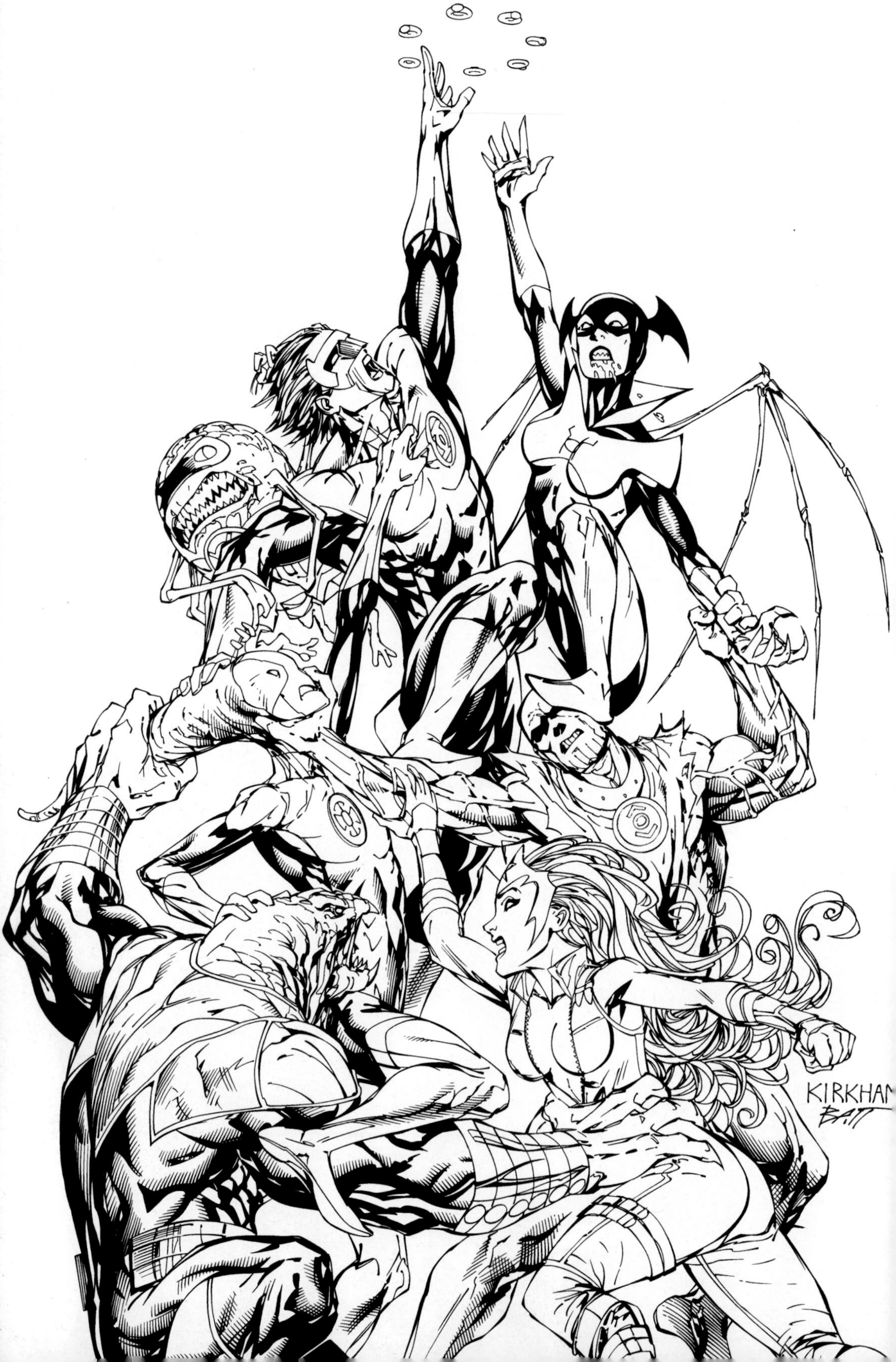

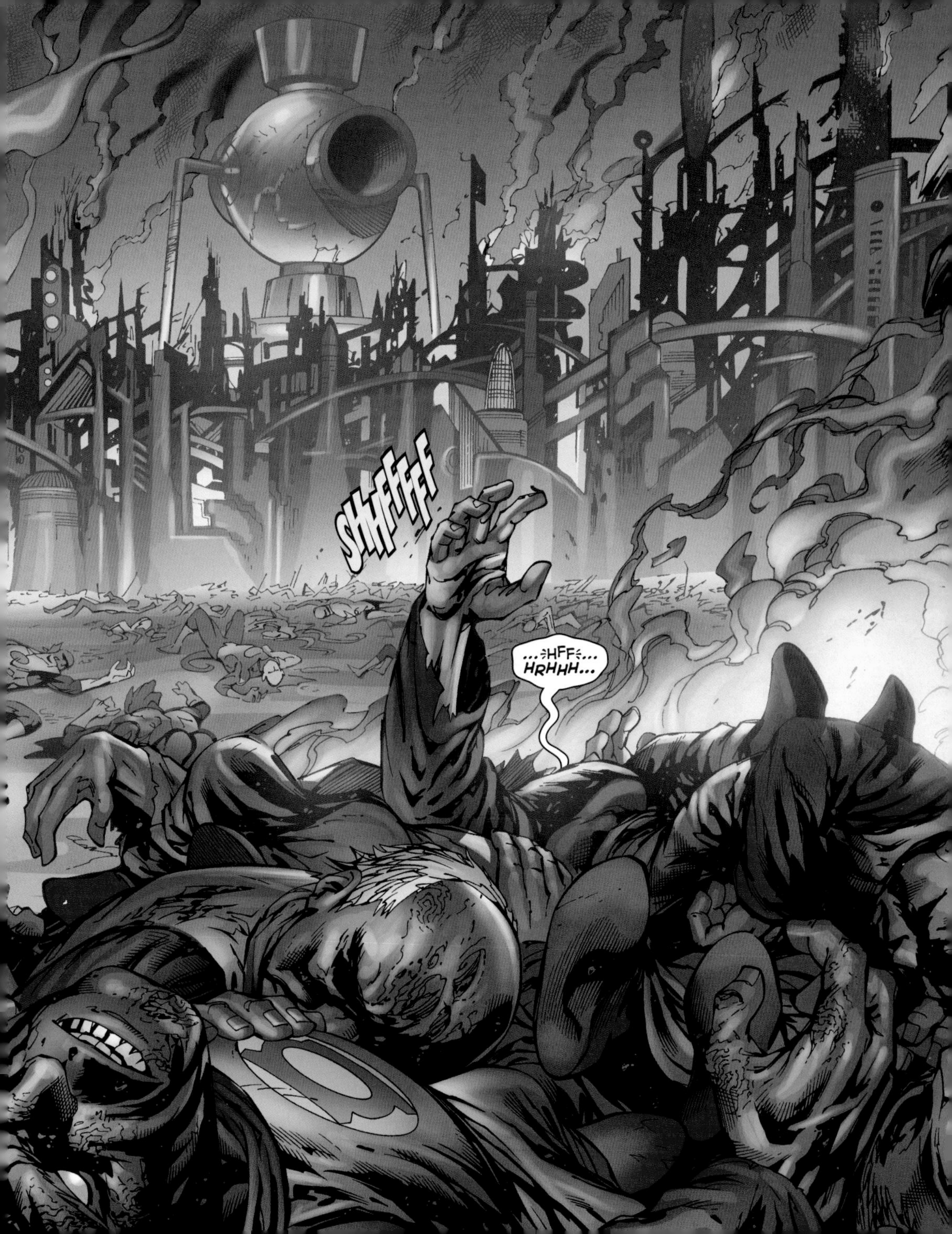
SHFFFFF
...HFF... HRHHH...

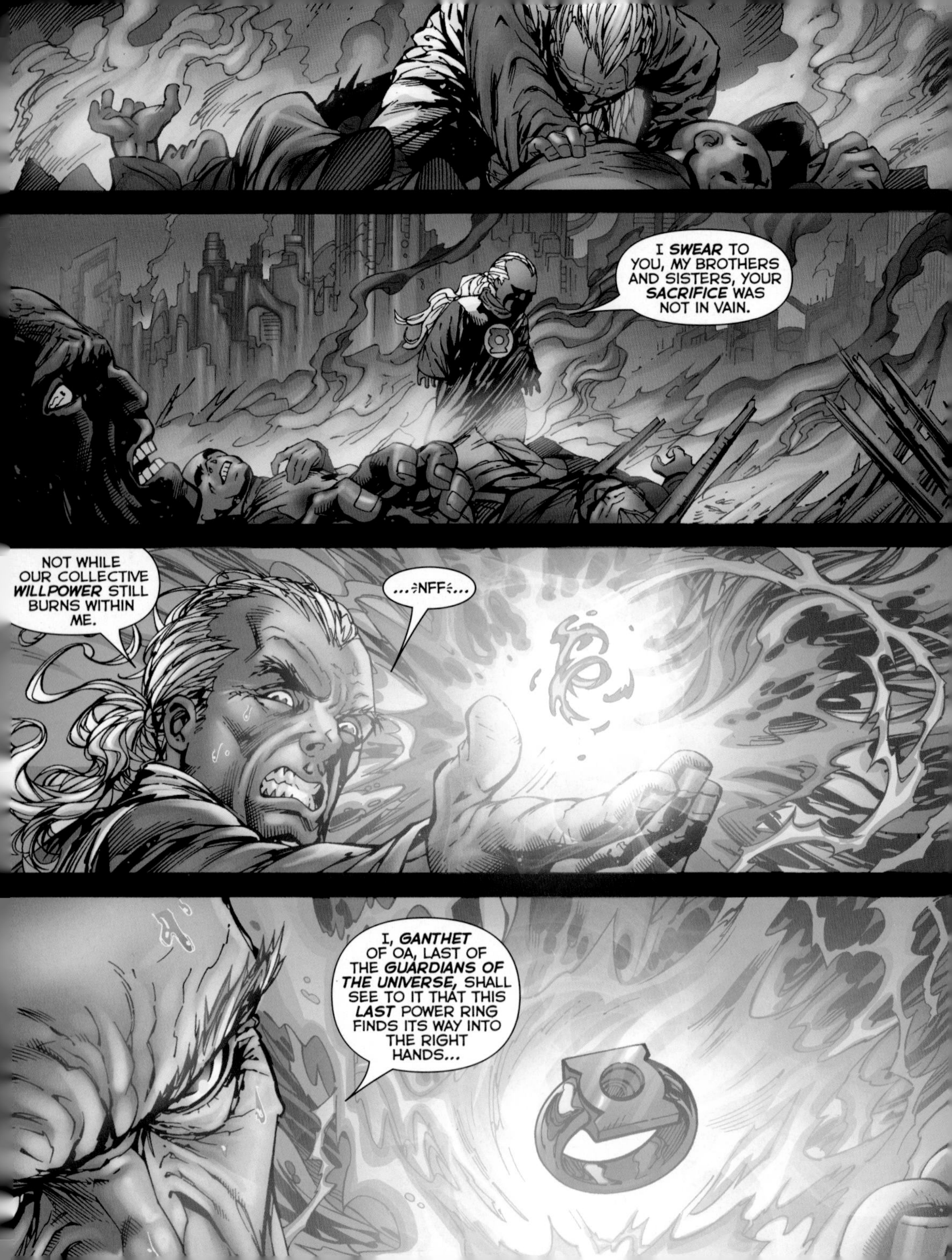
I SWEAR TO YOU, MY BROTHERS AND SISTERS, YOUR SACRIFICE WAS NOT IN VAIN.
NOT WHILE OUR COLLECTIVE WILLPOWER STILL BURNS WITHIN ME.
...NFF...
I, GANTHET OF OA, LAST OF THE GUARDIANS OF THE UNIVERSE, SHALL SEE TO IT THAT THIS LAST POWER RING FINDS ITS WAY INTO THE RIGHT HANDS...

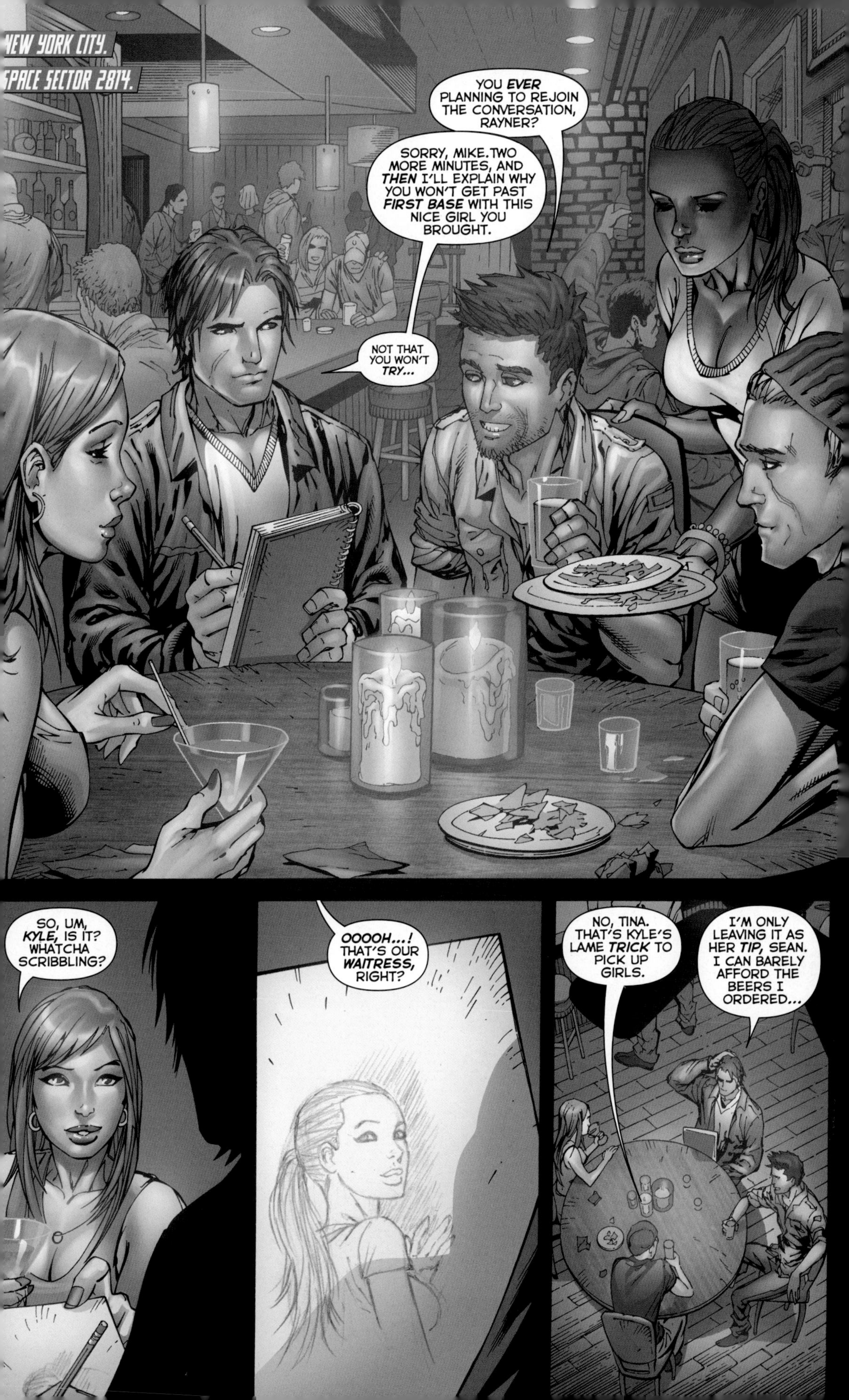
NEW YORK CITY.
SPACE SECTOR 2814.
YOU EVER PLANNING TO REJOIN THE CONVERSATION, RAYNER?
SORRY, MIKE. TWO MORE MINUTES, AND THEN I'LL EXPLAIN WHY YOU WON'T GET PAST FIRST BASE WITH THIS NICE GIRL YOU BROUGHT.
NOT THAT YOU WON'T TRY...
SO, UM, KYLE, IS IT? WHATCHA SCRIBBLING?
OOOOH...! THAT'S OUR WAITRESS, RIGHT?
NO, TINA. THAT'S KYLE'S LAME TRICK TO PICK UP GIRLS.
I'M ONLY LEAVING IT AS HER TIP, SEAN. I CAN BARELY AFFORD THE BEERS I ORDERED...

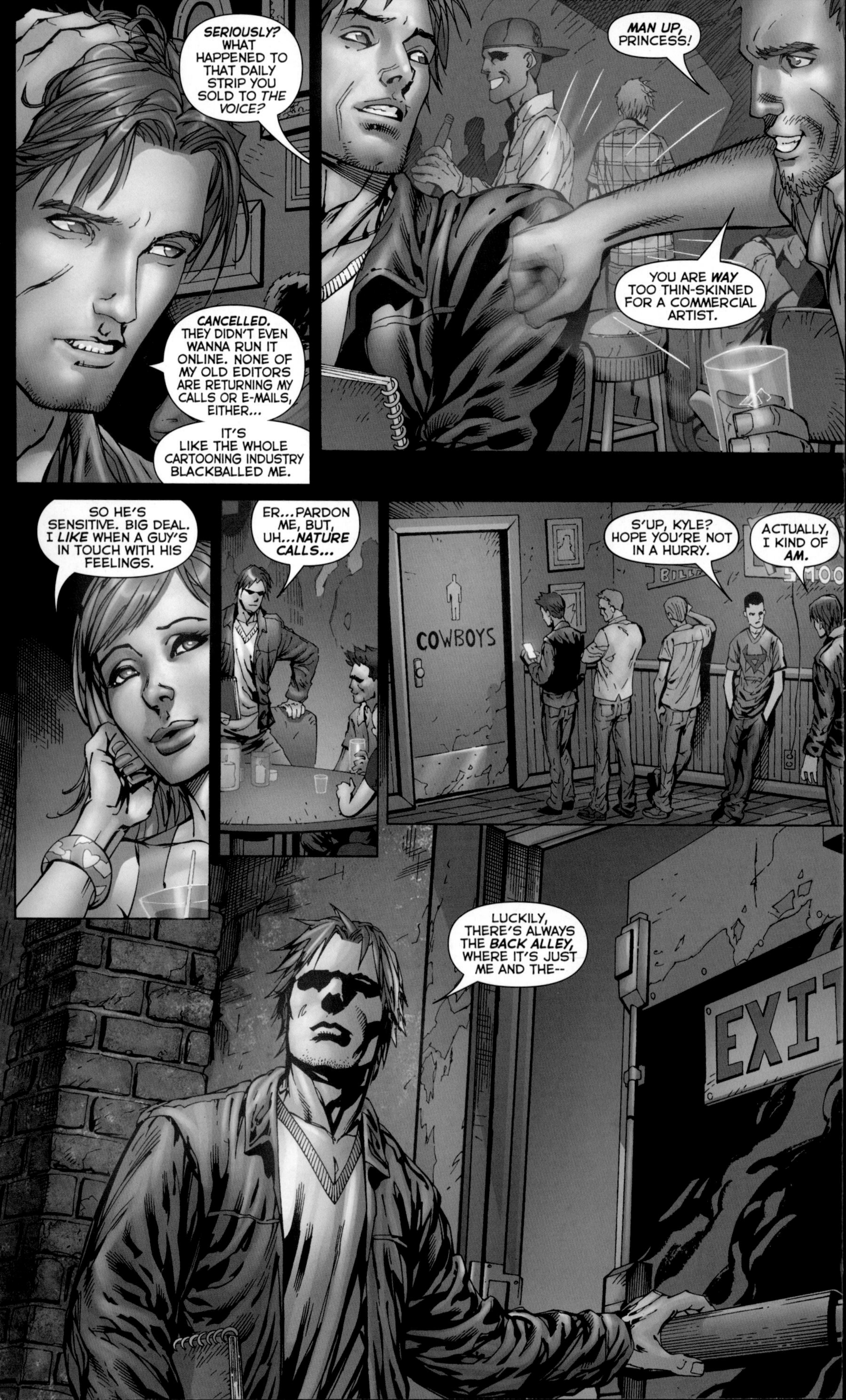
SERIOUSLY? WHAT HAPPENED TO THAT DAILY STRIP YOU SOLD TO THE VOICE?
CANCELLED. THEY DIDN'T EVEN WANNA RUN IT ONLINE. NONE OF MY OLD EDITORS ARE RETURNING MY CALLS OR E-MAILS, EITHER...
IT'S LIKE THE WHOLE CARTOONING INDUSTRY BLACKBALLED ME.
MAN UP, PRINCESS!
YOU ARE WAY TOO THIN-SKINNED FOR A COMMERCIAL ARTIST.
SO HE'S SENSITIVE. BIG DEAL. I LIKE WHEN A GUY'S IN TOUCH WITH HIS FEELINGS.
ER...PARDON ME, BUT, UH...NATURE CALLS...
COWBOYS
S'UP, KYLE? HOPE YOU'RE NOT IN A HURRY.
ACTUALLY, I KIND OF AM.
LUCKILY, THERE'S ALWAYS THE BACK ALLEY, WHERE IT'S JUST ME AND THE--
EXIT

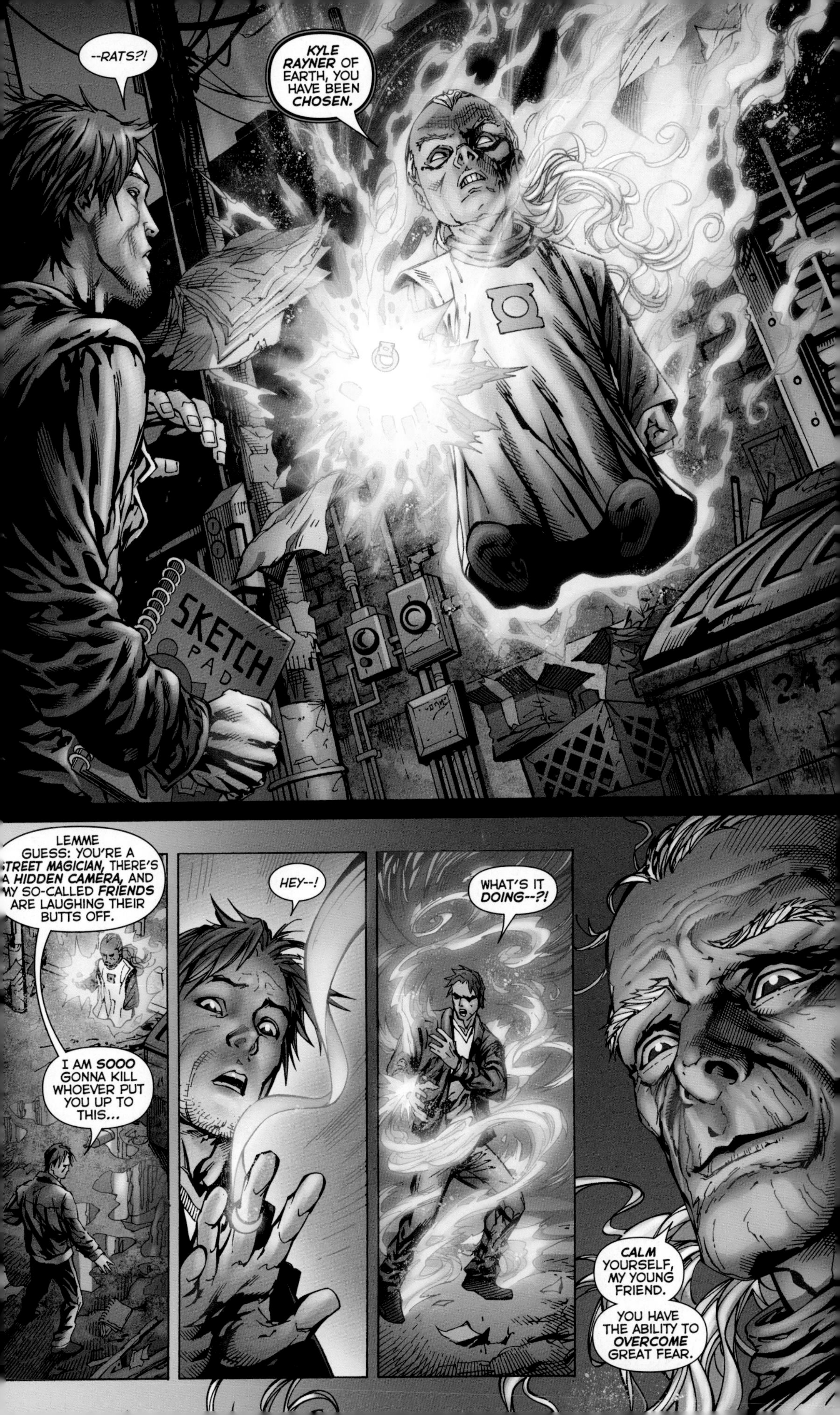
--RATS?!
KYLE RAYNER OF EARTH, YOU HAVE BEEN CHOSEN.
SKETCH PAD
LEMME GUESS: YOU'RE A STREET MAGICIAN, THERE'S A HIDDEN CAMERA, AND MY SO-CALLED FRIENDS ARE LAUGHING THEIR BUTTS OFF.
I AM SOOO GONNA KILL WHOEVER PUT YOU UP TO THIS...
HEY--!
WHAT'S IT DOING--?!
CALM YOURSELF, MY YOUNG FRIEND.
YOU HAVE THE ABILITY TO OVERCOME GREAT FEAR.

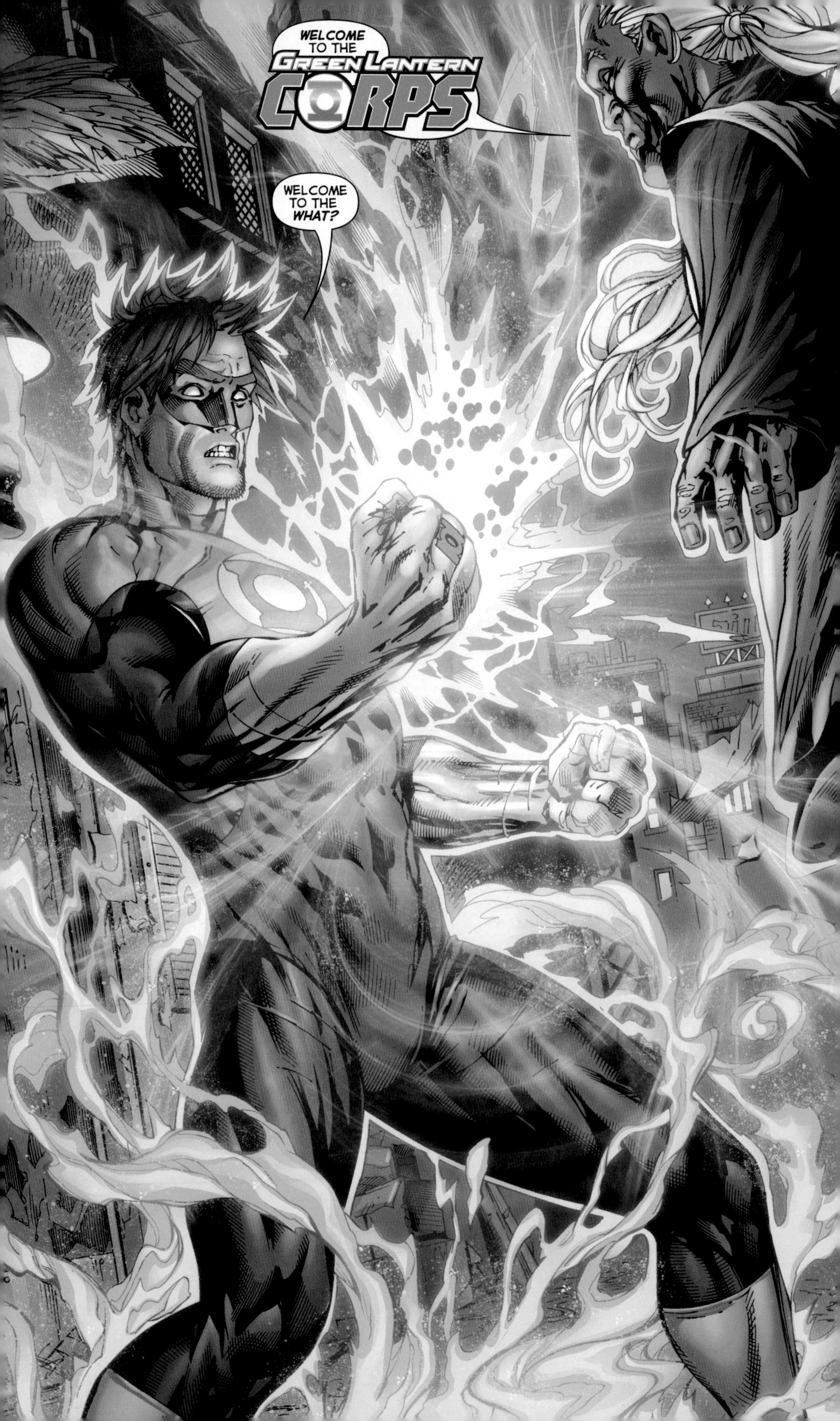
WELCOME TO THE GREEN LANTERN CORPS
WELCOME TO THE WHAT?

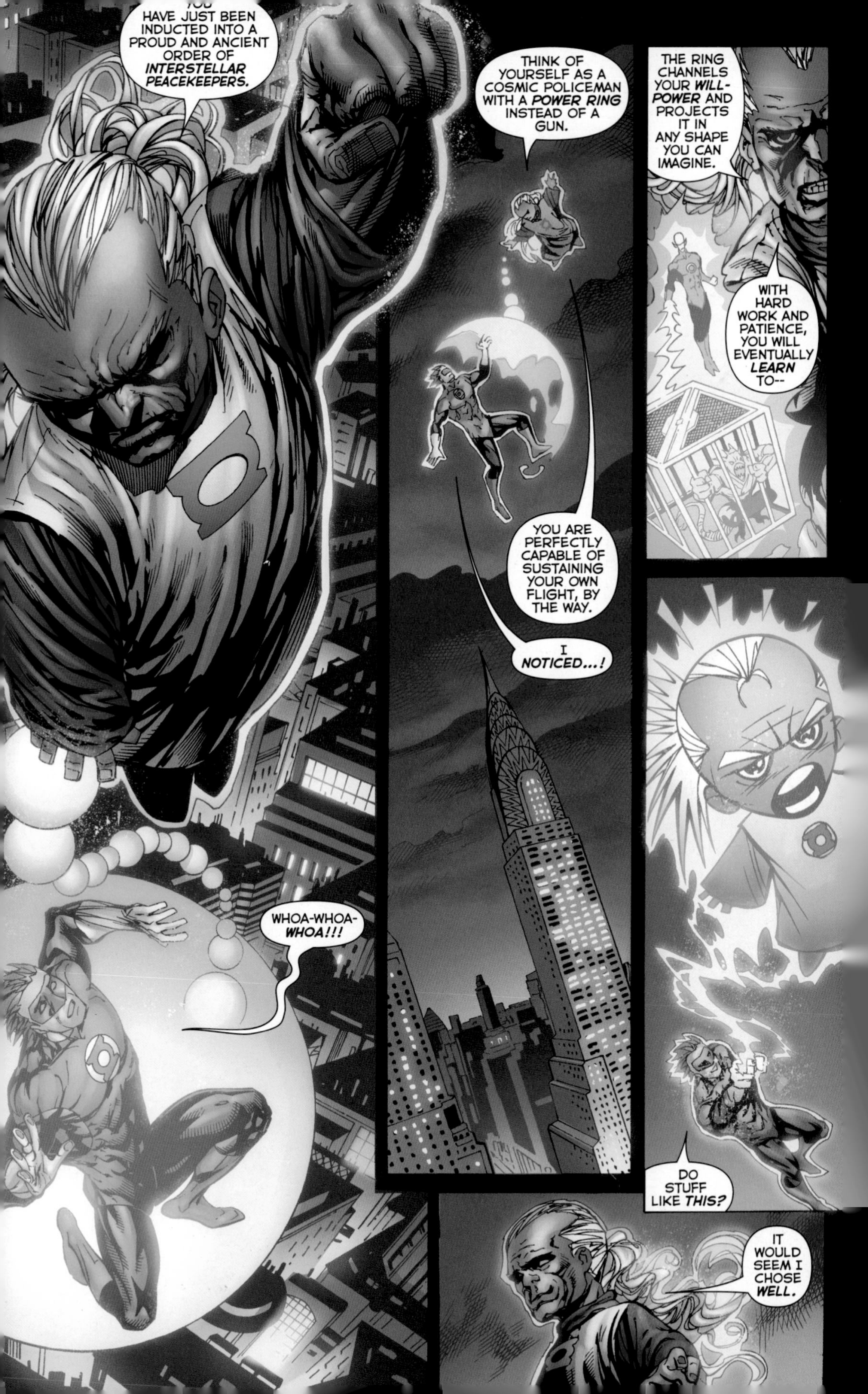
YOU HAVE JUST BEEN INDUCTED INTO A PROUD AND ANCIENT ORDER OF INTERSTELLAR PEACEKEEPERS.
WHOA-WHOA-WHOA!!!
THINK OF YOURSELF AS A COSMIC POLICEMAN WITH A POWER RING INSTEAD OF A GUN.
YOU ARE PERFECTLY CAPABLE OF SUSTAINING YOUR OWN FLIGHT, BY THE WAY.
I NOTICED...!
THE RING CHANNELS YOUR WILL-POWER AND PROJECTS IT IN ANY SHAPE YOU CAN IMAGINE.
WITH HARD WORK AND PATIENCE, YOU WILL EVENTUALLY LEARN TO--
DO STUFF LIKE THIS?
IT WOULD SEEM I CHOSE WELL.

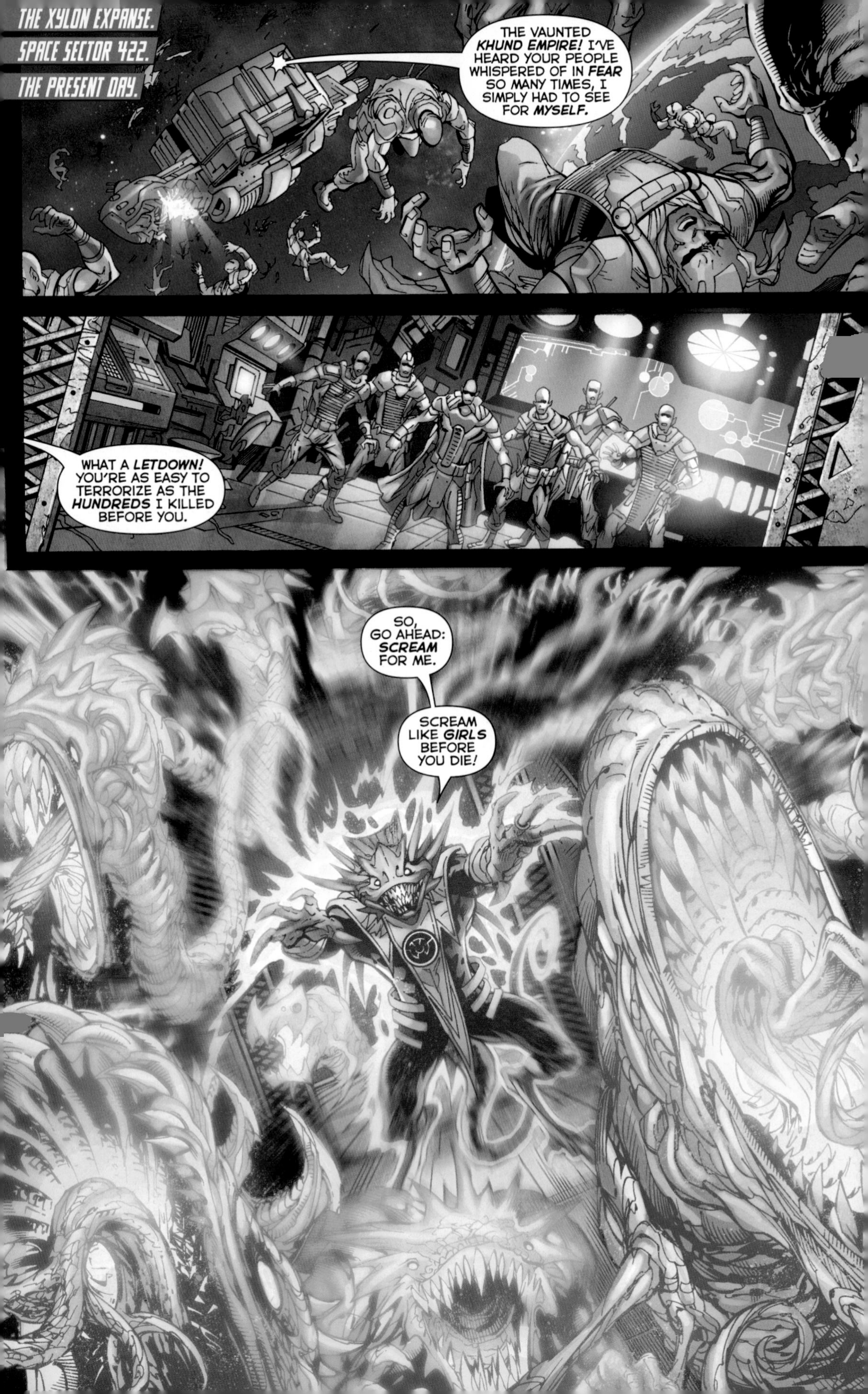

THE XYLON EXPANSE.
SPACE SECTOR 422.
THE PRESENT DAY.
THE VAUNTED KHUND EMPIRE! I'VE HEARD YOUR PEOPLE WHISPERED OF IN FEAR SO MANY TIMES, I SIMPLY HAD TO SEE FOR MYSELF.
WHAT A LETDOWN! YOU'RE AS EASY TO TERRORIZE AS THE HUNDREDS I KILLED BEFORE YOU.
SO, GO AHEAD: SCREAM FOR ME.
SCREAM LIKE GIRLS BEFORE YOU DIE!

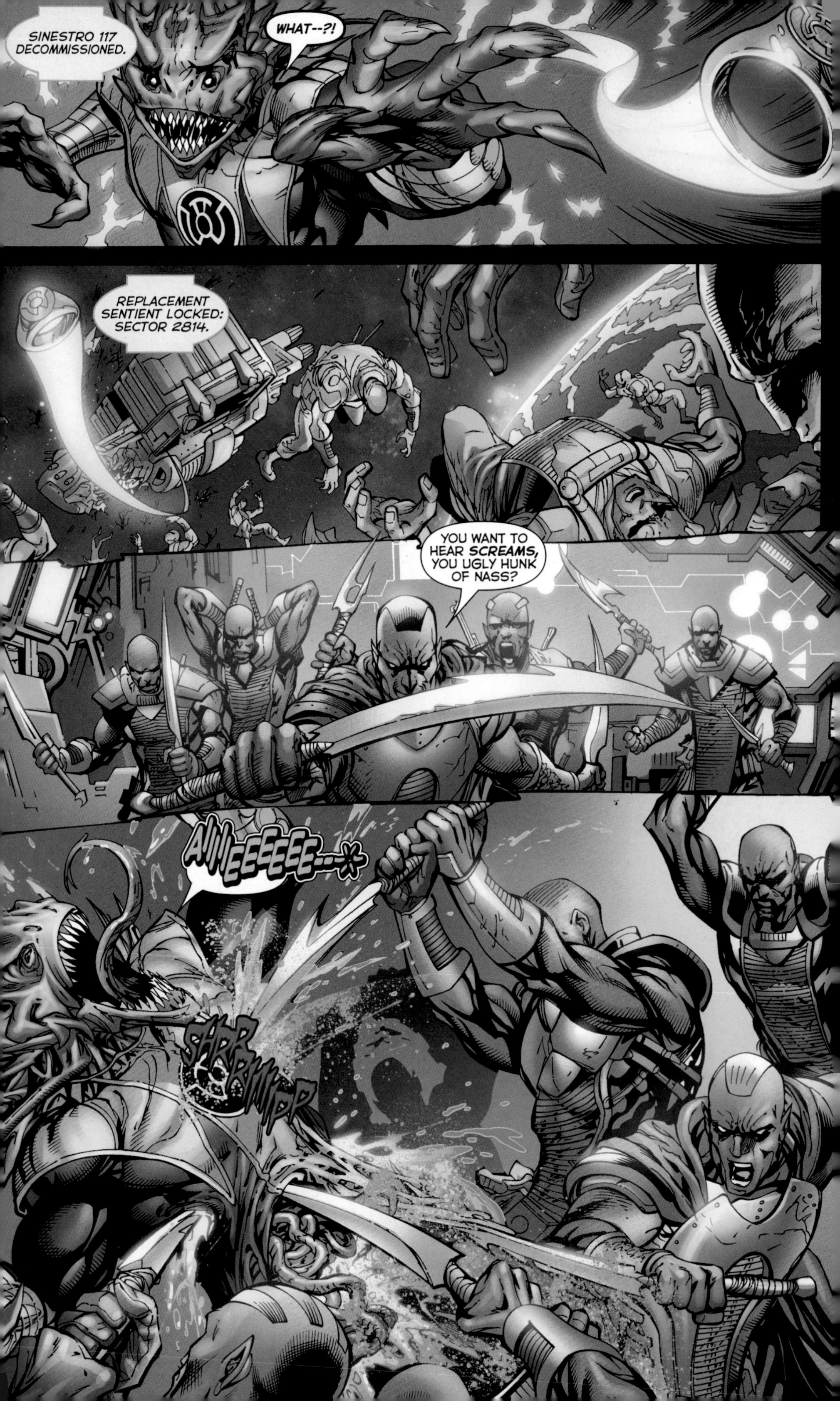

SINESTRO 117 DECOMMISSIONED.
WHAT--?!
REPLACEMENT SENTIENT LOCKED: SECTOR 2814.
YOU WANT TO HEAR SCREAMS, YOU UGLY HUNK OF NASS?
AIIIEEEEEE--*
SHRRRUNNNPP

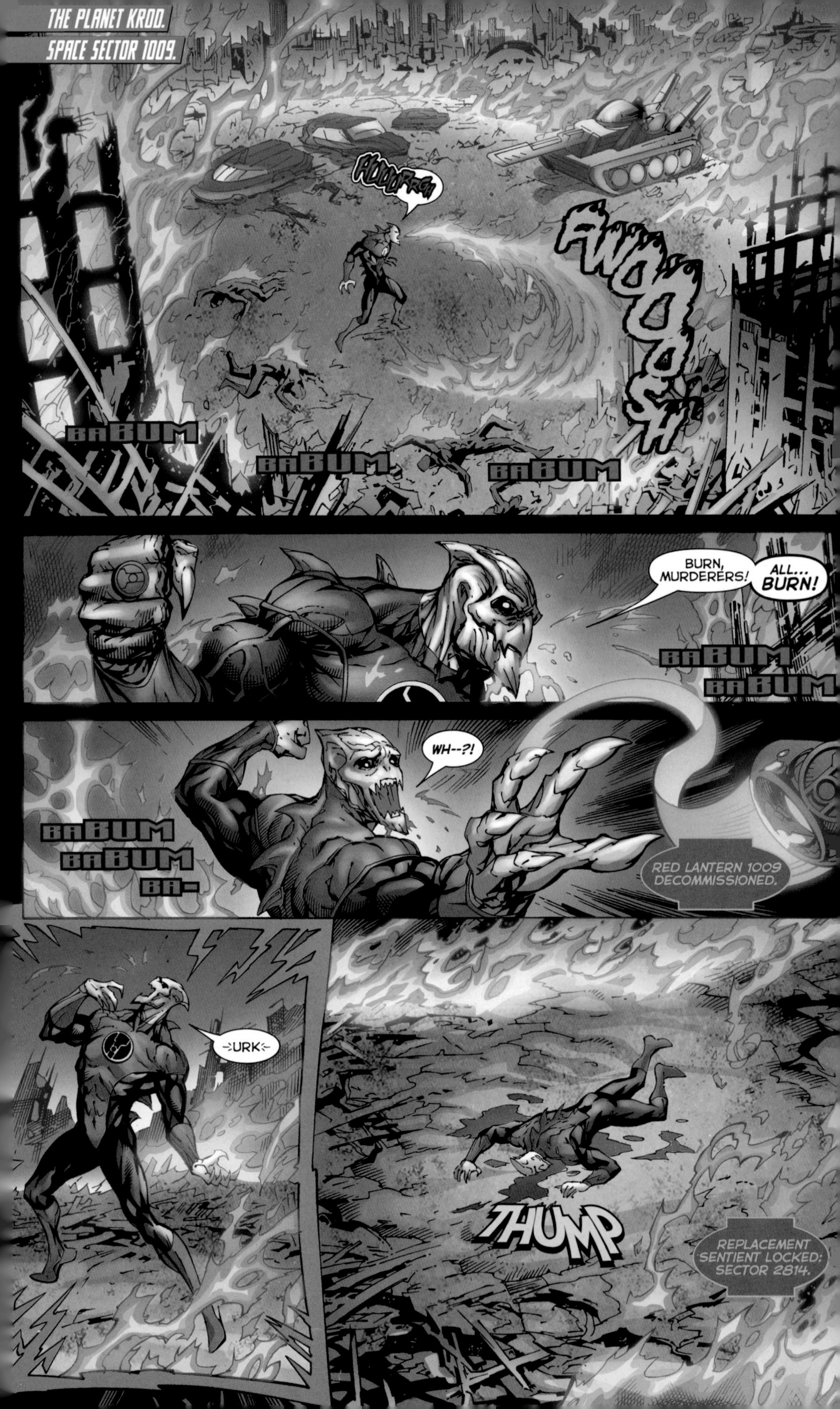
THE PLANET KROD.
SPACE SECTOR 1009.
FWOOOSH
BABUM
BABUM
BABUM
BURN, MURDERERS!
ALL... BURN!
BABUM
BABUM
WH--?!
BABUM
BABUM
BA-
RED LANTERN 1009 DECOMMISSIONED.
URK
THUMP
REPLACEMENT SENTIENT LOCKED: SECTOR 2814.

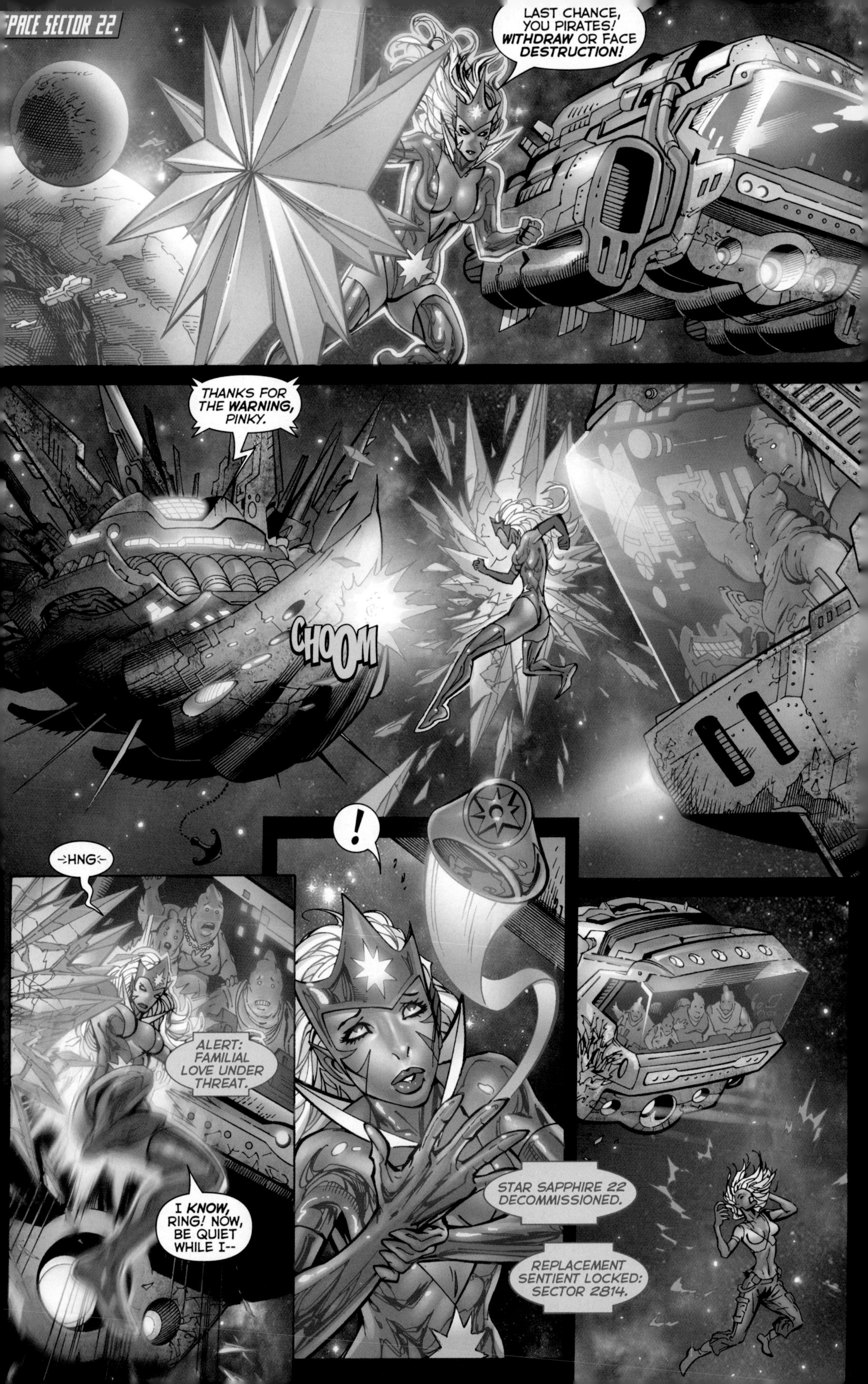
SPACE SECTOR 22
LAST CHANCE, YOU PIRATES! WITHDRAW OR FACE DESTRUCTION!
THANKS FOR THE WARNING, PINKY.
CHOOM
HNG
ALERT: FAMILIAL LOVE UNDER THREAT.
I KNOW, RING! NOW, BE QUIET WHILE I--
!
STAR SAPPHIRE 22 DECOMMISSIONED.
REPLACEMENT SENTIENT LOCKED: SECTOR 2814.

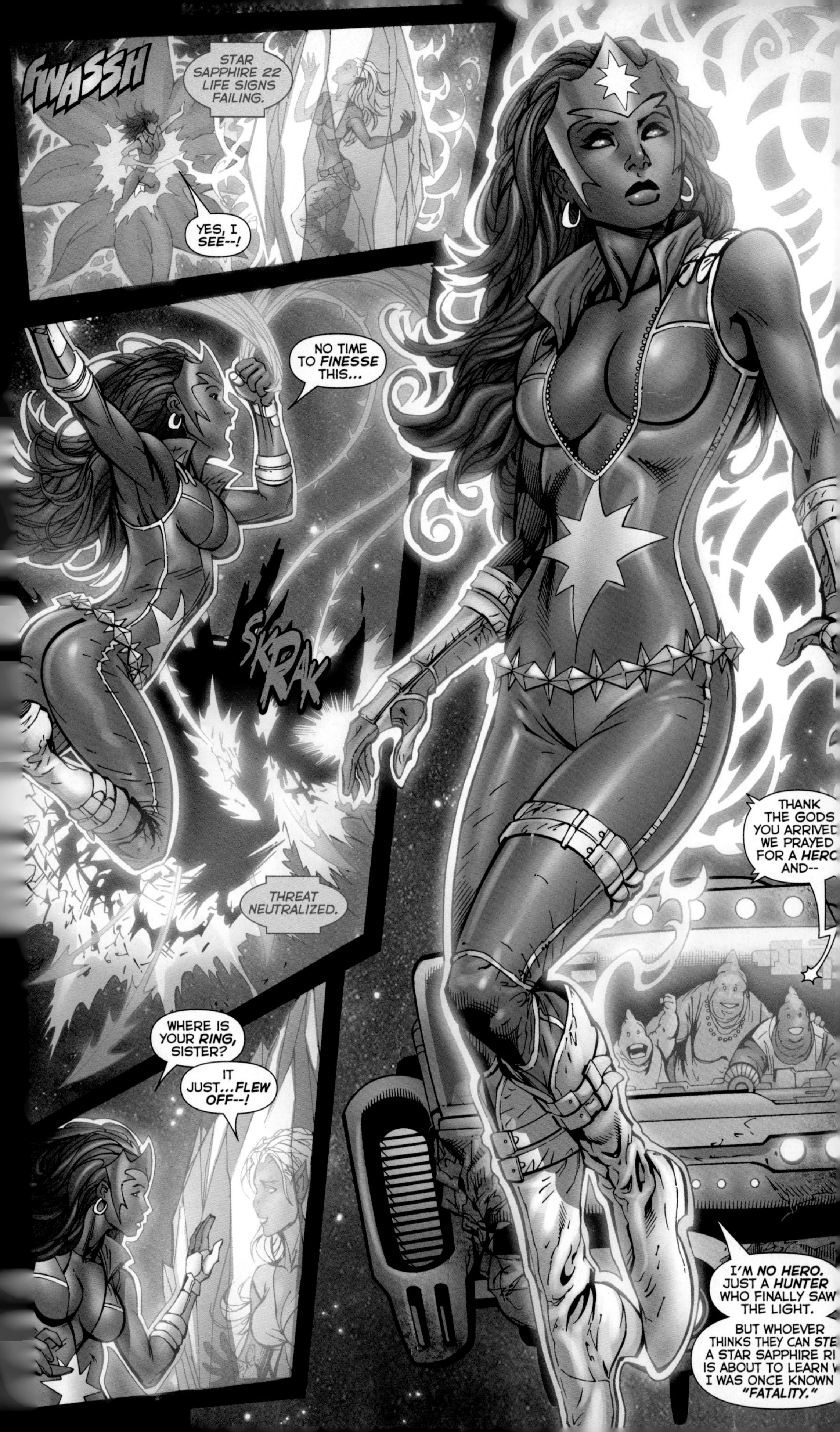
FWASSH
STAR SAPPHIRE 22 LIFE SIGNS FAILING.
YES, I SEE--!
NO TIME TO FINESSE THIS...
SKRAK
THREAT NEUTRALIZED.
WHERE IS YOUR RING, SISTER?
IT JUST...FLEW OFF--!
THANK THE GODS YOU ARRIVED WE PRAYED FOR A HERO AND--
I'M NO HERO. JUST A HUNTER WHO FINALLY SAW THE LIGHT.
BUT WHOEVER THINKS THEY CAN STE A STAR SAPPHIRE RI IS ABOUT TO LEARN I WAS ONCE KNOWN "FATALITY."

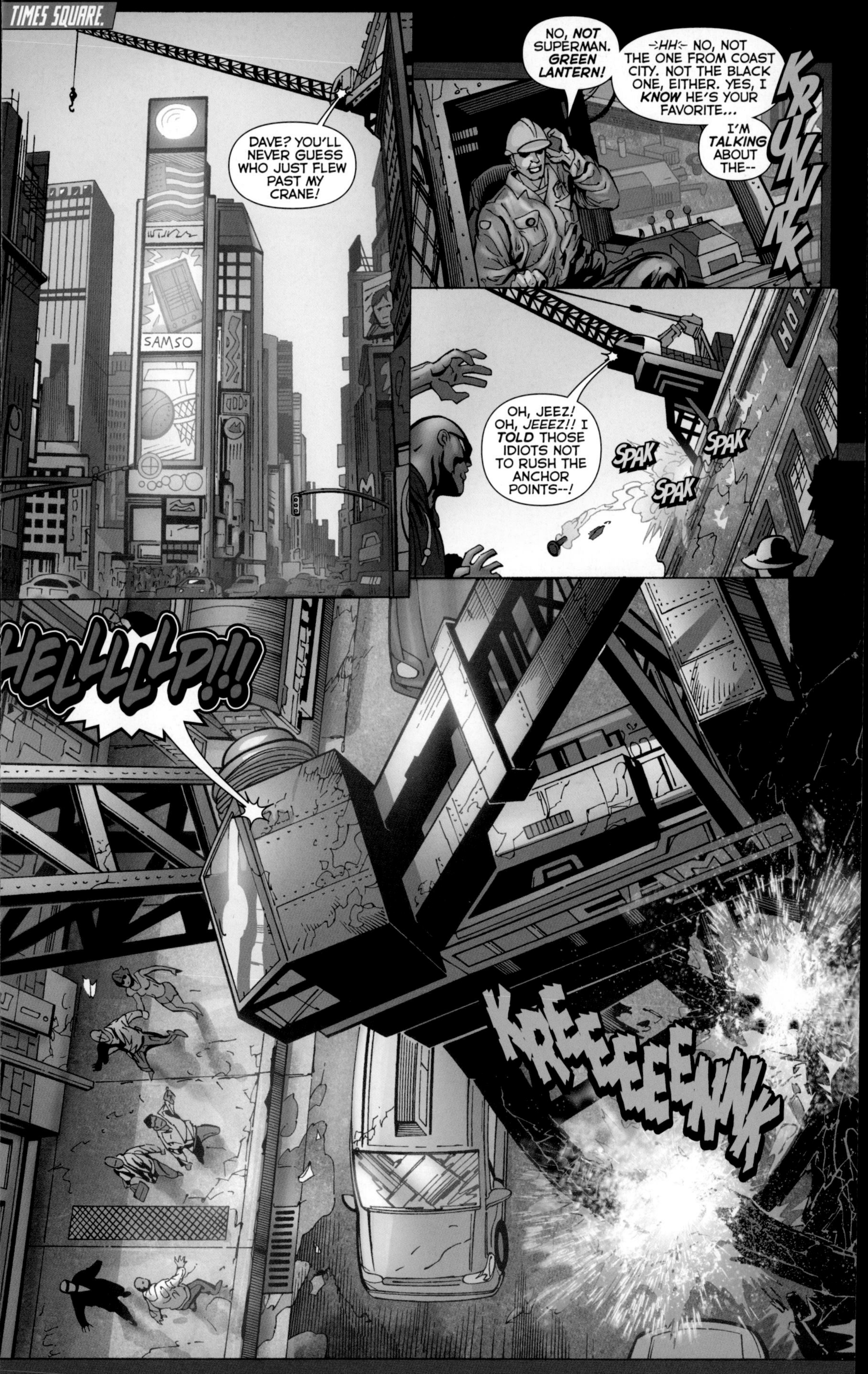
TIMES SQUARE.
DAVE? YOU'LL NEVER GUESS WHO JUST FLEW PAST MY CRANE!
NO, NOT SUPERMAN. GREEN LANTERN!
-HH- NO, NOT THE ONE FROM COAST CITY. NOT THE BLACK ONE, EITHER. YES, I KNOW HE'S YOUR FAVORITE...
I'M TALKING ABOUT THE--
KRUNNNK
OH, JEEZ! OH, JEEEZ!! I TOLD THOSE IDIOTS NOT TO RUSH THE ANCHOR POINTS--!
SPAK
SPAK
SPAK
HELLLLLP!!!
KREEEEEENNK

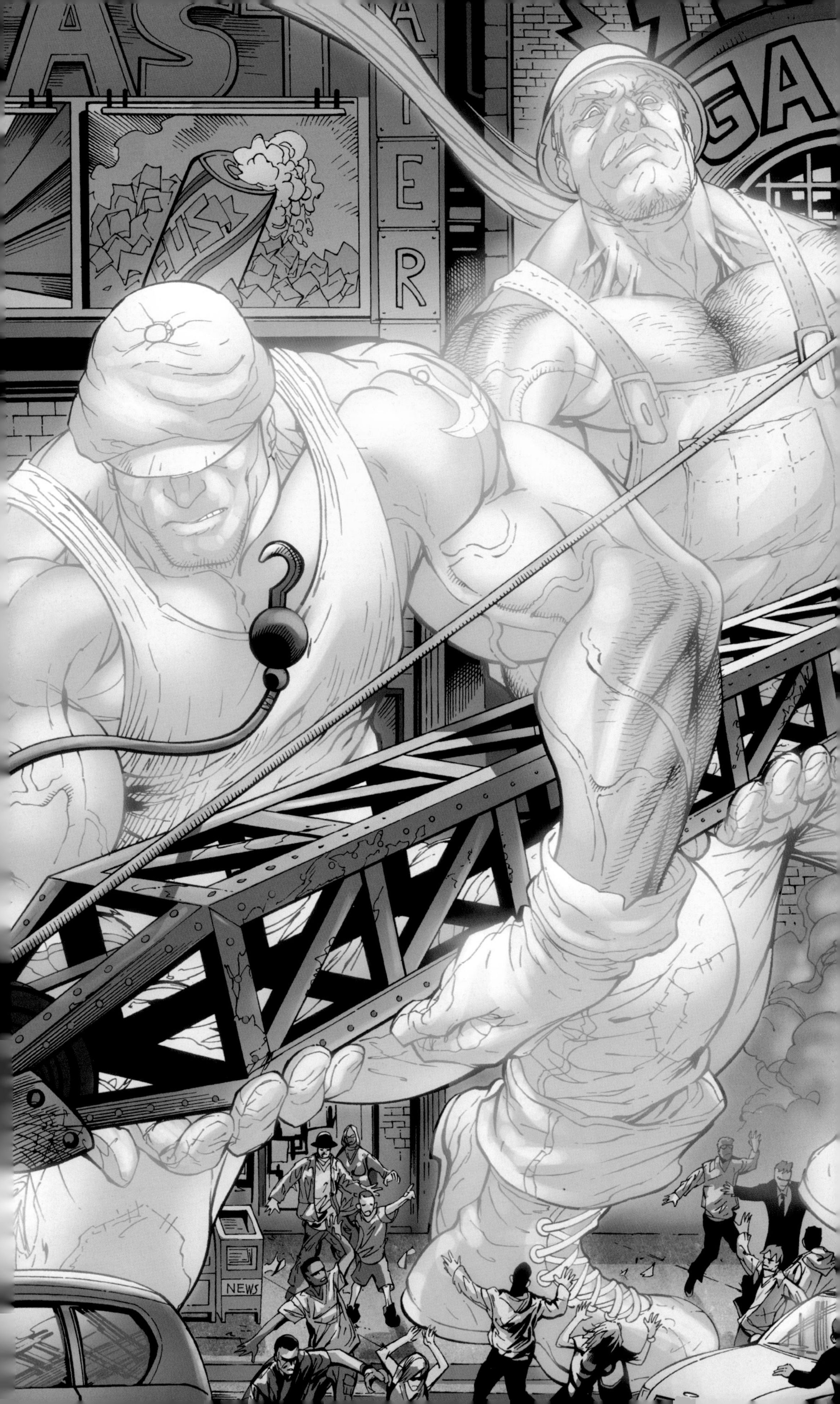
NEWS

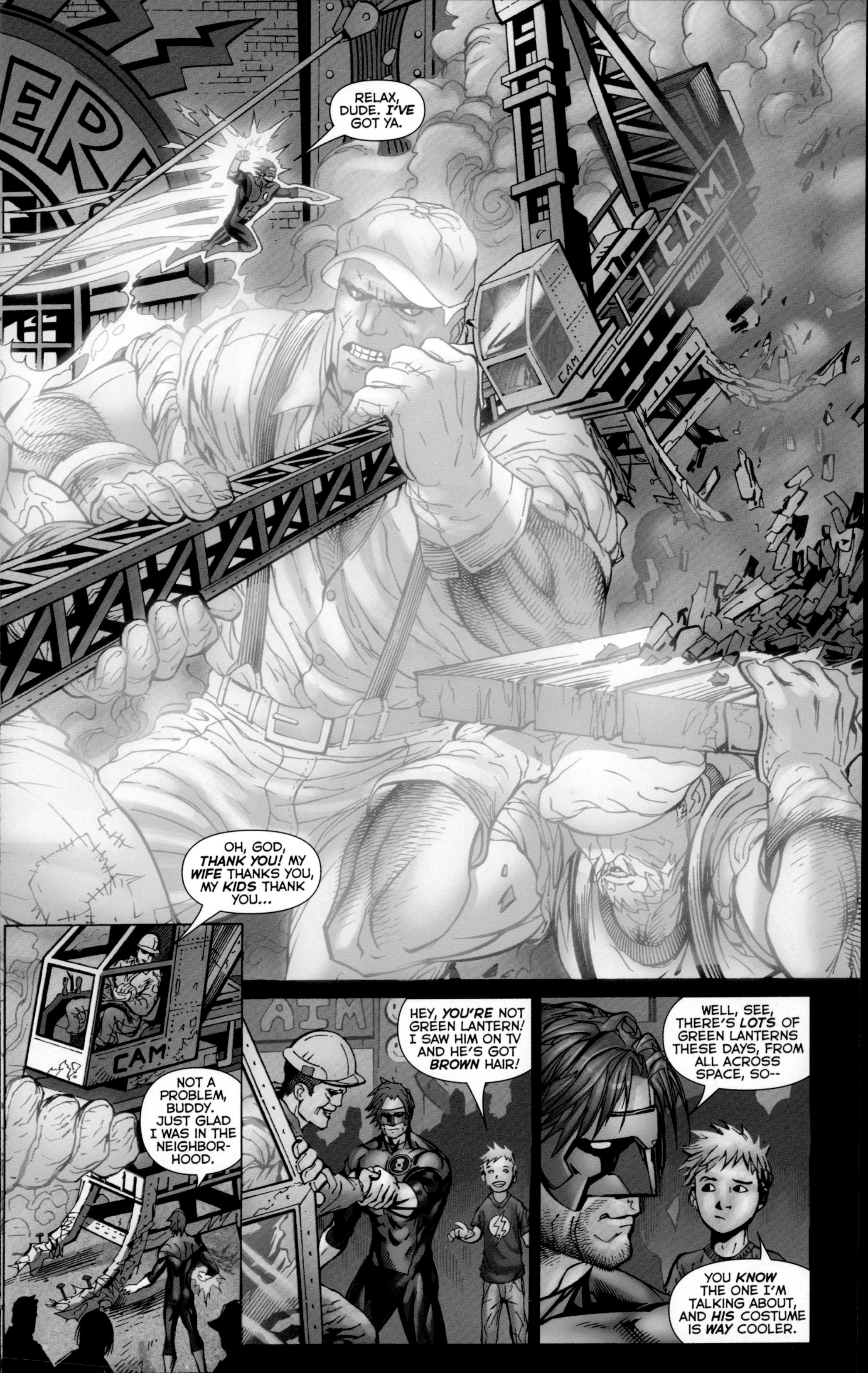
RELAX, DUDE. I'VE GOT YA.
OH, GOD, THANK YOU! MY WIFE THANKS YOU, MY KIDS THANK YOU...
NOT A PROBLEM, BUDDY. JUST GLAD I WAS IN THE NEIGHBOR-HOOD.
CAM
HEY, YOU'RE NOT GREEN LANTERN! I SAW HIM ON TV AND HE'S GOT BROWN HAIR!
WELL, SEE, THERE'S LOTS OF GREEN LANTERNS THESE DAYS, FROM ALL ACROSS SPACE, SO--
YOU KNOW THE ONE I'M TALKING ABOUT, AND HIS COSTUME IS WAY COOLER.

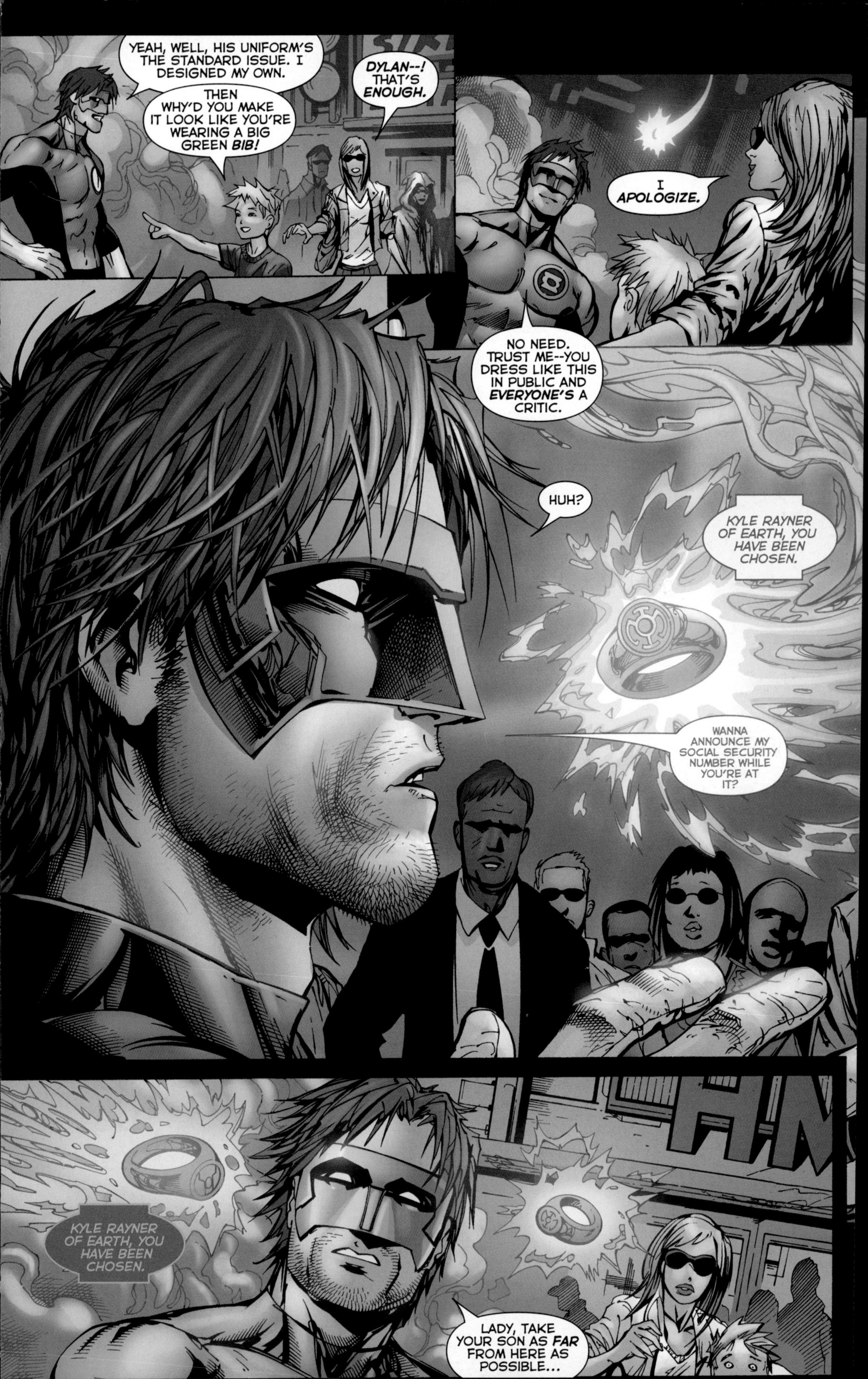
YEAH, WELL, HIS UNIFORM'S THE STANDARD ISSUE. I DESIGNED MY OWN.
THEN WHY'D YOU MAKE IT LOOK LIKE YOU'RE WEARING A BIG GREEN BIB!
DYLAN--! THAT'S ENOUGH.
I APOLOGIZE.
NO NEED. TRUST ME--YOU DRESS LIKE THIS IN PUBLIC AND EVERYONE'S A CRITIC.
HUH?
KYLE RAYNER OF EARTH, YOU HAVE BEEN CHOSEN.
WANNA ANNOUNCE MY SOCIAL SECURITY NUMBER WHILE YOU'RE AT IT?
KYLE RAYNER OF EARTH, YOU HAVE BEEN CHOSEN.
LADY, TAKE YOUR SON AS FAR FROM HERE AS POSSIBLE...

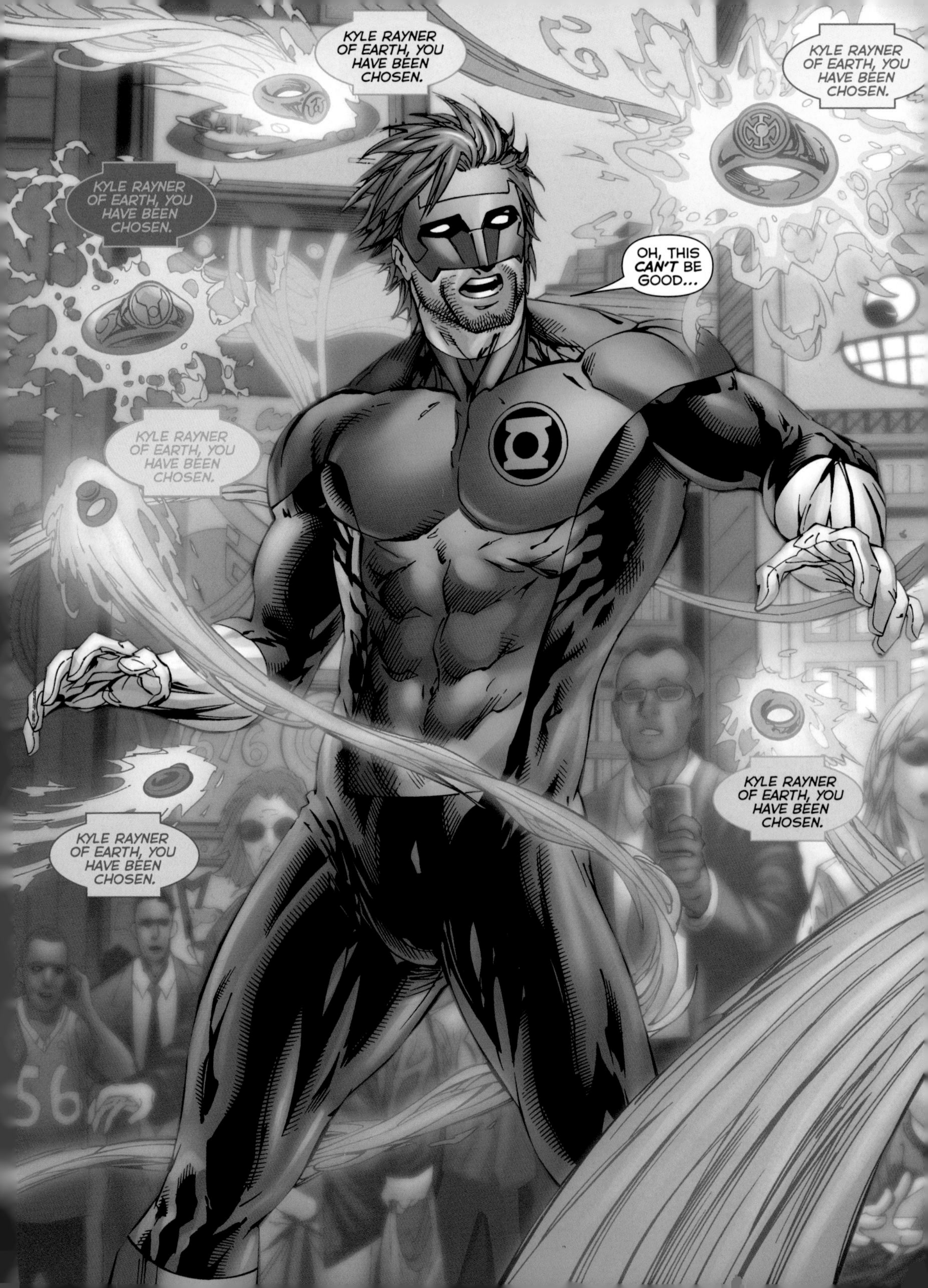
KYLE RAYNER OF EARTH, YOU HAVE BEEN CHOSEN.
KYLE RAYNER OF EARTH, YOU HAVE BEEN CHOSEN.
KYLE RAYNER OF EARTH, YOU HAVE BEEN CHOSEN.
OH, THIS CAN'T BE GOOD...
KYLE RAYNER OF EARTH, YOU HAVE BEEN CHOSEN.
KYLE RAYNER OF EARTH, YOU HAVE BEEN CHOSEN.
KYLE RAYNER OF EARTH, YOU HAVE BEEN CHOSEN.

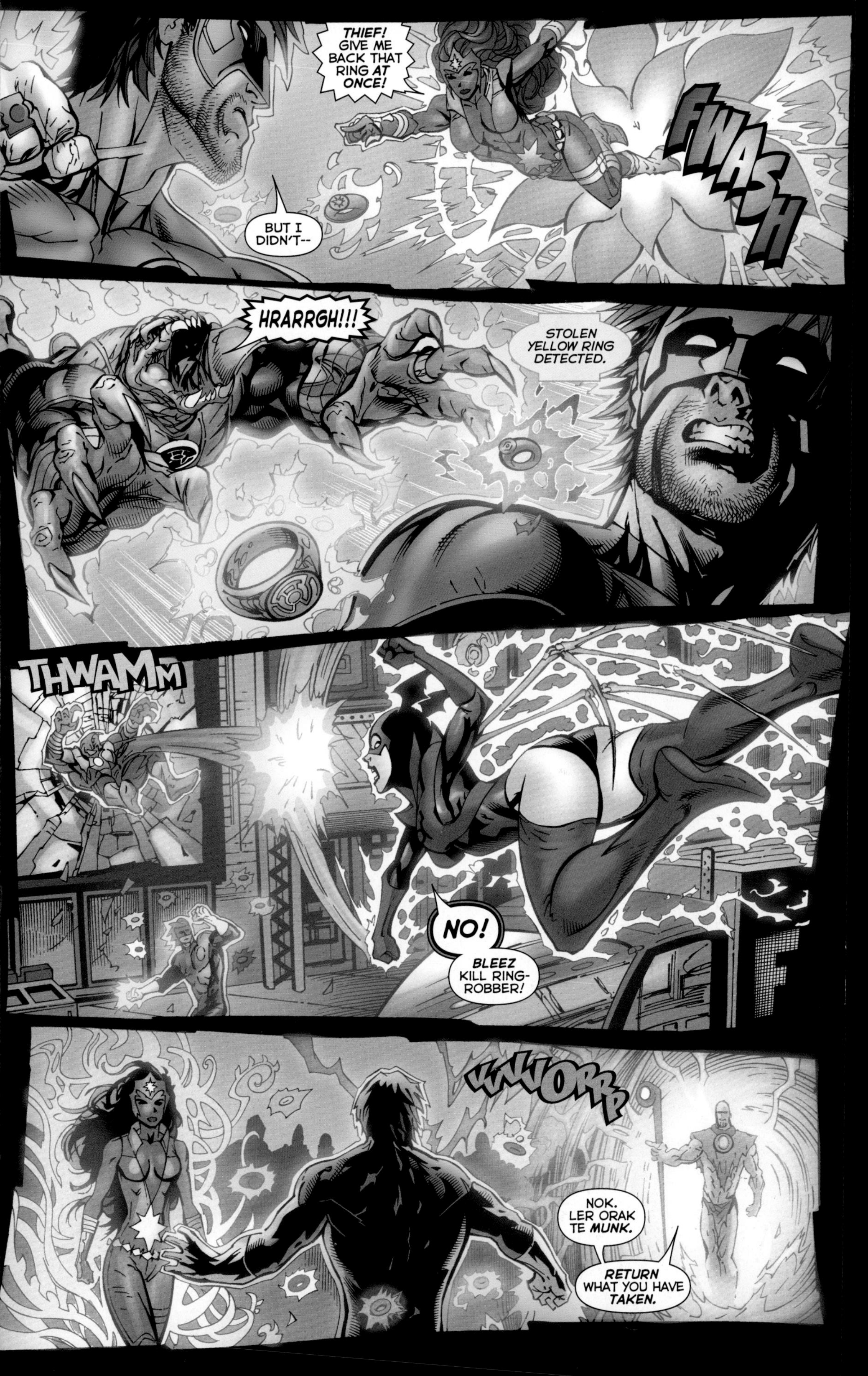
THIEF! GIVE ME BACK THAT RING AT ONCE!
FWASH
BUT I DIDN'T--
HRARRGH!!!
STOLEN YELLOW RING DETECTED.
THWAMM
NO!
BLEEZ KILL RING-ROBBER!
VVVVORRP
NOK. LER ORAK TE MUNK.
RETURN WHAT YOU HAVE TAKEN.

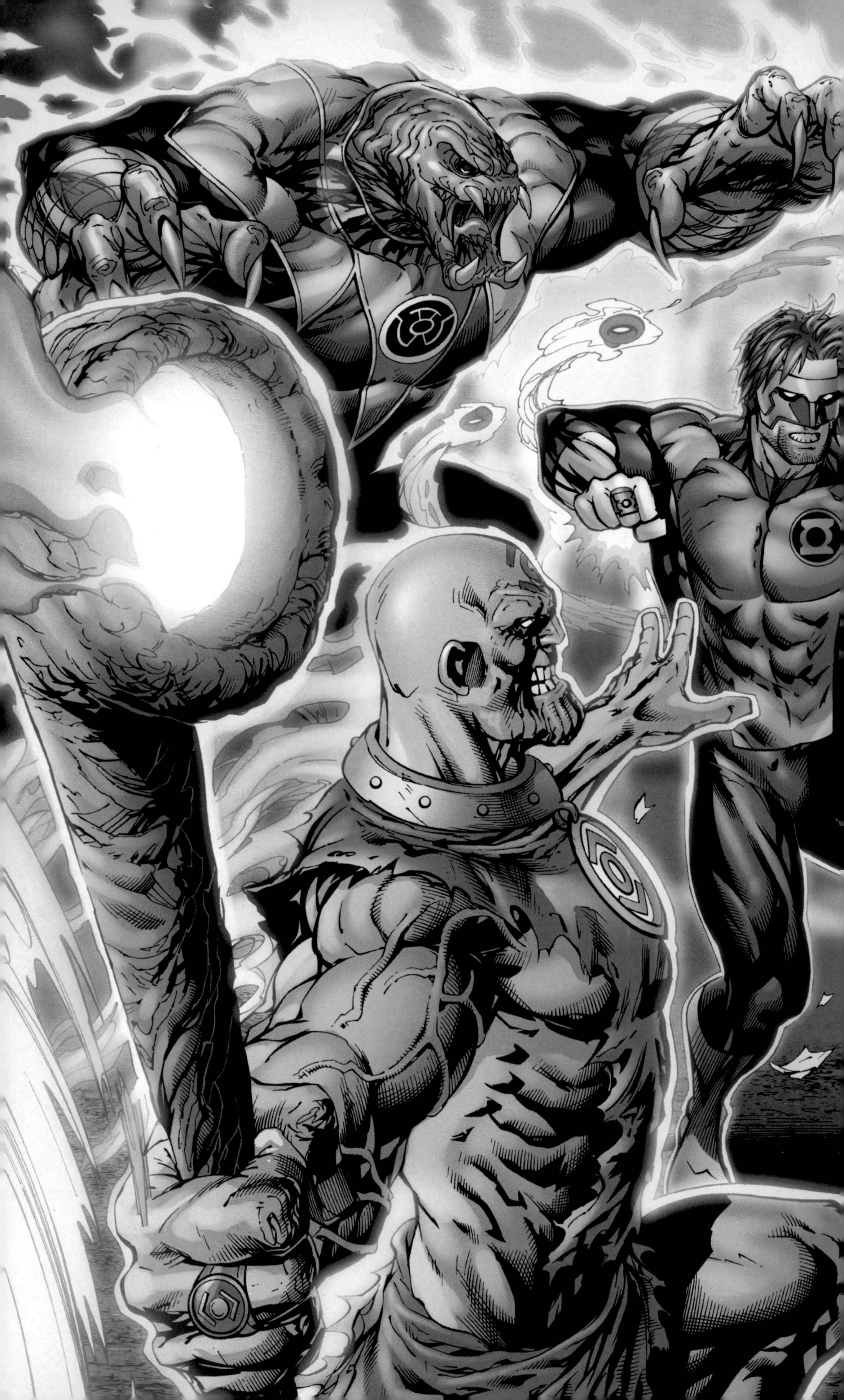

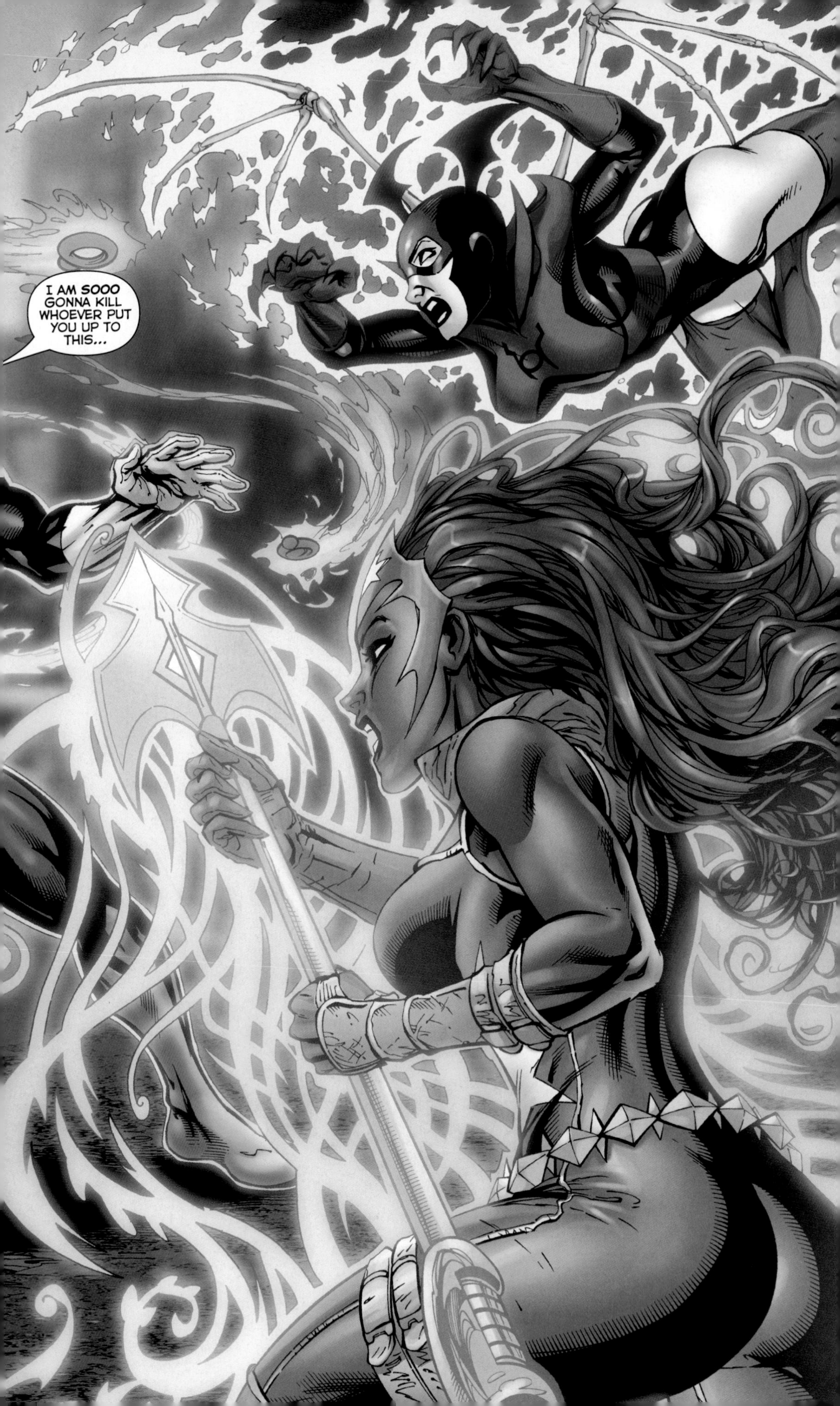
I AM *SOOO* GONNA KILL WHOEVER PUT YOU UP TO THIS...

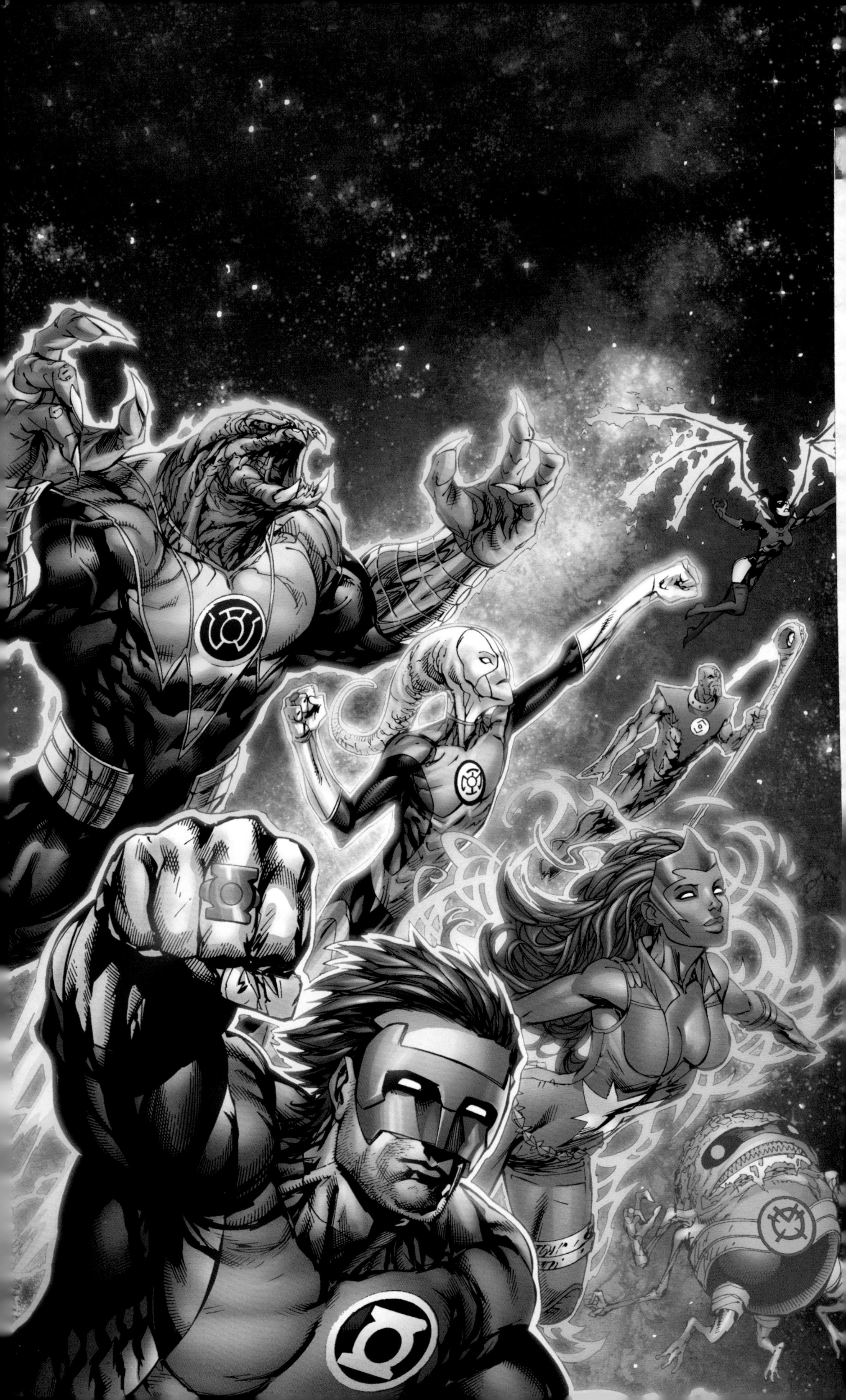

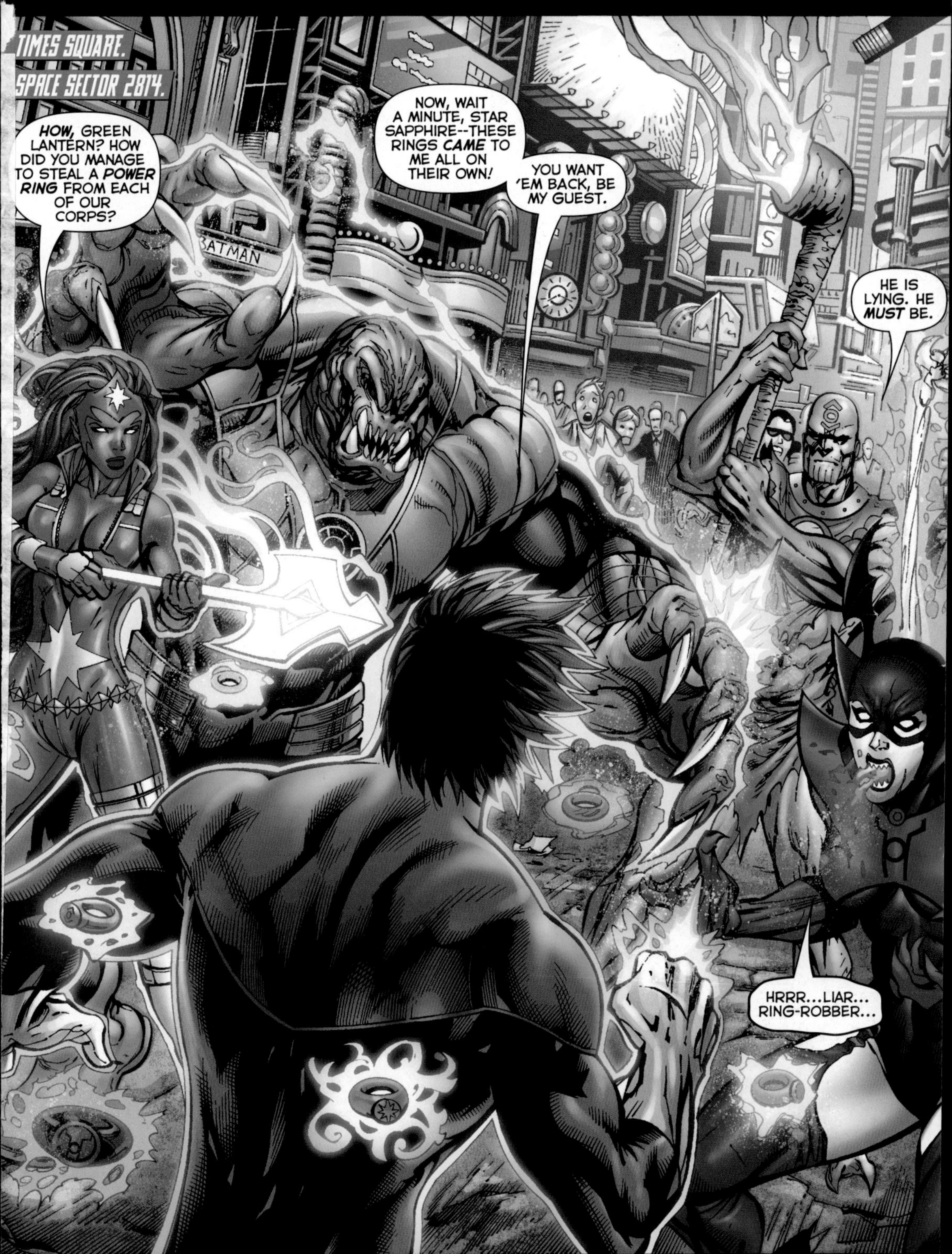
TIMES SQUARE.
SPACE SECTOR 2814.
HOW, GREEN LANTERN? HOW DID YOU MANAGE TO STEAL A POWER RING FROM EACH OF OUR CORPS?
NOW, WAIT A MINUTE, STAR SAPPHIRE--THESE RINGS CAME TO ME ALL ON THEIR OWN!
YOU WANT 'EM BACK, BE MY GUEST.
HE IS LYING. HE MUST BE.
HRRR...LIAR... RING-ROBBER...
BATMAN

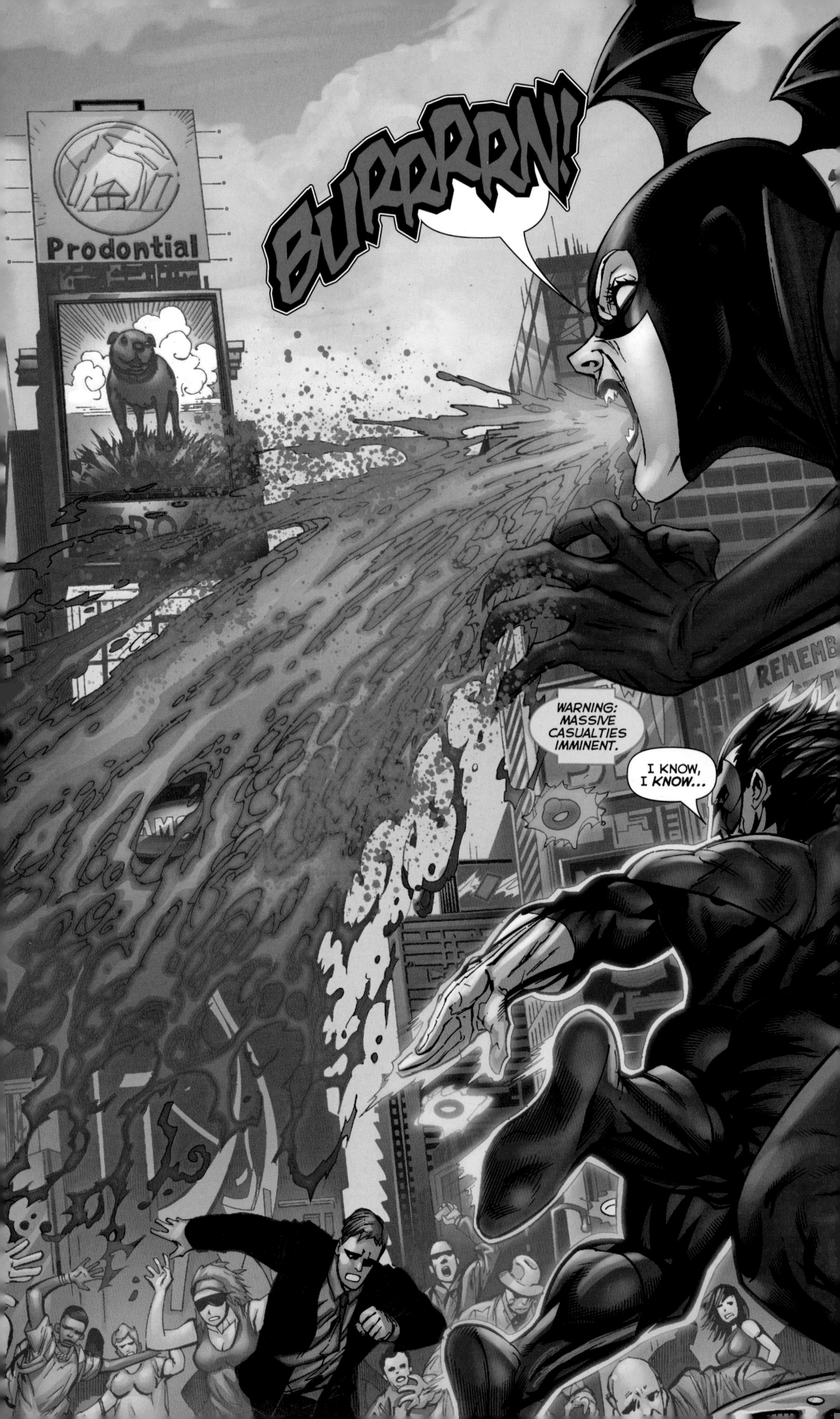
Prodontial
BURRRRN!
WARNING: MASSIVE CASUALTIES IMMINENT.
I KNOW, I KNOW...

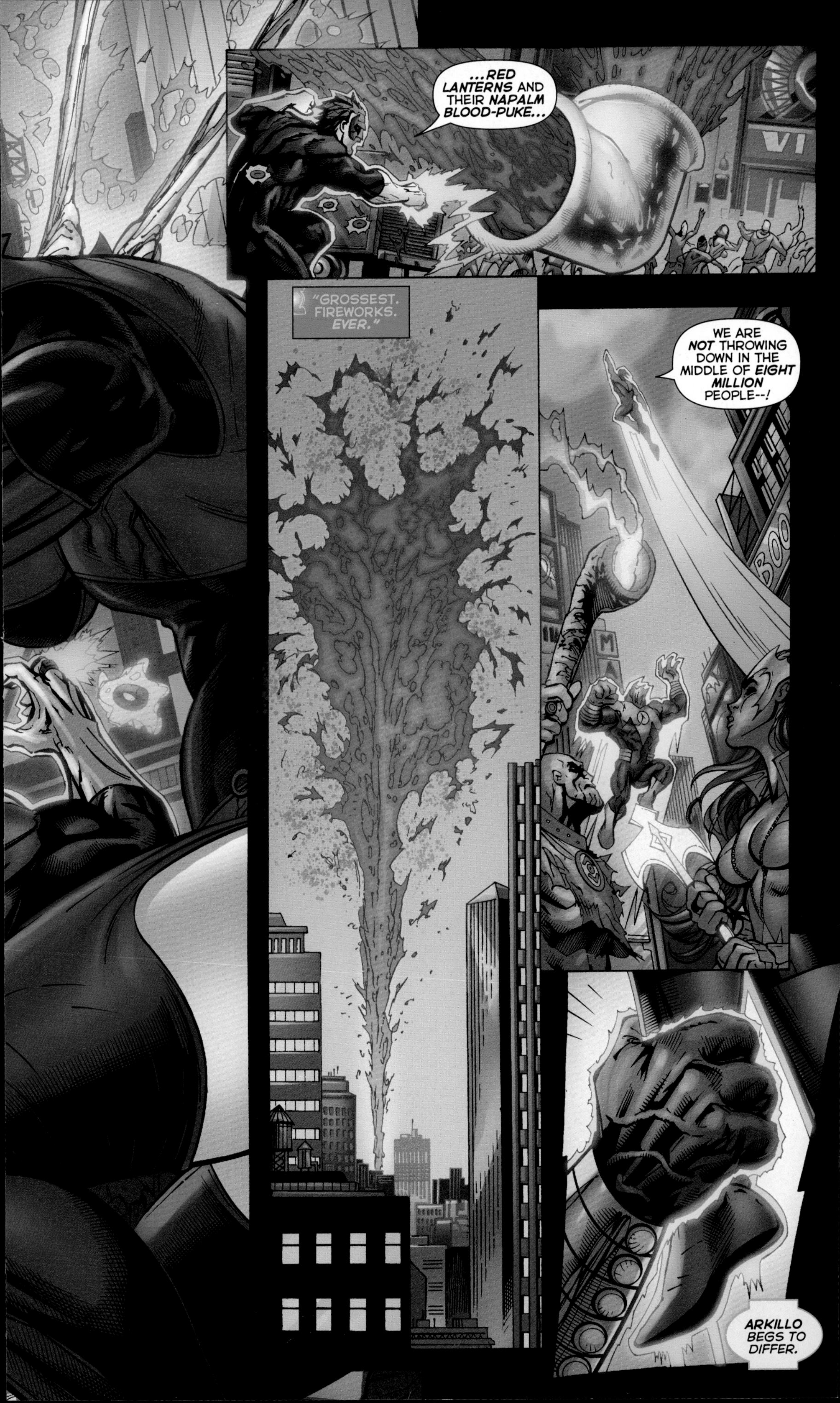
...RED LANTERNS AND THEIR NAPALM BLOOD-PUKE...
"GROSSEST. FIREWORKS. EVER."
WE ARE NOT THROWING DOWN IN THE MIDDLE OF EIGHT MILLION PEOPLE--!
ARKILLO BEGS TO DIFFER.

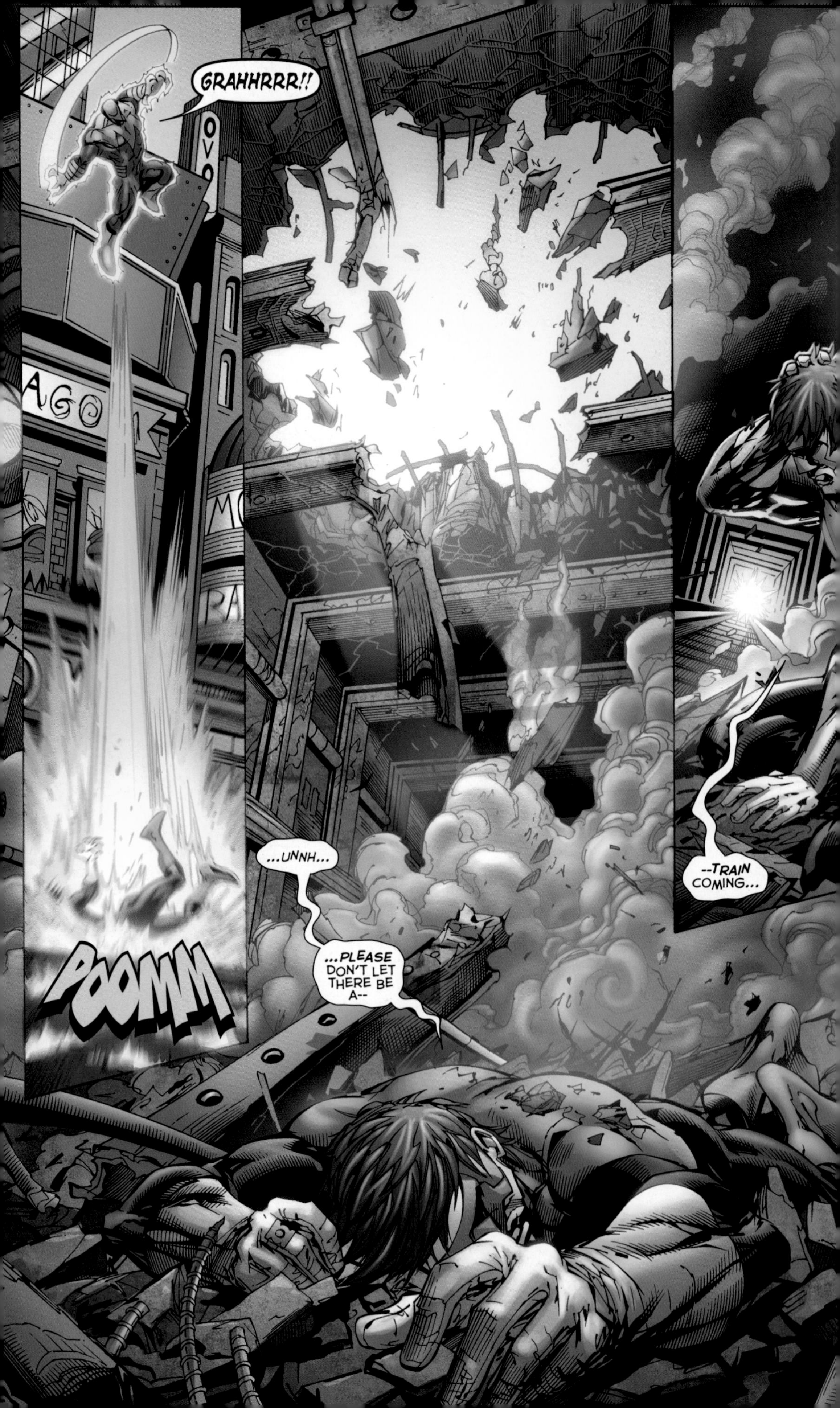

GRAHHRRR!!
POOMM
...UNNH...
...PLEASE DON'T LET THERE BE A--
--TRAIN COMING...

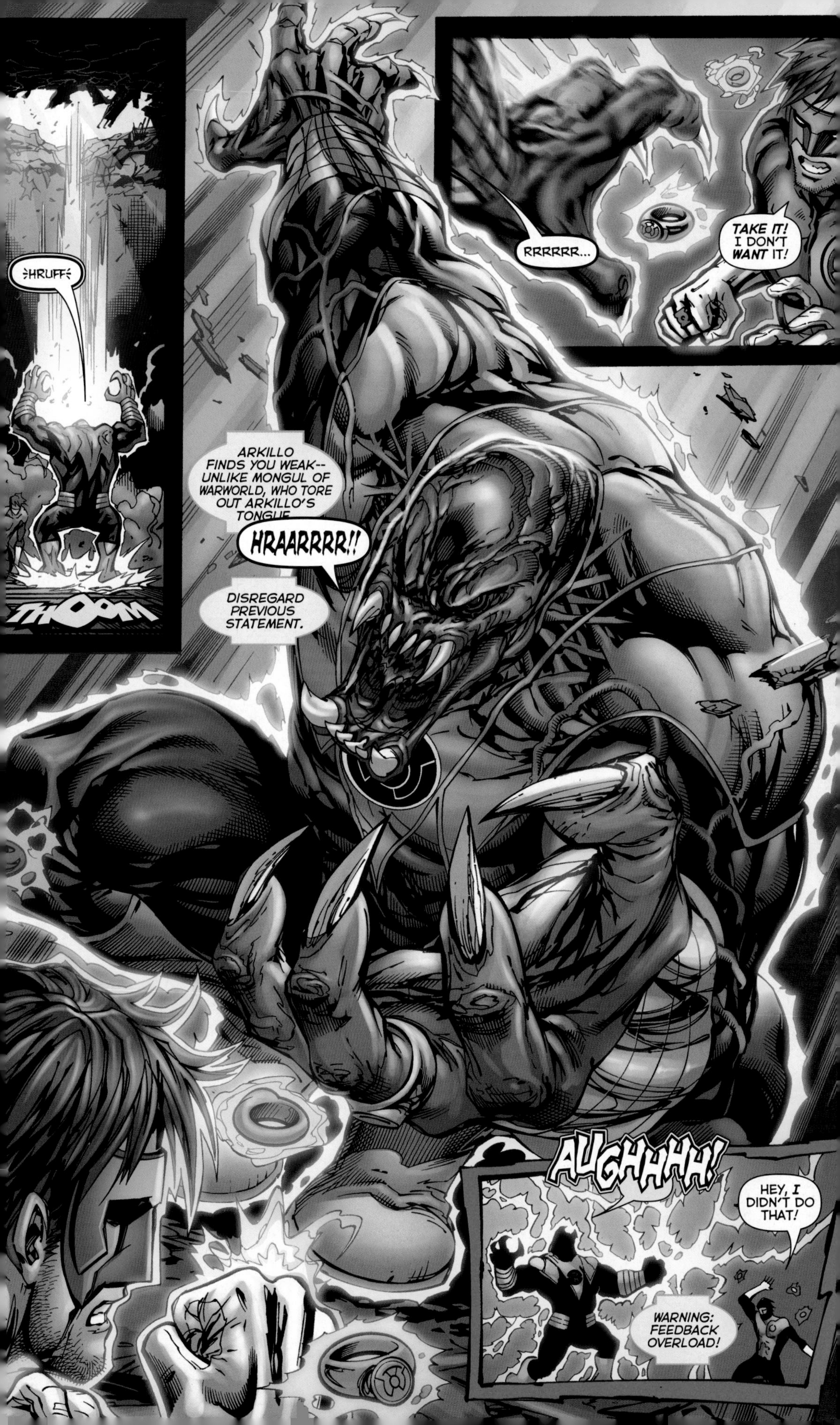
HRUFF
THOOM
RRRRRR...
TAKE IT! I DON'T WANT IT!
ARKILLO FINDS YOU WEAK-- UNLIKE MONGUL OF WARWORLD, WHO TORE OUT ARKILLO'S TONGUE
HRAARRRR!!
DISREGARD PREVIOUS STATEMENT.
AUGHHHH!
HEY, I DIDN'T DO THAT!
WARNING: FEEDBACK OVERLOAD!

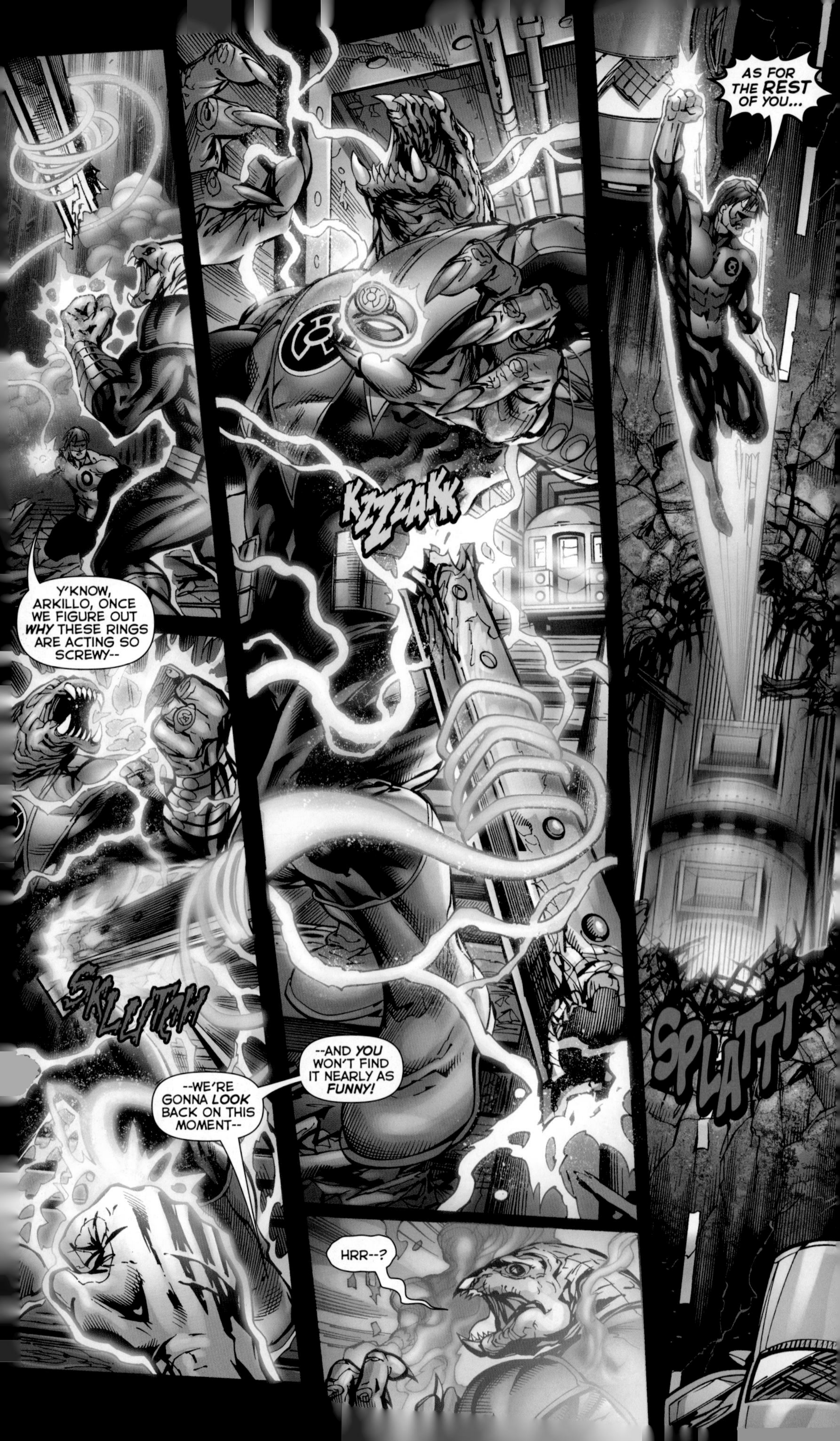
Y'KNOW, ARKILLO, ONCE WE FIGURE OUT WHY THESE RINGS ARE ACTING SO SCREWY--
SKLITCH
--WE'RE GONNA LOOK BACK ON THIS MOMENT--
KZZZAKK
--AND YOU WON'T FIND IT NEARLY AS FUNNY!
HRR--?
AS FOR THE REST OF YOU...
SPLATTT

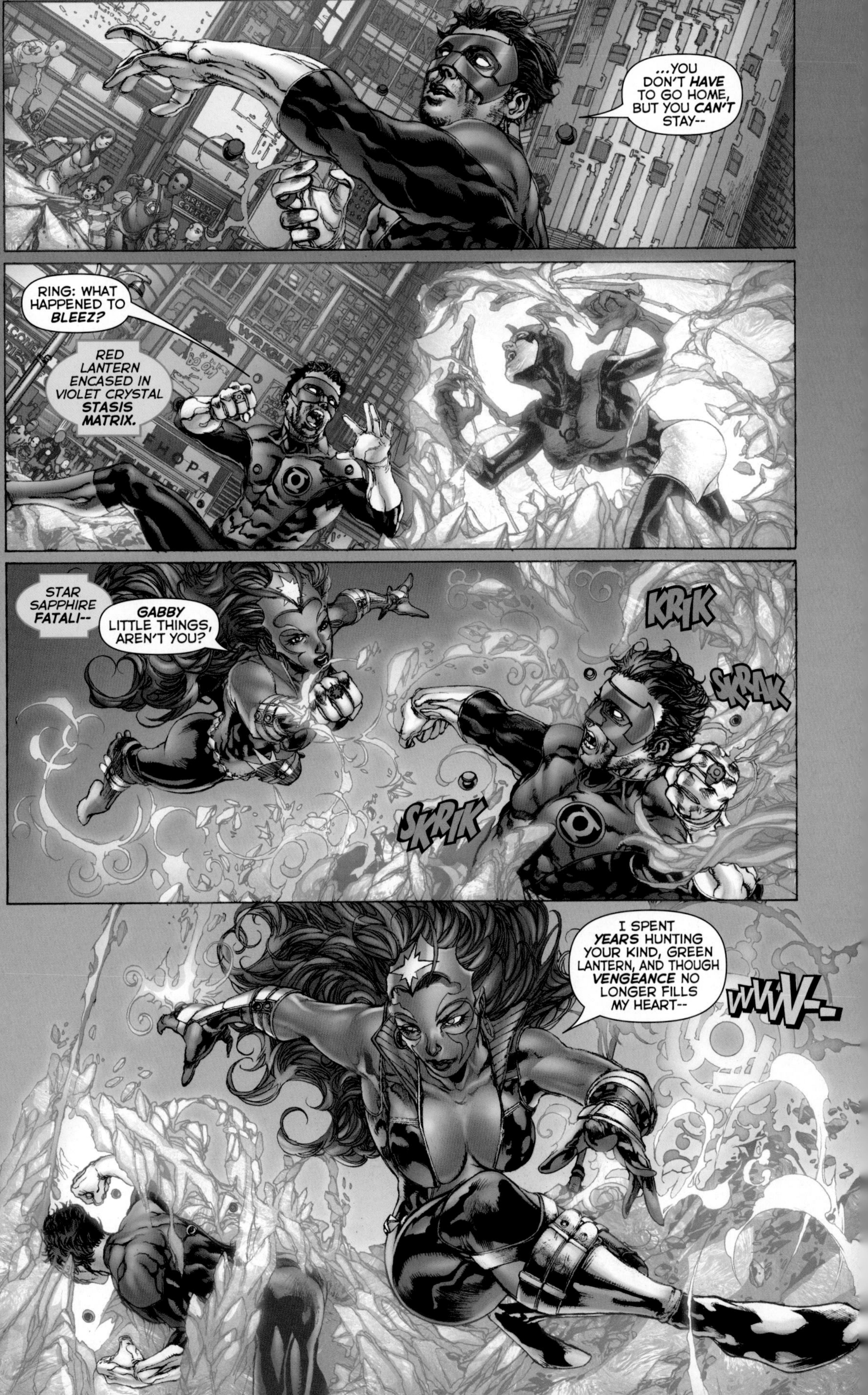
...YOU DON'T HAVE TO GO HOME, BUT YOU CAN'T STAY--
RING: WHAT HAPPENED TO BLEEZ?
RED LANTERN ENCASED IN VIOLET CRYSTAL STASIS MATRIX.
STAR SAPPHIRE FATALI--
GABBY LITTLE THINGS, AREN'T YOU?
KRIK
SKRAK
SKRIK
I SPENT YEARS HUNTING YOUR KIND, GREEN LANTERN, AND THOUGH VENGEANCE NO LONGER FILLS MY HEART--
VVVVV--

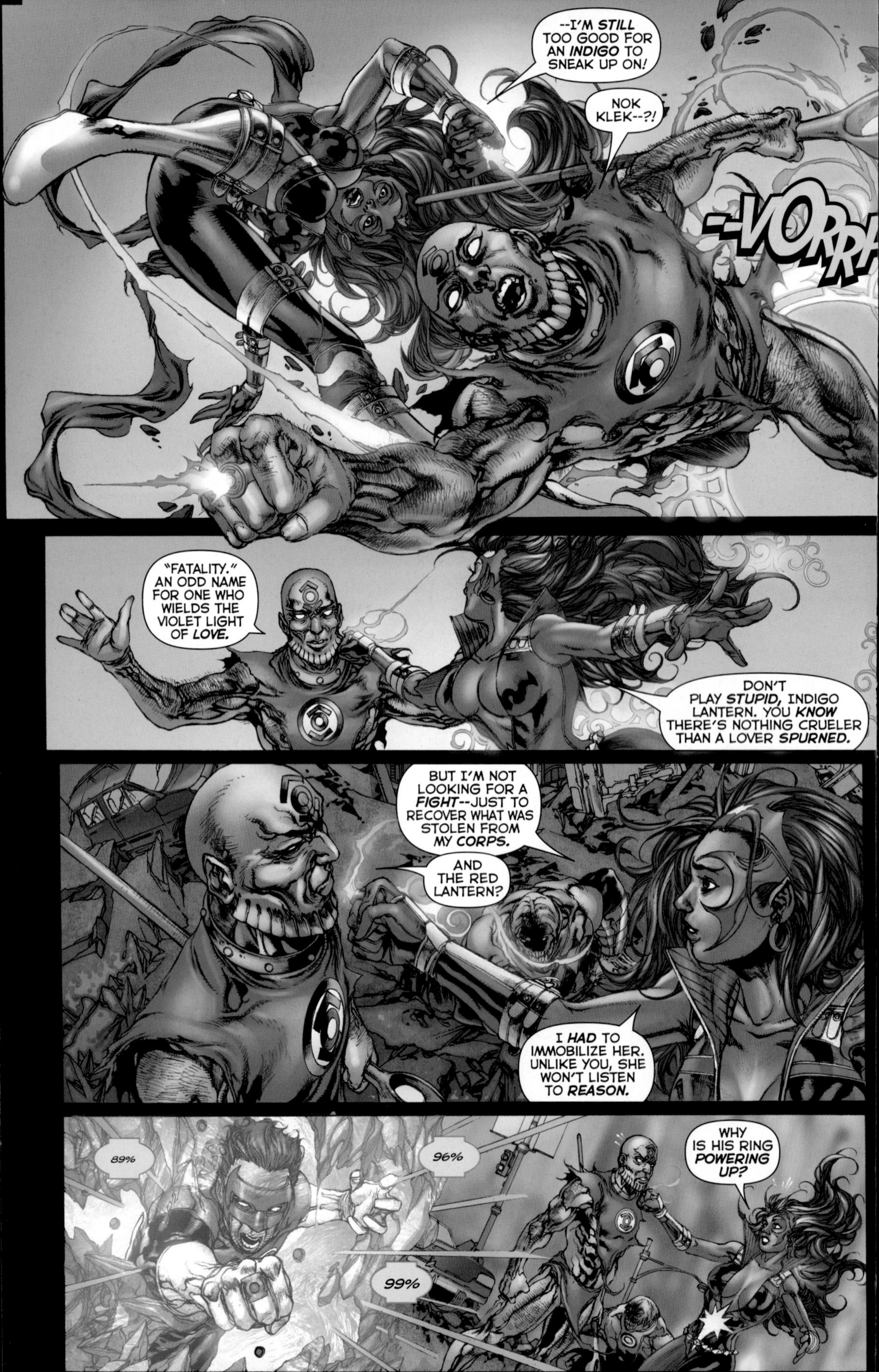
--I'M STILL TOO GOOD FOR AN INDIGO TO SNEAK UP ON!
NOK KLEK--?!
--VORR
"FATALITY." AN ODD NAME FOR ONE WHO WIELDS THE VIOLET LIGHT OF LOVE.
DON'T PLAY STUPID, INDIGO LANTERN. YOU KNOW THERE'S NOTHING CRUELER THAN A LOVER SPURNED.
BUT I'M NOT LOOKING FOR A FIGHT--JUST TO RECOVER WHAT WAS STOLEN FROM MY CORPS.
AND THE RED LANTERN?
I HAD TO IMMOBILIZE HER. UNLIKE YOU, SHE WON'T LISTEN TO REASON.
89%
96%
WHY IS HIS RING POWERING UP?
99%

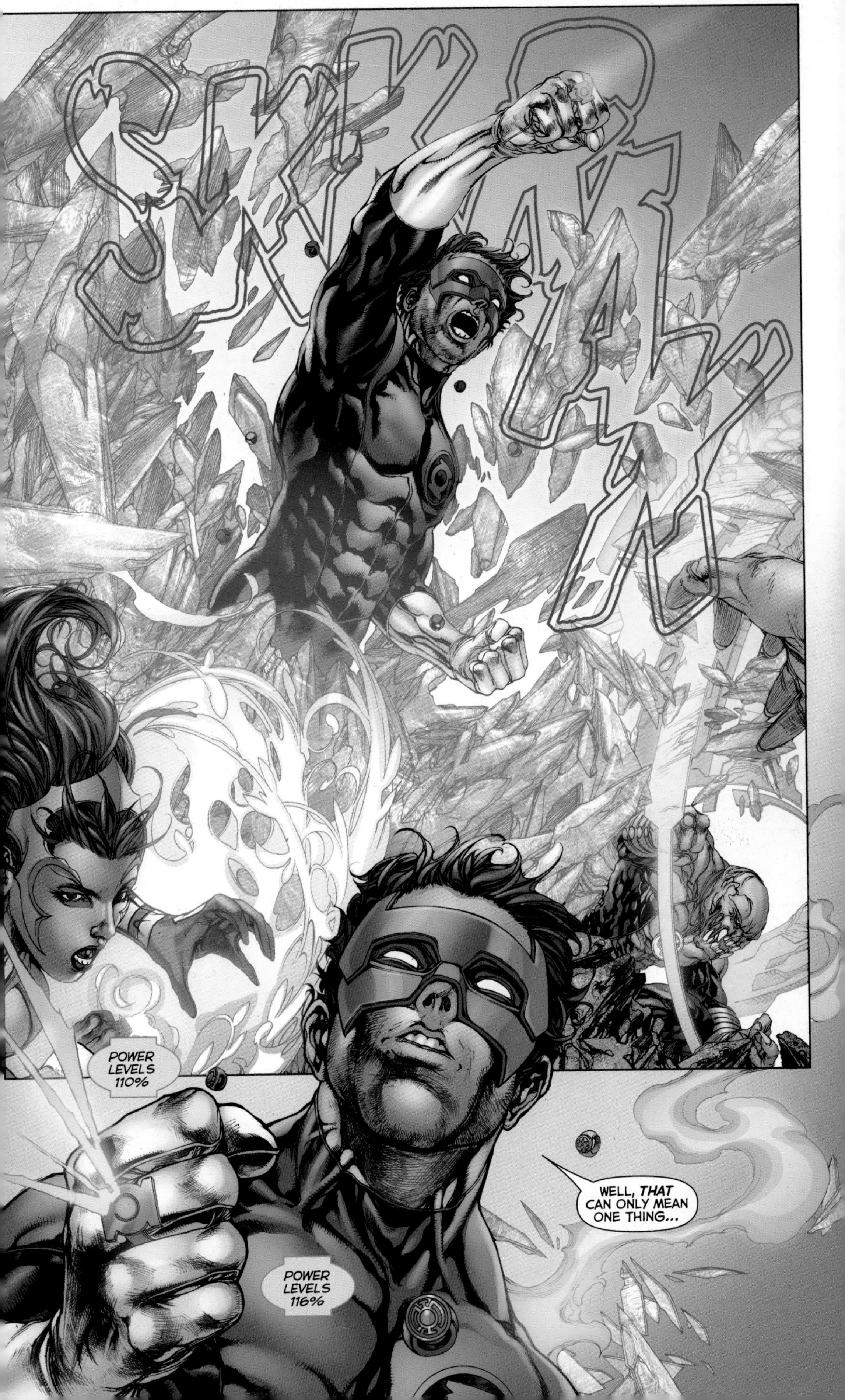
POWER LEVELS 110%
WELL, *THAT* CAN ONLY MEAN ONE THING...
POWER LEVELS 116%

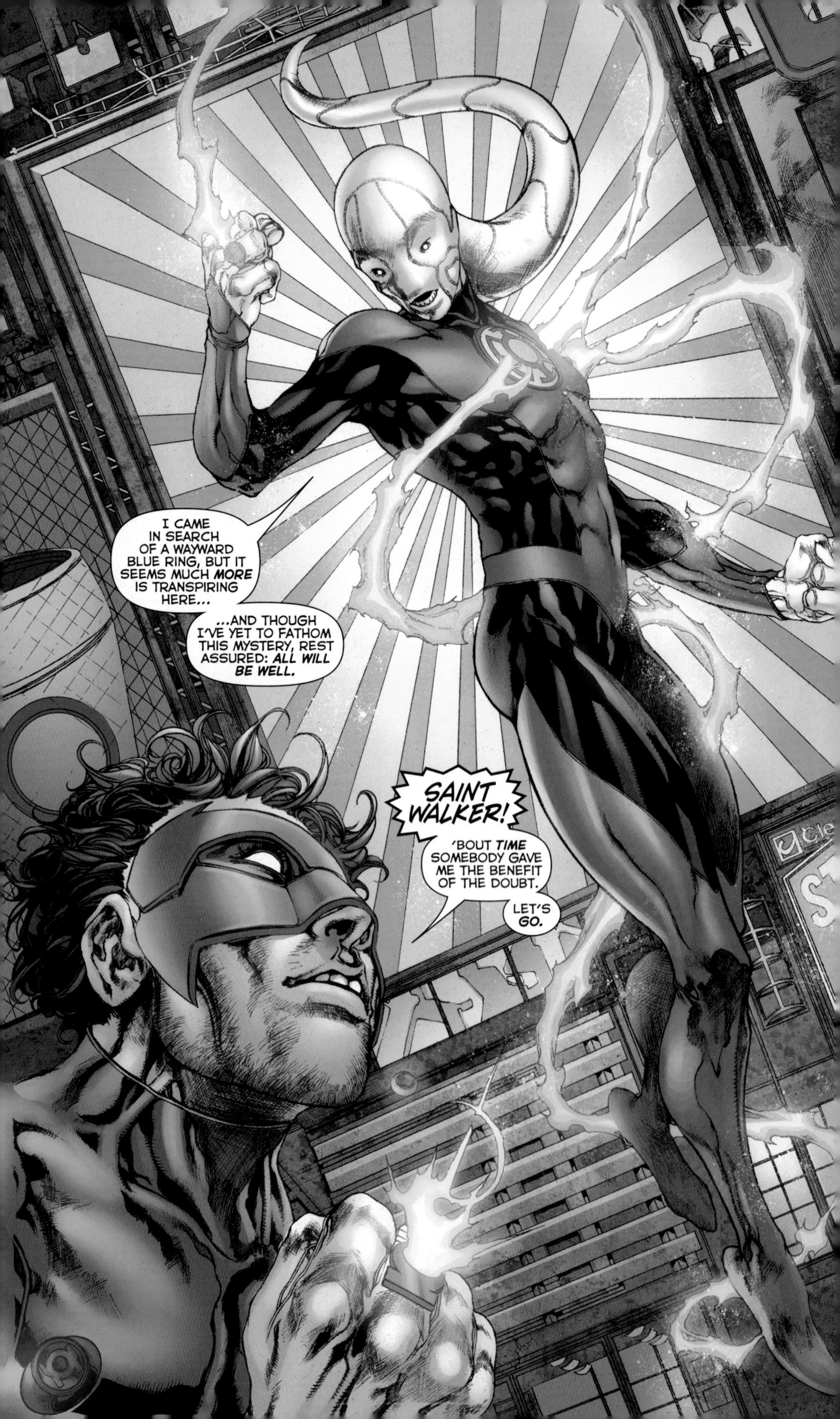
I CAME IN SEARCH OF A WAYWARD BLUE RING, BUT IT SEEMS MUCH *MORE* IS TRANSPIRING HERE...
...AND THOUGH I'VE YET TO FATHOM THIS MYSTERY, REST ASSURED: *ALL WILL BE WELL.*
SAINT WALKER!
'BOUT *TIME* SOMEBODY GAVE ME THE BENEFIT OF THE DOUBT.
LET'S *GO.*

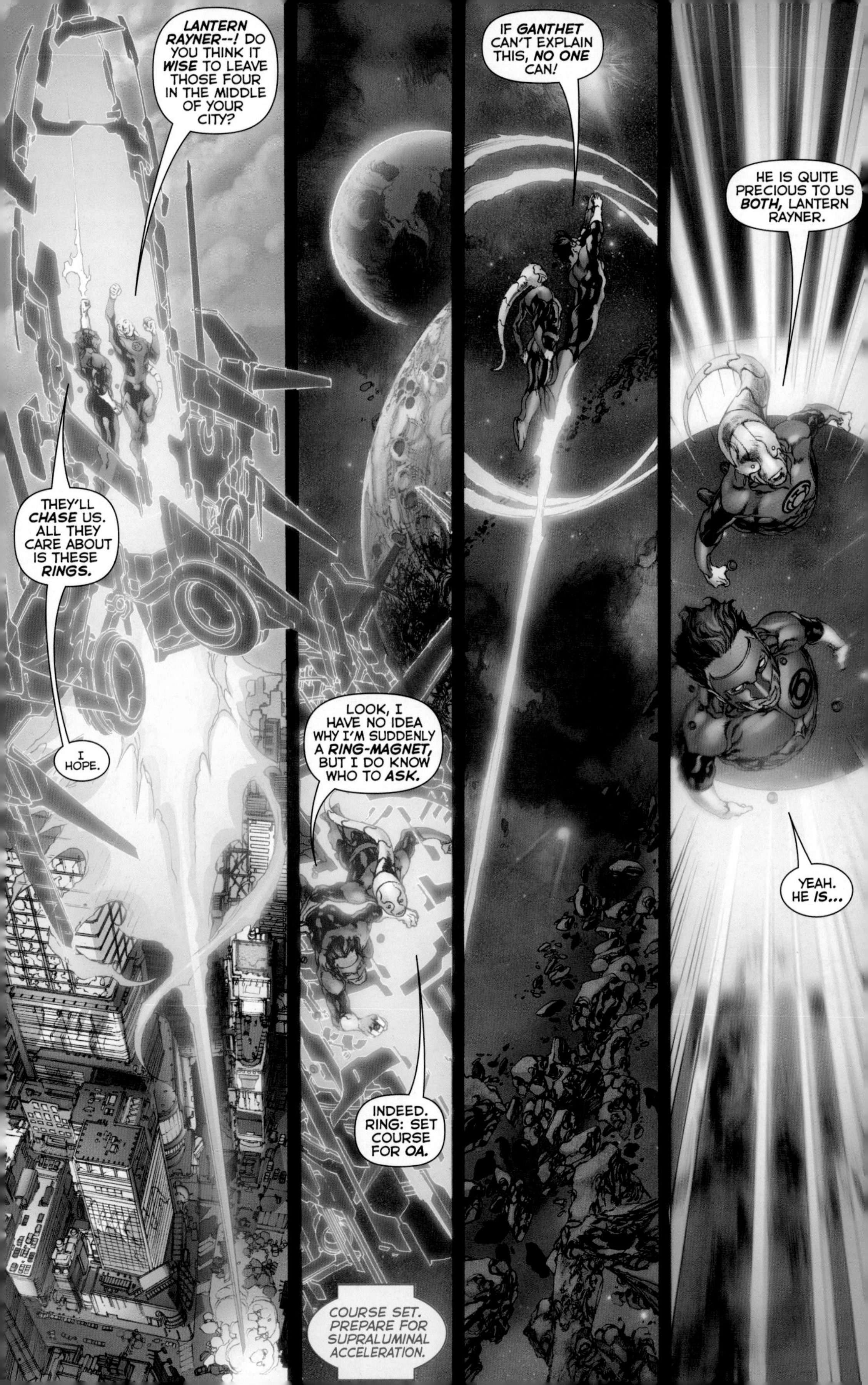
LANTERN RAYNER--! DO YOU THINK IT WISE TO LEAVE THOSE FOUR IN THE MIDDLE OF YOUR CITY?
THEY'LL CHASE US. ALL THEY CARE ABOUT IS THESE RINGS.
I HOPE.
LOOK, I HAVE NO IDEA WHY I'M SUDDENLY A RING-MAGNET, BUT I DO KNOW WHO TO ASK.
INDEED. RING: SET COURSE FOR OA.
COURSE SET. PREPARE FOR SUPRALUMINAL ACCELERATION.
IF GANTHET CAN'T EXPLAIN THIS, NO ONE CAN!
HE IS QUITE PRECIOUS TO US BOTH, LANTERN RAYNER.
YEAH. HE IS...

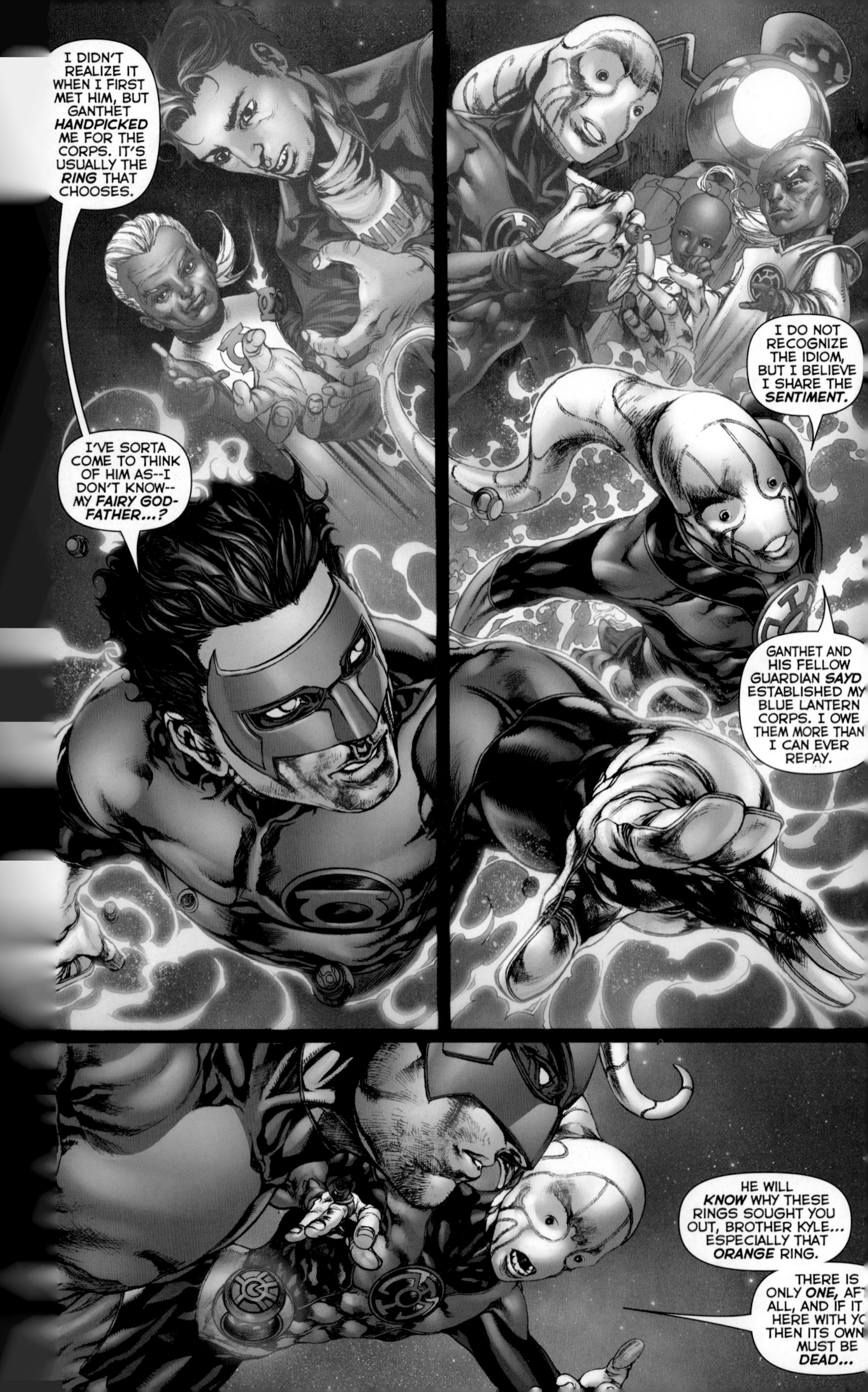
I DIDN'T REALIZE IT WHEN I FIRST MET HIM, BUT GANTHET *HANDPICKED* ME FOR THE CORPS. IT'S USUALLY THE *RING* THAT CHOOSES.
I'VE SORTA COME TO THINK OF HIM AS--I DON'T KNOW--MY *FAIRY GOD-FATHER...?*
I DO NOT RECOGNIZE THE IDIOM, BUT I BELIEVE I SHARE THE *SENTIMENT.*
GANTHET AND HIS FELLOW GUARDIAN *SAYD* ESTABLISHED MY BLUE LANTERN CORPS. I OWE THEM MORE THAN I CAN EVER REPAY.
HE WILL *KNOW* WHY THESE RINGS SOUGHT YOU OUT, BROTHER KYLE... ESPECIALLY THAT *ORANGE* RING.
THERE IS ONLY *ONE,* AF ALL, AND IF IT HERE WITH YO THEN ITS OWN MUST BE *DEAD...*

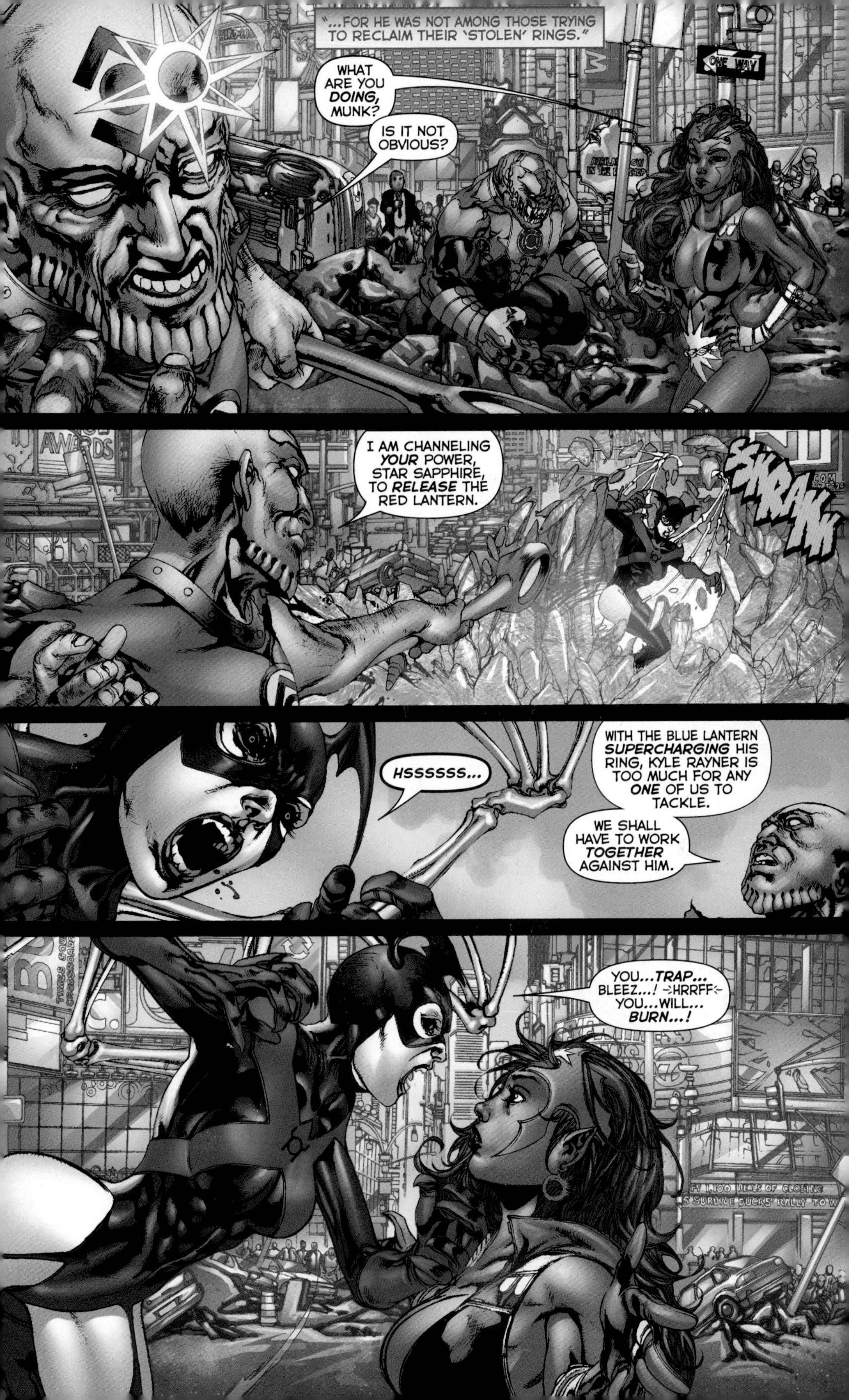
"...FOR HE WAS NOT AMONG THOSE TRYING TO RECLAIM THEIR 'STOLEN' RINGS."
ONE WAY
WHAT ARE YOU *DOING,* MUNK?
IS IT NOT OBVIOUS?
AWARDS
I AM CHANNELING *YOUR* POWER, STAR SAPPHIRE, TO *RELEASE* THE RED LANTERN.
SSHRAKK
HSSSSSS...
WITH THE BLUE LANTERN *SUPERCHARGING* HIS RING, KYLE RAYNER IS TOO MUCH FOR ANY *ONE* OF US TO TACKLE.
WE SHALL HAVE TO WORK *TOGETHER* AGAINST HIM.
YOU...*TRAP...* BLEEZ...! ⇾HRRFF⇽ YOU...WILL... *BURN...!*

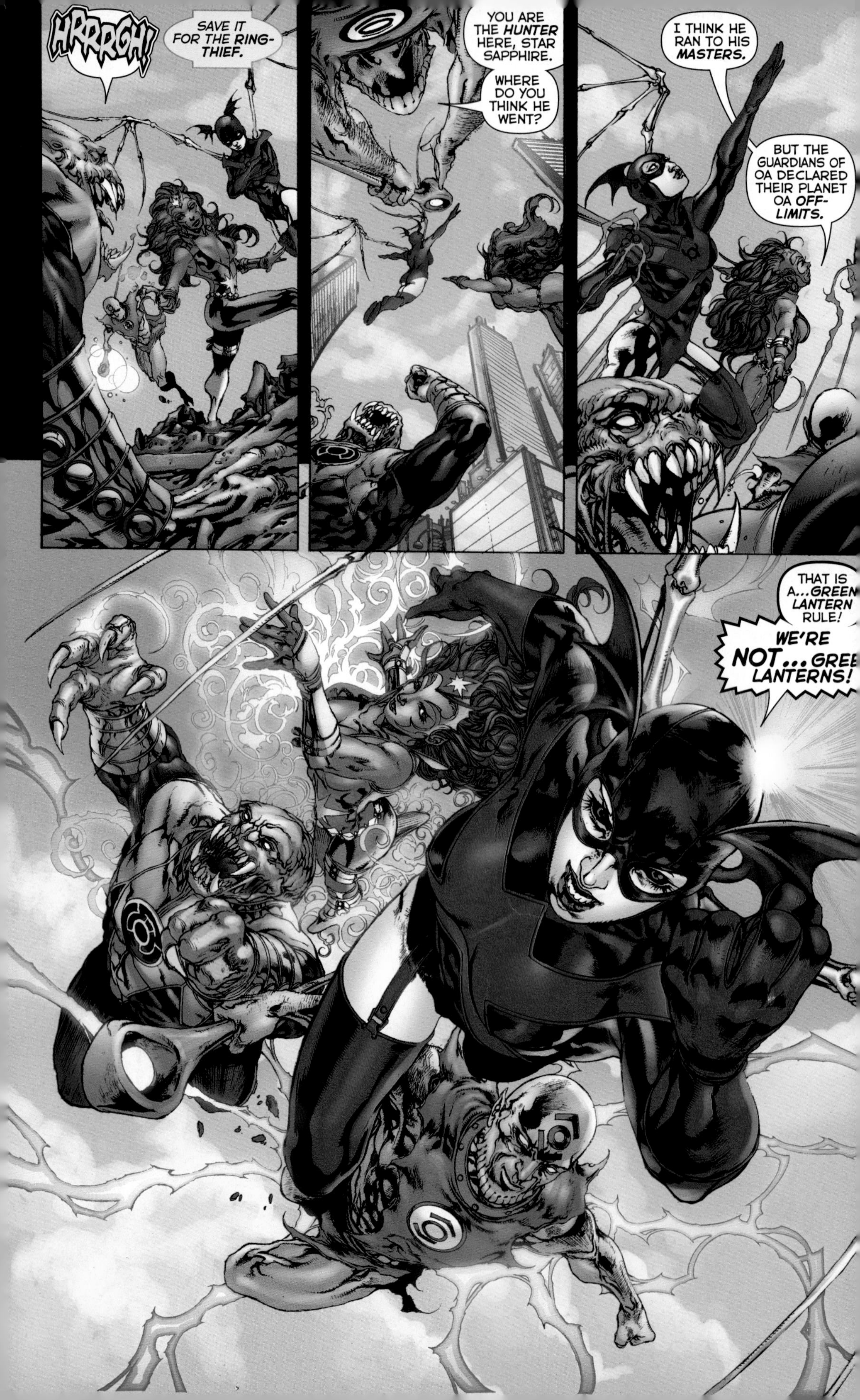
HRRRGH!
SAVE IT FOR THE RING-THIEF.
YOU ARE THE HUNTER HERE, STAR SAPPHIRE.
WHERE DO YOU THINK HE WENT?
I THINK HE RAN TO HIS MASTERS.
BUT THE GUARDIANS OF OA DECLARED THEIR PLANET OA OFF-LIMITS.
THAT IS A...GREEN LANTERN RULE!
WE'RE NOT...GREE LANTERNS!

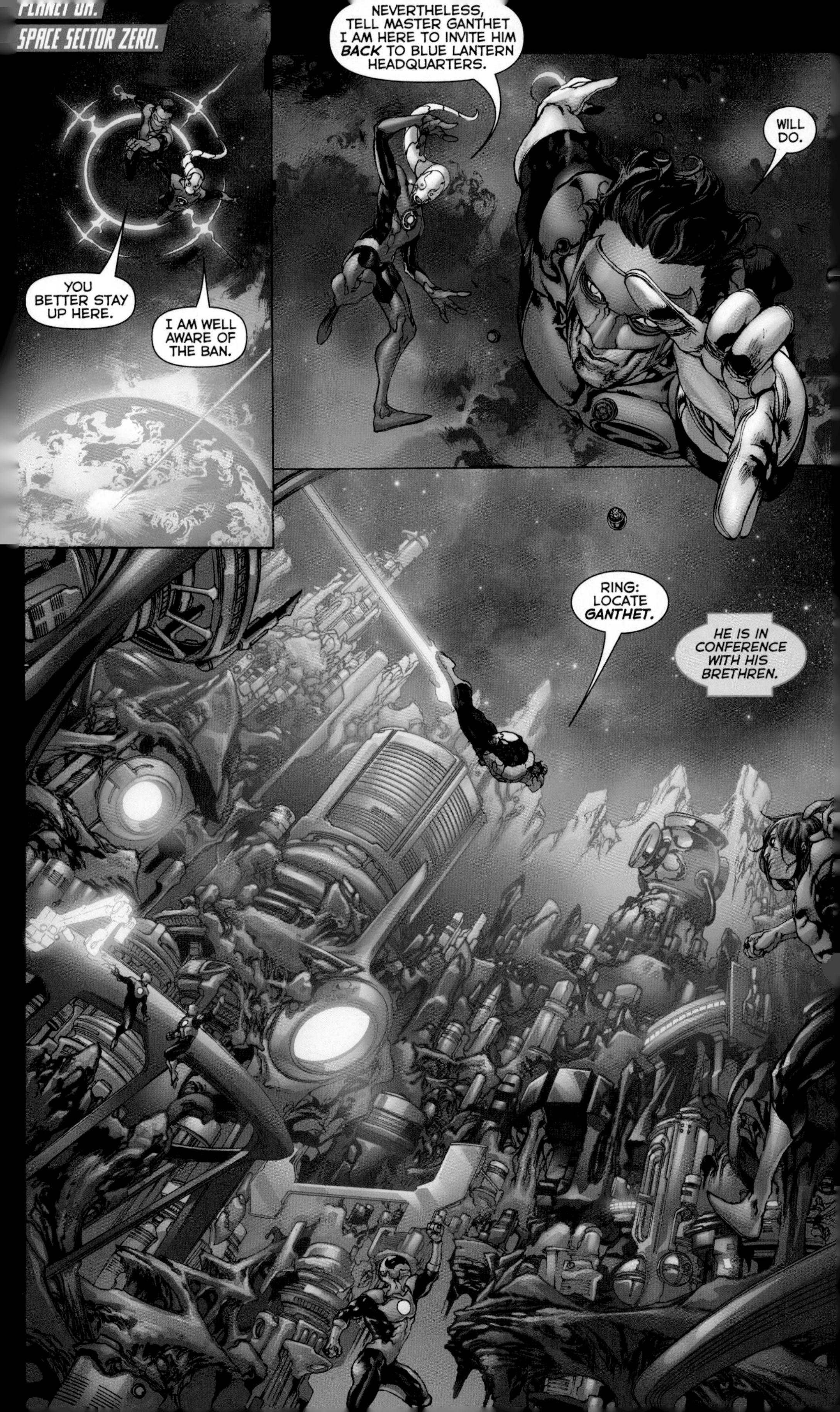

SPACE SECTOR ZERO.
YOU BETTER STAY UP HERE.
I AM WELL AWARE OF THE BAN.
NEVERTHELESS, TELL MASTER GANTHET I AM HERE TO INVITE HIM *BACK* TO BLUE LANTERN HEADQUARTERS.
WILL DO.
RING: LOCATE *GANTHET.*
HE IS IN CONFERENCE WITH HIS BRETHREN.

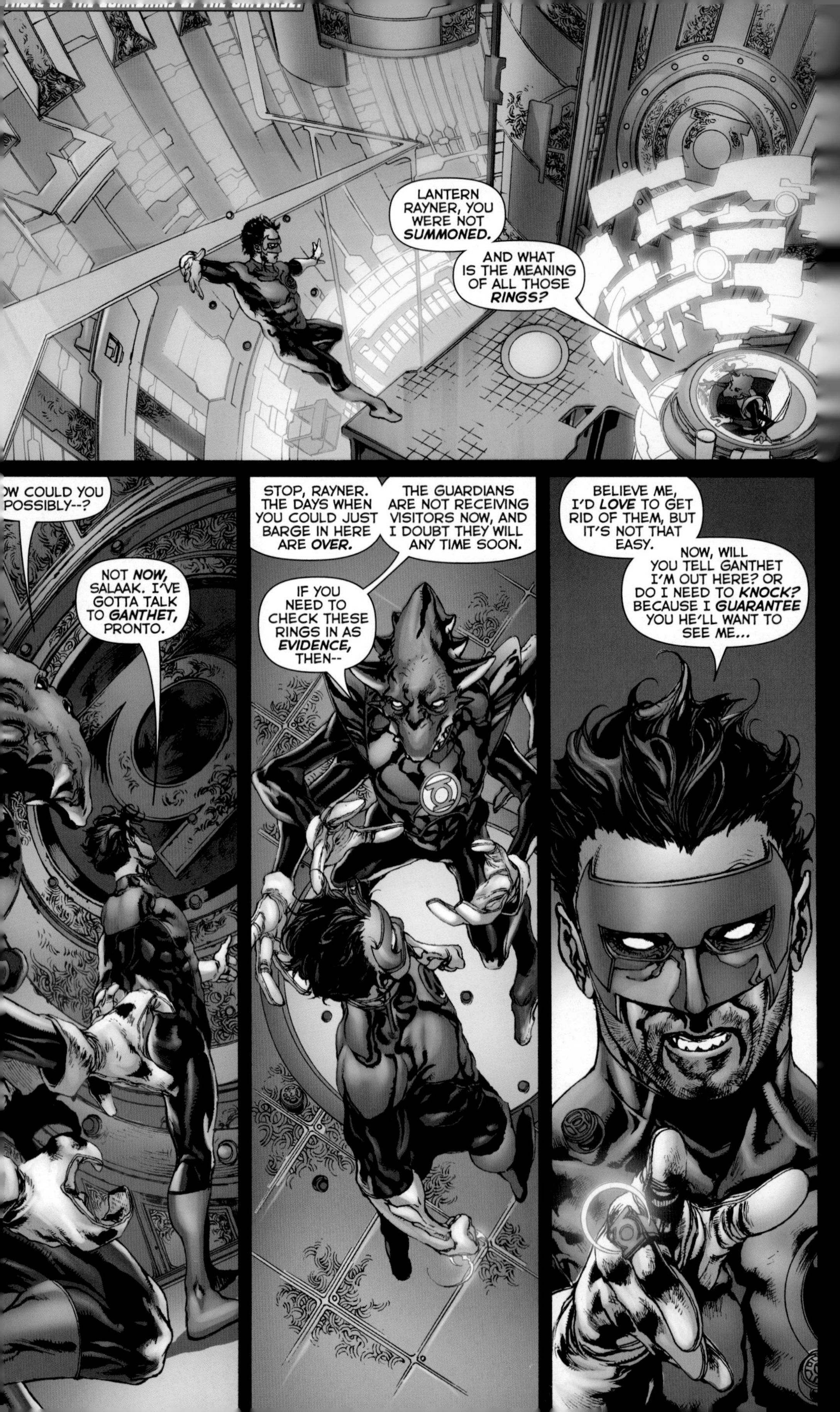
LANTERN RAYNER, YOU WERE NOT SUMMONED.
AND WHAT IS THE MEANING OF ALL THOSE RINGS?
OW COULD YOU POSSIBLY--?
NOT NOW, SALAAK. I'VE GOTTA TALK TO GANTHET, PRONTO.
STOP, RAYNER. THE DAYS WHEN YOU COULD JUST BARGE IN HERE ARE OVER.
THE GUARDIANS ARE NOT RECEIVING VISITORS NOW, AND I DOUBT THEY WILL ANY TIME SOON.
IF YOU NEED TO CHECK THESE RINGS IN AS EVIDENCE, THEN--
BELIEVE ME, I'D LOVE TO GET RID OF THEM, BUT IT'S NOT THAT EASY.
NOW, WILL YOU TELL GANTHET I'M OUT HERE? OR DO I NEED TO KNOCK? BECAUSE I GUARANTEE YOU HE'LL WANT TO SEE ME...

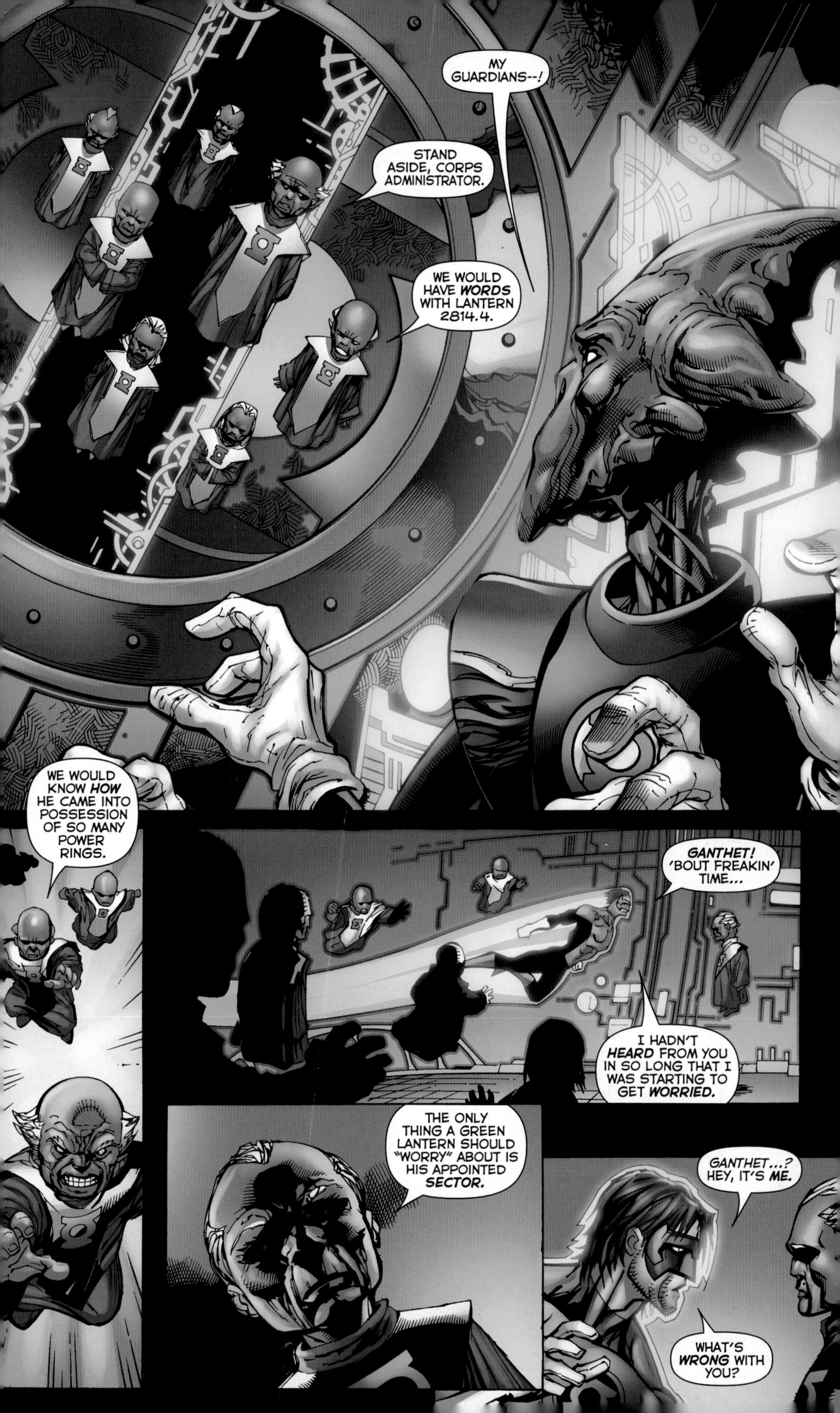

MY GUARDIANS--!
STAND ASIDE, CORPS ADMINISTRATOR.
WE WOULD HAVE **WORDS** WITH LANTERN 2814.4.
WE WOULD KNOW **HOW** HE CAME INTO POSSESSION OF SO MANY POWER RINGS.
GANTHET! 'BOUT FREAKIN' TIME...
I HADN'T **HEARD** FROM YOU IN SO LONG THAT I WAS STARTING TO GET **WORRIED.**
THE ONLY THING A GREEN LANTERN SHOULD "WORRY" ABOUT IS HIS APPOINTED **SECTOR.**
GANTHET...? HEY, IT'S **ME.**
WHAT'S **WRONG** WITH YOU?

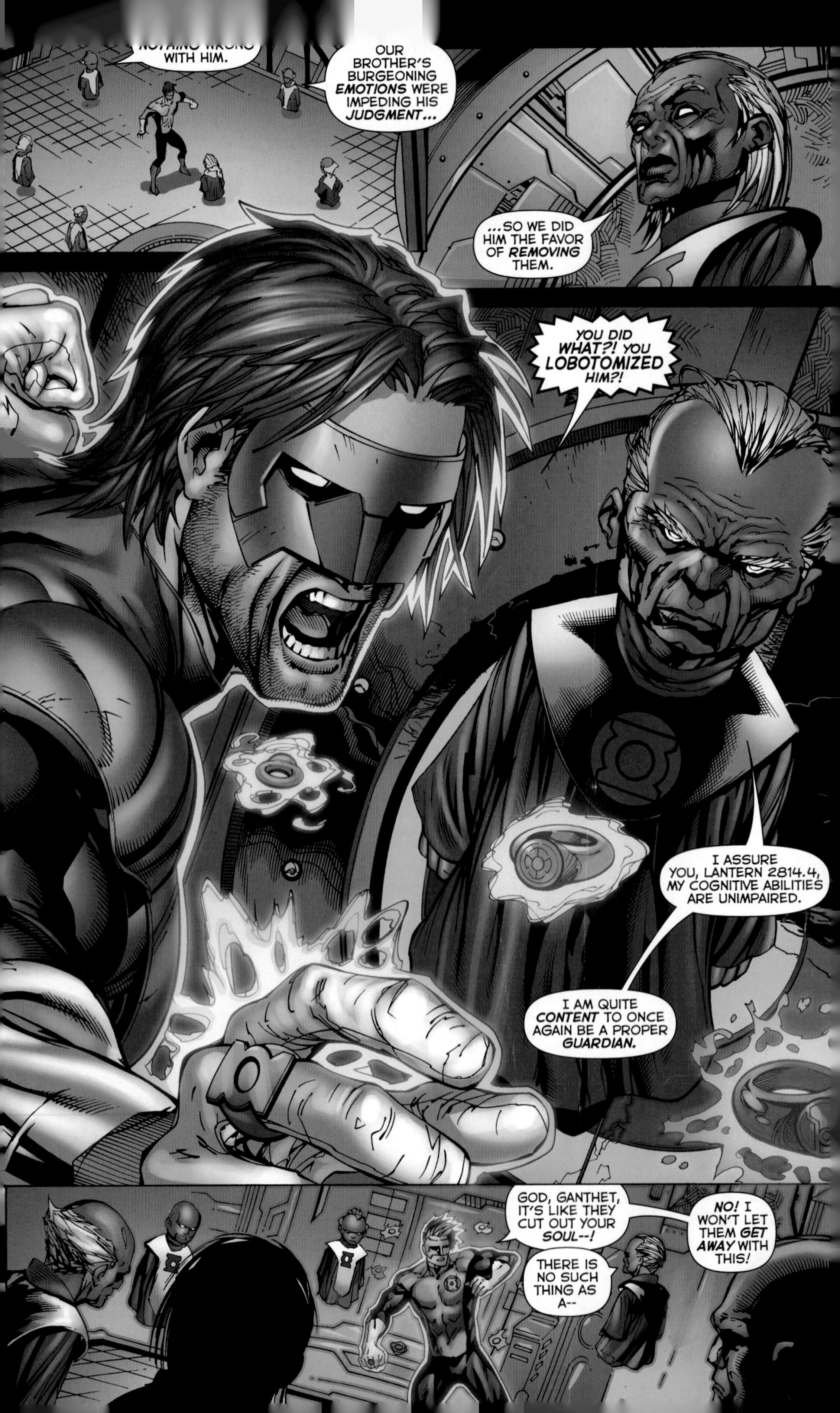
WITH HIM.
OUR BROTHER'S BURGEONING EMOTIONS WERE IMPEDING HIS JUDGMENT...
...SO WE DID HIM THE FAVOR OF REMOVING THEM.
YOU DID WHAT?! YOU LOBOTOMIZED HIM?!
I ASSURE YOU, LANTERN 2814.4, MY COGNITIVE ABILITIES ARE UNIMPAIRED.
I AM QUITE CONTENT TO ONCE AGAIN BE A PROPER GUARDIAN.
GOD, GANTHET, IT'S LIKE THEY CUT OUT YOUR SOUL--!
THERE IS NO SUCH THING AS A--
NO! I WON'T LET THEM GET AWAY WITH THIS!

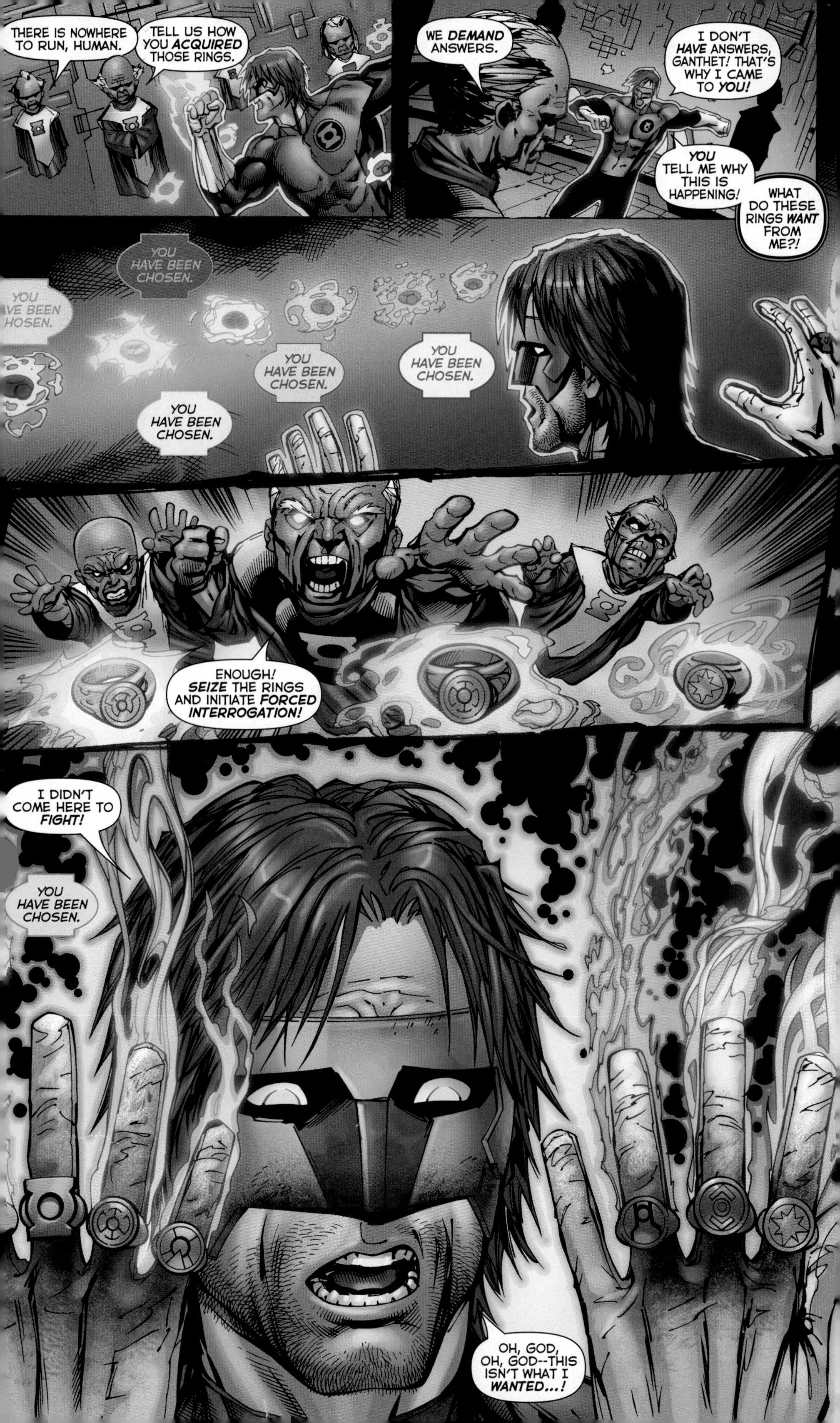
THERE IS NOWHERE TO RUN, HUMAN.
TELL US HOW YOU ACQUIRED THOSE RINGS.
WE DEMAND ANSWERS.
I DON'T HAVE ANSWERS, GANTHET! THAT'S WHY I CAME TO YOU!
YOU TELL ME WHY THIS IS HAPPENING!
WHAT DO THESE RINGS WANT FROM ME?!
YOU HAVE BEEN CHOSEN.
YOU HAVE BEEN CHOSEN.
YOU HAVE BEEN CHOSEN.
YOU HAVE BEEN CHOSEN.
YOU HAVE BEEN CHOSEN.
ENOUGH! SEIZE THE RINGS AND INITIATE FORCED INTERROGATION!
I DIDN'T COME HERE TO FIGHT!
YOU HAVE BEEN CHOSEN.
OH, GOD, OH, GOD--THIS ISN'T WHAT I WANTED...!

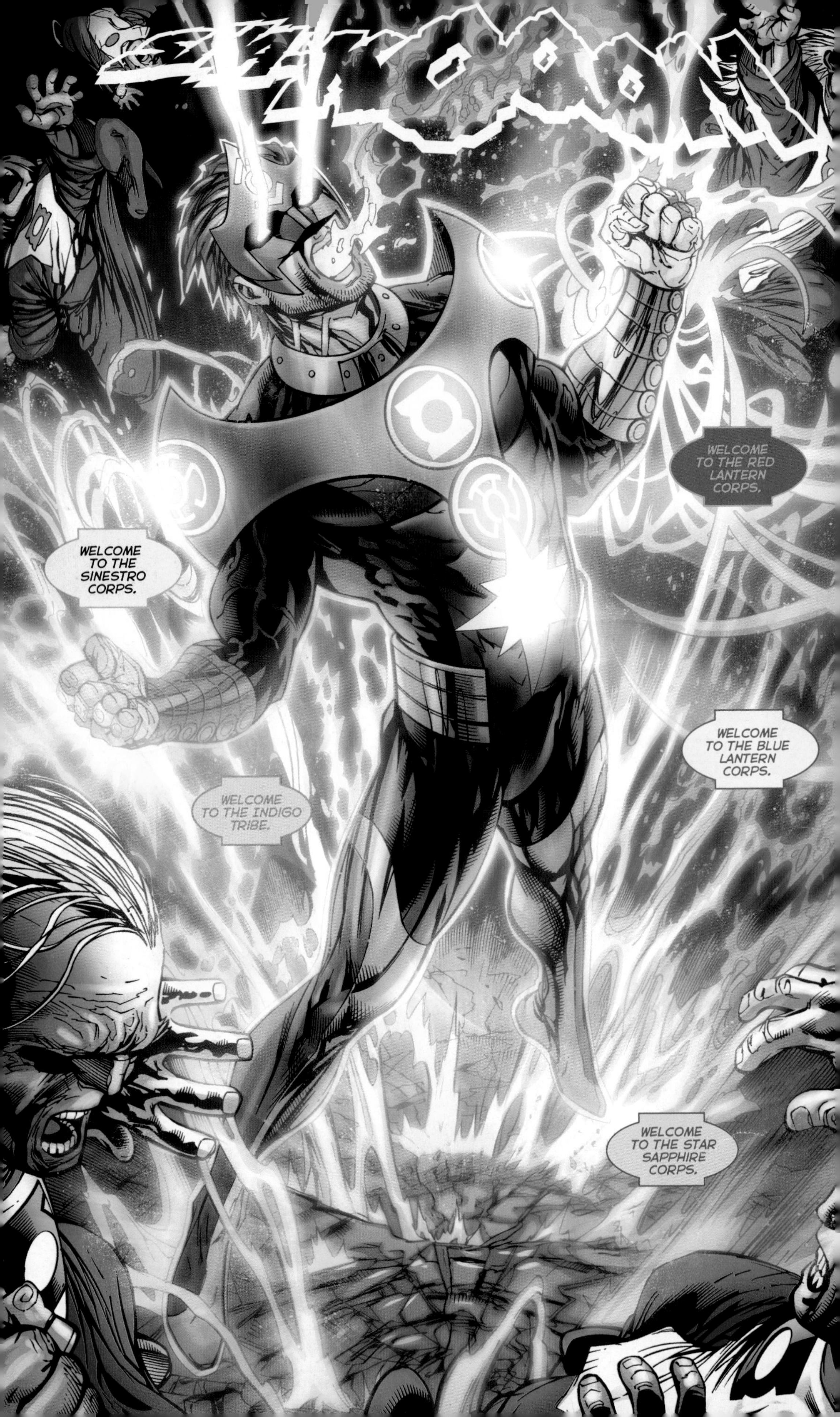
WELCOME TO THE RED LANTERN CORPS.
WELCOME TO THE SINESTRO CORPS.
WELCOME TO THE BLUE LANTERN CORPS.
WELCOME TO THE INDIGO TRIBE.
WELCOME TO THE STAR SAPPHIRE CORPS.

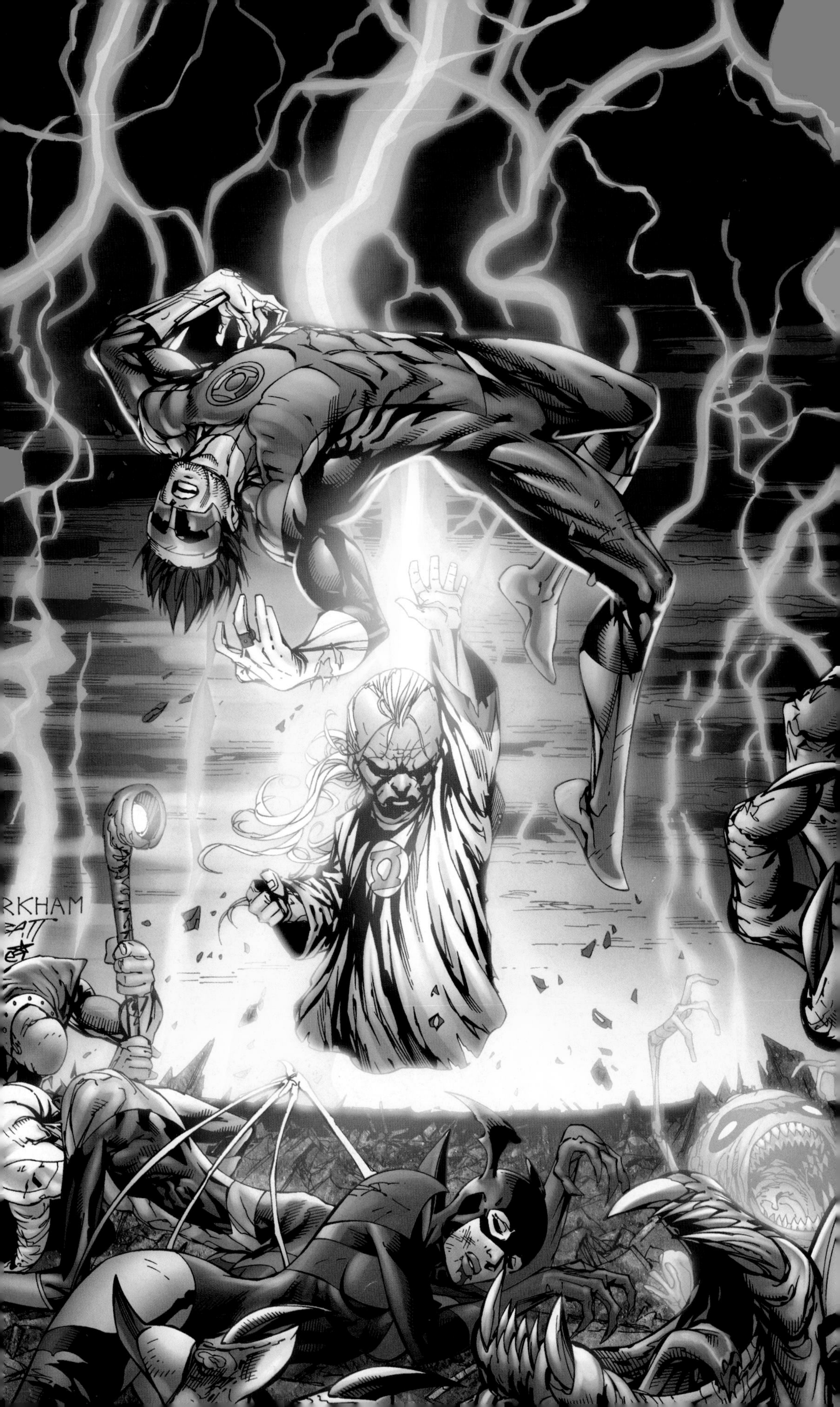

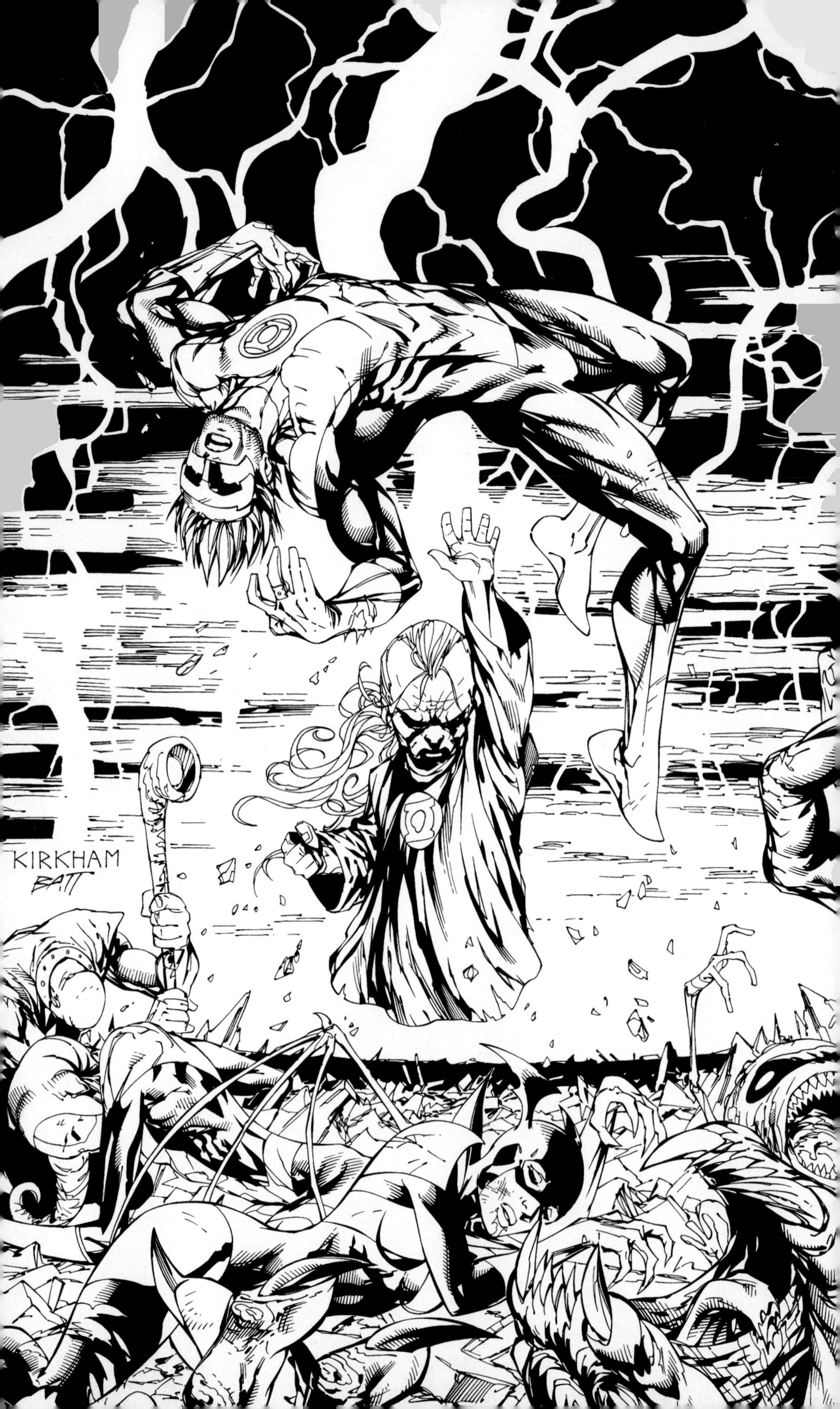
KIRKHAM
BATT

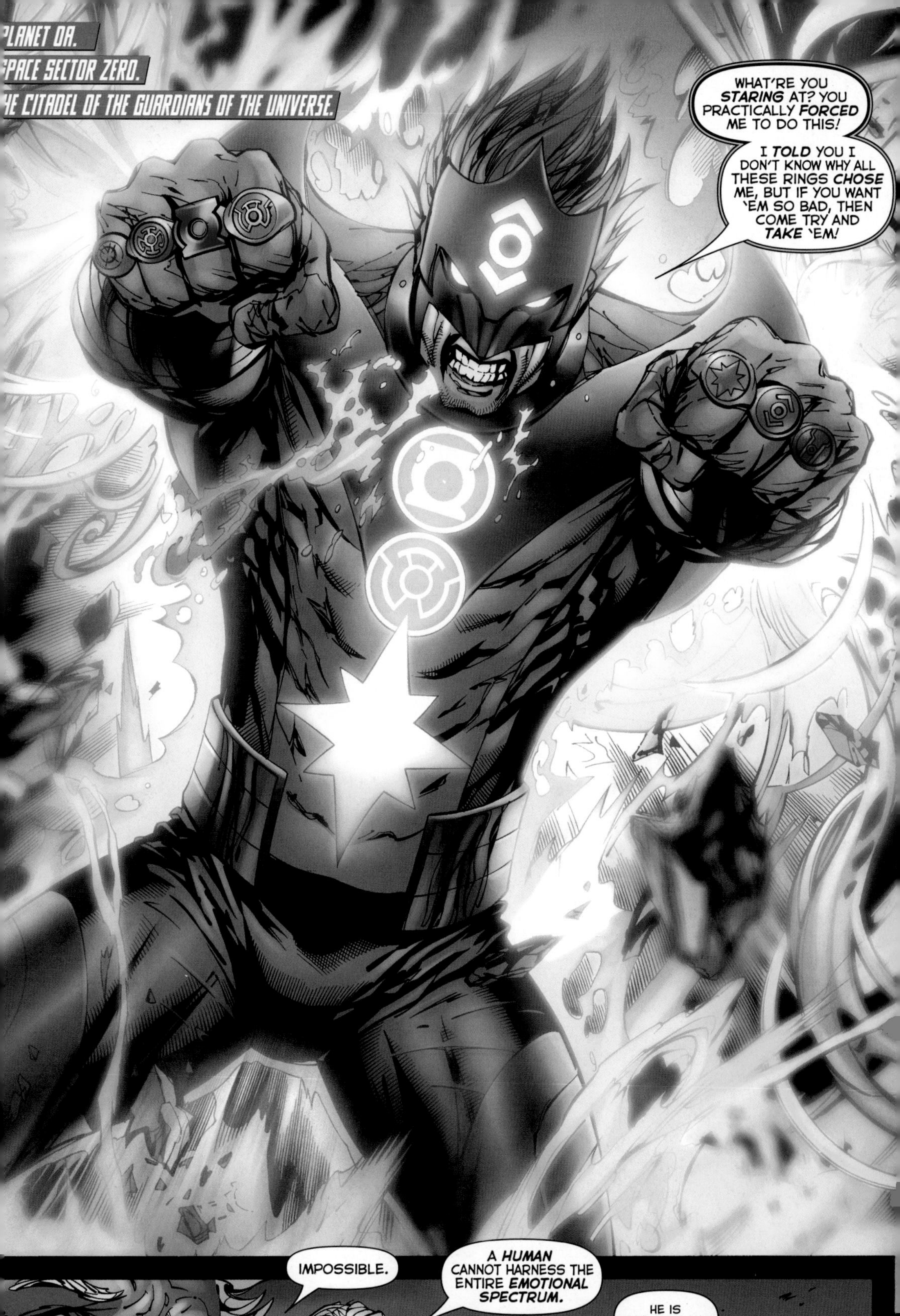
PLANET OA.
SPACE SECTOR ZERO.
THE CITADEL OF THE GUARDIANS OF THE UNIVERSE.
WHAT'RE YOU STARING AT? YOU PRACTICALLY FORCED ME TO DO THIS!
I TOLD YOU I DON'T KNOW WHY ALL THESE RINGS CHOSE ME, BUT IF YOU WANT 'EM SO BAD, THEN COME TRY AND TAKE 'EM!

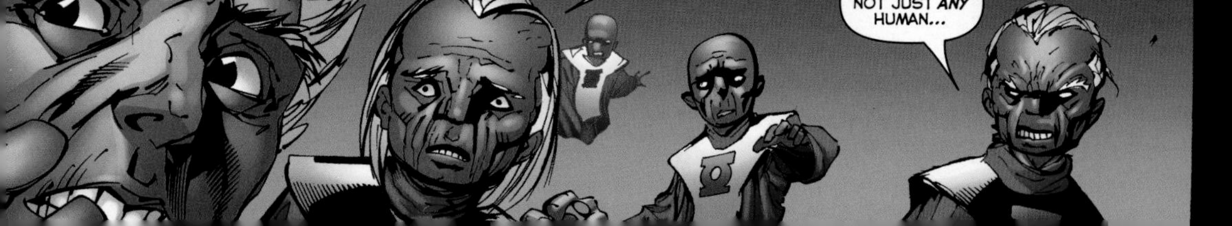
IMPOSSIBLE.
A HUMAN CANNOT HARNESS THE ENTIRE EMOTIONAL SPECTRUM.
HE IS NOT JUST ANY HUMAN...

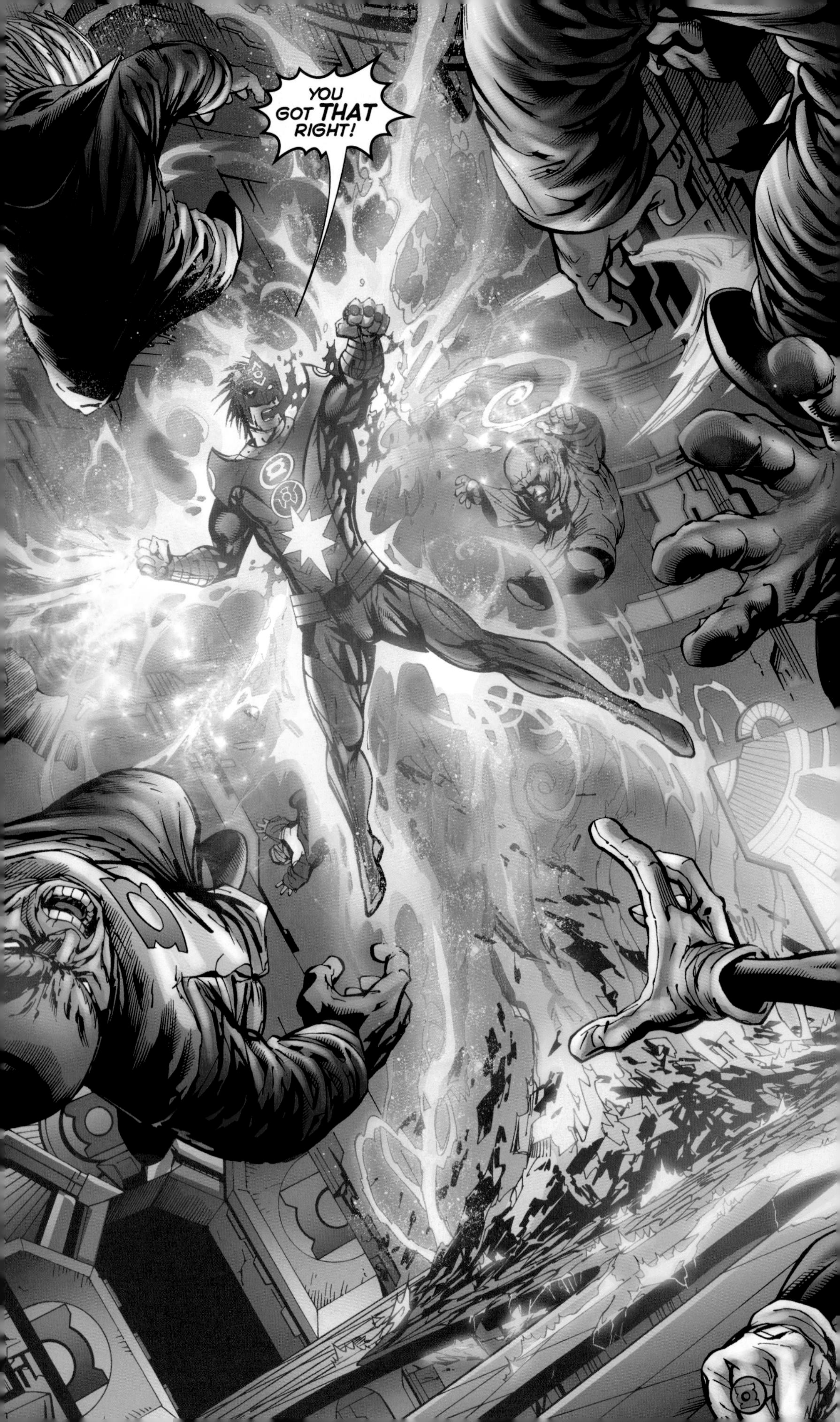
YOU GOT THAT RIGHT!

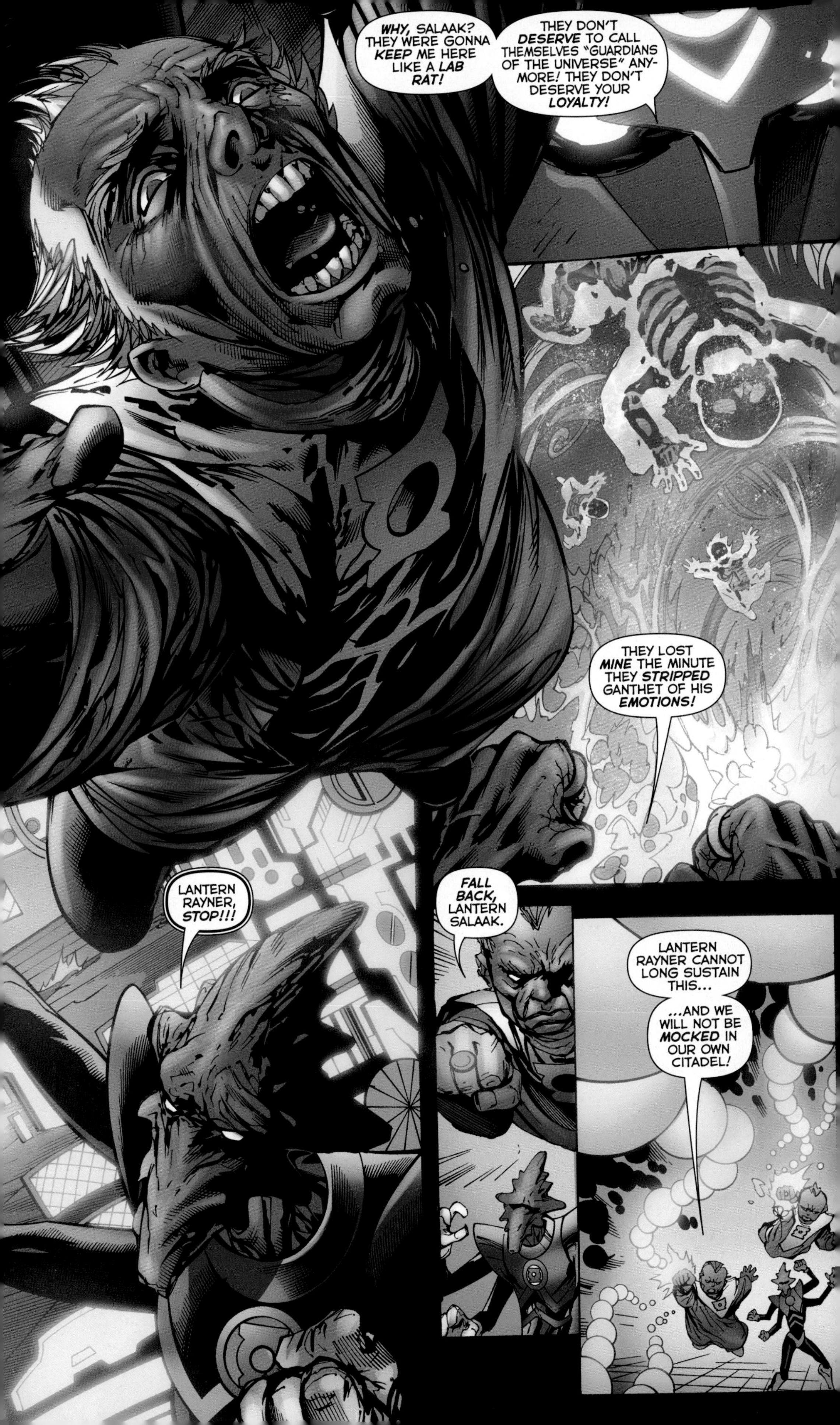
WHY, SALAAK? THEY WERE GONNA KEEP ME HERE LIKE A LAB RAT!
THEY DON'T DESERVE TO CALL THEMSELVES "GUARDIANS OF THE UNIVERSE" ANY-MORE! THEY DON'T DESERVE YOUR LOYALTY!
THEY LOST MINE THE MINUTE THEY STRIPPED GANTHET OF HIS EMOTIONS!
LANTERN RAYNER, STOP!!!
FALL BACK, LANTERN SALAAK.
LANTERN RAYNER CANNOT LONG SUSTAIN THIS...
...AND WE WILL NOT BE MOCKED IN OUR OWN CITADEL!

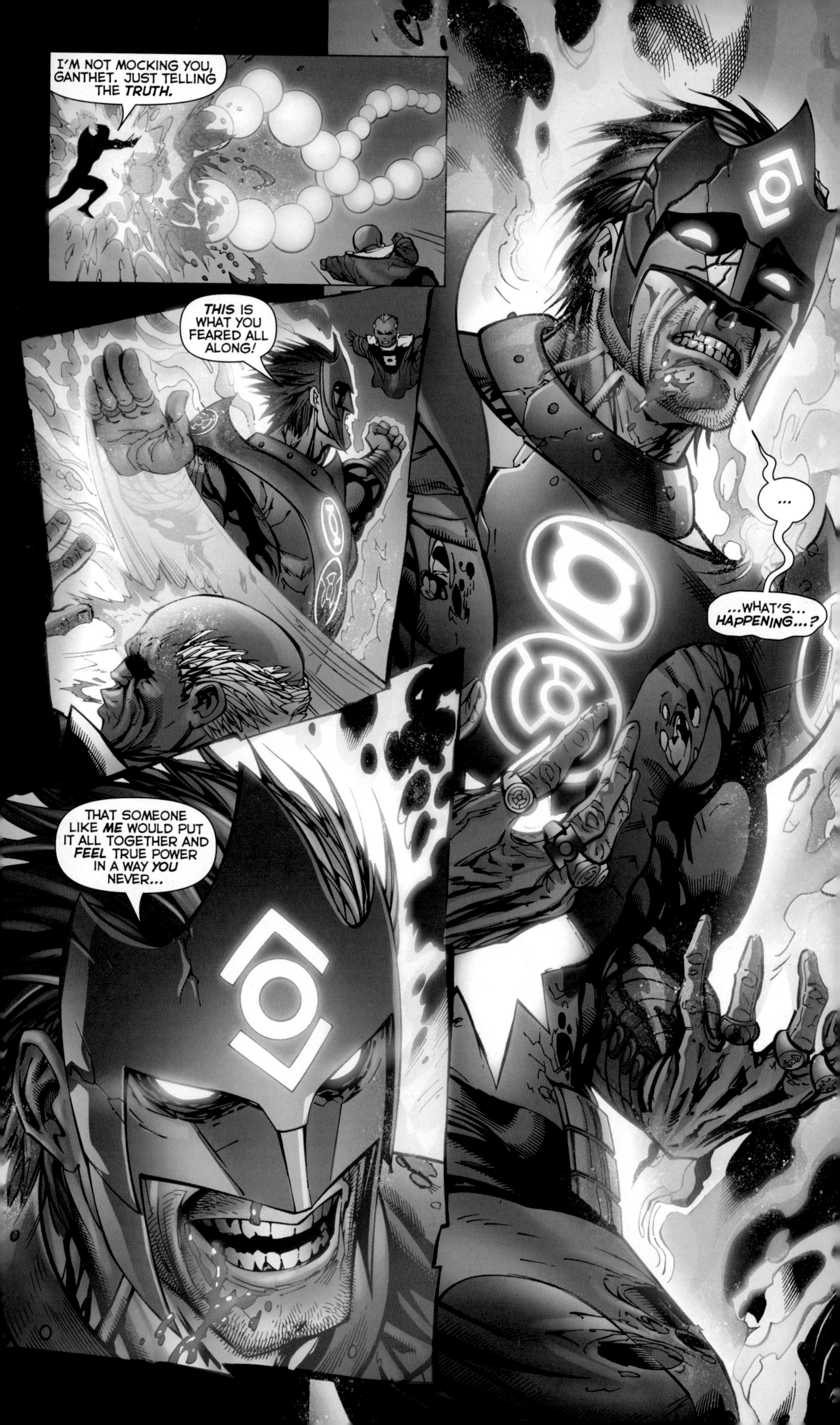
I'M NOT MOCKING YOU, GANTHET. JUST TELLING THE TRUTH.
THIS IS WHAT YOU FEARED ALL ALONG!
...
...WHAT'S... HAPPENING...?
THAT SOMEONE LIKE ME WOULD PUT IT ALL TOGETHER AND FEEL TRUE POWER IN A WAY YOU NEVER...

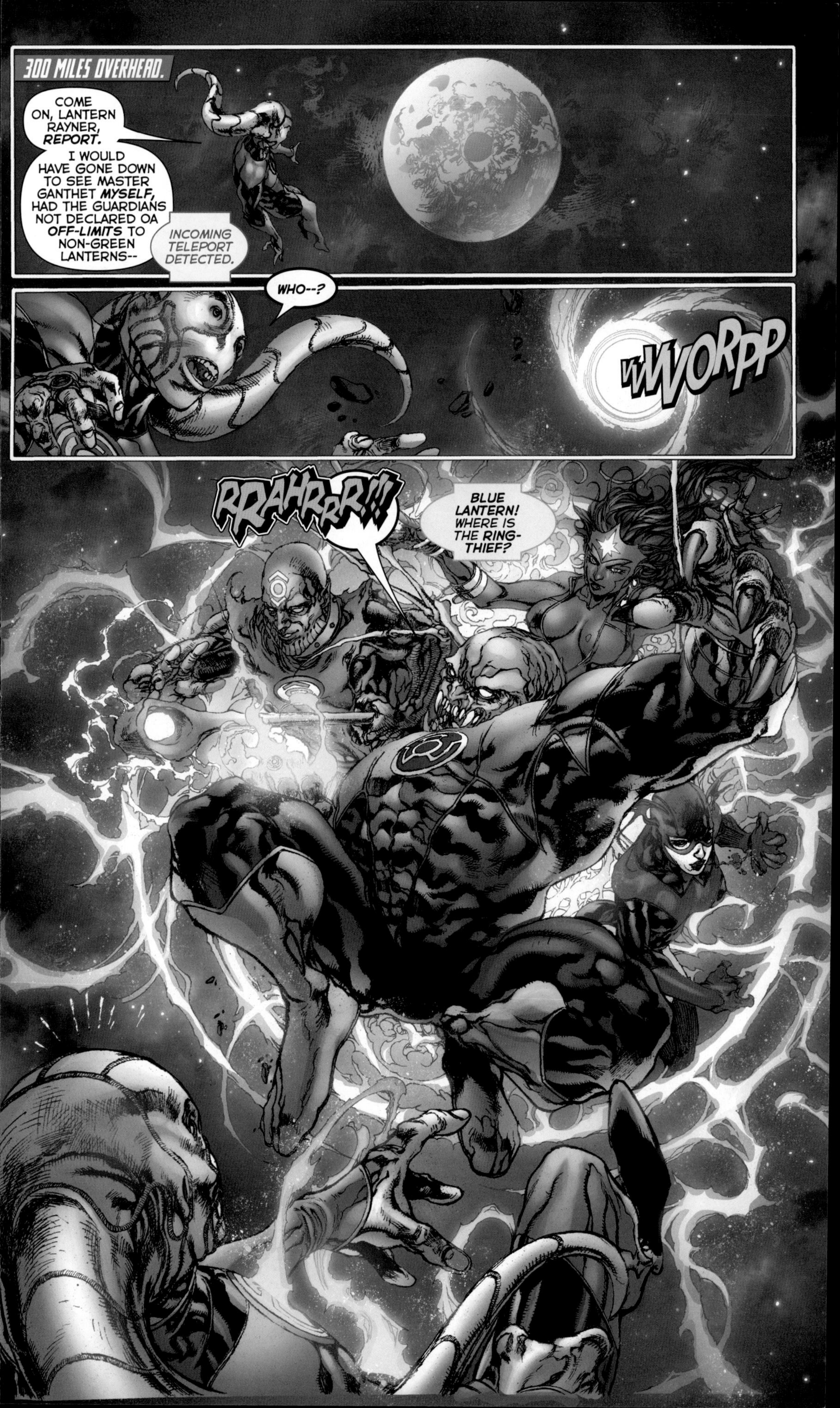
300 MILES OVERHEAD.
COME ON, LANTERN RAYNER, REPORT.
I WOULD HAVE GONE DOWN TO SEE MASTER GANTHET MYSELF, HAD THE GUARDIANS NOT DECLARED OA OFF-LIMITS TO NON-GREEN LANTERNS--
INCOMING TELEPORT DETECTED.
WHO--?
VVVVORPP
RRAHRRR!!!
BLUE LANTERN! WHERE IS THE RING-THIEF?
!!!

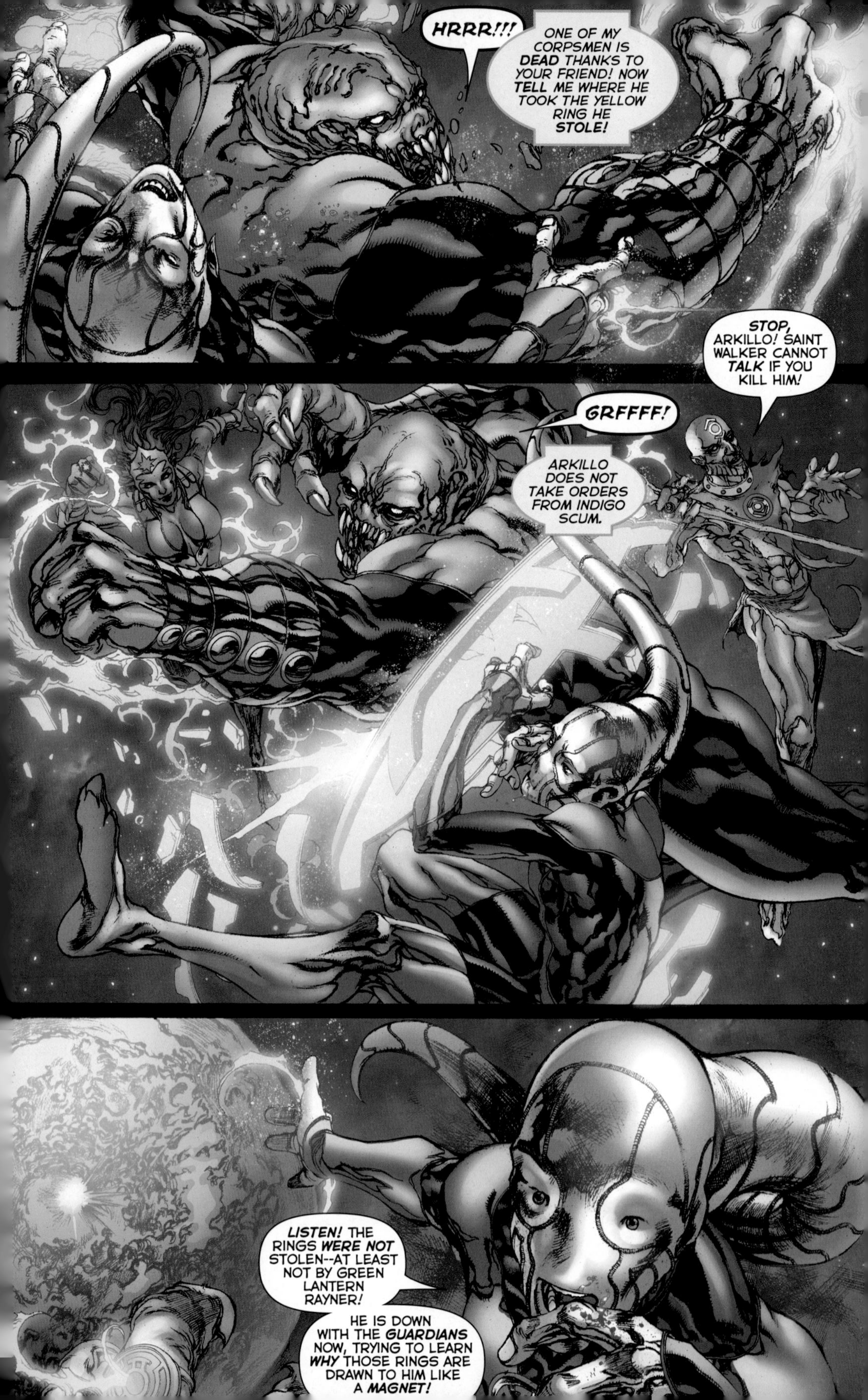
HRRR!!!
ONE OF MY CORPSMEN IS DEAD THANKS TO YOUR FRIEND! NOW TELL ME WHERE HE TOOK THE YELLOW RING HE STOLE!
STOP, ARKILLO! SAINT WALKER CANNOT TALK IF YOU KILL HIM!
GRFFFF!
ARKILLO DOES NOT TAKE ORDERS FROM INDIGO SCUM.
LISTEN! THE RINGS WERE NOT STOLEN--AT LEAST NOT BY GREEN LANTERN RAYNER!
HE IS DOWN WITH THE GUARDIANS NOW, TRYING TO LEARN WHY THOSE RINGS ARE DRAWN TO HIM LIKE A MAGNET!

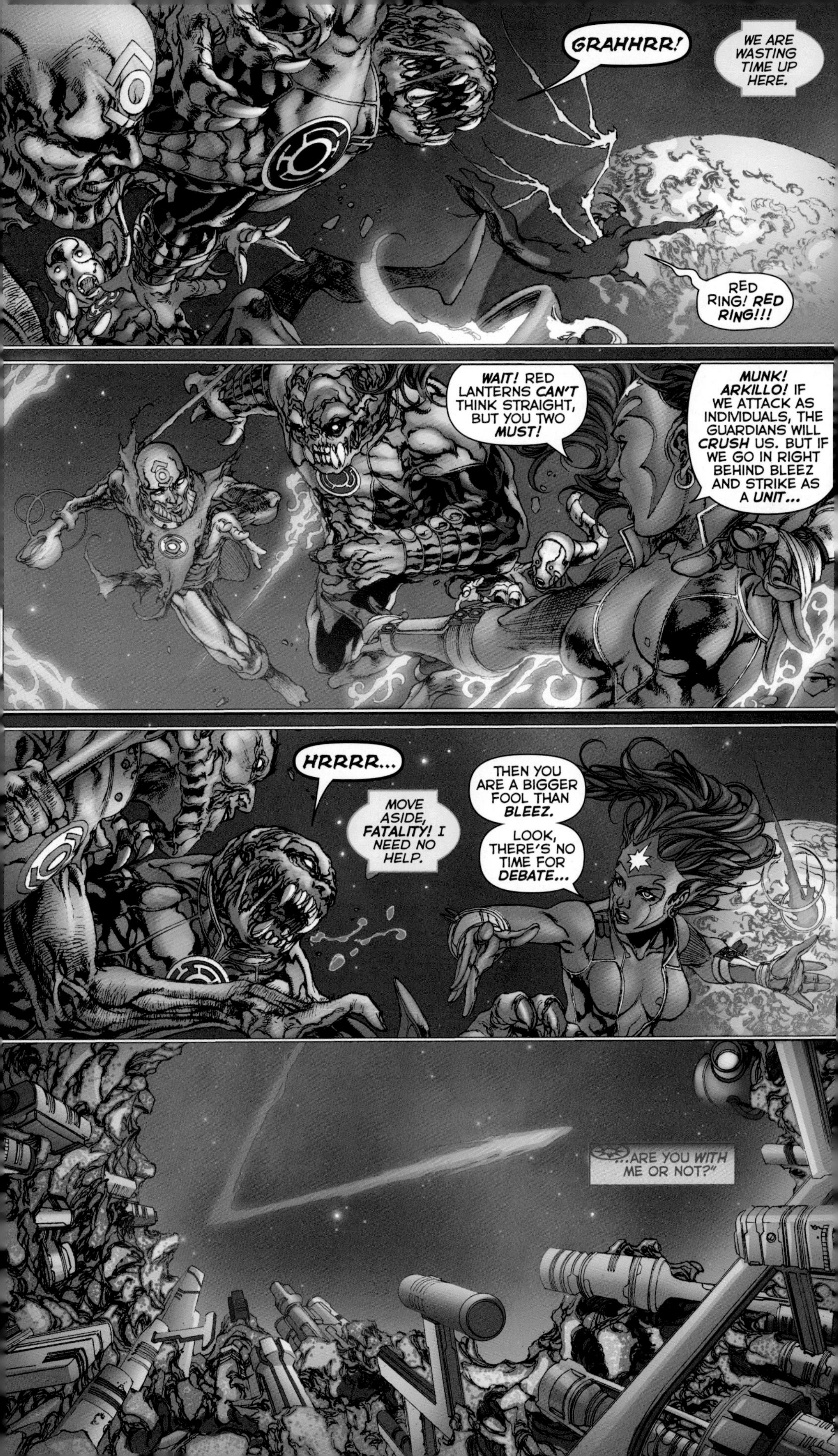
GRAHHRR!
WE ARE WASTING TIME UP HERE.
RED RING! RED RING!!!
WAIT! RED LANTERNS CAN'T THINK STRAIGHT, BUT YOU TWO MUST!
MUNK! ARKILLO! IF WE ATTACK AS INDIVIDUALS, THE GUARDIANS WILL CRUSH US. BUT IF WE GO IN RIGHT BEHIND BLEEZ AND STRIKE AS A UNIT...
HRRRR...
MOVE ASIDE, FATALITY! I NEED NO HELP.
THEN YOU ARE A BIGGER FOOL THAN BLEEZ.
LOOK, THERE'S NO TIME FOR DEBATE...
"...ARE YOU WITH ME OR NOT?"

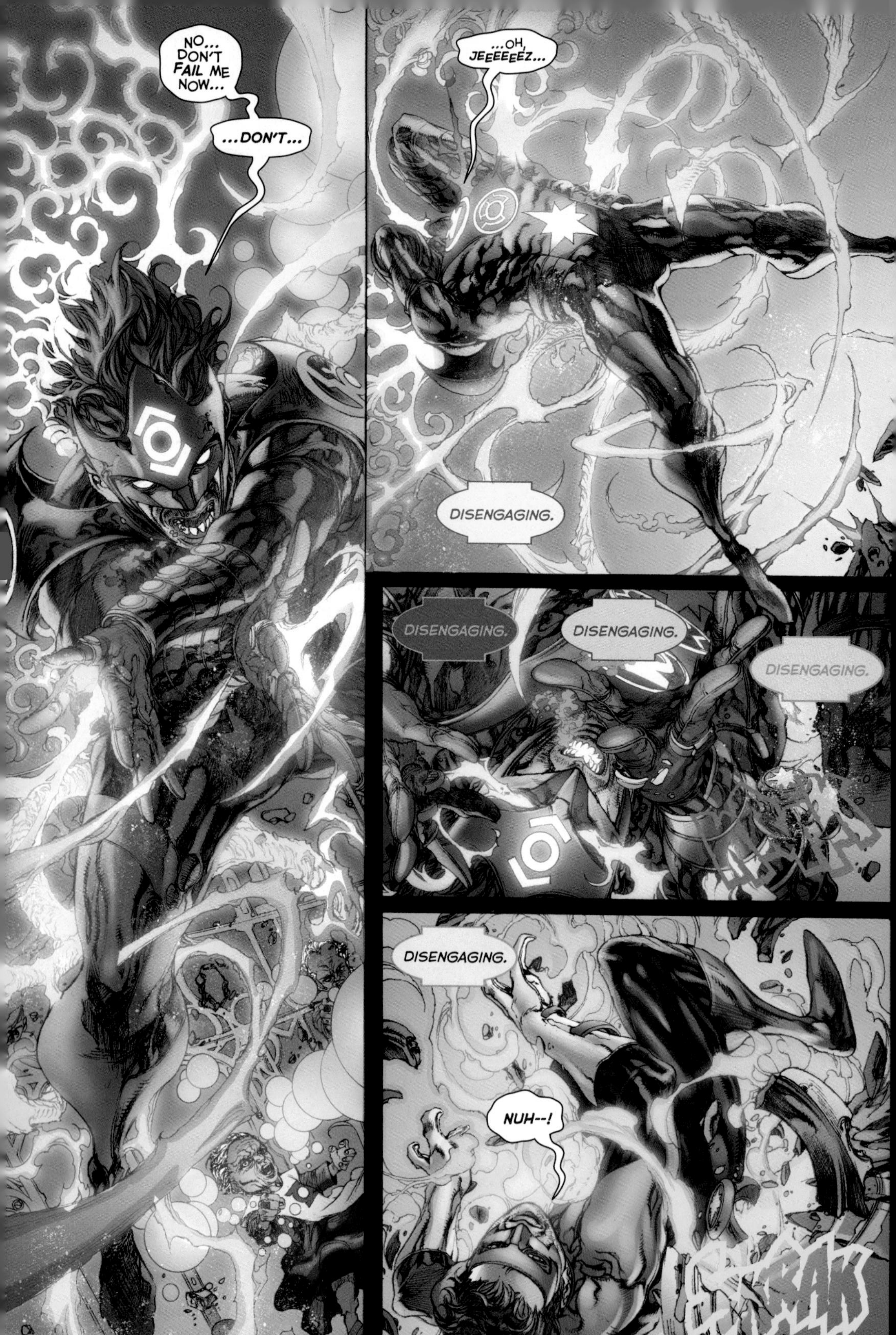
NO... DON'T FAIL ME NOW...
...DON'T...
...OH, JEEEEEEZ...
DISENGAGING.
DISENGAGING.
DISENGAGING.
DISENGAGING.
DISENGAGING.
NUH--!
KRAK

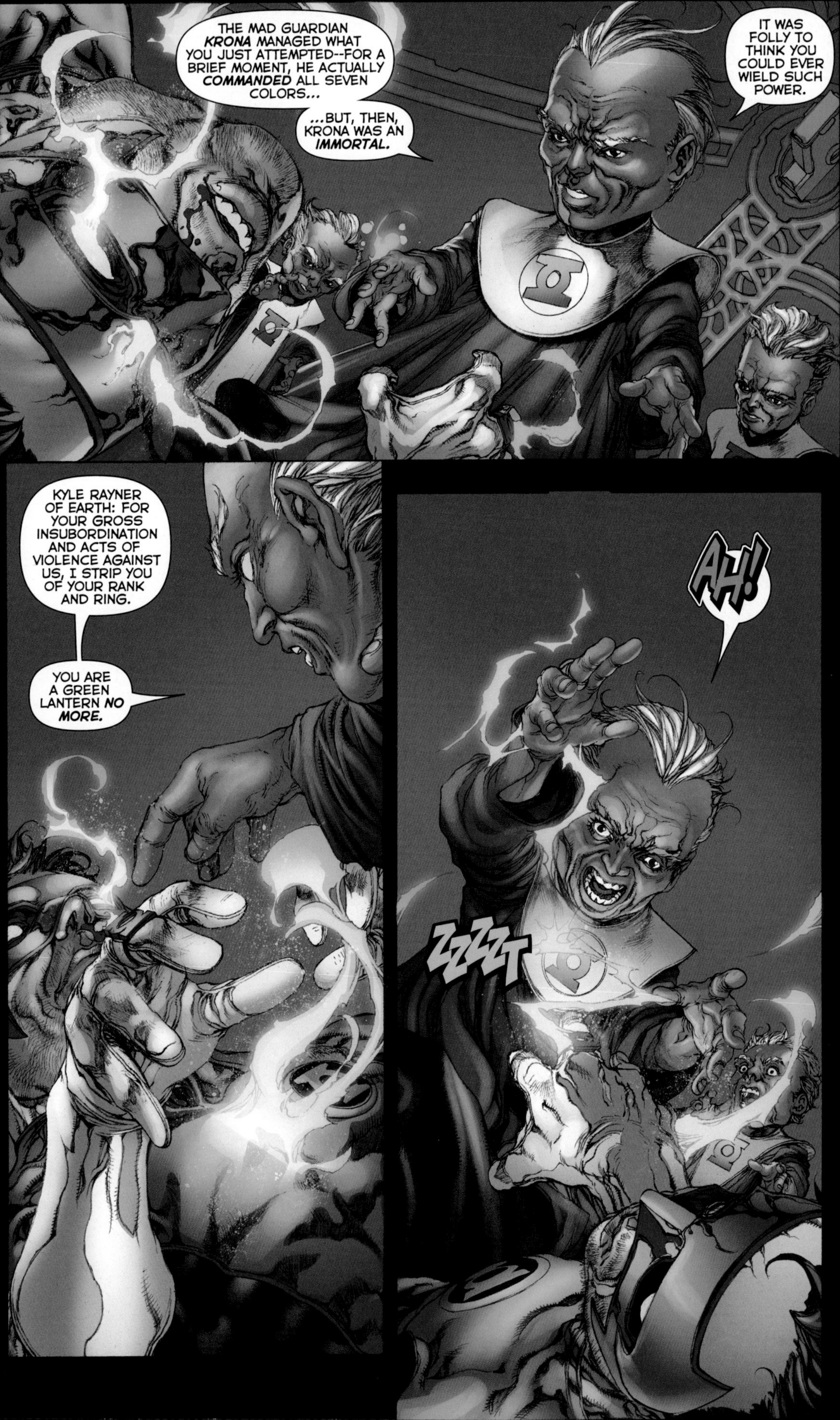
THE MAD GUARDIAN KRONA MANAGED WHAT YOU JUST ATTEMPTED--FOR A BRIEF MOMENT, HE ACTUALLY COMMANDED ALL SEVEN COLORS...
...BUT, THEN, KRONA WAS AN IMMORTAL.
IT WAS FOLLY TO THINK YOU COULD EVER WIELD SUCH POWER.
KYLE RAYNER OF EARTH: FOR YOUR GROSS INSUBORDINATION AND ACTS OF VIOLENCE AGAINST US, I STRIP YOU OF YOUR RANK AND RING.
YOU ARE A GREEN LANTERN NO MORE.
AH!
ZZZZZT

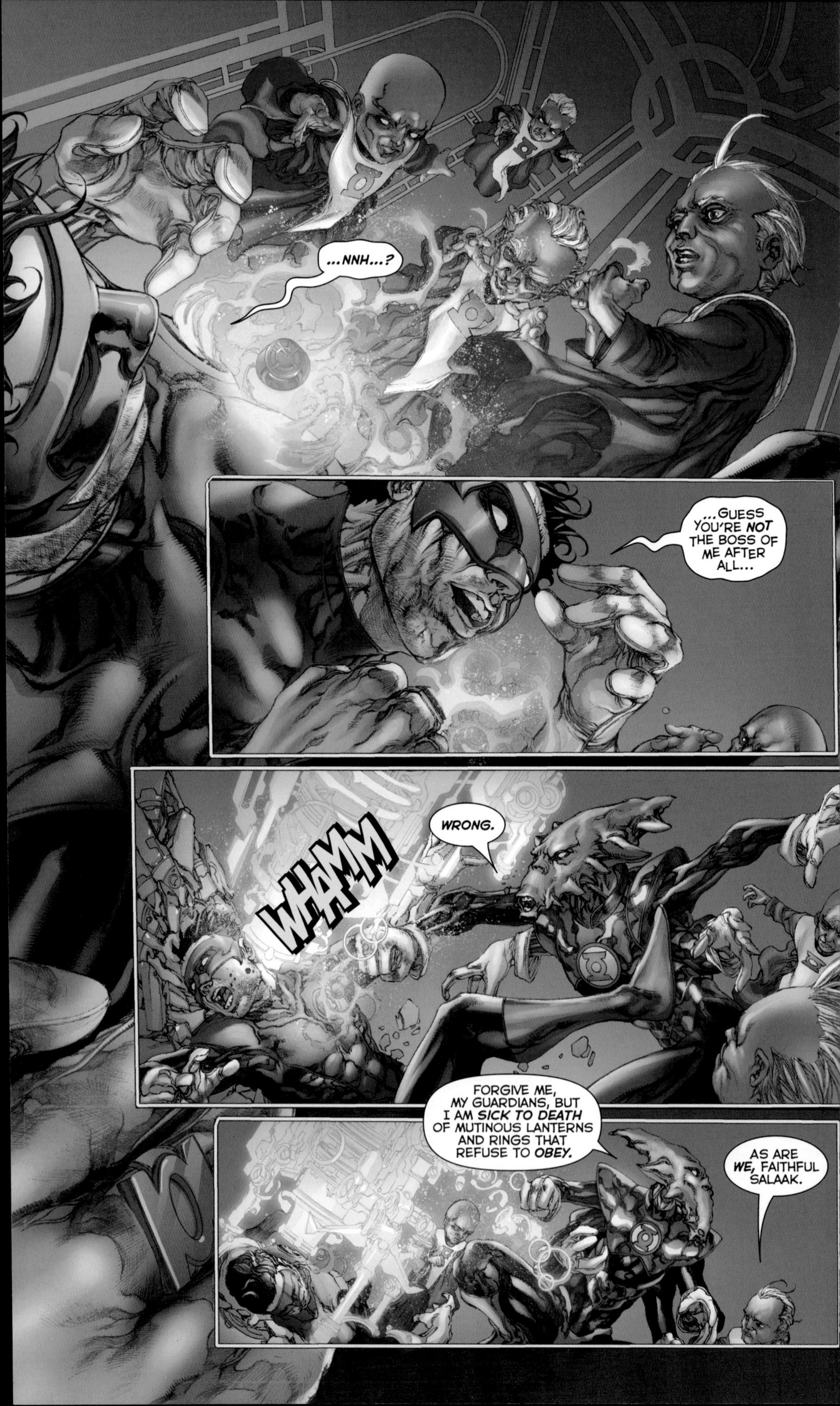
...NNH...?
...GUESS YOU'RE NOT THE BOSS OF ME AFTER ALL...
WRONG.
WHAMM
FORGIVE ME, MY GUARDIANS, BUT I AM SICK TO DEATH OF MUTINOUS LANTERNS AND RINGS THAT REFUSE TO OBEY.
AS ARE WE, FAITHFUL SALAAK.

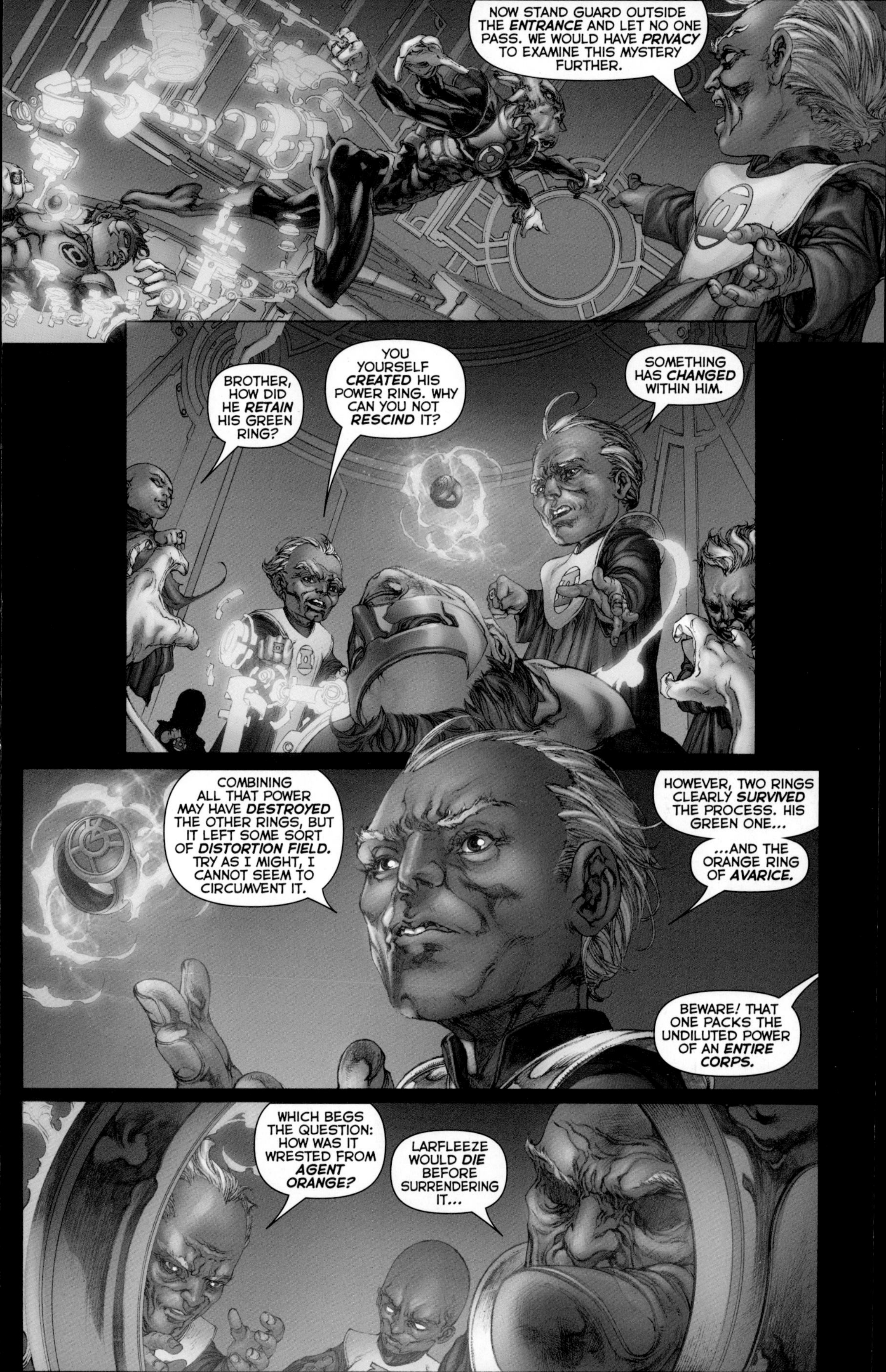
NOW STAND GUARD OUTSIDE THE ENTRANCE AND LET NO ONE PASS. WE WOULD HAVE PRIVACY TO EXAMINE THIS MYSTERY FURTHER.
BROTHER, HOW DID HE RETAIN HIS GREEN RING?
YOU YOURSELF CREATED HIS POWER RING. WHY CAN YOU NOT RESCIND IT?
SOMETHING HAS CHANGED WITHIN HIM.
COMBINING ALL THAT POWER MAY HAVE DESTROYED THE OTHER RINGS, BUT IT LEFT SOME SORT OF DISTORTION FIELD. TRY AS I MIGHT, I CANNOT SEEM TO CIRCUMVENT IT.
HOWEVER, TWO RINGS CLEARLY SURVIVED THE PROCESS. HIS GREEN ONE...
...AND THE ORANGE RING OF AVARICE.
BEWARE! THAT ONE PACKS THE UNDILUTED POWER OF AN ENTIRE CORPS.
WHICH BEGS THE QUESTION: HOW WAS IT WRESTED FROM AGENT ORANGE?
LARFLEEZE WOULD DIE BEFORE SURRENDERING IT...

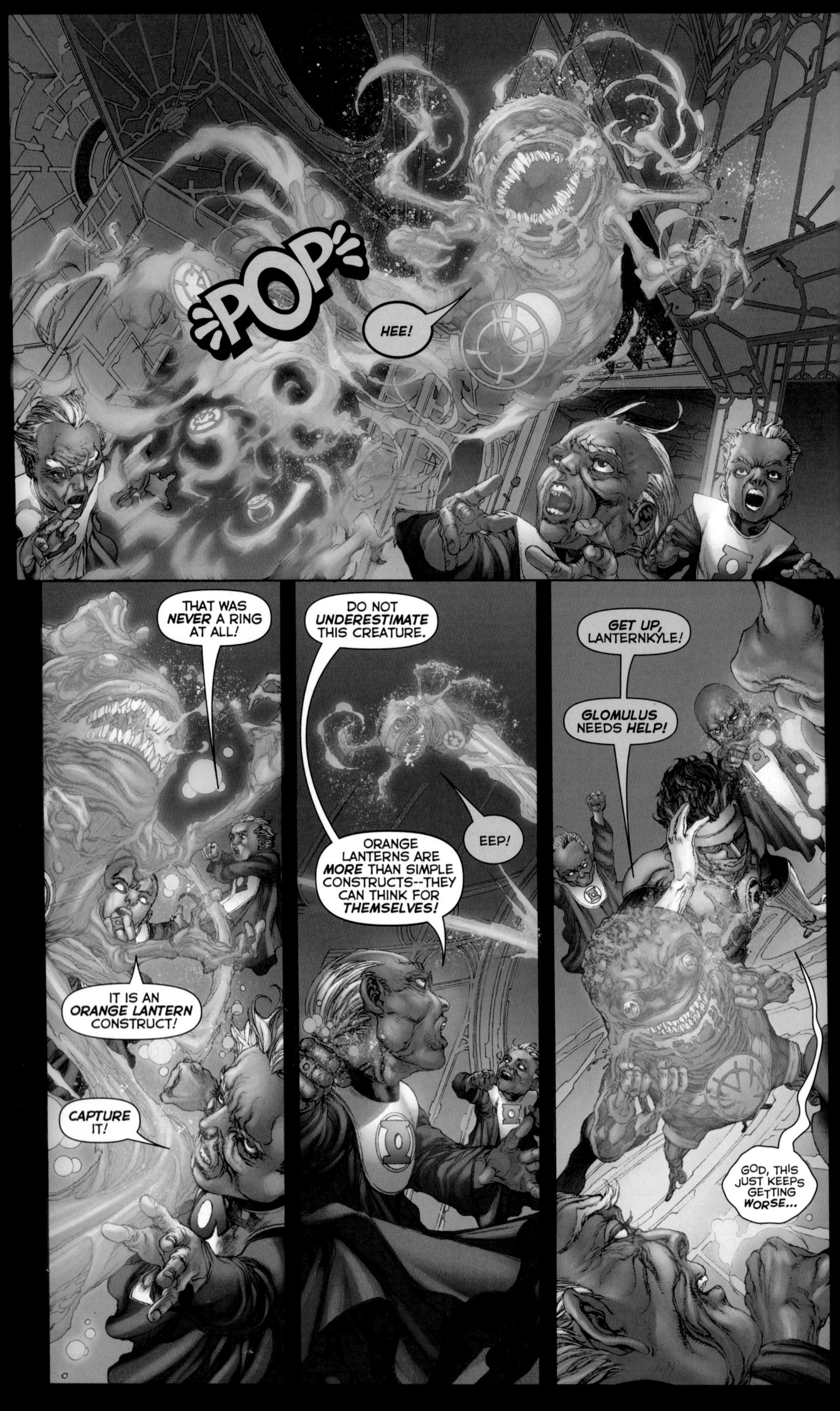
POP
HEE!
THAT WAS NEVER A RING AT ALL!
IT IS AN ORANGE LANTERN CONSTRUCT!
CAPTURE IT!
DO NOT UNDERESTIMATE THIS CREATURE.
EEP!
ORANGE LANTERNS ARE MORE THAN SIMPLE CONSTRUCTS--THEY CAN THINK FOR THEMSELVES!
GET UP, LANTERNKYLE!
GLOMULUS NEEDS HELP!
GOD, THIS JUST KEEPS GETTING WORSE...

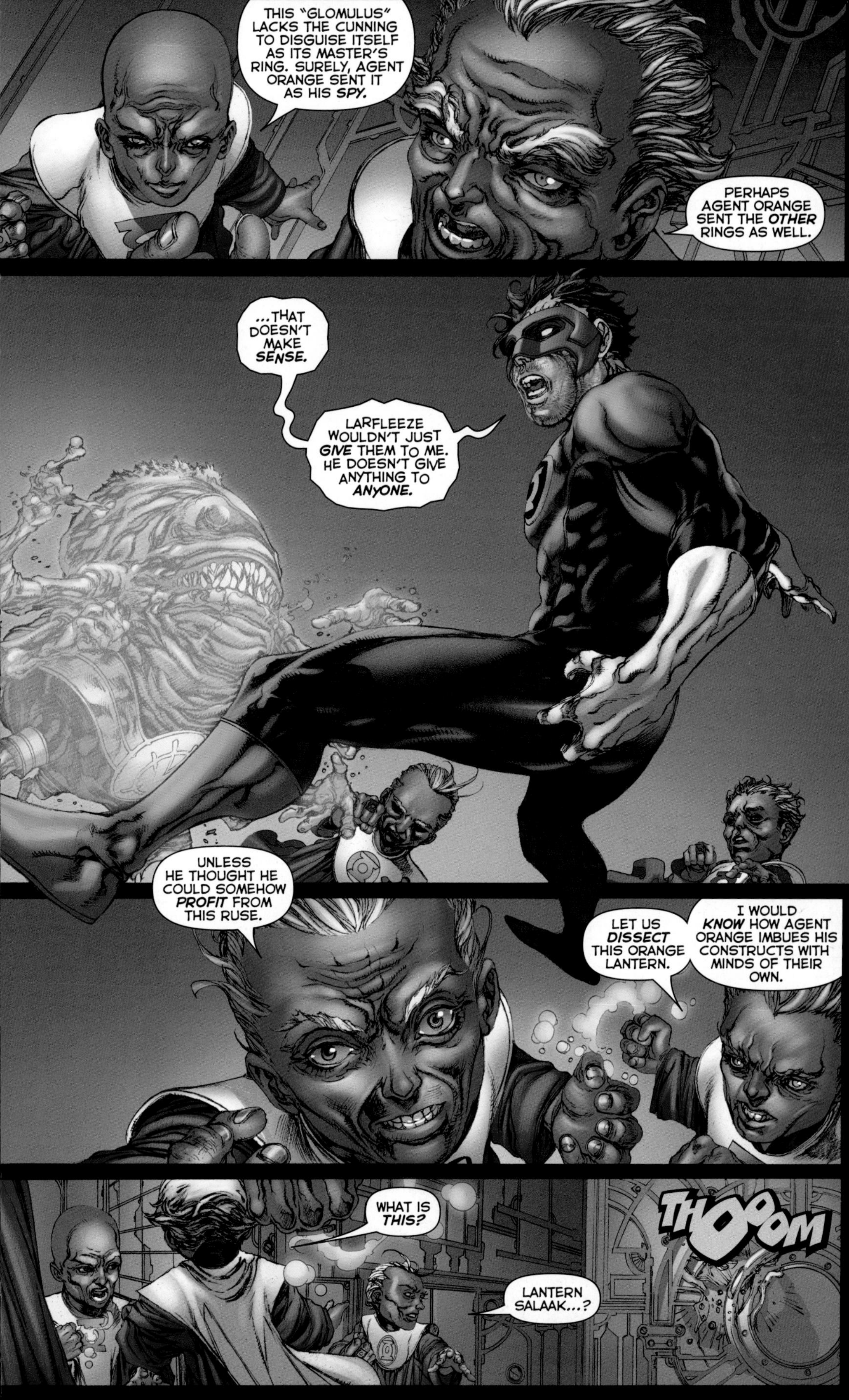
THIS "GLOMULUS" LACKS THE CUNNING TO DISGUISE ITSELF AS ITS MASTER'S RING. SURELY, AGENT ORANGE SENT IT AS HIS SPY.
PERHAPS AGENT ORANGE SENT THE OTHER RINGS AS WELL.
...THAT DOESN'T MAKE SENSE.
LARFLEEZE WOULDN'T JUST GIVE THEM TO ME. HE DOESN'T GIVE ANYTHING TO ANYONE.
UNLESS HE THOUGHT HE COULD SOMEHOW PROFIT FROM THIS RUSE.
LET US DISSECT THIS ORANGE LANTERN.
I WOULD KNOW HOW AGENT ORANGE IMBUES HIS CONSTRUCTS WITH MINDS OF THEIR OWN.
WHAT IS THIS?
THOOOM
LANTERN SALAAK...?

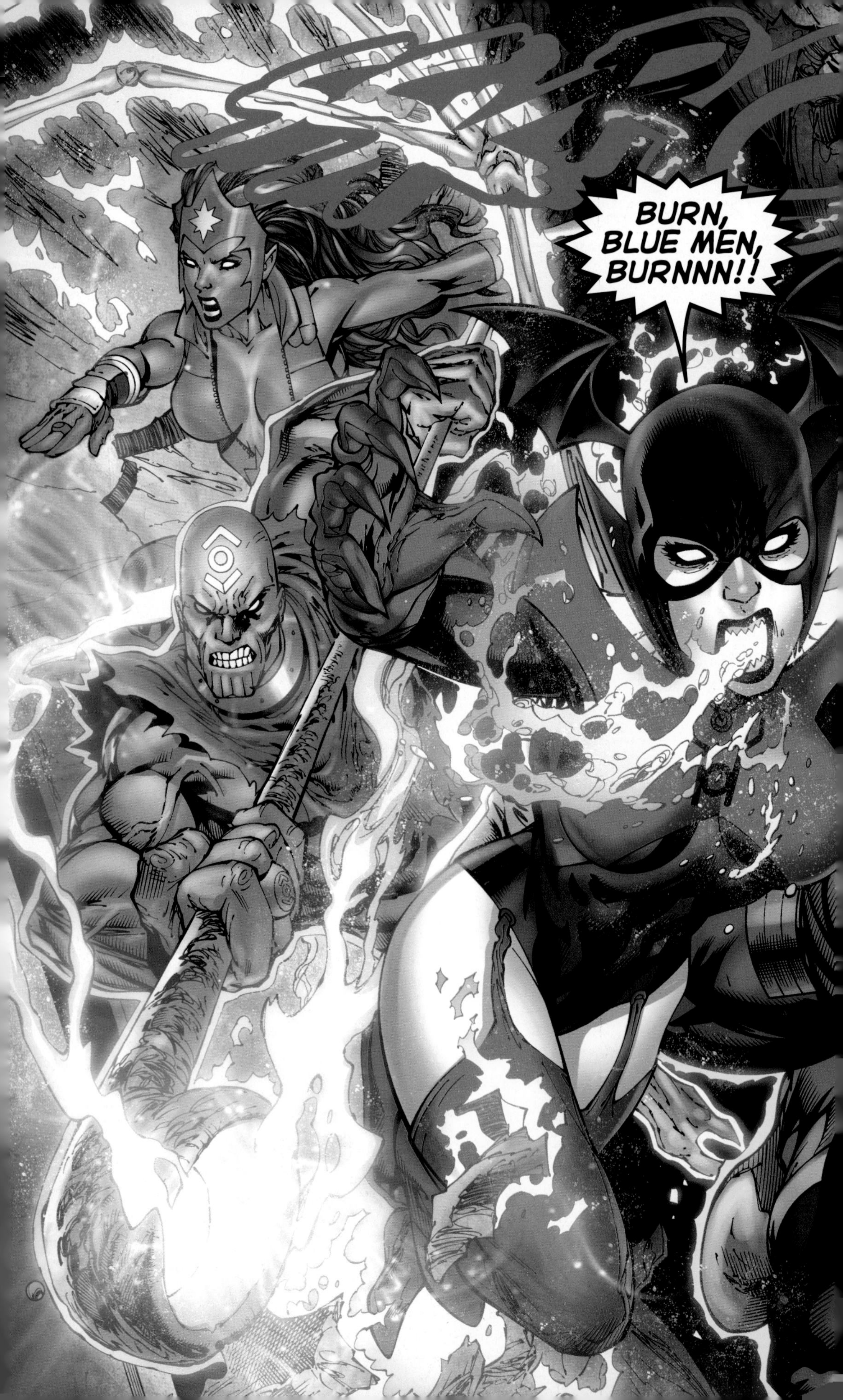
BURN, BLUE MEN, BURNNN!!

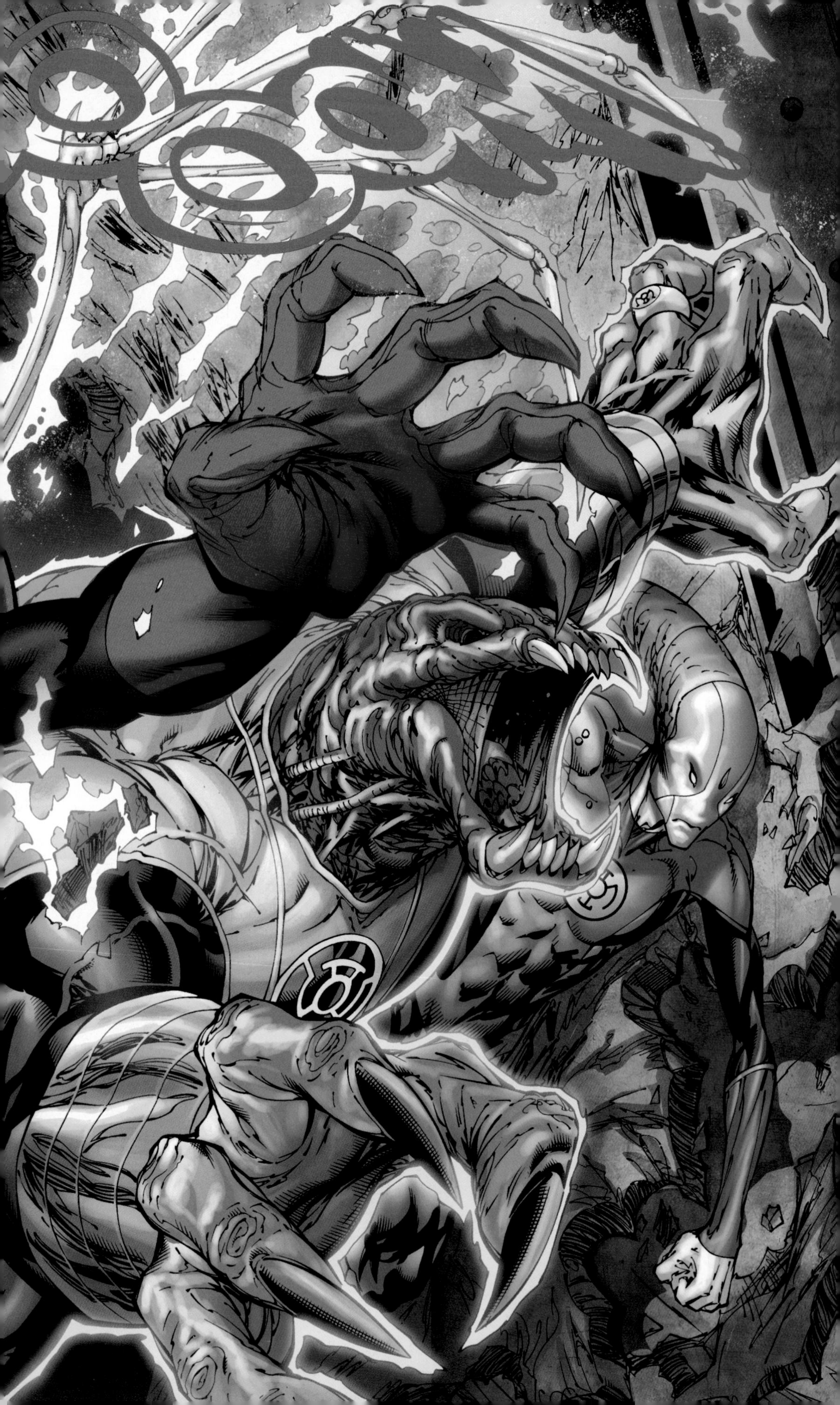

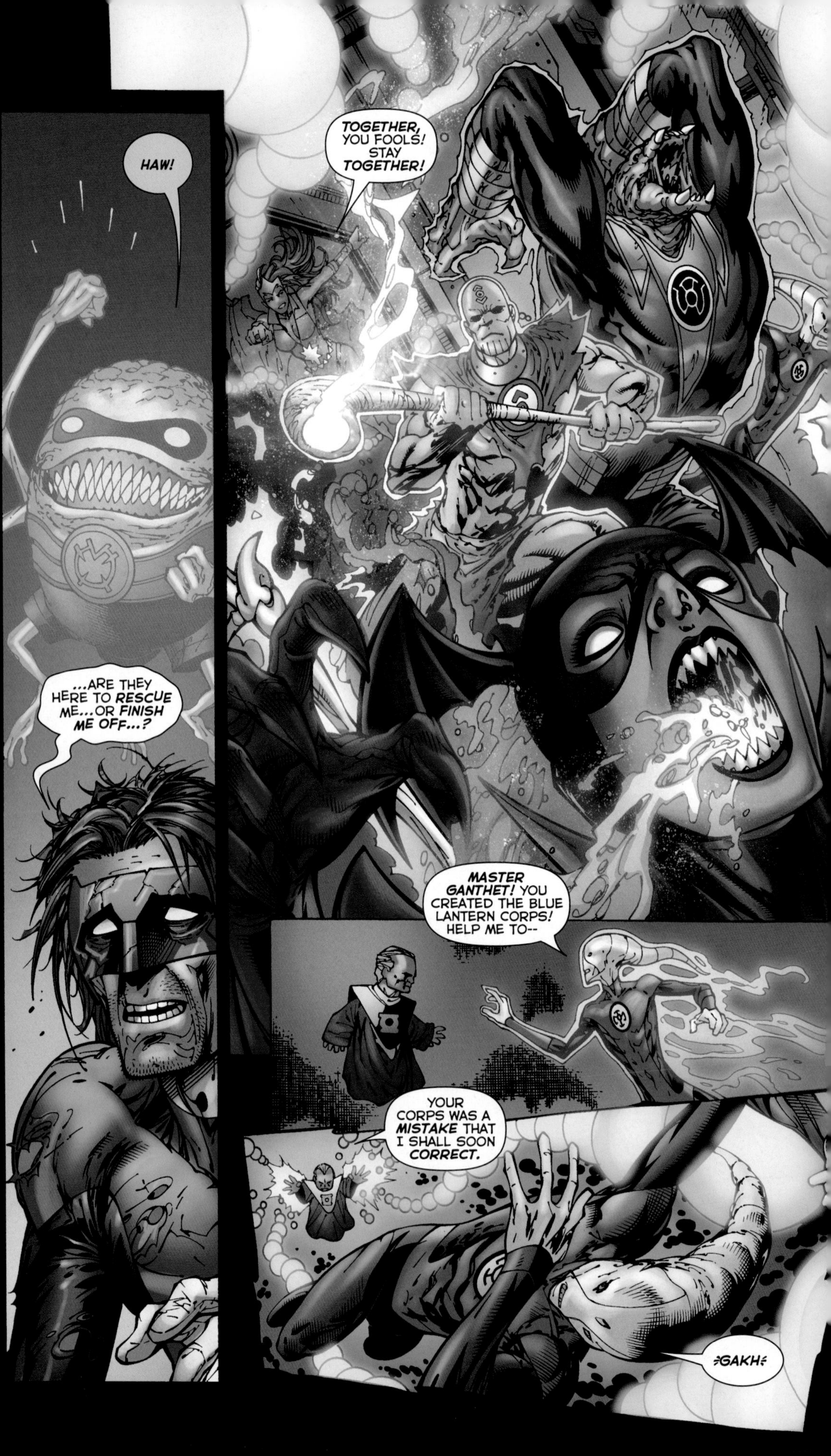

HAW!
TOGETHER, YOU FOOLS! STAY TOGETHER!
...ARE THEY HERE TO RESCUE ME...OR FINISH ME OFF...?
MASTER GANTHET! YOU CREATED THE BLUE LANTERN CORPS! HELP ME TO--
YOUR CORPS WAS A MISTAKE THAT I SHALL SOON CORRECT.
GAKH

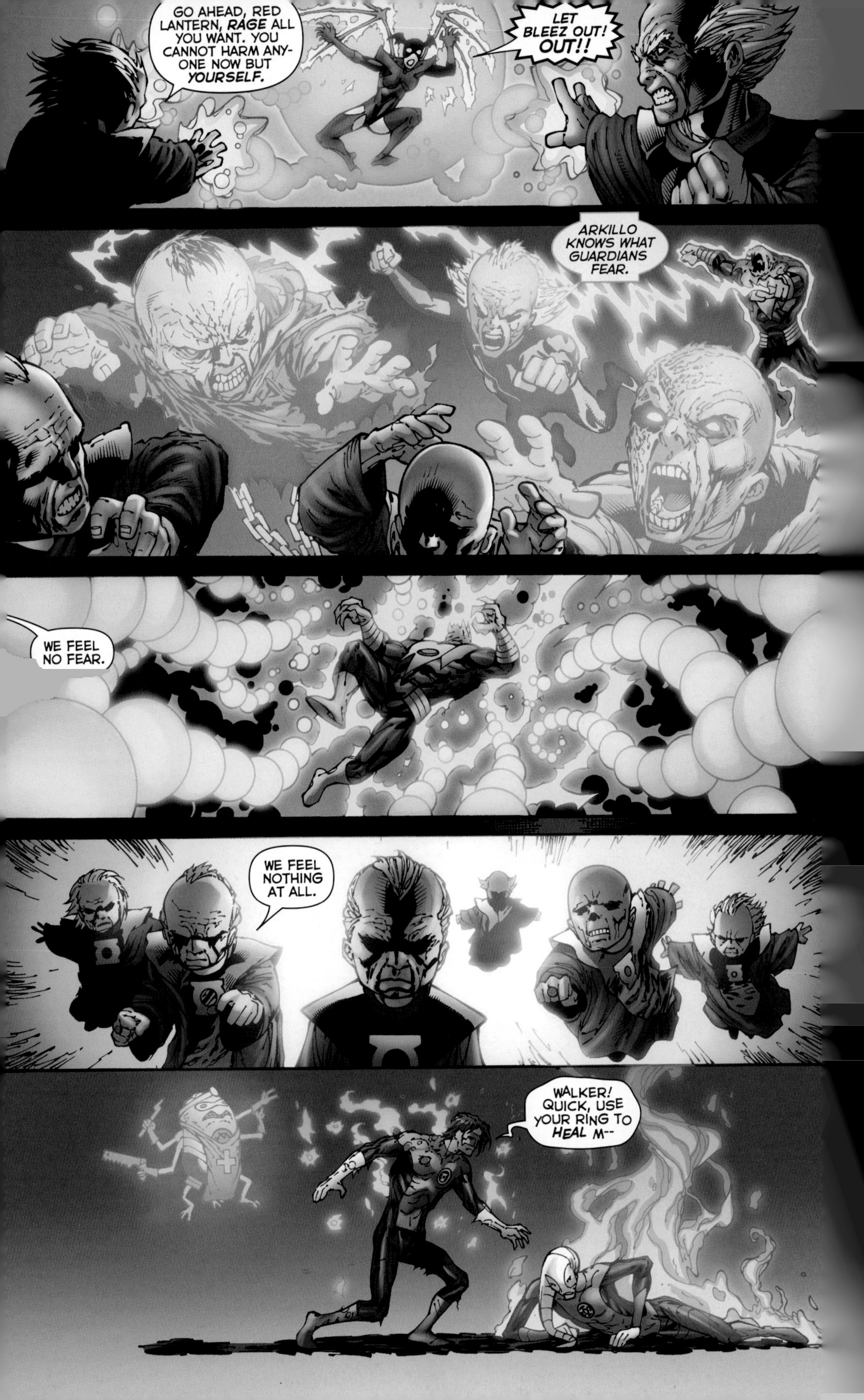
GO AHEAD, RED LANTERN, RAGE ALL YOU WANT. YOU CANNOT HARM ANY-ONE NOW BUT YOURSELF.
LET BLEEZ OUT! OUT!!
ARKILLO KNOWS WHAT GUARDIANS FEAR.
WE FEEL NO FEAR.
WE FEEL NOTHING AT ALL.
WALKER! QUICK, USE YOUR RING TO HEAL M--

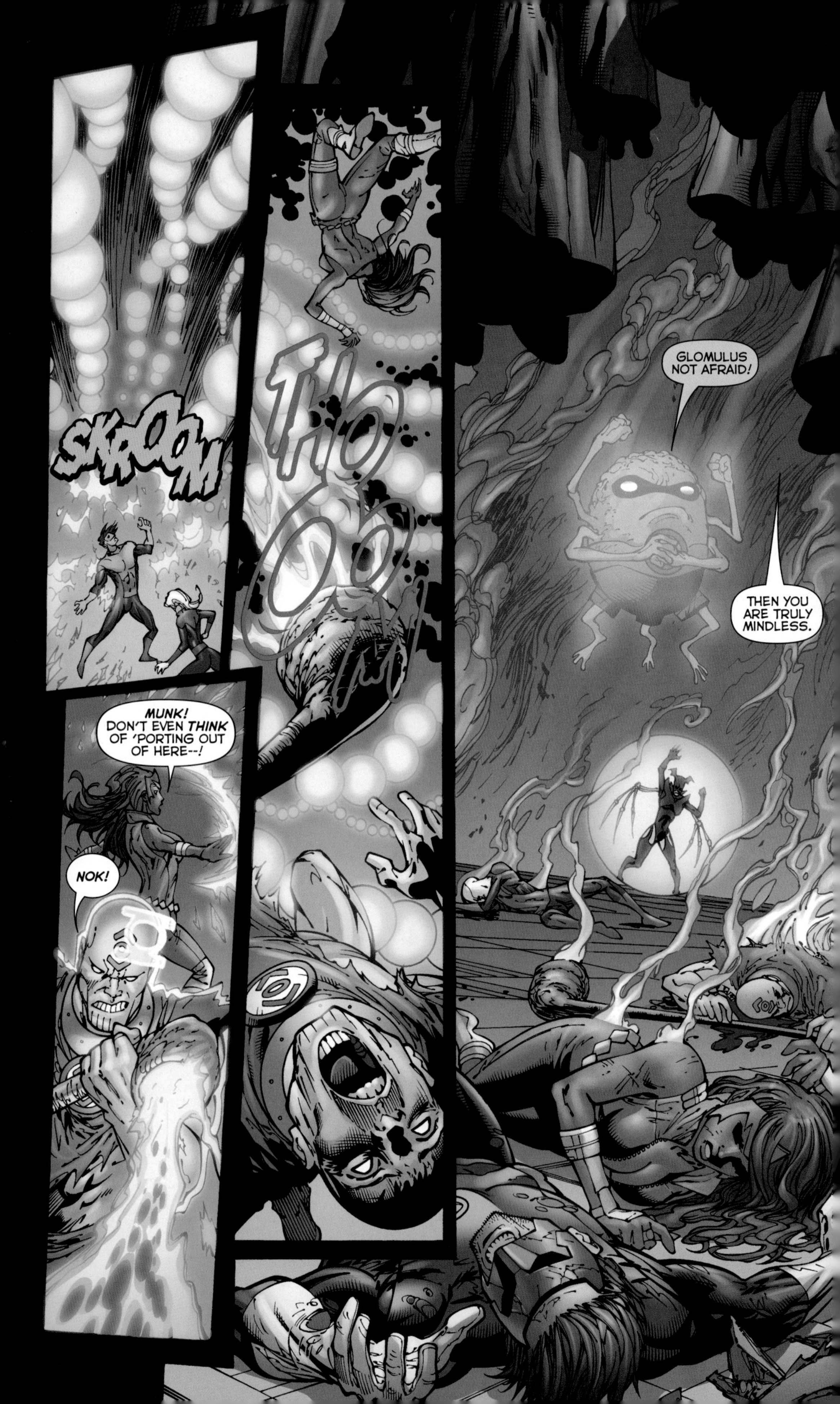

SKROOM
THOOOM
MUNK! DON'T EVEN THINK OF 'PORTING OUT OF HERE--!
NOK!
GLOMULUS NOT AFRAID!
THEN YOU ARE TRULY MINDLESS.

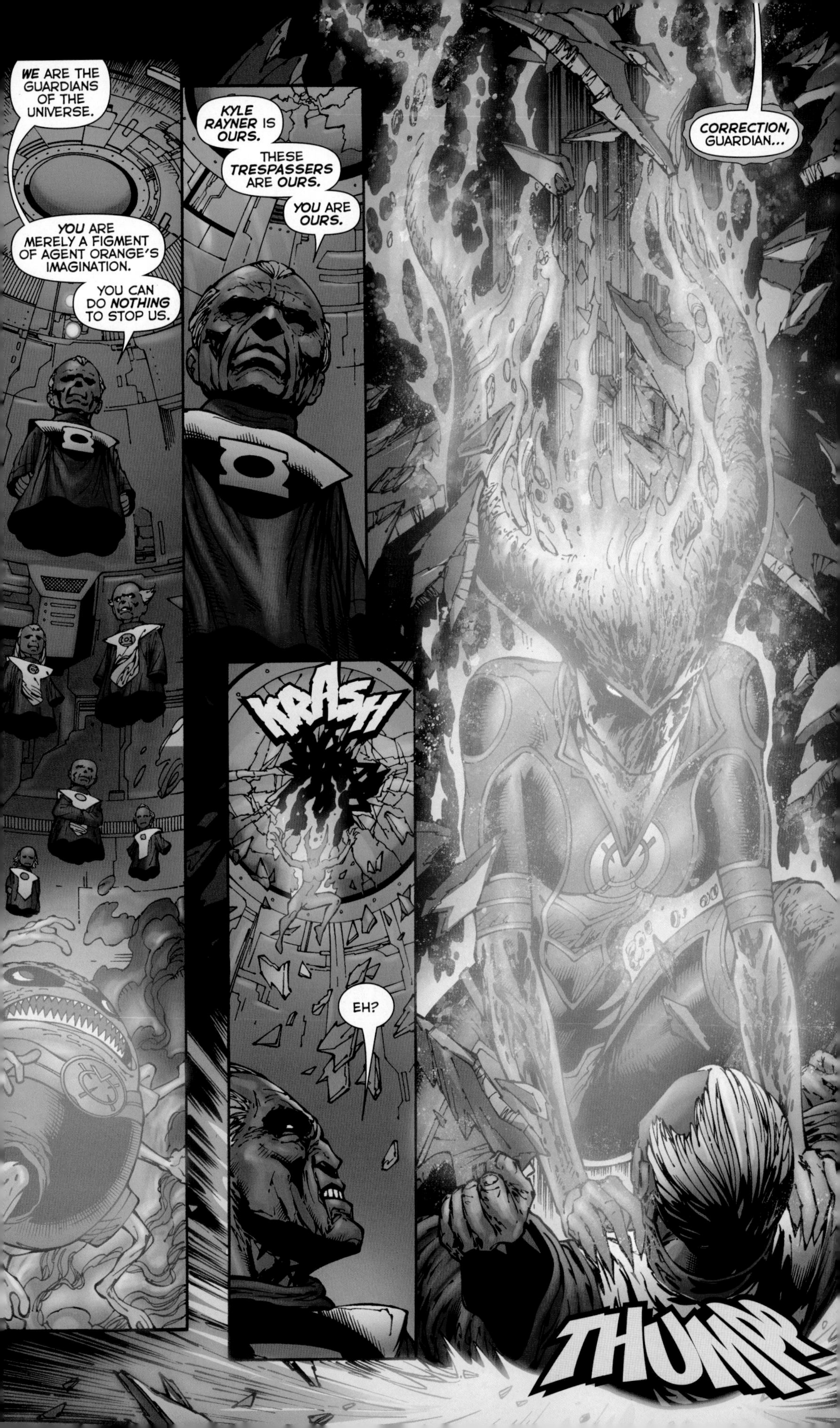
WE ARE THE GUARDIANS OF THE UNIVERSE.
YOU ARE MERELY A FIGMENT OF AGENT ORANGE'S IMAGINATION.
YOU CAN DO NOTHING TO STOP US.
KYLE RAYNER IS OURS.
THESE TRESPASSERS ARE OURS.
YOU ARE OURS.
KRASH
EH?
CORRECTION, GUARDIAN...
THUMP

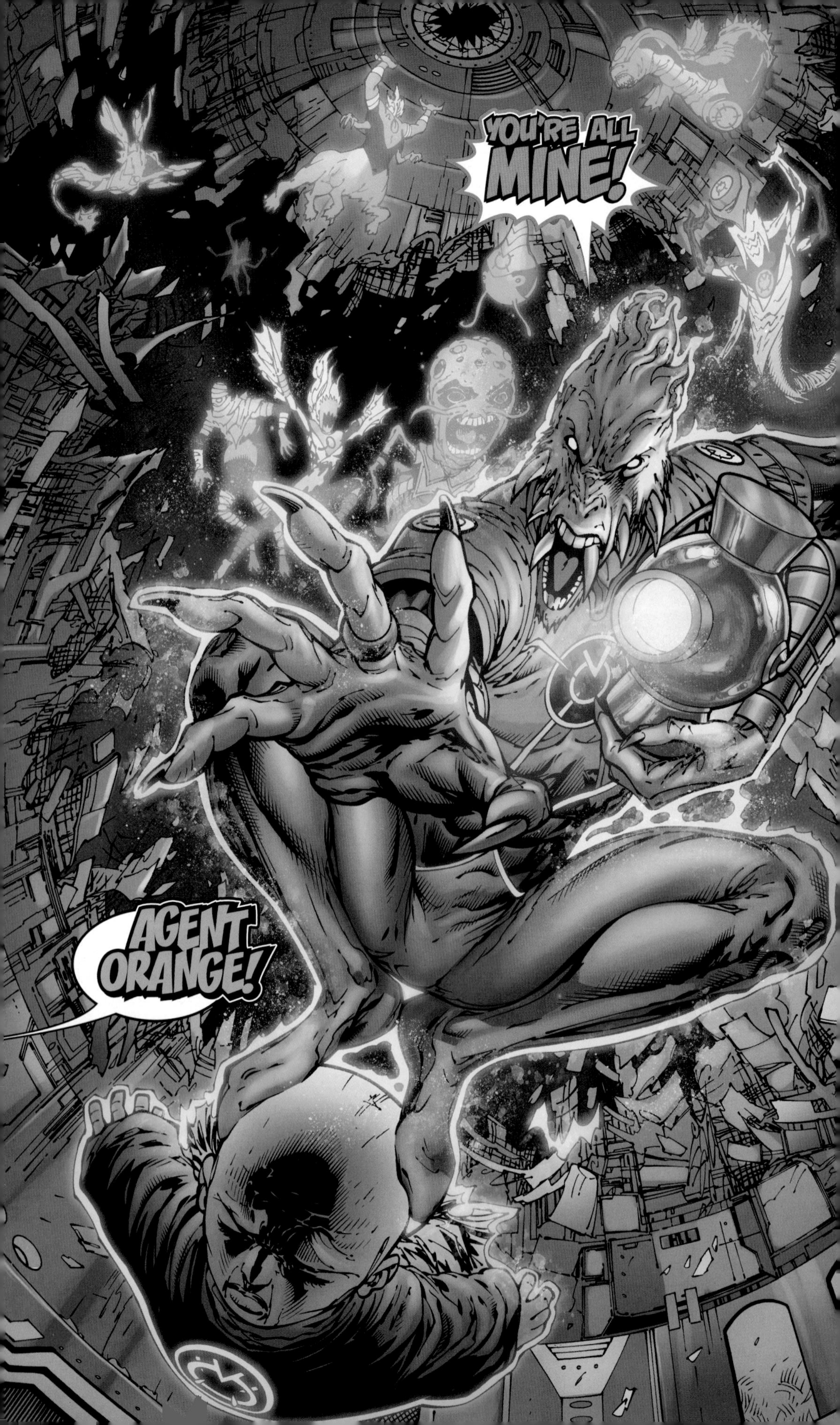
YOU'RE ALL MINE!
AGENT ORANGE!

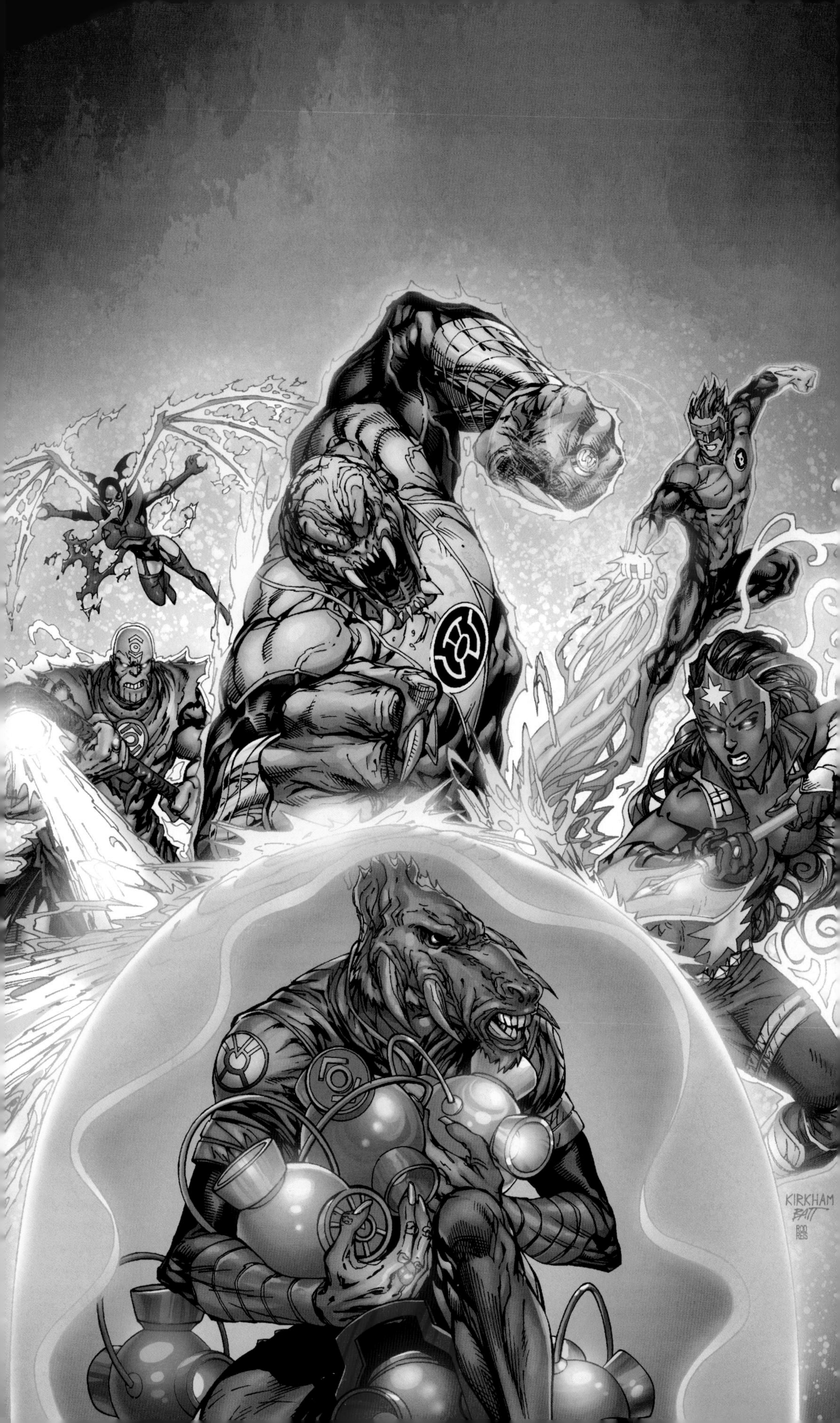
KIRKHAM
BATT
ROD REIS

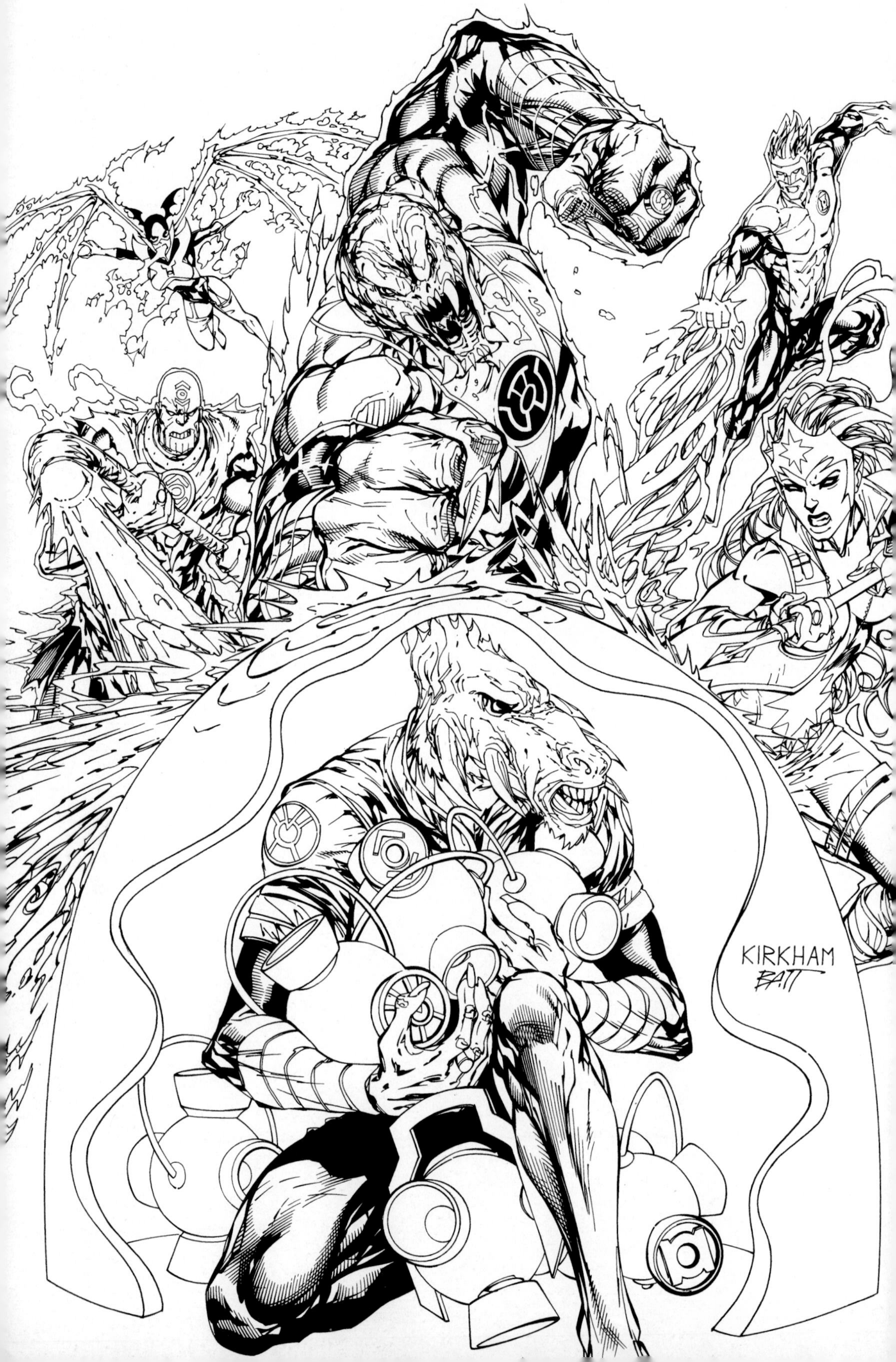
KIRKHAM
BATT

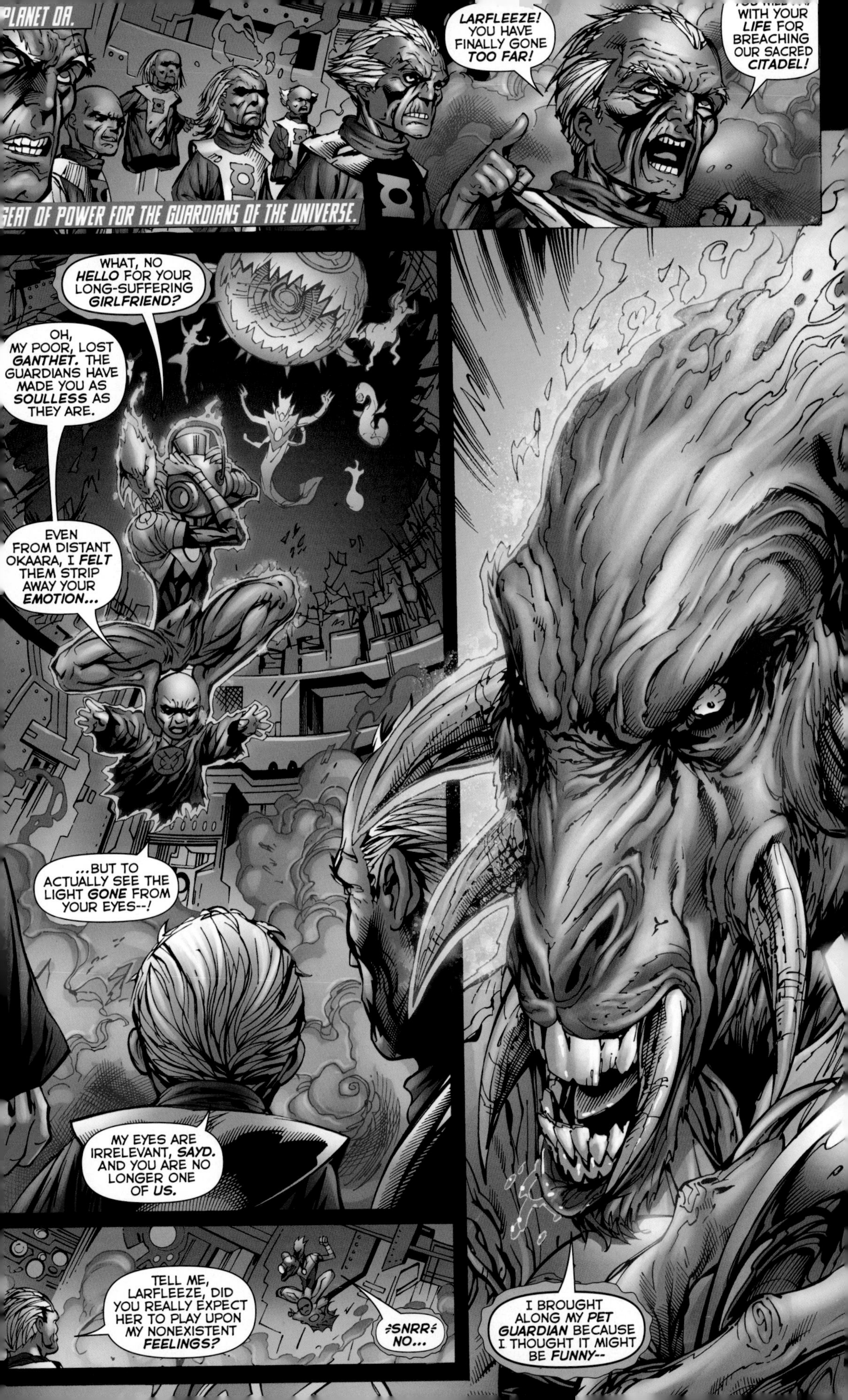
PLANET OA.
SEAT OF POWER FOR THE GUARDIANS OF THE UNIVERSE.
LARFLEEZE! YOU HAVE FINALLY GONE TOO FAR!
WITH YOUR LIFE FOR BREACHING OUR SACRED CITADEL!
WHAT, NO HELLO FOR YOUR LONG-SUFFERING GIRLFRIEND?
OH, MY POOR, LOST GANTHET. THE GUARDIANS HAVE MADE YOU AS SOULLESS AS THEY ARE.
EVEN FROM DISTANT OKAARA, I FELT THEM STRIP AWAY YOUR EMOTION...
...BUT TO ACTUALLY SEE THE LIGHT GONE FROM YOUR EYES--!
MY EYES ARE IRRELEVANT, SAYD. AND YOU ARE NO LONGER ONE OF US.
TELL ME, LARFLEEZE, DID YOU REALLY EXPECT HER TO PLAY UPON MY NONEXISTENT FEELINGS?
SNRR NO...
I BROUGHT ALONG MY PET GUARDIAN BECAUSE I THOUGHT IT MIGHT BE FUNNY--

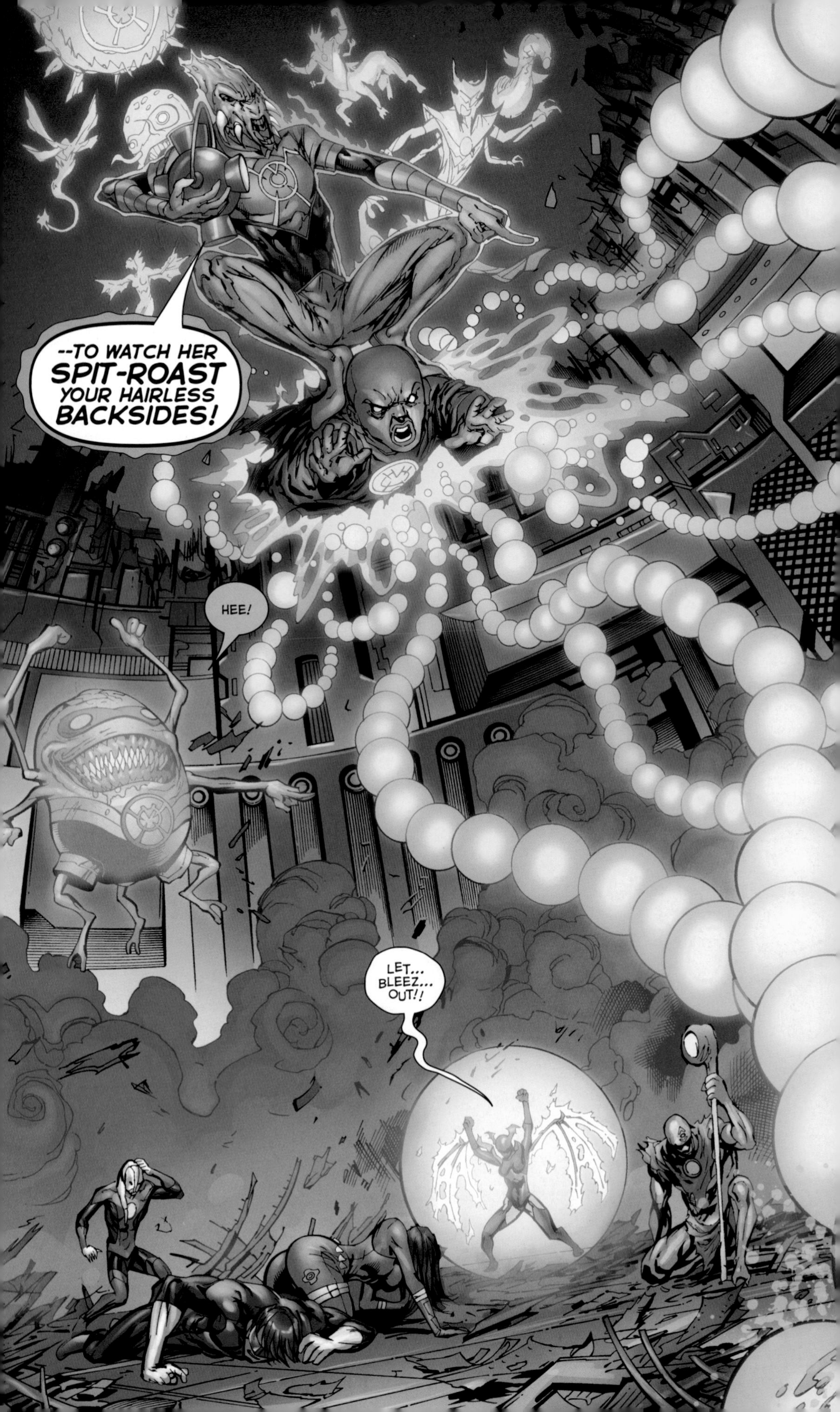
--TO WATCH HER SPIT-ROAST YOUR HAIRLESS BACKSIDES!
HEE!
LET... BLEEZ... OUT!!

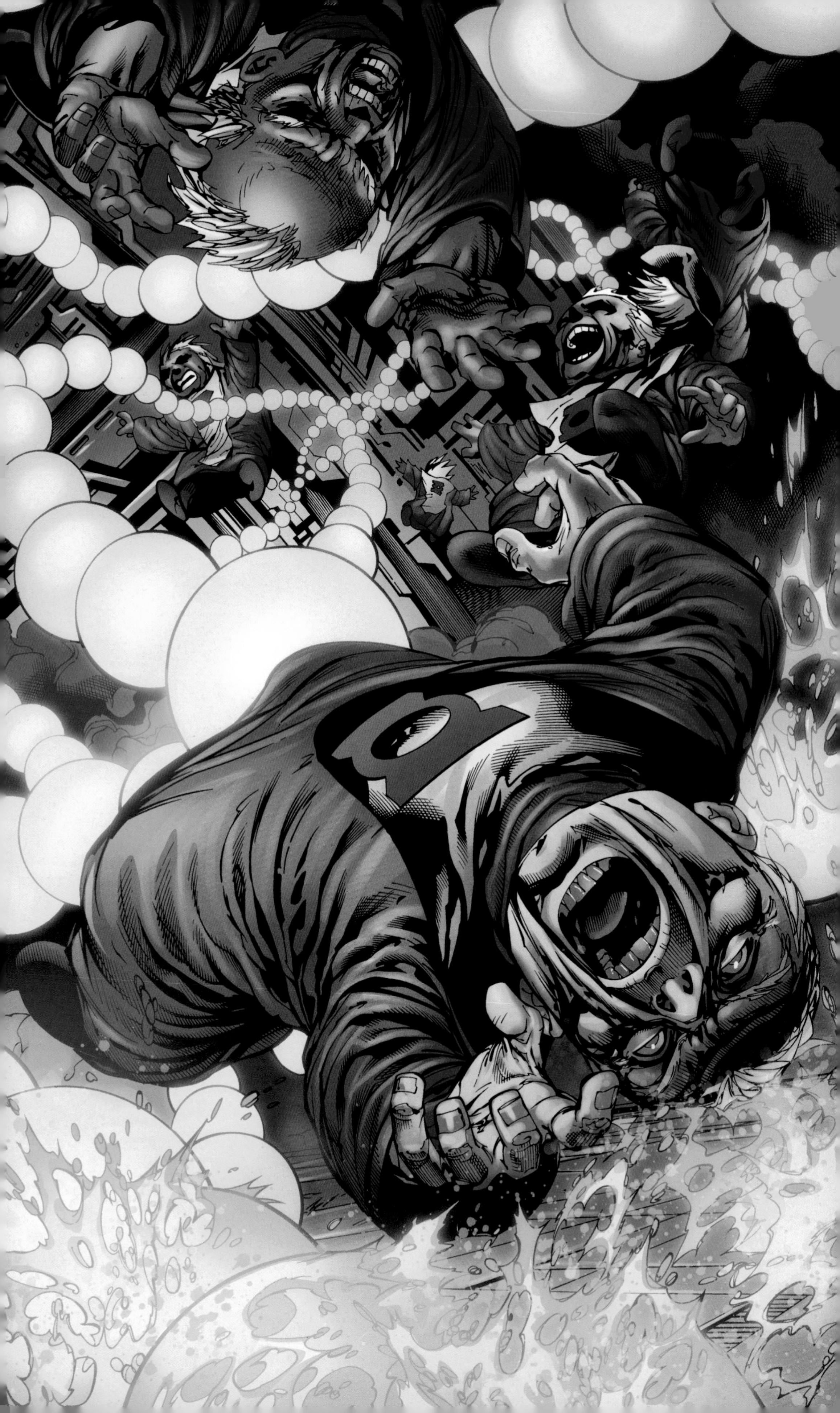

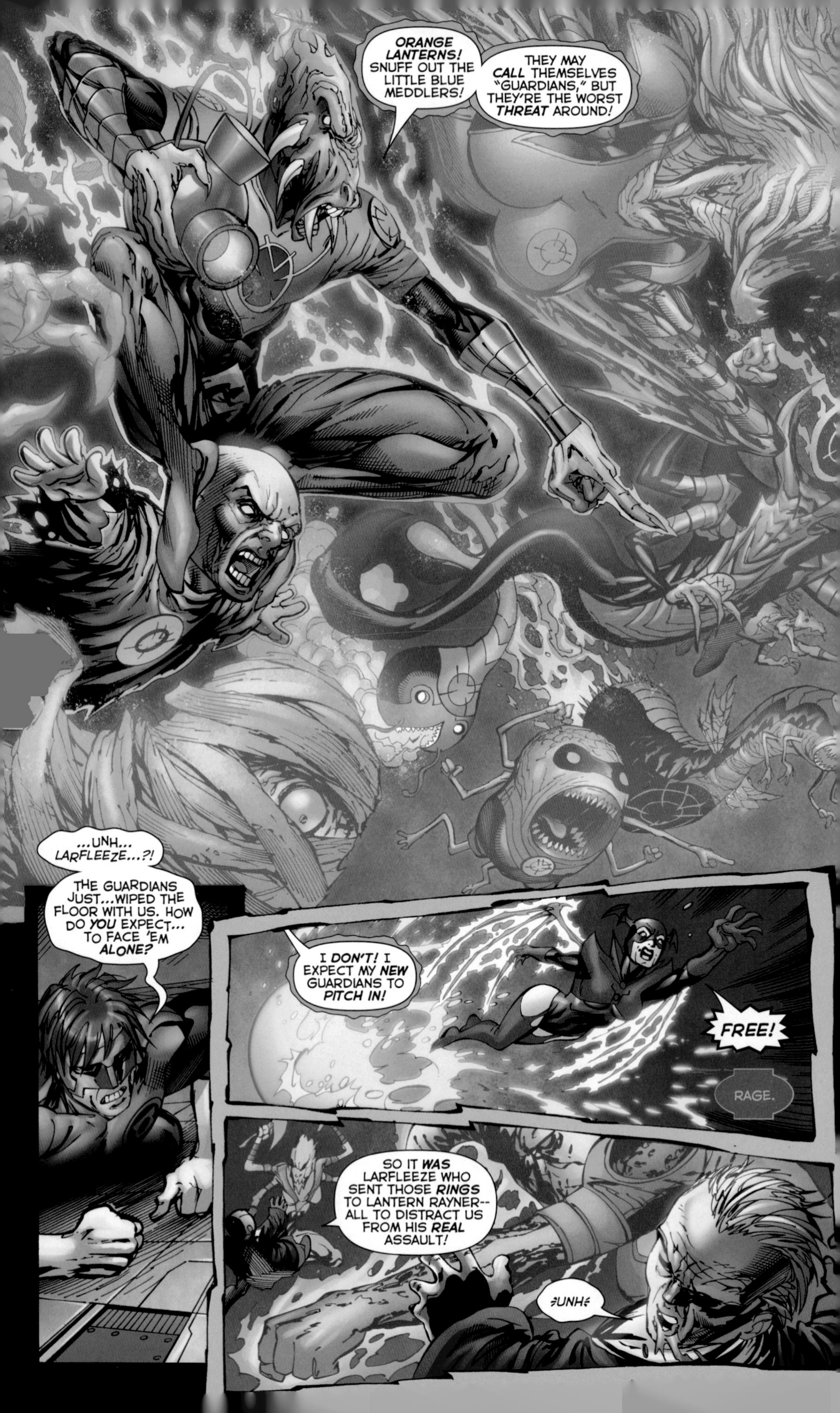
ORANGE LANTERNS! SNUFF OUT THE LITTLE BLUE MEDDLERS!
THEY MAY CALL THEMSELVES "GUARDIANS," BUT THEY'RE THE WORST THREAT AROUND!
...UNH... LARFLEEZE...?!
THE GUARDIANS JUST...WIPED THE FLOOR WITH US. HOW DO YOU EXPECT... TO FACE 'EM ALONE?
I DON'T! I EXPECT MY NEW GUARDIANS TO PITCH IN!
FREE!
RAGE.
SO IT WAS LARFLEEZE WHO SENT THOSE RINGS TO LANTERN RAYNER-- ALL TO DISTRACT US FROM HIS REAL ASSAULT!
UNH

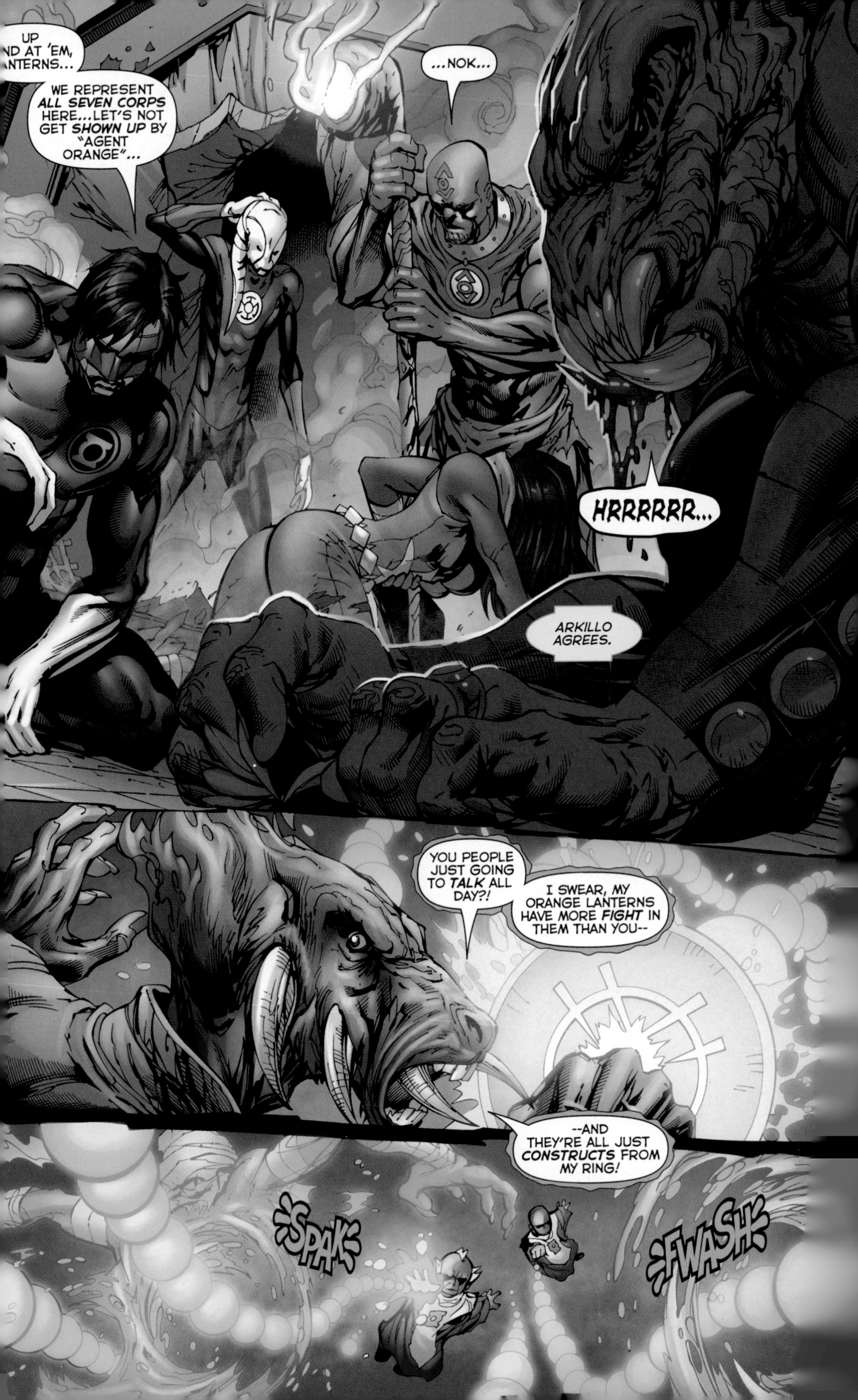
UP
ND AT 'EM,
ANTERNS...
WE REPRESENT ALL SEVEN CORPS HERE...LET'S NOT GET SHOWN UP BY "AGENT ORANGE"...
...NOK...
HRRRRRR...
ARKILLO AGREES.
YOU PEOPLE JUST GOING TO TALK ALL DAY?!
I SWEAR, MY ORANGE LANTERNS HAVE MORE FIGHT IN THEM THAN YOU--
--AND THEY'RE ALL JUST CONSTRUCTS FROM MY RING!
SPAK
FWASH

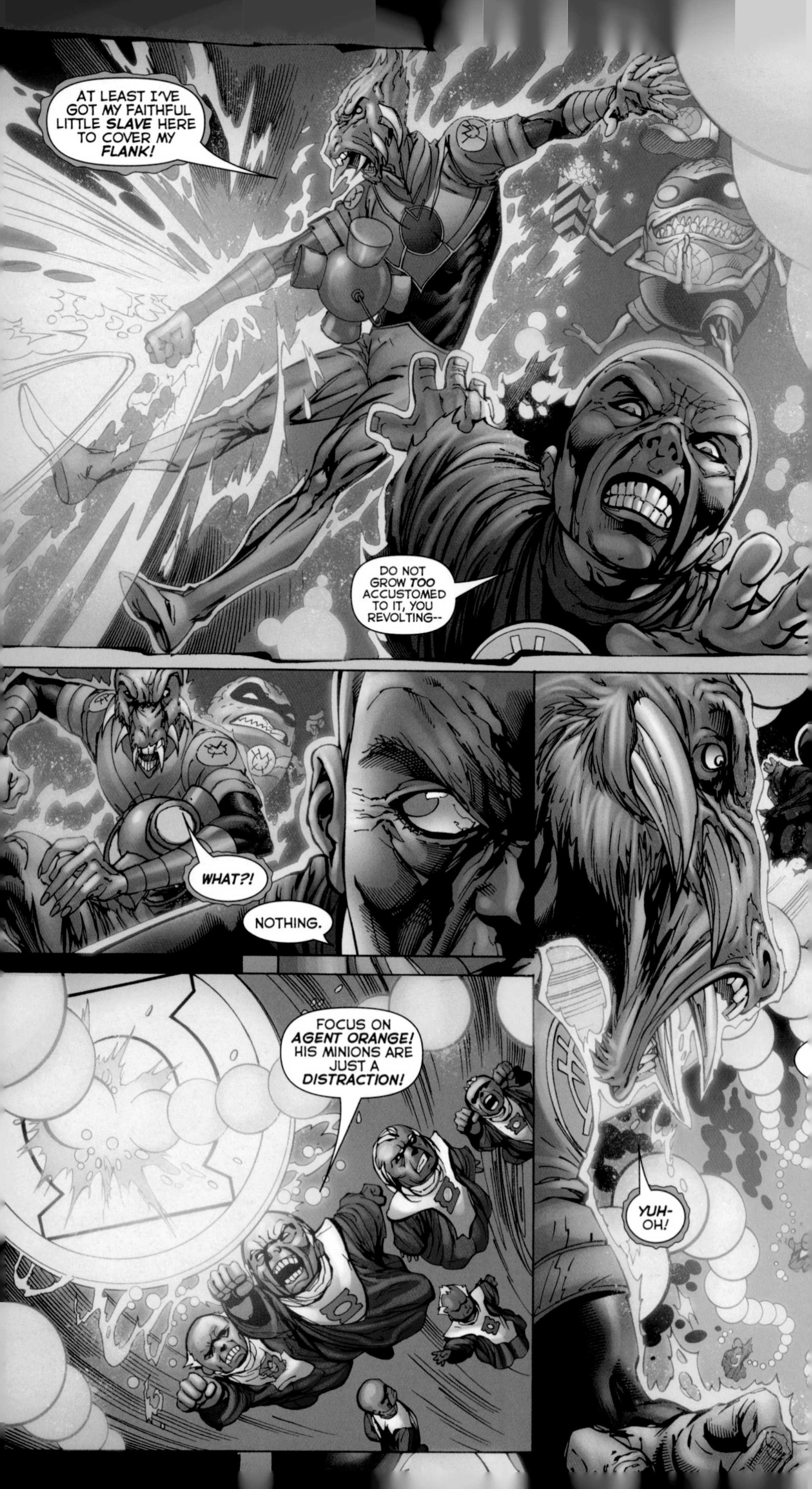

AT LEAST I'VE GOT MY FAITHFUL LITTLE SLAVE HERE TO COVER MY FLANK!
DO NOT GROW TOO ACCUSTOMED TO IT, YOU REVOLTING--
WHAT?!
NOTHING.
FOCUS ON AGENT ORANGE! HIS MINIONS ARE JUST A DISTRACTION!
YUH-OH!

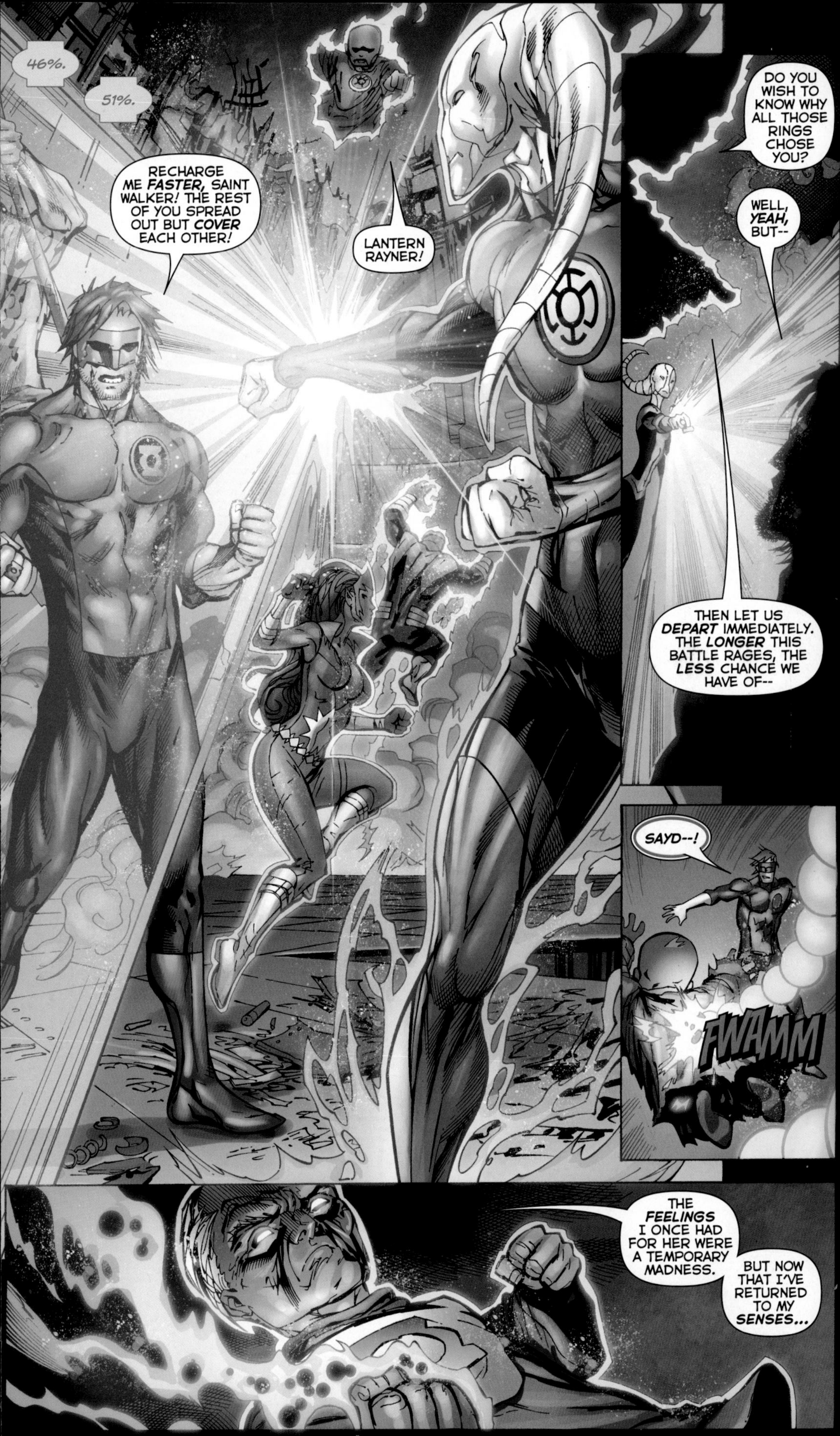
46%.
51%.
RECHARGE ME FASTER, SAINT WALKER! THE REST OF YOU SPREAD OUT BUT COVER EACH OTHER!
LANTERN RAYNER!
DO YOU WISH TO KNOW WHY ALL THOSE RINGS CHOSE YOU?
WELL, YEAH, BUT--
THEN LET US DEPART IMMEDIATELY. THE LONGER THIS BATTLE RAGES, THE LESS CHANCE WE HAVE OF--
SAYD--!
FWAMM
THE FEELINGS I ONCE HAD FOR HER WERE A TEMPORARY MADNESS.
BUT NOW THAT I'VE RETURNED TO MY SENSES...

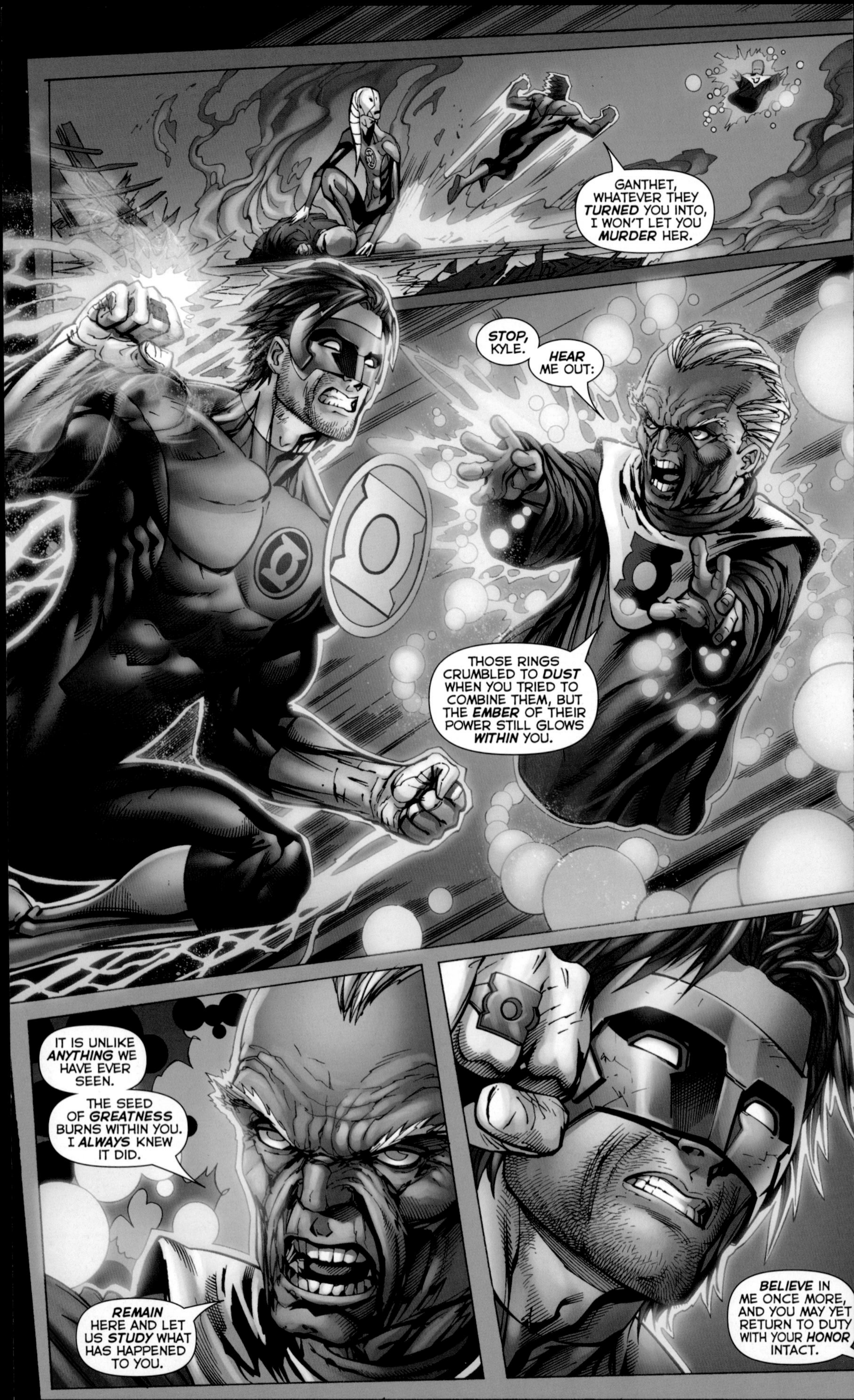
GANTHET, WHATEVER THEY TURNED YOU INTO, I WON'T LET YOU MURDER HER.
STOP, KYLE.
HEAR ME OUT:
THOSE RINGS CRUMBLED TO DUST WHEN YOU TRIED TO COMBINE THEM, BUT THE EMBER OF THEIR POWER STILL GLOWS WITHIN YOU.
IT IS UNLIKE ANYTHING WE HAVE EVER SEEN.
THE SEED OF GREATNESS BURNS WITHIN YOU. I ALWAYS KNEW IT DID.
REMAIN HERE AND LET US STUDY WHAT HAS HAPPENED TO YOU.
BELIEVE IN ME ONCE MORE, AND YOU MAY YET RETURN TO DUTY WITH YOUR HONOR INTACT.

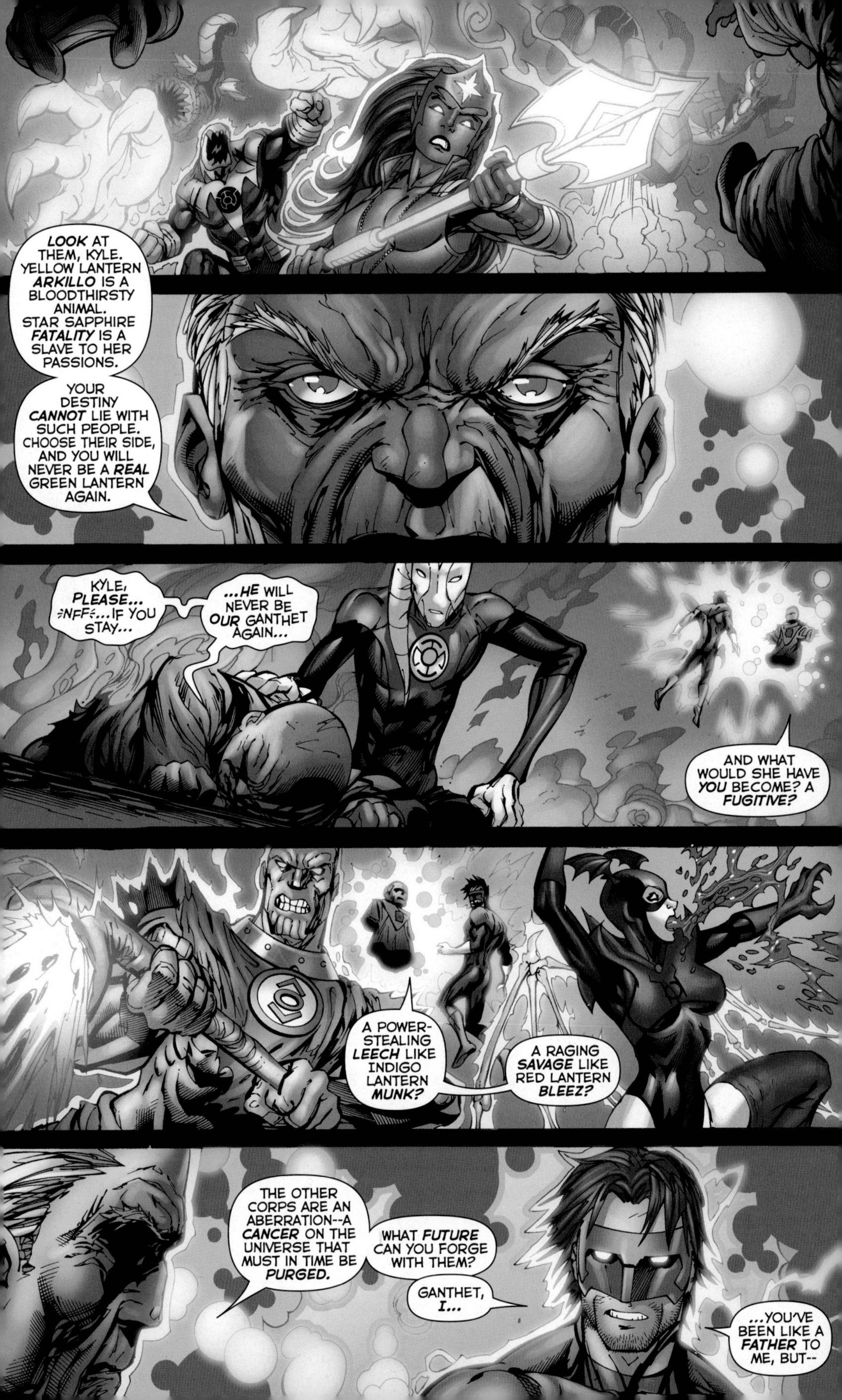
LOOK AT THEM, KYLE. YELLOW LANTERN ARKILLO IS A BLOODTHIRSTY ANIMAL. STAR SAPPHIRE FATALITY IS A SLAVE TO HER PASSIONS.
YOUR DESTINY CANNOT LIE WITH SUCH PEOPLE. CHOOSE THEIR SIDE, AND YOU WILL NEVER BE A REAL GREEN LANTERN AGAIN.
KYLE, PLEASE... NFF...IF YOU STAY...
...HE WILL NEVER BE OUR GANTHET AGAIN...
AND WHAT WOULD SHE HAVE YOU BECOME? A FUGITIVE?
A POWER-STEALING LEECH LIKE INDIGO LANTERN MUNK?
A RAGING SAVAGE LIKE RED LANTERN BLEEZ?
THE OTHER CORPS ARE AN ABERRATION--A CANCER ON THE UNIVERSE THAT MUST IN TIME BE PURGED.
WHAT FUTURE CAN YOU FORGE WITH THEM?
GANTHET, I...
...YOU'VE BEEN LIKE A FATHER TO ME, BUT--

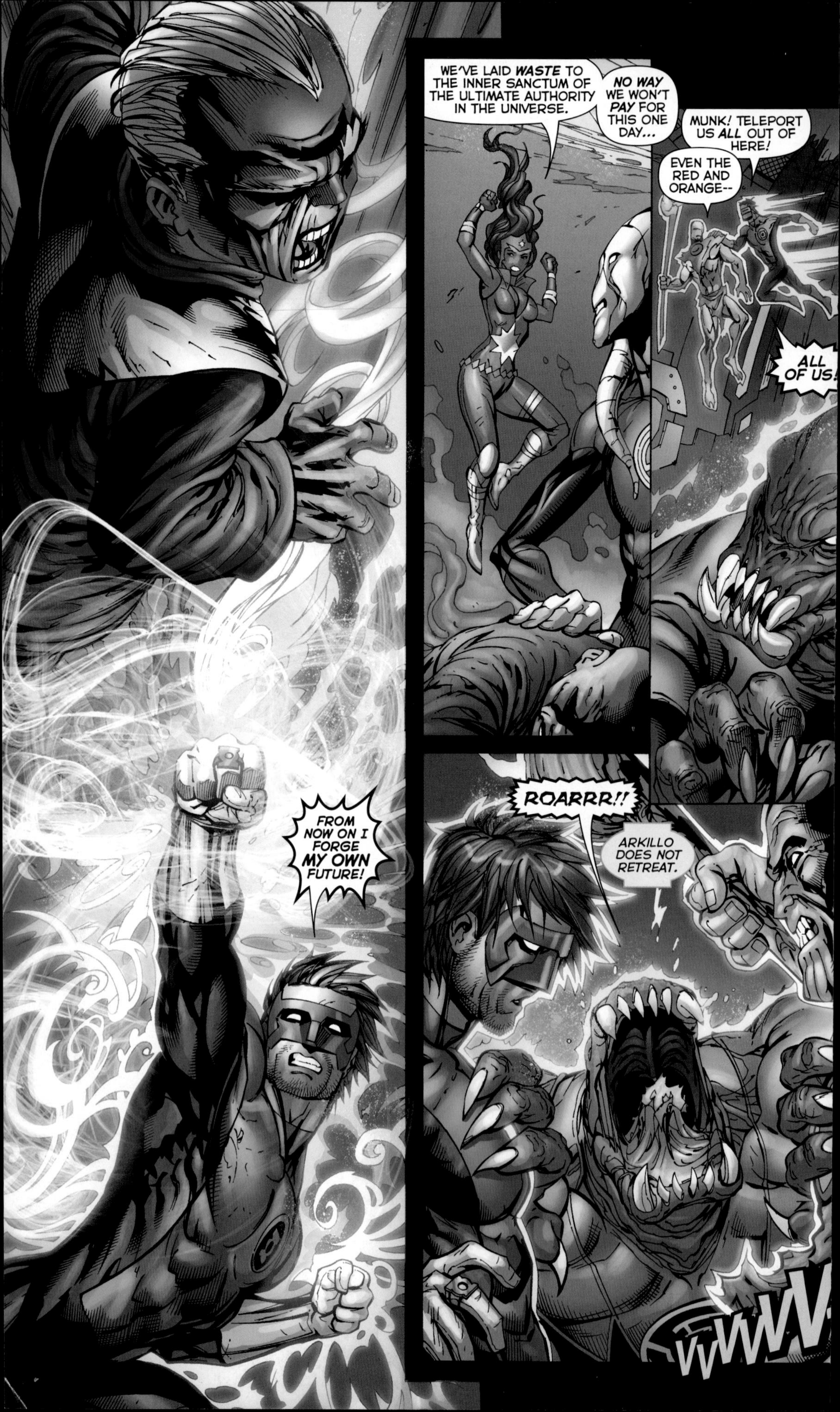

FROM NOW ON I FORGE MY OWN FUTURE!
WE'VE LAID WASTE TO THE INNER SANCTUM OF THE ULTIMATE AUTHORITY IN THE UNIVERSE.
NO WAY WE WON'T PAY FOR THIS ONE DAY...
MUNK! TELEPORT US ALL OUT OF HERE!
EVEN THE RED AND ORANGE--
ALL OF US!
ROARRR!!
ARKILLO DOES NOT RETREAT.
VVVVVV

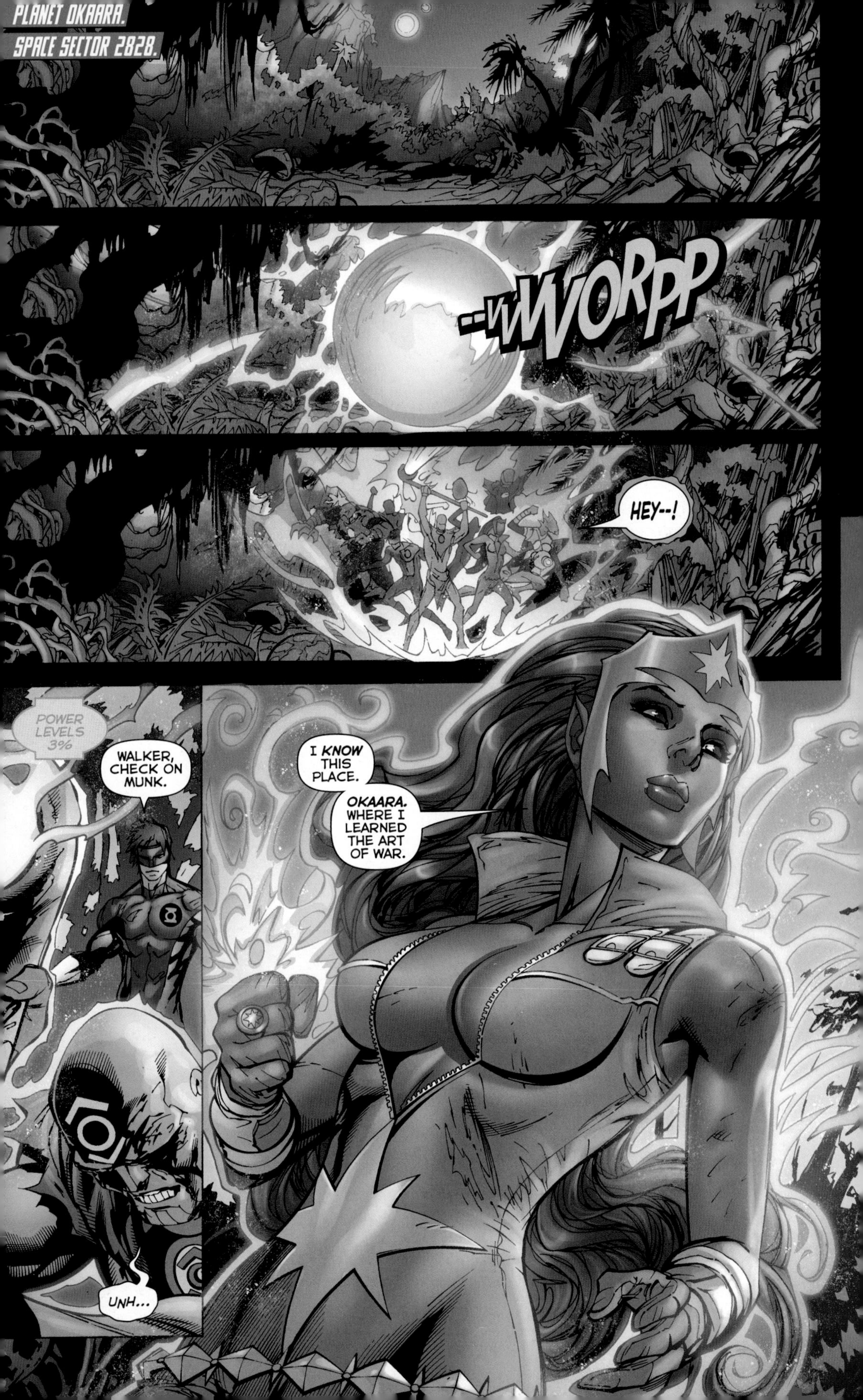
PLANET OKAARA.
SPACE SECTOR 2828.
--VVVWORPP
HEY--!
POWER LEVELS 3%
WALKER, CHECK ON MUNK.
UNH...
I KNOW THIS PLACE.
OKAARA. WHERE I LEARNED THE ART OF WAR.

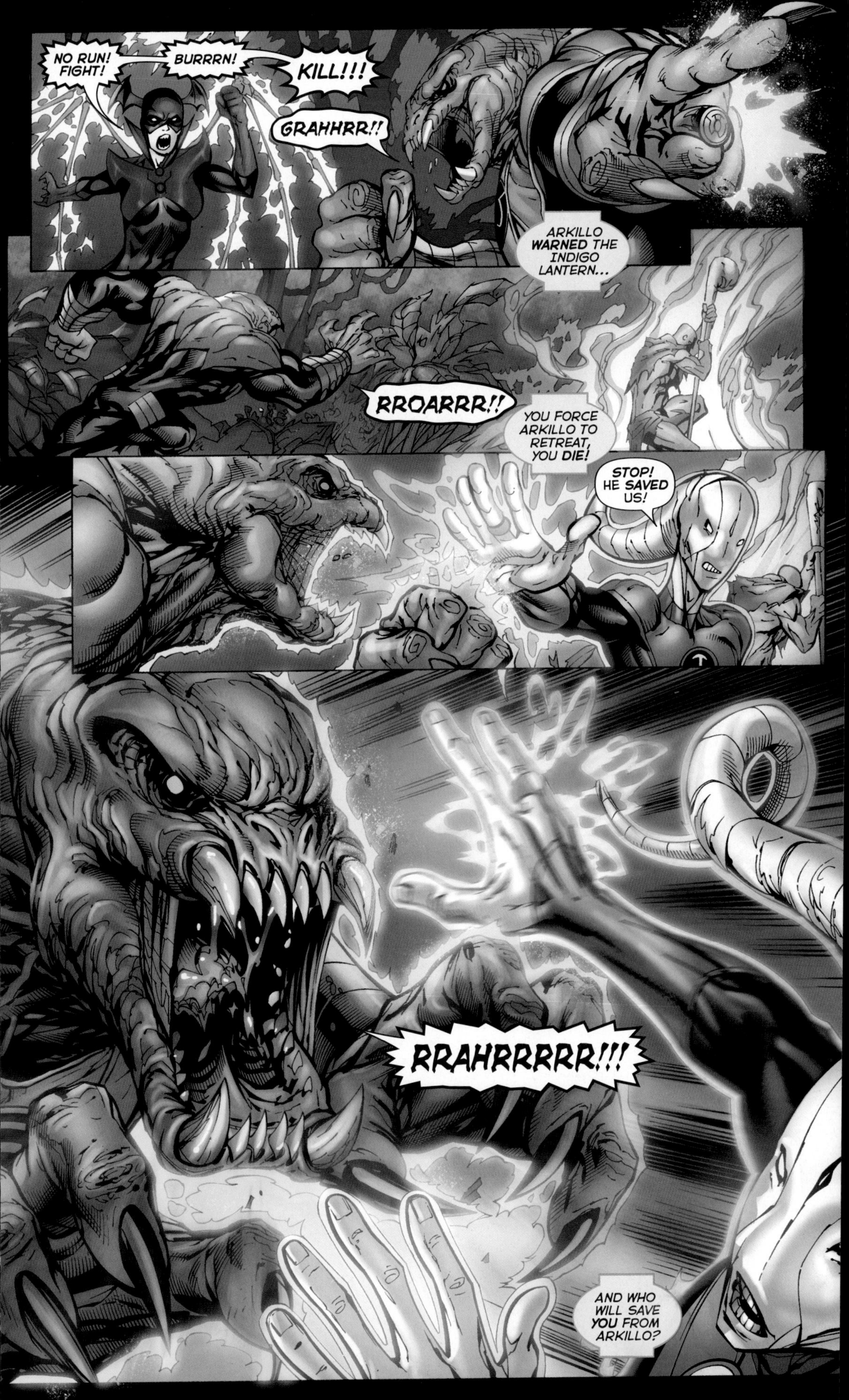
NO RUN! FIGHT!
BURRRN!
KILL!!!
GRAHHRR!!
ARKILLO WARNED THE INDIGO LANTERN...
RROARRR!!
YOU FORCE ARKILLO TO RETREAT, YOU DIE!
STOP! HE SAVED US!
RRAHRRRRR!!!
AND WHO WILL SAVE YOU FROM ARKILLO?

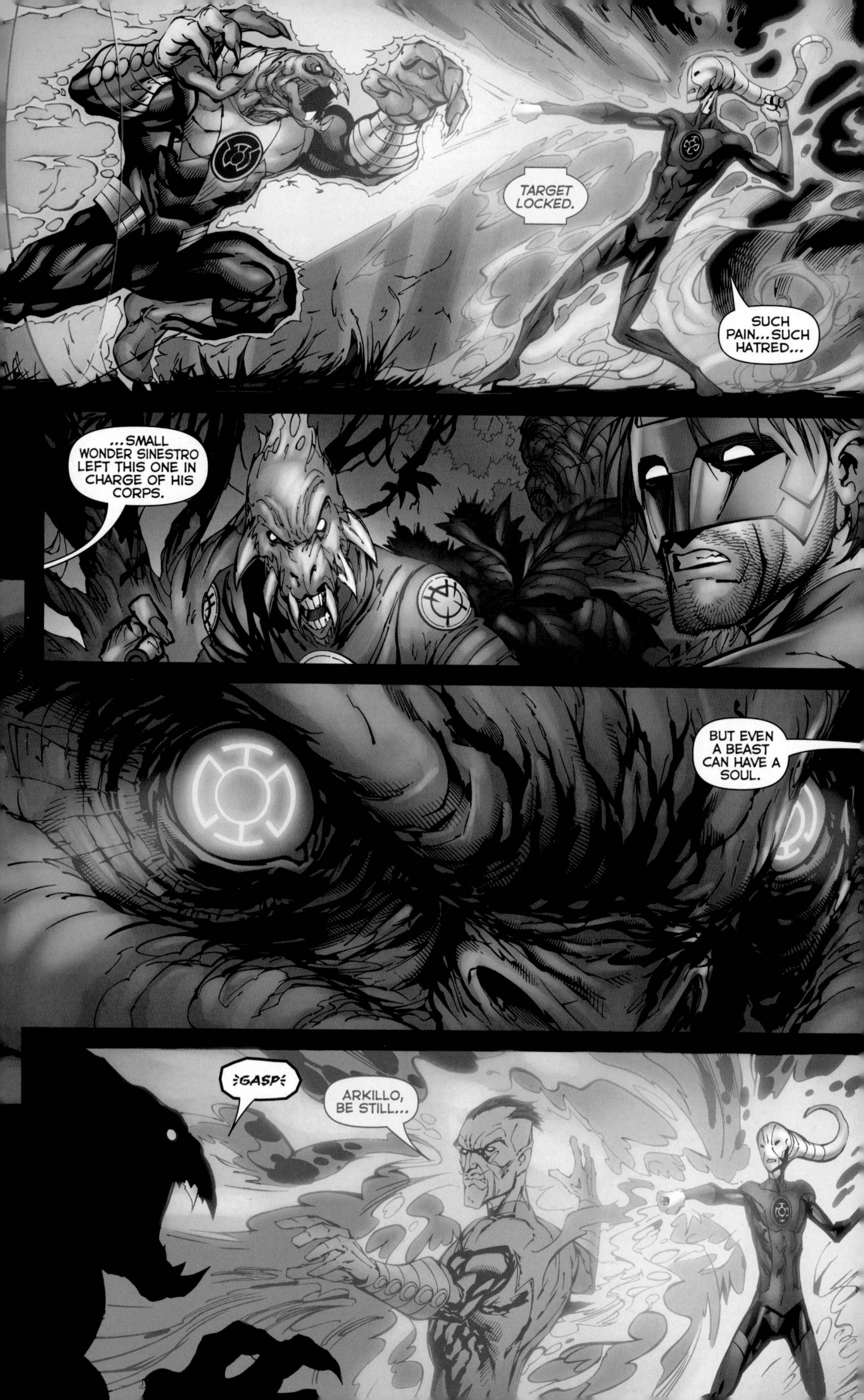
TARGET LOCKED.
SUCH PAIN...SUCH HATRED...
...SMALL WONDER SINESTRO LEFT THIS ONE IN CHARGE OF HIS CORPS.
BUT EVEN A BEAST CAN HAVE A SOUL.
GASP
ARKILLO, BE STILL...

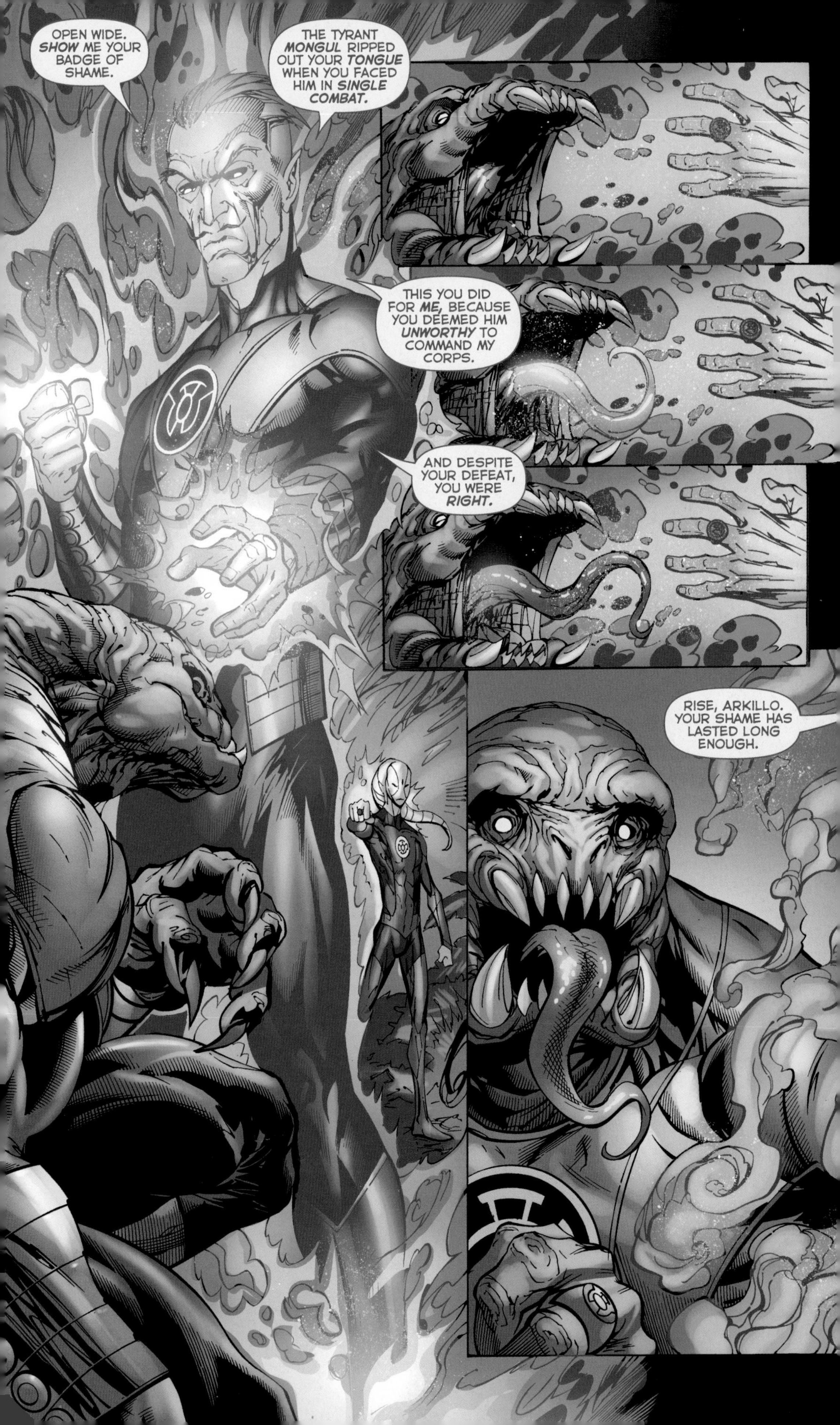
OPEN WIDE. SHOW ME YOUR BADGE OF SHAME.
THE TYRANT MONGUL RIPPED OUT YOUR TONGUE WHEN YOU FACED HIM IN SINGLE COMBAT.
THIS YOU DID FOR ME, BECAUSE YOU DEEMED HIM UNWORTHY TO COMMAND MY CORPS.
AND DESPITE YOUR DEFEAT, YOU WERE RIGHT.
RISE, ARKILLO. YOUR SHAME HAS LASTED LONG ENOUGH.

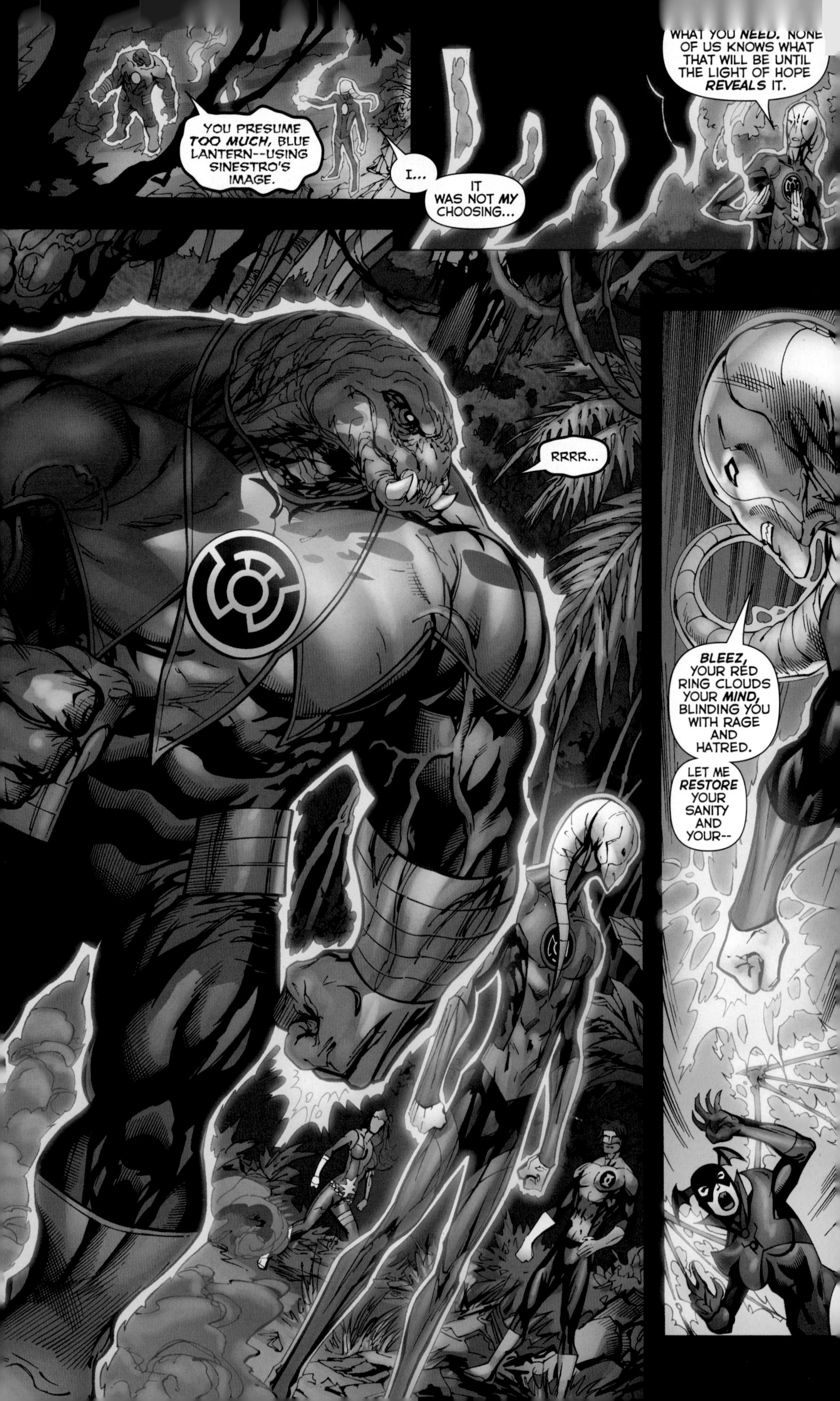

WHAT YOU NEED. NONE OF US KNOWS WHAT THAT WILL BE UNTIL THE LIGHT OF HOPE REVEALS IT.
YOU PRESUME TOO MUCH, BLUE LANTERN--USING SINESTRO'S IMAGE.
I...
IT WAS NOT MY CHOOSING...
RRRR...
BLEEZ, YOUR RED RING CLOUDS YOUR MIND, BLINDING YOU WITH RAGE AND HATRED.
LET ME RESTORE YOUR SANITY AND YOUR--

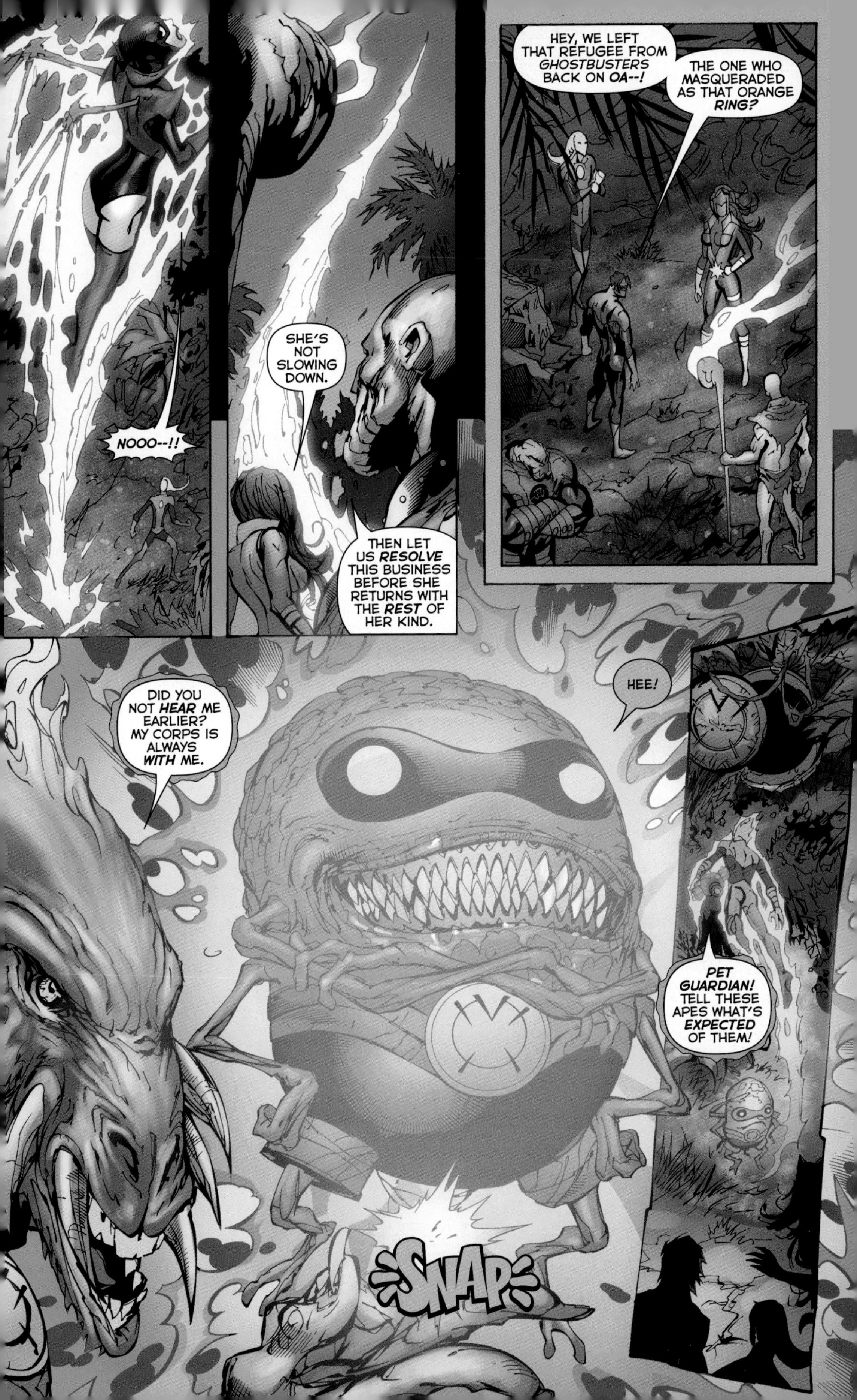
NOOO--!!
SHE'S NOT SLOWING DOWN.
THEN LET US RESOLVE THIS BUSINESS BEFORE SHE RETURNS WITH THE REST OF HER KIND.
HEY, WE LEFT THAT REFUGEE FROM GHOSTBUSTERS BACK ON OA--!
THE ONE WHO MASQUERADED AS THAT ORANGE RING?
DID YOU NOT HEAR ME EARLIER? MY CORPS IS ALWAYS WITH ME.
HEE!
PET GUARDIAN! TELL THESE APES WHAT'S EXPECTED OF THEM!
SNAP

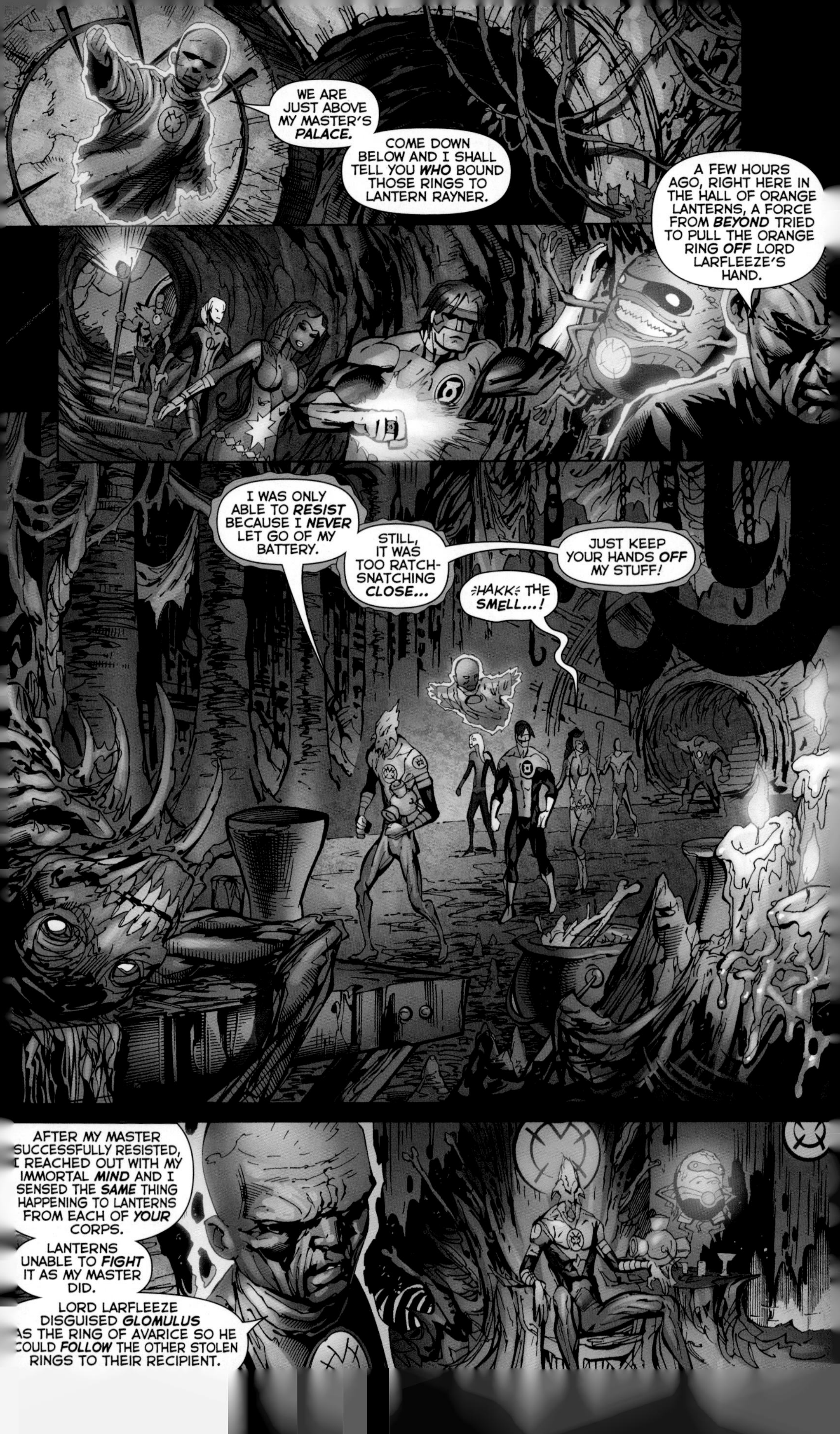
WE ARE JUST ABOVE MY MASTER'S *PALACE.*
COME DOWN BELOW AND I SHALL TELL YOU *WHO* BOUND THOSE RINGS TO LANTERN RAYNER.
A FEW HOURS AGO, RIGHT HERE IN THE HALL OF ORANGE LANTERNS, A FORCE FROM *BEYOND* TRIED TO PULL THE ORANGE RING *OFF* LORD LARFLEEZE'S HAND.
I WAS ONLY ABLE TO *RESIST* BECAUSE I *NEVER* LET GO OF MY BATTERY.
STILL, IT WAS TOO RATCH-SNATCHING *CLOSE...*
JUST KEEP YOUR HANDS *OFF* MY STUFF!
=HAKK= THE *SMELL...!*
AFTER MY MASTER SUCCESSFULLY RESISTED, I REACHED OUT WITH MY IMMORTAL *MIND* AND I SENSED THE *SAME* THING HAPPENING TO LANTERNS FROM EACH OF *YOUR* CORPS.
LANTERNS UNABLE TO *FIGHT* IT AS MY MASTER DID.
LORD LARFLEEZE DISGUISED *GLOMULUS* AS THE RING OF AVARICE SO HE COULD *FOLLOW* THE OTHER STOLEN RINGS TO THEIR RECIPIENT.

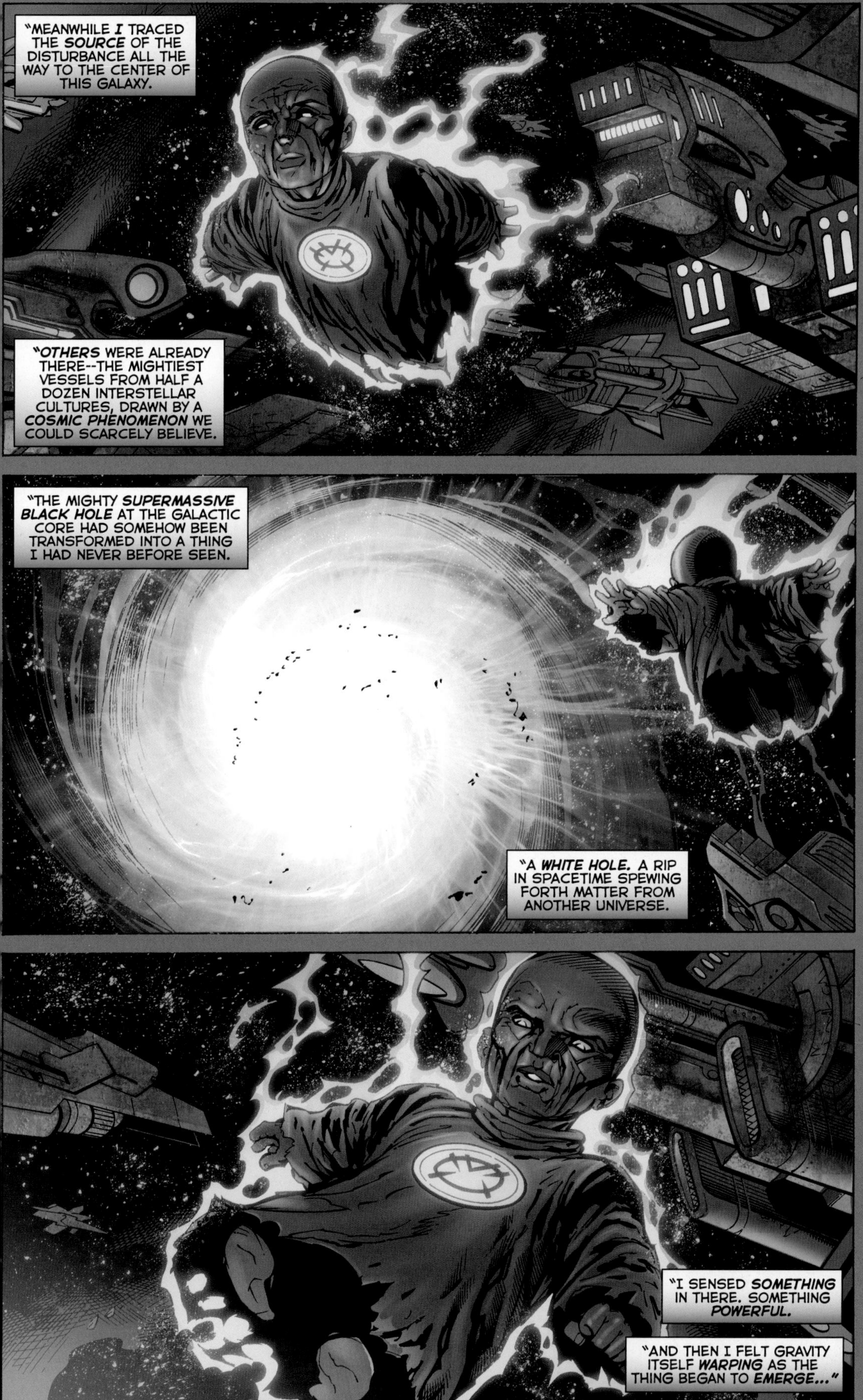
"MEANWHILE *I* TRACED THE *SOURCE* OF THE DISTURBANCE ALL THE WAY TO THE CENTER OF THIS GALAXY.
"*OTHERS* WERE ALREADY THERE--THE MIGHTIEST VESSELS FROM HALF A DOZEN INTERSTELLAR CULTURES, DRAWN BY A *COSMIC PHENOMENON* WE COULD SCARCELY BELIEVE.
"THE MIGHTY *SUPERMASSIVE BLACK HOLE* AT THE GALACTIC CORE HAD SOMEHOW BEEN TRANSFORMED INTO A THING I HAD NEVER BEFORE SEEN.
"A *WHITE HOLE.* A RIP IN SPACETIME SPEWING FORTH MATTER FROM ANOTHER UNIVERSE.
"I SENSED *SOMETHING* IN THERE. SOMETHING *POWERFUL.*
"AND THEN I FELT GRAVITY ITSELF *WARPING* AS THE THING BEGAN TO *EMERGE...*"

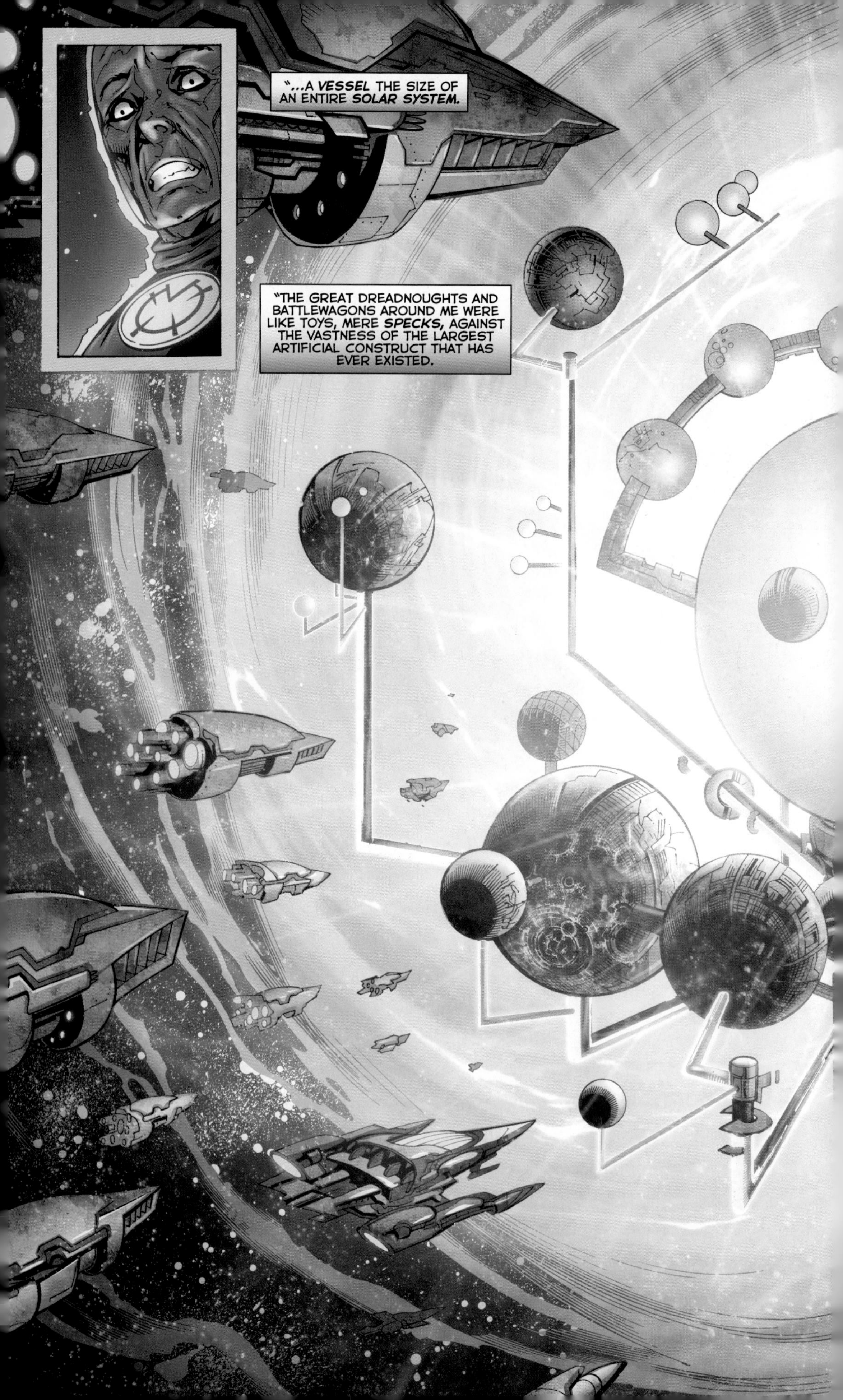

"...A VESSEL THE SIZE OF AN ENTIRE SOLAR SYSTEM.
"THE GREAT DREADNOUGHTS AND BATTLEWAGONS AROUND ME WERE LIKE TOYS, MERE SPECKS, AGAINST THE VASTNESS OF THE LARGEST ARTIFICIAL CONSTRUCT THAT HAS EVER EXISTED.

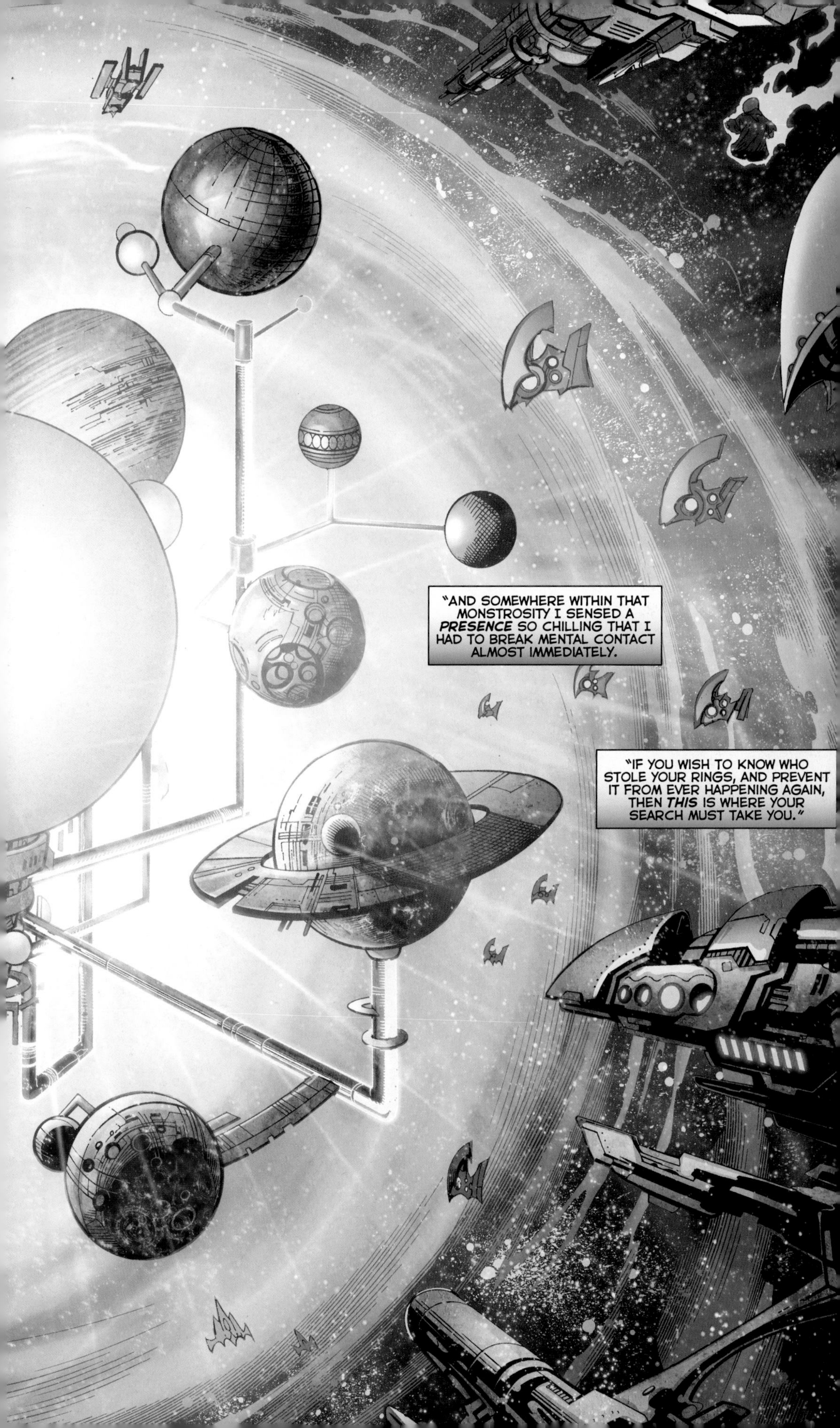
"AND SOMEWHERE WITHIN THAT MONSTROSITY I SENSED A *PRESENCE* SO CHILLING THAT I HAD TO BREAK MENTAL CONTACT ALMOST IMMEDIATELY.
"IF YOU WISH TO KNOW WHO STOLE YOUR RINGS, AND PREVENT IT FROM EVER HAPPENING AGAIN, THEN *THIS* IS WHERE YOUR SEARCH MUST TAKE YOU."

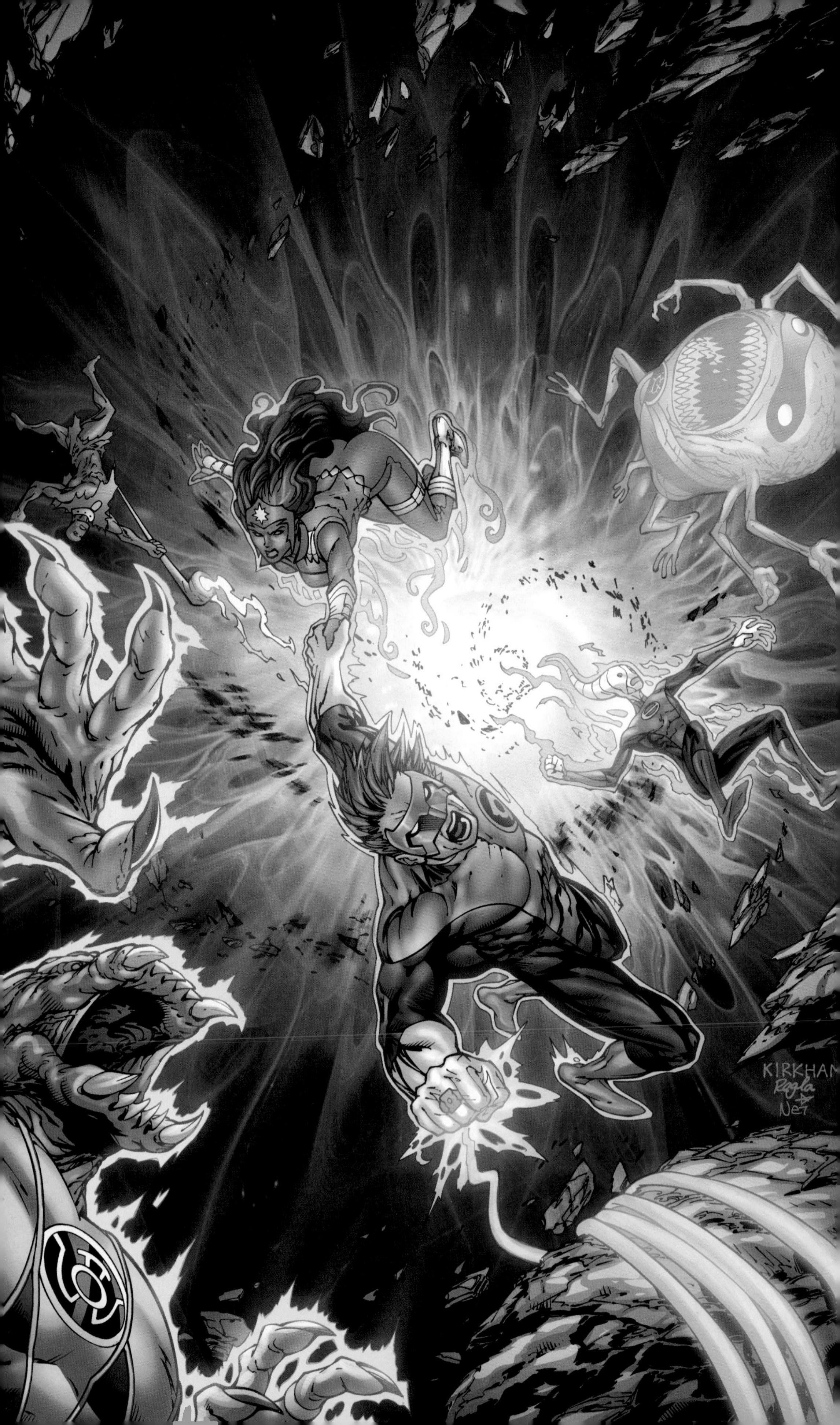
KIRKHAM

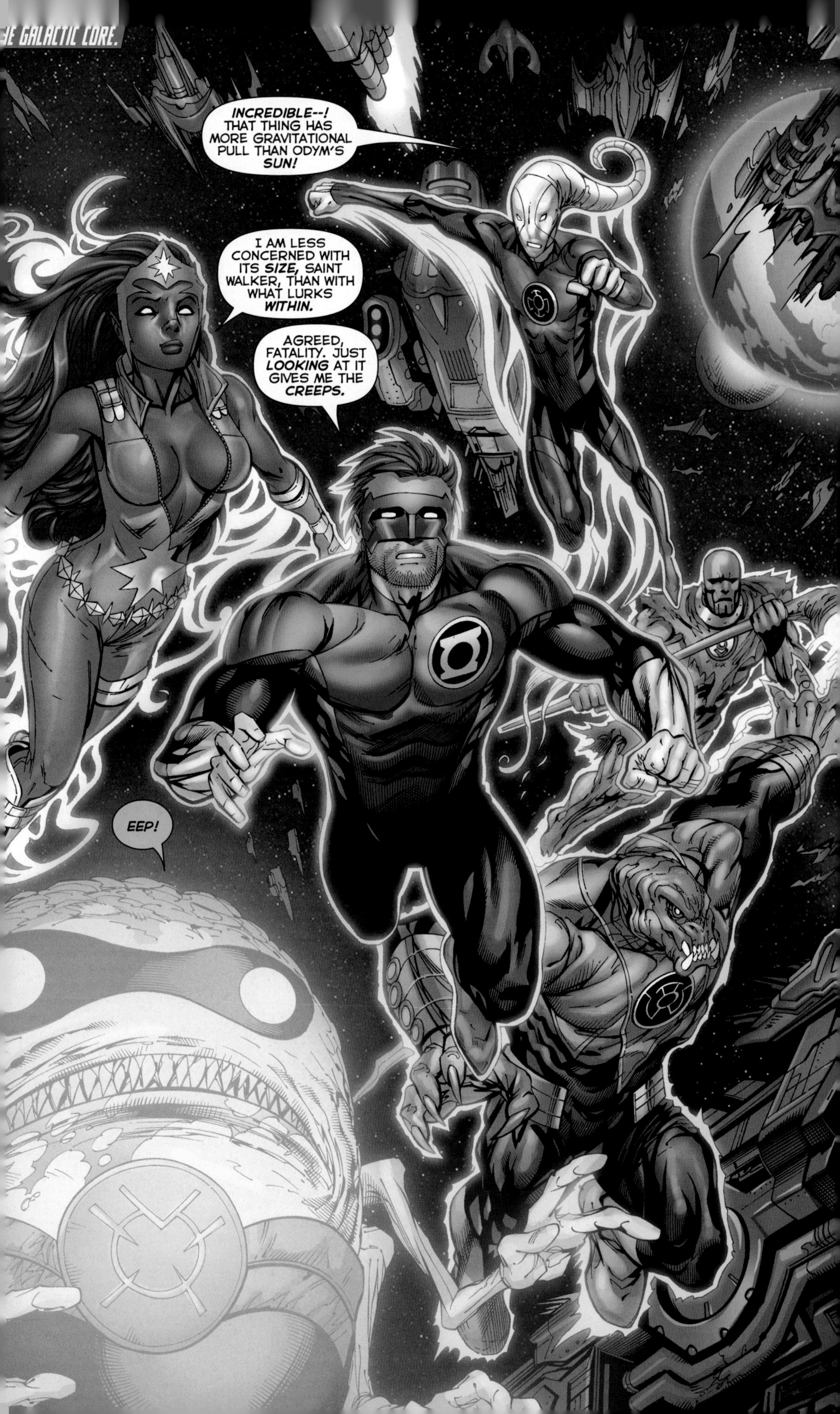

...E GALACTIC CORE.
INCREDIBLE--! THAT THING HAS MORE GRAVITATIONAL PULL THAN ODYM'S SUN!
I AM LESS CONCERNED WITH ITS SIZE, SAINT WALKER, THAN WITH WHAT LURKS WITHIN.
AGREED, FATALITY. JUST LOOKING AT IT GIVES ME THE CREEPS.
EEP!

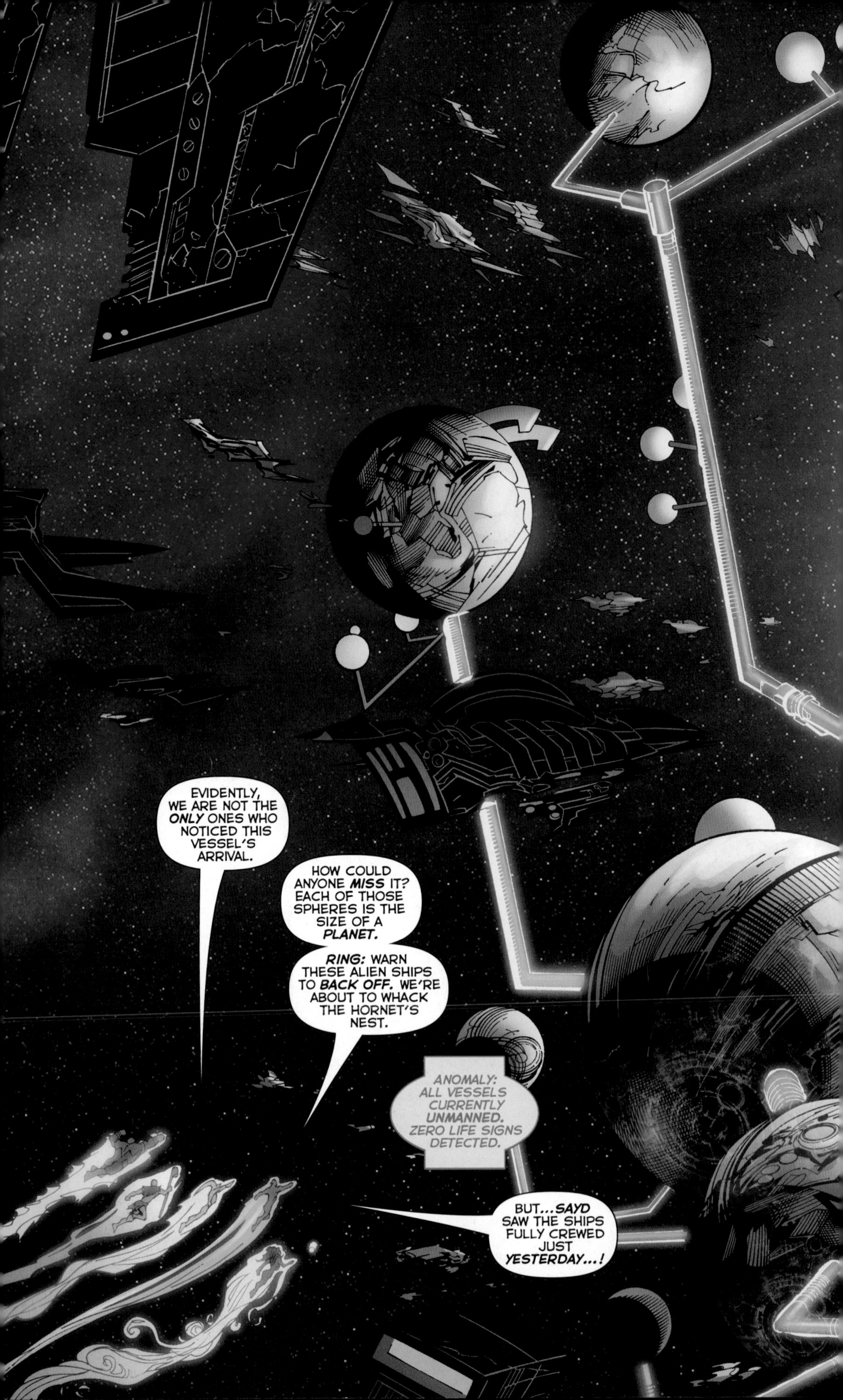
EVIDENTLY, WE ARE NOT THE ONLY ONES WHO NOTICED THIS VESSEL'S ARRIVAL.
HOW COULD ANYONE MISS IT? EACH OF THOSE SPHERES IS THE SIZE OF A PLANET.
RING: WARN THESE ALIEN SHIPS TO BACK OFF. WE'RE ABOUT TO WHACK THE HORNET'S NEST.
ANOMALY: ALL VESSELS CURRENTLY UNMANNED. ZERO LIFE SIGNS DETECTED.
BUT...SAYD SAW THE SHIPS FULLY CREWED JUST YESTERDAY...!

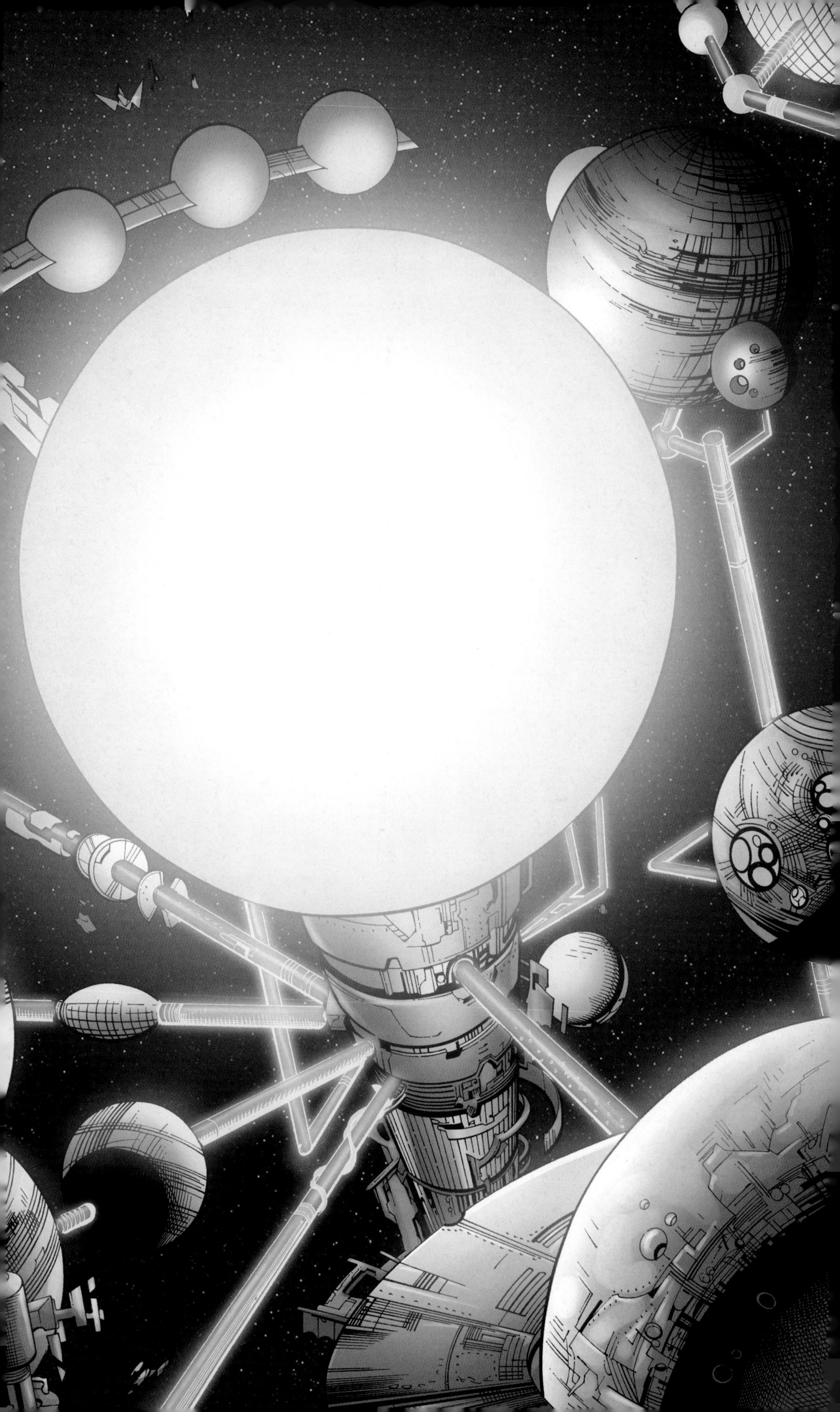

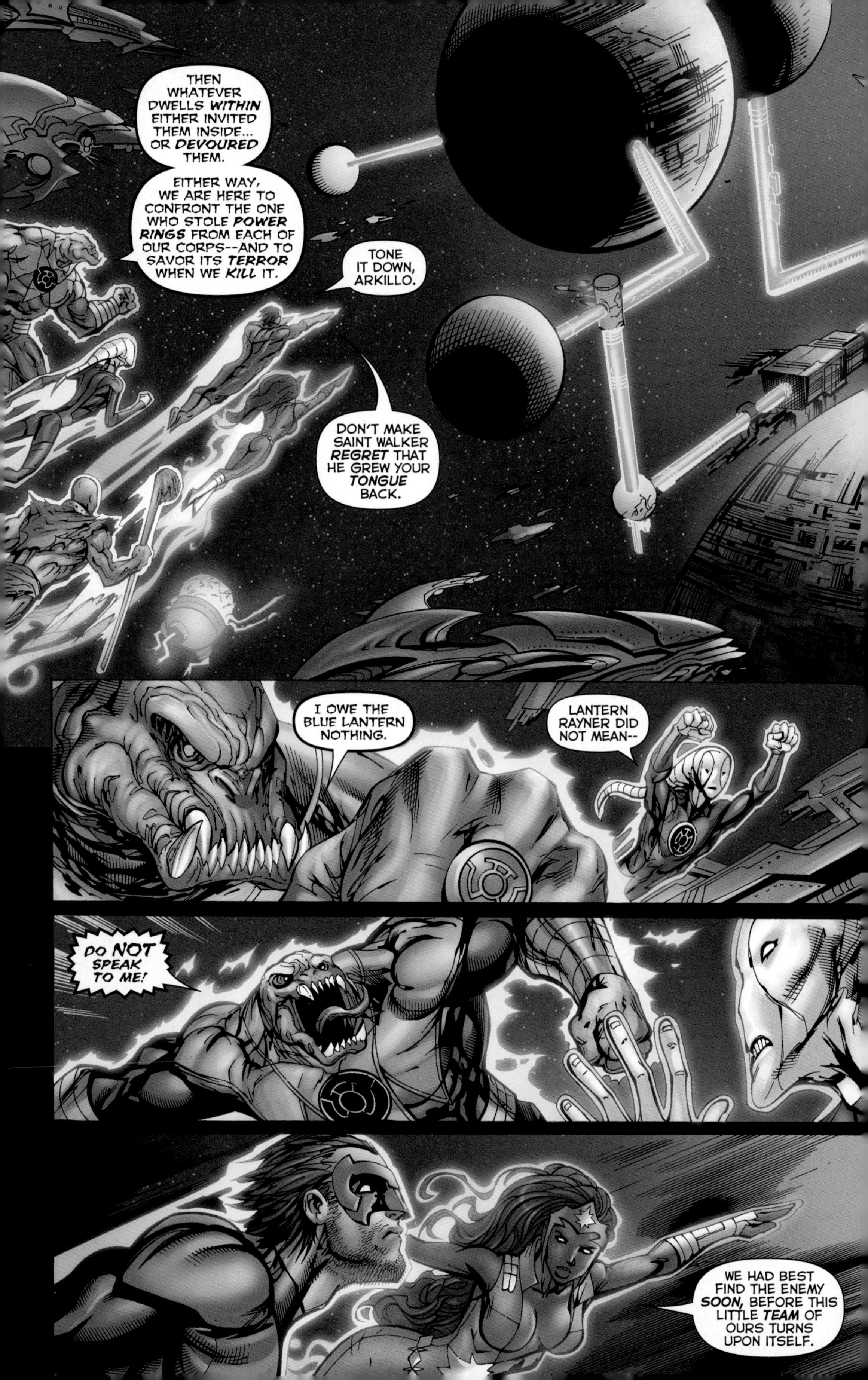
THEN WHATEVER DWELLS *WITHIN* EITHER INVITED THEM INSIDE... OR *DEVOURED* THEM.
EITHER WAY, WE ARE HERE TO CONFRONT THE ONE WHO STOLE *POWER RINGS* FROM EACH OF OUR CORPS--AND TO SAVOR ITS *TERROR* WHEN WE *KILL* IT.
TONE IT DOWN, ARKILLO.
DON'T MAKE SAINT WALKER *REGRET* THAT HE GREW YOUR *TONGUE* BACK.
I OWE THE BLUE LANTERN NOTHING.
LANTERN RAYNER DID NOT MEAN--
DO *NOT* SPEAK TO ME!
WE HAD BEST FIND THE ENEMY *SOON,* BEFORE THIS LITTLE *TEAM* OF OURS TURNS UPON ITSELF.

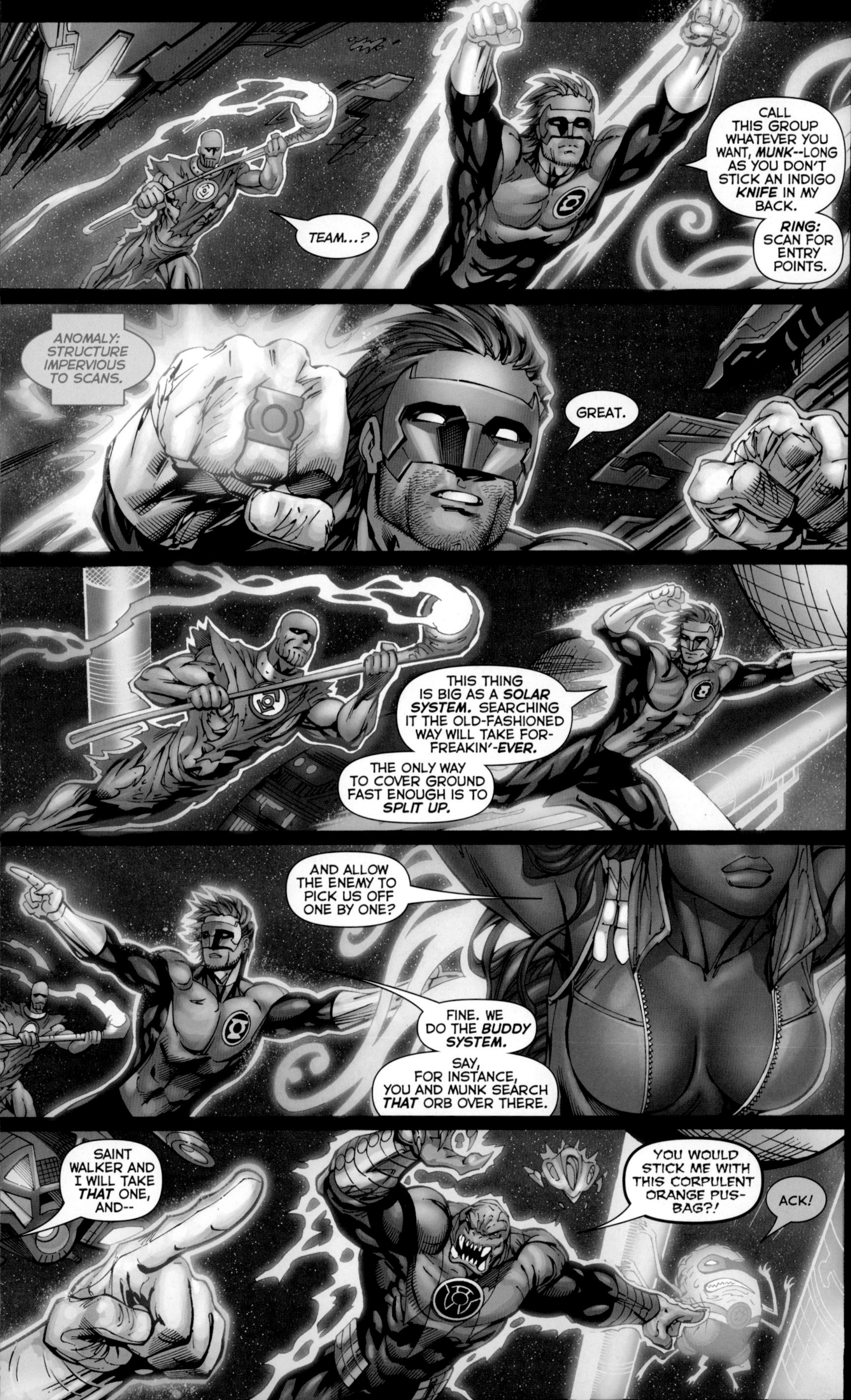
CALL THIS GROUP WHATEVER YOU WANT, MUNK--LONG AS YOU DON'T STICK AN INDIGO KNIFE IN MY BACK.
TEAM...?
RING: SCAN FOR ENTRY POINTS.
ANOMALY: STRUCTURE IMPERVIOUS TO SCANS.
GREAT.
THIS THING IS BIG AS A SOLAR SYSTEM. SEARCHING IT THE OLD-FASHIONED WAY WILL TAKE FOR-FREAKIN'-EVER.
THE ONLY WAY TO COVER GROUND FAST ENOUGH IS TO SPLIT UP.
AND ALLOW THE ENEMY TO PICK US OFF ONE BY ONE?
FINE. WE DO THE BUDDY SYSTEM.
SAY, FOR INSTANCE, YOU AND MUNK SEARCH THAT ORB OVER THERE.
SAINT WALKER AND I WILL TAKE THAT ONE, AND--
YOU WOULD STICK ME WITH THIS CORPULENT ORANGE PUS-BAG?!
ACK!

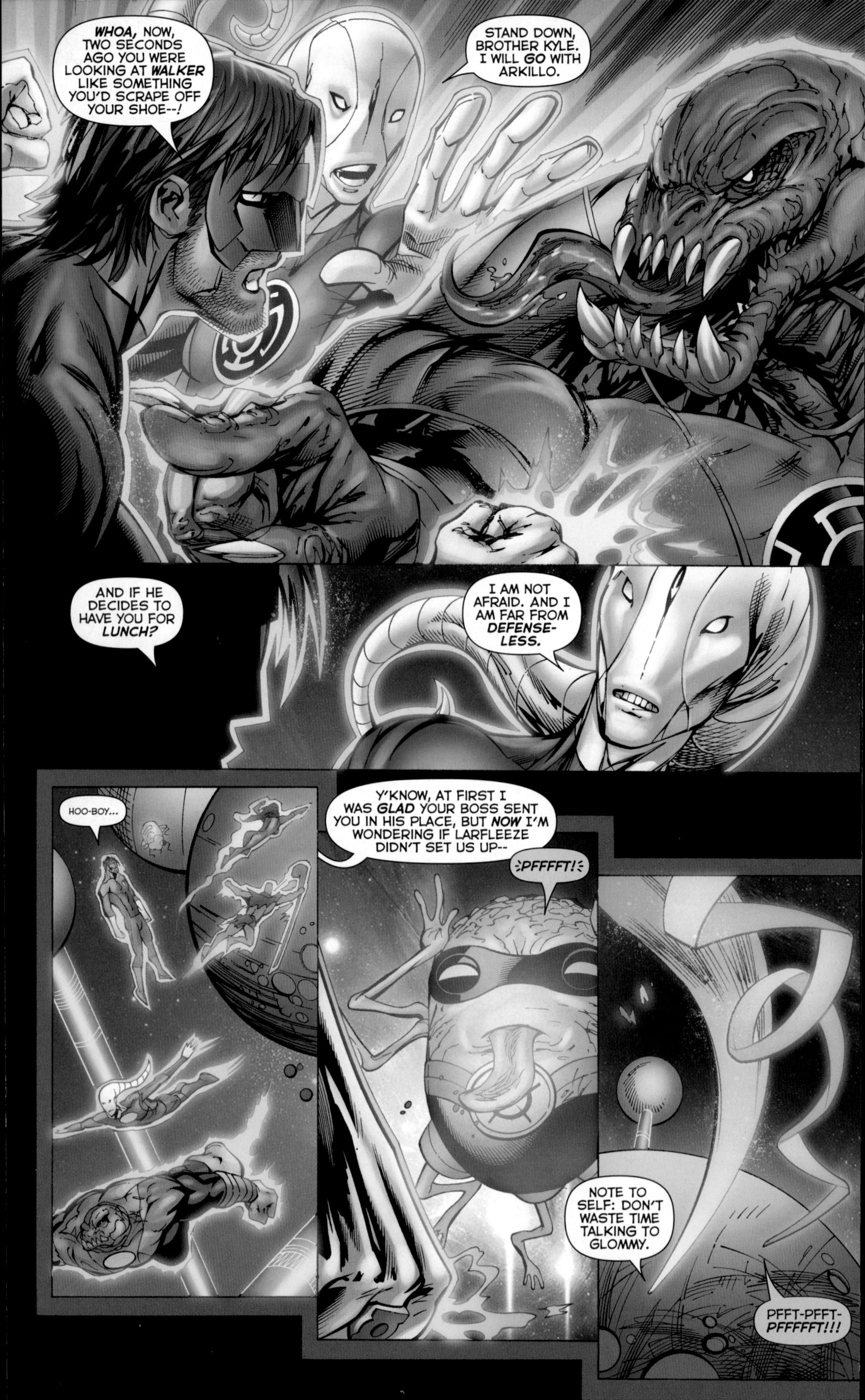
WHOA, NOW, TWO SECONDS AGO YOU WERE LOOKING AT WALKER LIKE SOMETHING YOU'D SCRAPE OFF YOUR SHOE--!
STAND DOWN, BROTHER KYLE. I WILL GO WITH ARKILLO.
AND IF HE DECIDES TO HAVE YOU FOR LUNCH?
I AM NOT AFRAID. AND I AM FAR FROM DEFENSE-LESS.
HOO-BOY...
Y'KNOW, AT FIRST I WAS GLAD YOUR BOSS SENT YOU IN HIS PLACE, BUT NOW I'M WONDERING IF LARFLEEZE DIDN'T SET US UP--
PFFFFT!
NOTE TO SELF: DON'T WASTE TIME TALKING TO GLOMMY.
PFFT-PFFT-PFFFFFT!!!

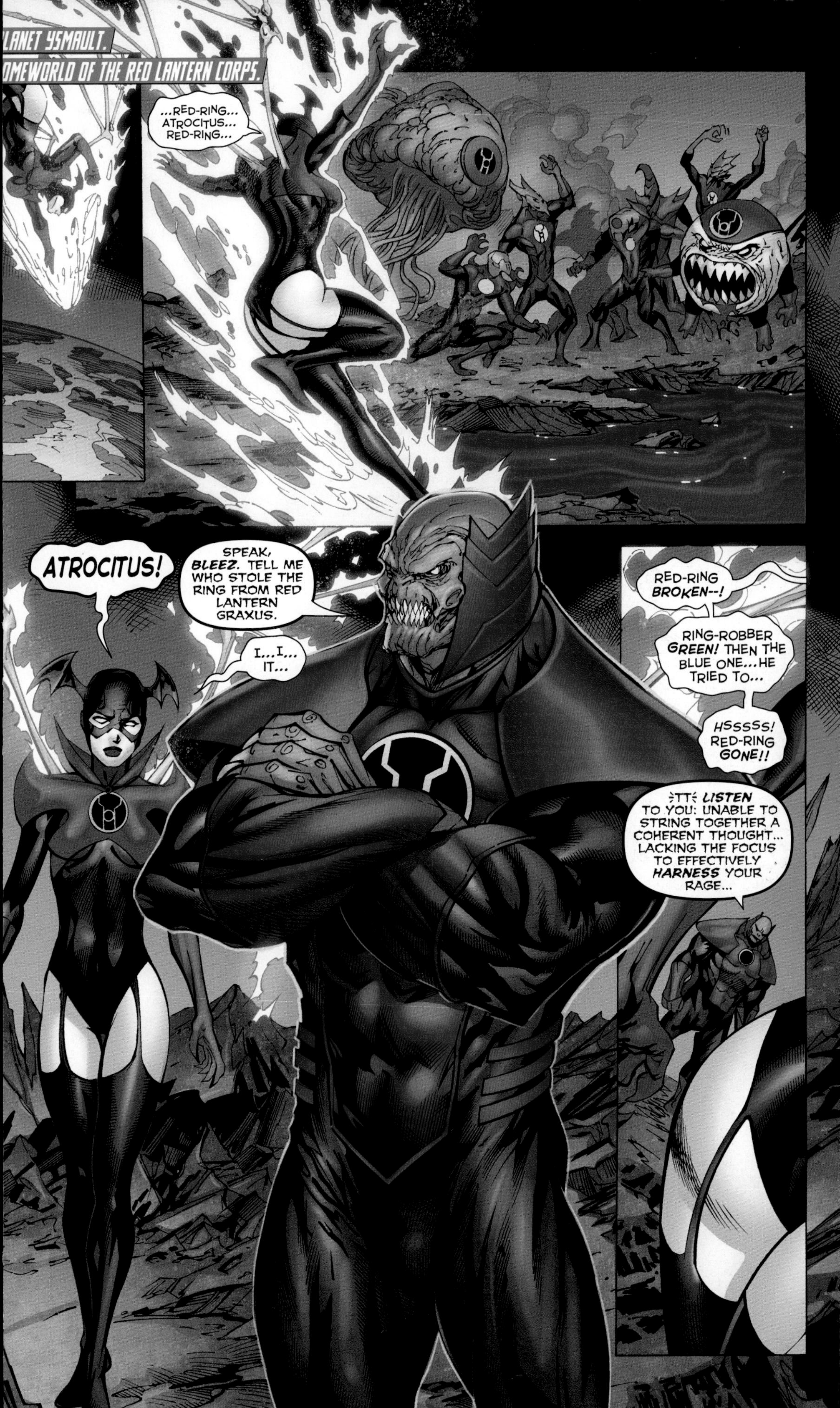

LANET YSMAULT.
OMEWORLD OF THE RED LANTERN CORPS.
...RED-RING... ATROCITUS... RED-RING...
ATROCITUS!
SPEAK, BLEEZ. TELL ME WHO STOLE THE RING FROM RED LANTERN GRAXUS.
I...I... IT...
RED-RING BROKEN--!
RING-ROBBER GREEN! THEN THE BLUE ONE...HE TRIED TO...
HSSSSS! RED-RING GONE!!
TT LISTEN TO YOU: UNABLE TO STRING TOGETHER A COHERENT THOUGHT... LACKING THE FOCUS TO EFFECTIVELY HARNESS YOUR RAGE...

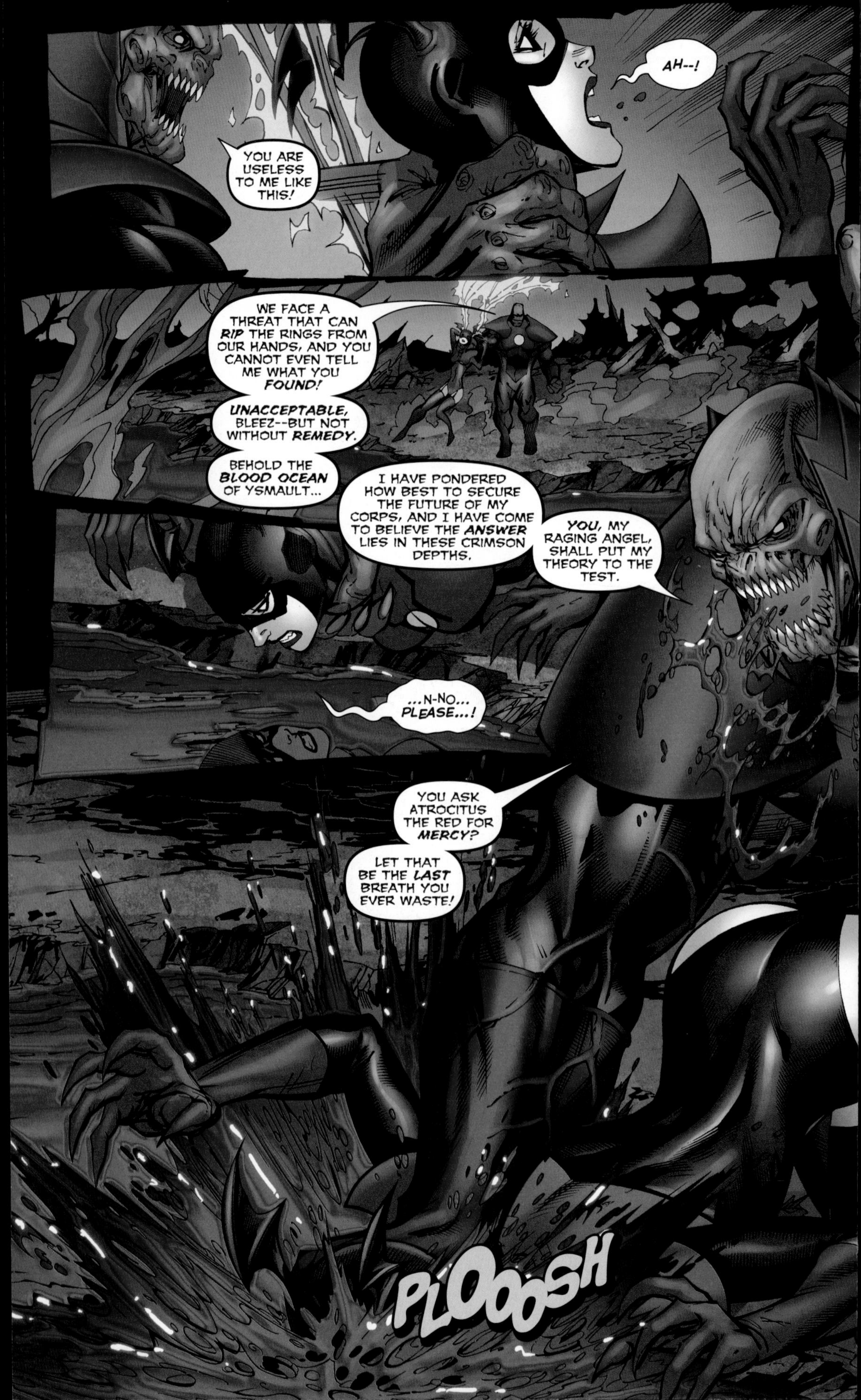
AH--!
YOU ARE USELESS TO ME LIKE THIS!
WE FACE A THREAT THAT CAN RIP THE RINGS FROM OUR HANDS, AND YOU CANNOT EVEN TELL ME WHAT YOU FOUND!
UNACCEPTABLE, BLEEZ--BUT NOT WITHOUT REMEDY.
BEHOLD THE BLOOD OCEAN OF YSMAULT...
I HAVE PONDERED HOW BEST TO SECURE THE FUTURE OF MY CORPS, AND I HAVE COME TO BELIEVE THE ANSWER LIES IN THESE CRIMSON DEPTHS.
YOU, MY RAGING ANGEL, SHALL PUT MY THEORY TO THE TEST.
...N-NO... PLEASE...!
YOU ASK ATROCITUS THE RED FOR MERCY?
LET THAT BE THE LAST BREATH YOU EVER WASTE!
PLOOOOSH

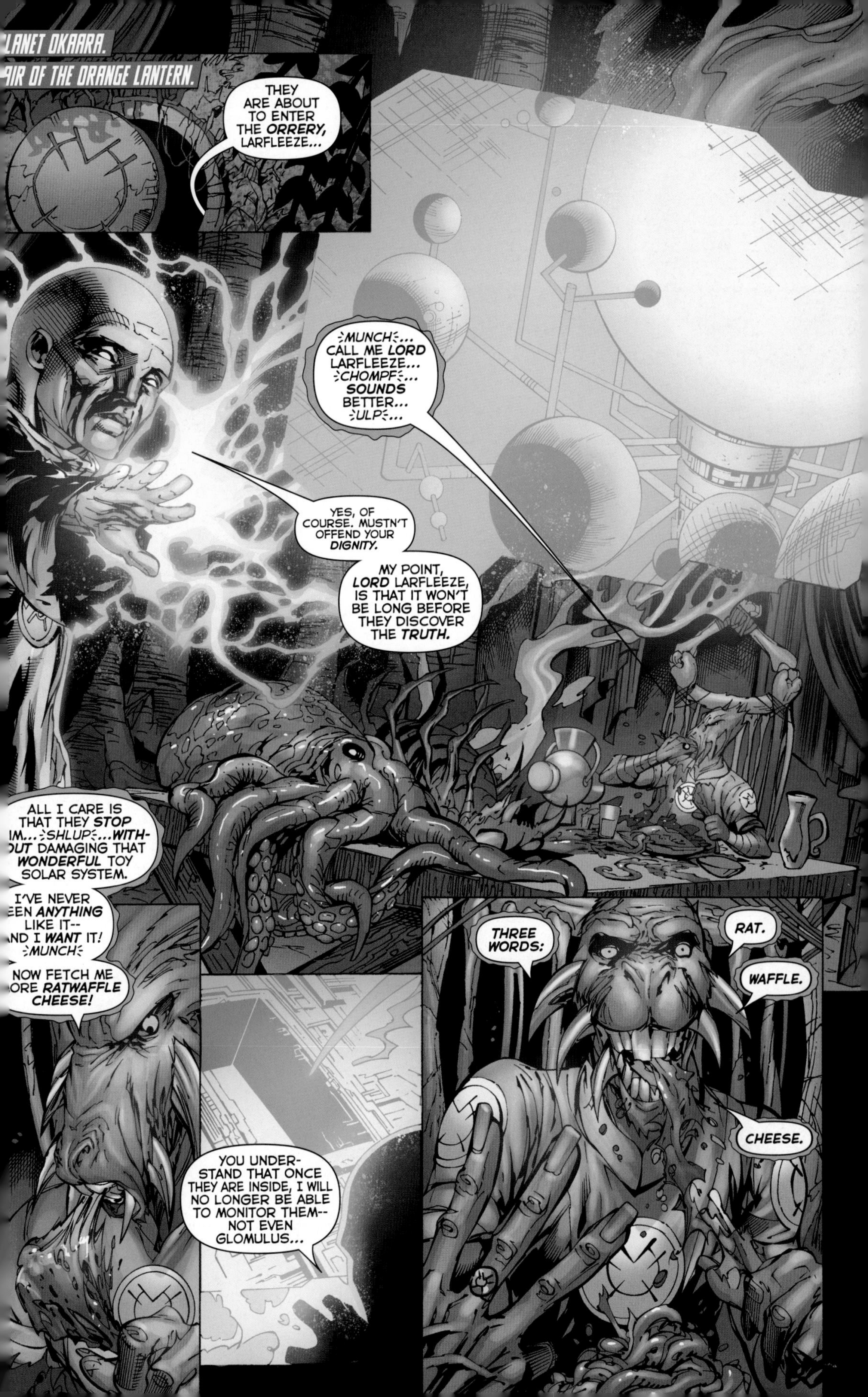

LANET OKAARA.
AIR OF THE ORANGE LANTERN.
THEY ARE ABOUT TO ENTER THE *ORRERY,* LARFLEEZE...
MUNCH... CALL ME *LORD* LARFLEEZE... *CHOMPF*... *SOUNDS* BETTER... *ULP*...
YES, OF COURSE. MUSTN'T OFFEND YOUR *DIGNITY.*
MY POINT, *LORD* LARFLEEZE, IS THAT IT WON'T BE LONG BEFORE THEY DISCOVER THE *TRUTH.*
ALL I CARE IS THAT THEY *STOP* IM... *SHLUP*... *WITH-OUT* DAMAGING THAT *WONDERFUL* TOY SOLAR SYSTEM.
I'VE NEVER EEN *ANYTHING* LIKE IT-- ND I *WANT* IT! *MUNCH*
NOW FETCH ME ORE *RATWAFFLE CHEESE!*
YOU UNDER-STAND THAT ONCE THEY ARE INSIDE, I WILL NO LONGER BE ABLE TO MONITOR THEM-- NOT EVEN GLOMULUS...
THREE WORDS:
RAT.
WAFFLE.
CHEESE.

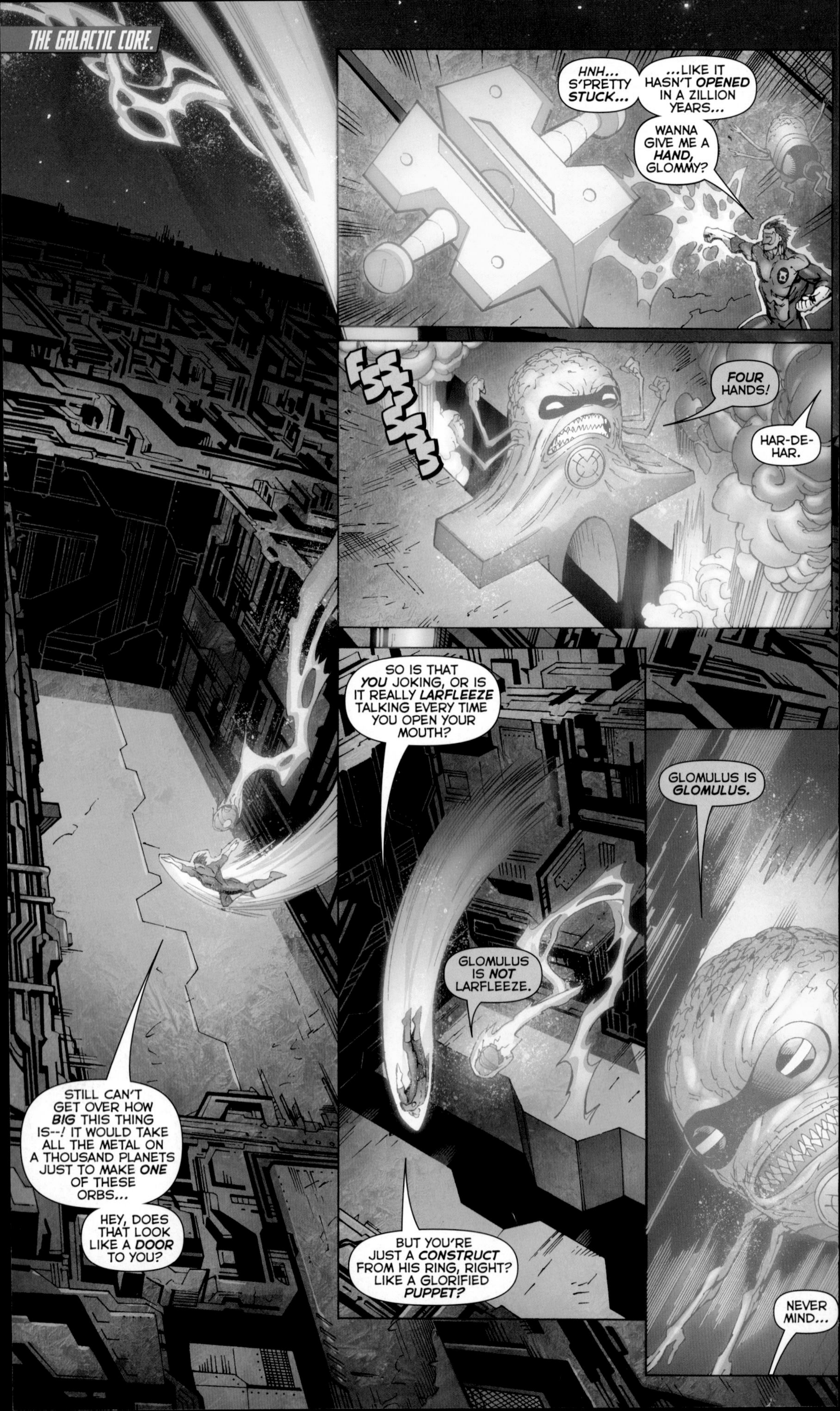
THE GALACTIC CORE.
HNH... S'PRETTY STUCK...
...LIKE IT HASN'T OPENED IN A ZILLION YEARS...
WANNA GIVE ME A HAND, GLOMMY?
FSSSHHH
FOUR HANDS!
HAR-DE-HAR.
STILL CAN'T GET OVER HOW BIG THIS THING IS--! IT WOULD TAKE ALL THE METAL ON A THOUSAND PLANETS JUST TO MAKE ONE OF THESE ORBS...
HEY, DOES THAT LOOK LIKE A DOOR TO YOU?
SO IS THAT YOU JOKING, OR IS IT REALLY LARFLEEZE TALKING EVERY TIME YOU OPEN YOUR MOUTH?
GLOMULUS IS NOT LARFLEEZE.
BUT YOU'RE JUST A CONSTRUCT FROM HIS RING, RIGHT? LIKE A GLORIFIED PUPPET?
GLOMULUS IS GLOMULUS.
NEVER MIND...

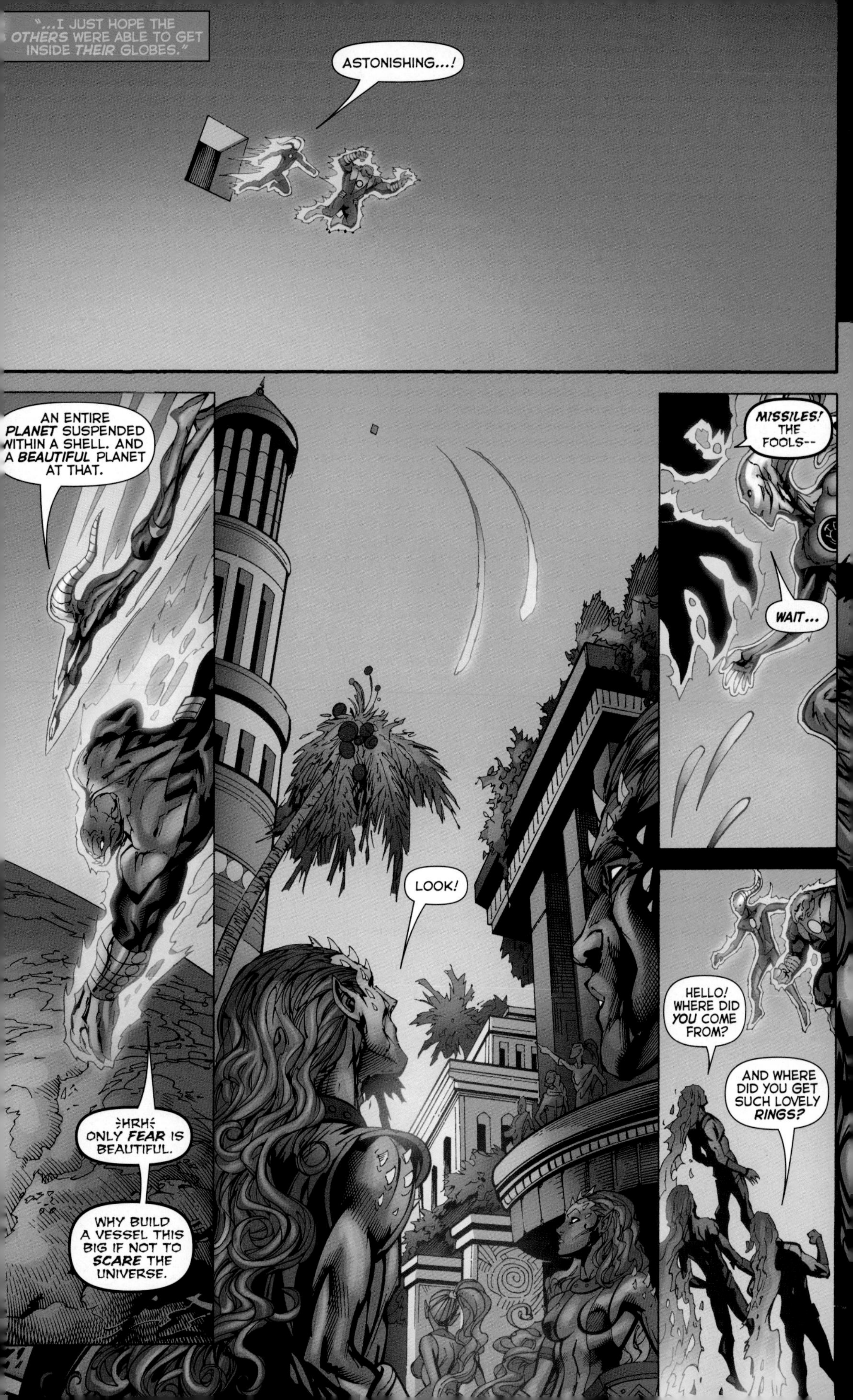
"...I JUST HOPE THE OTHERS WERE ABLE TO GET INSIDE THEIR GLOBES."
ASTONISHING...!
AN ENTIRE PLANET SUSPENDED WITHIN A SHELL. AND A BEAUTIFUL PLANET AT THAT.
HRH ONLY FEAR IS BEAUTIFUL.
WHY BUILD A VESSEL THIS BIG IF NOT TO SCARE THE UNIVERSE.
LOOK!
MISSILES! THE FOOLS--
WAIT...
HELLO! WHERE DID YOU COME FROM?
AND WHERE DID YOU GET SUCH LOVELY RINGS?

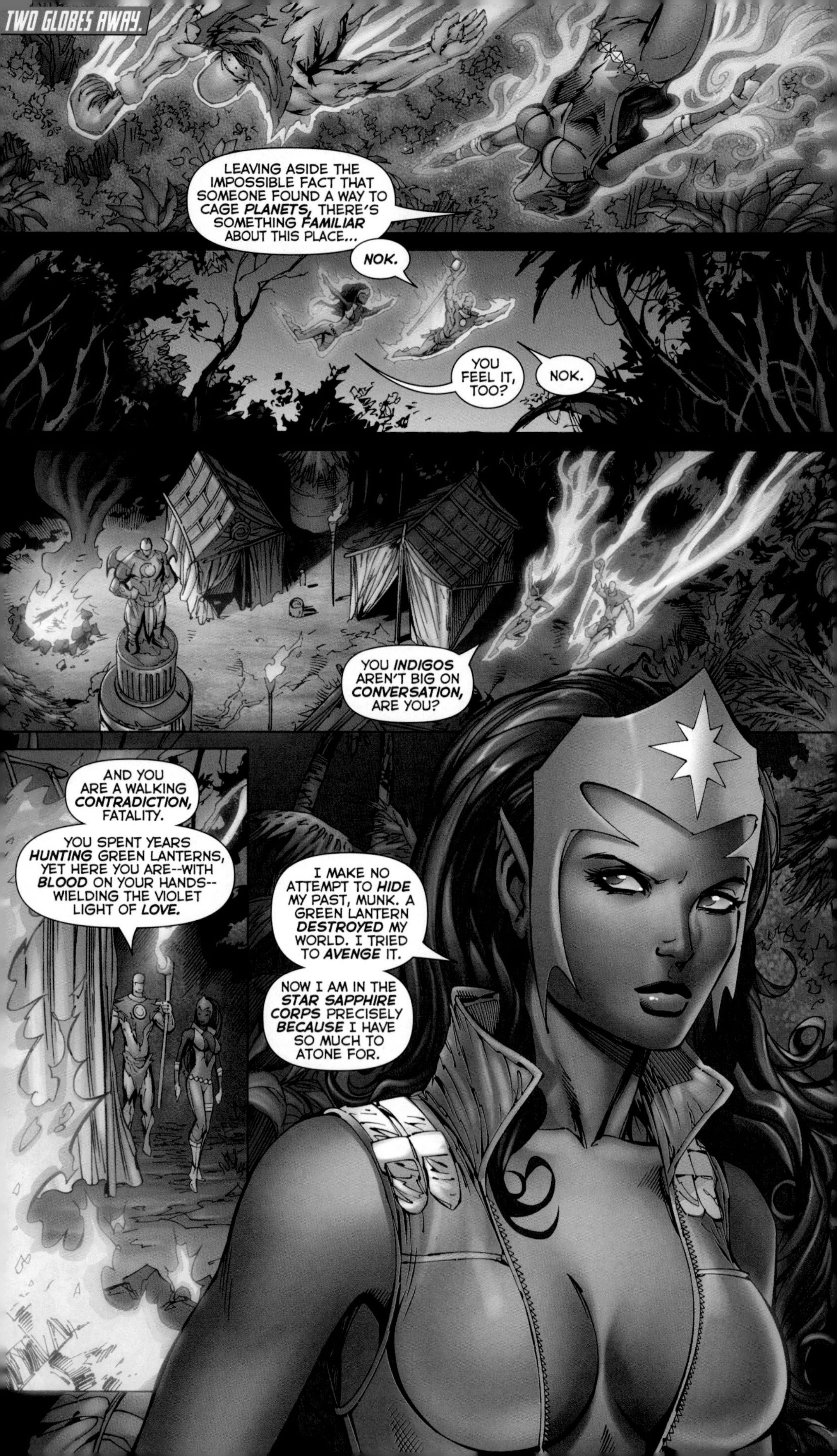
TWO GLOBES AWAY.
LEAVING ASIDE THE IMPOSSIBLE FACT THAT SOMEONE FOUND A WAY TO CAGE PLANETS, THERE'S SOMETHING FAMILIAR ABOUT THIS PLACE...
NOK.
YOU FEEL IT, TOO?
NOK.
YOU INDIGOS AREN'T BIG ON CONVERSATION, ARE YOU?
AND YOU ARE A WALKING CONTRADICTION, FATALITY.
YOU SPENT YEARS HUNTING GREEN LANTERNS, YET HERE YOU ARE--WITH BLOOD ON YOUR HANDS--WIELDING THE VIOLET LIGHT OF LOVE.
I MAKE NO ATTEMPT TO HIDE MY PAST, MUNK. A GREEN LANTERN DESTROYED MY WORLD. I TRIED TO AVENGE IT.
NOW I AM IN THE STAR SAPPHIRE CORPS PRECISELY BECAUSE I HAVE SO MUCH TO ATONE FOR.

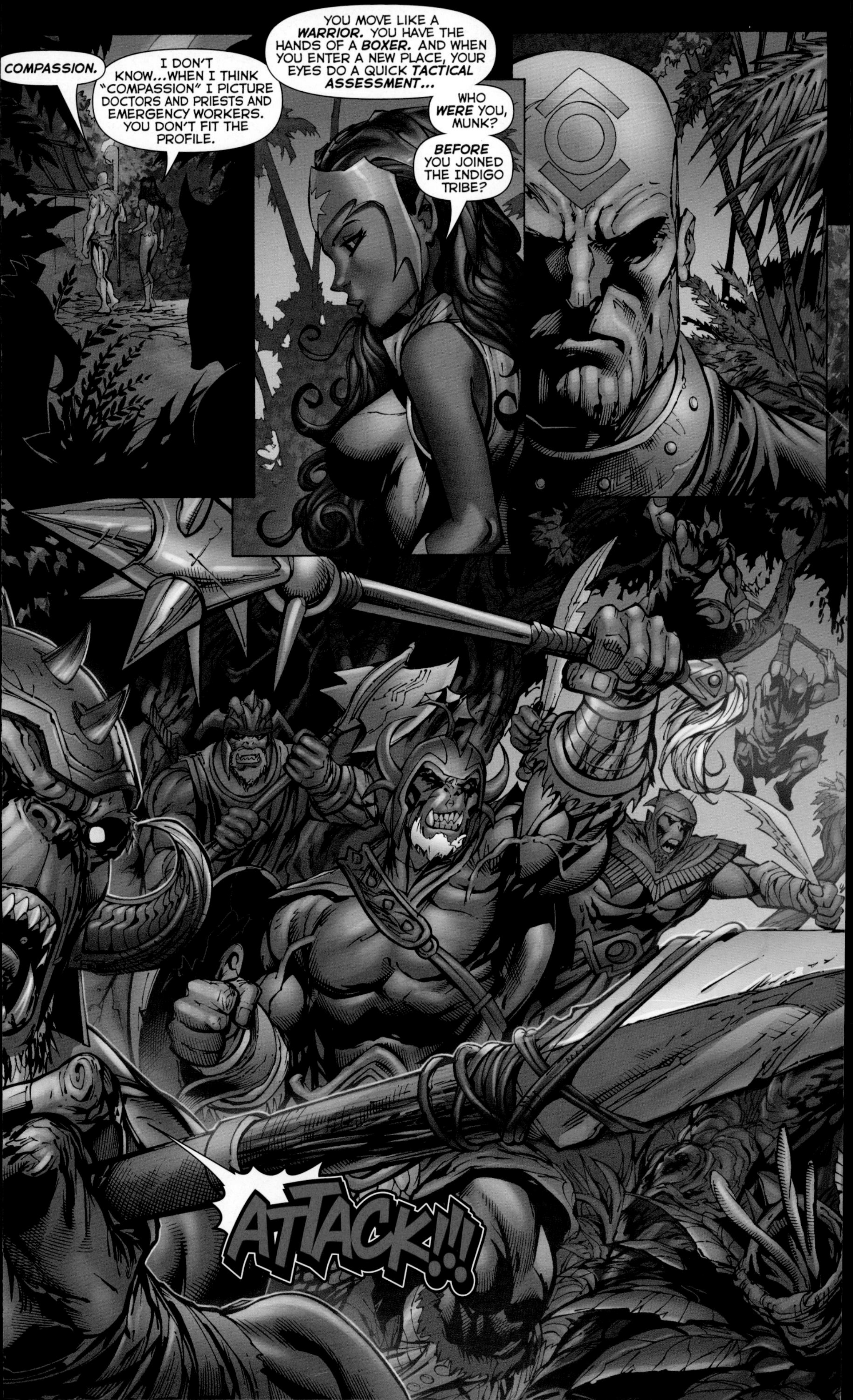

COMPASSION.
I DON'T KNOW...WHEN I THINK "COMPASSION" I PICTURE DOCTORS AND PRIESTS AND EMERGENCY WORKERS. YOU DON'T FIT THE PROFILE.
YOU MOVE LIKE A WARRIOR. YOU HAVE THE HANDS OF A BOXER. AND WHEN YOU ENTER A NEW PLACE, YOUR EYES DO A QUICK TACTICAL ASSESSMENT...
WHO WERE YOU, MUNK?
BEFORE YOU JOINED THE INDIGO TRIBE?
ATTACK!!!

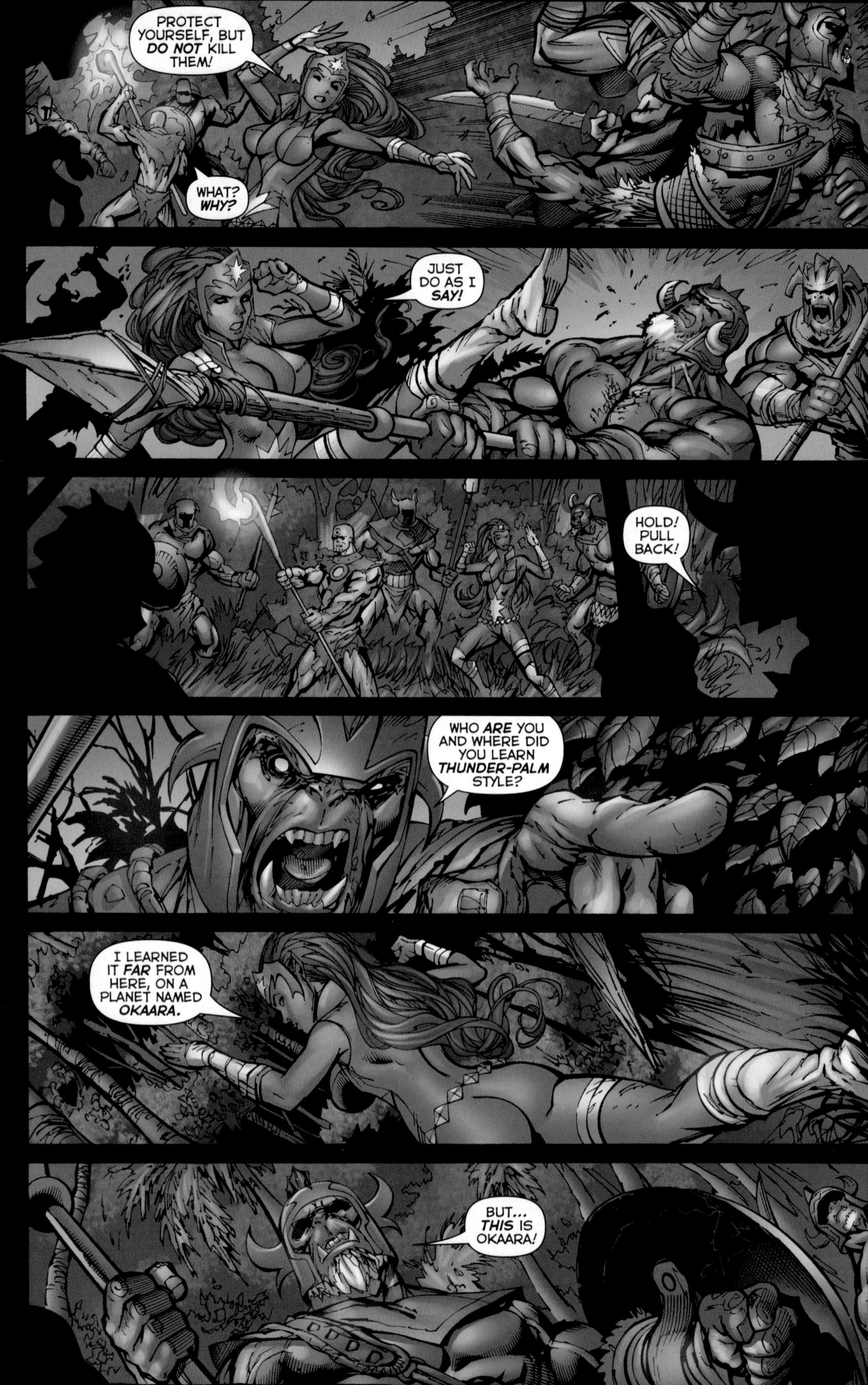

PROTECT YOURSELF, BUT DO NOT KILL THEM!
WHAT? WHY?
JUST DO AS I SAY!
HOLD! PULL BACK!
WHO ARE YOU AND WHERE DID YOU LEARN THUNDER-PALM STYLE?
I LEARNED IT FAR FROM HERE, ON A PLANET NAMED OKAARA.
BUT... THIS IS OKAARA!

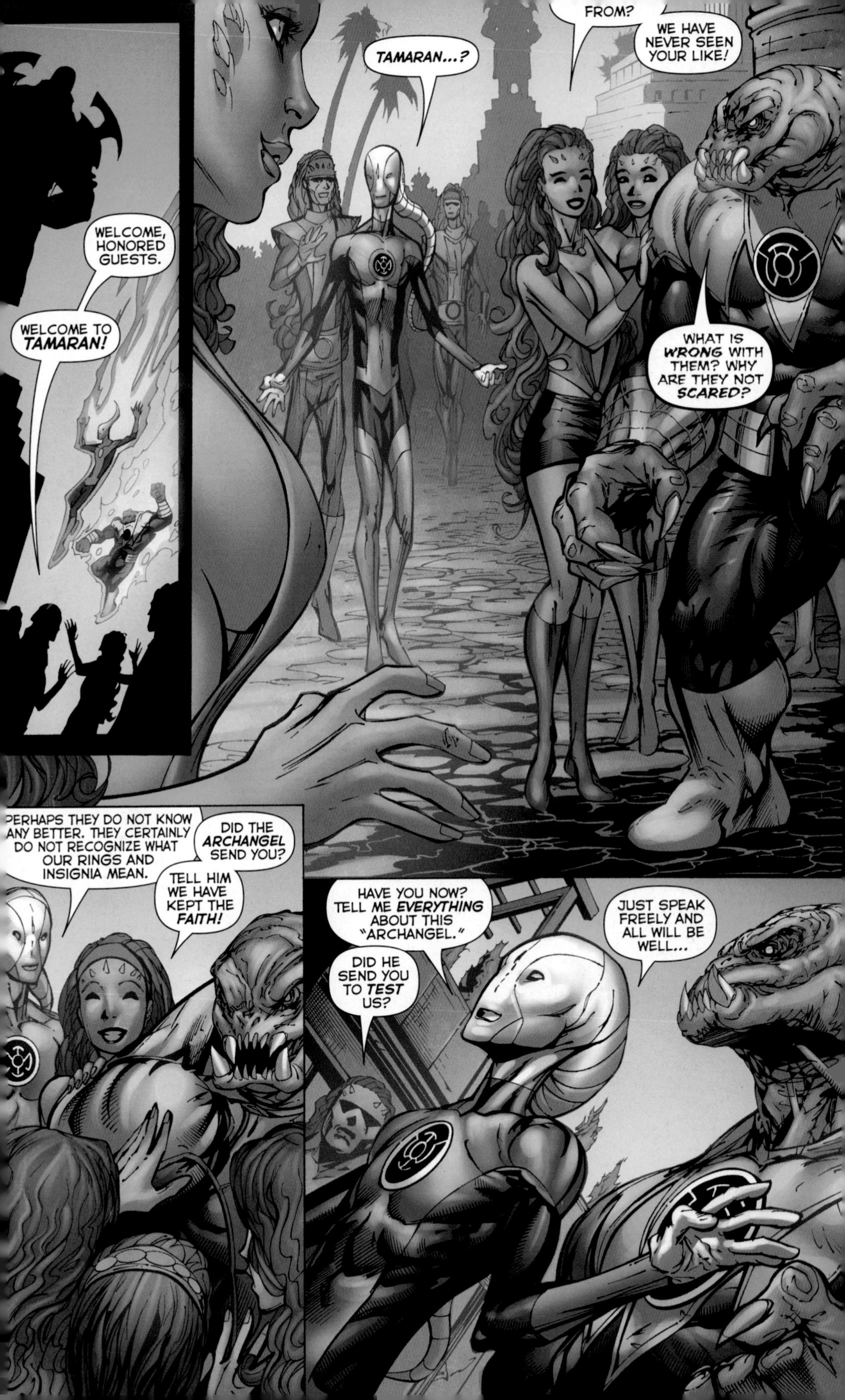

TAMARAN...?
FROM?
WE HAVE NEVER SEEN YOUR LIKE!
WELCOME, HONORED GUESTS.
WELCOME TO TAMARAN!
WHAT IS WRONG WITH THEM? WHY ARE THEY NOT SCARED?
PERHAPS THEY DO NOT KNOW ANY BETTER. THEY CERTAINLY DO NOT RECOGNIZE WHAT OUR RINGS AND INSIGNIA MEAN.
DID THE ARCHANGEL SEND YOU?
TELL HIM WE HAVE KEPT THE FAITH!
HAVE YOU NOW? TELL ME EVERYTHING ABOUT THIS "ARCHANGEL."
DID HE SEND YOU TO TEST US?
JUST SPEAK FREELY AND ALL WILL BE WELL...

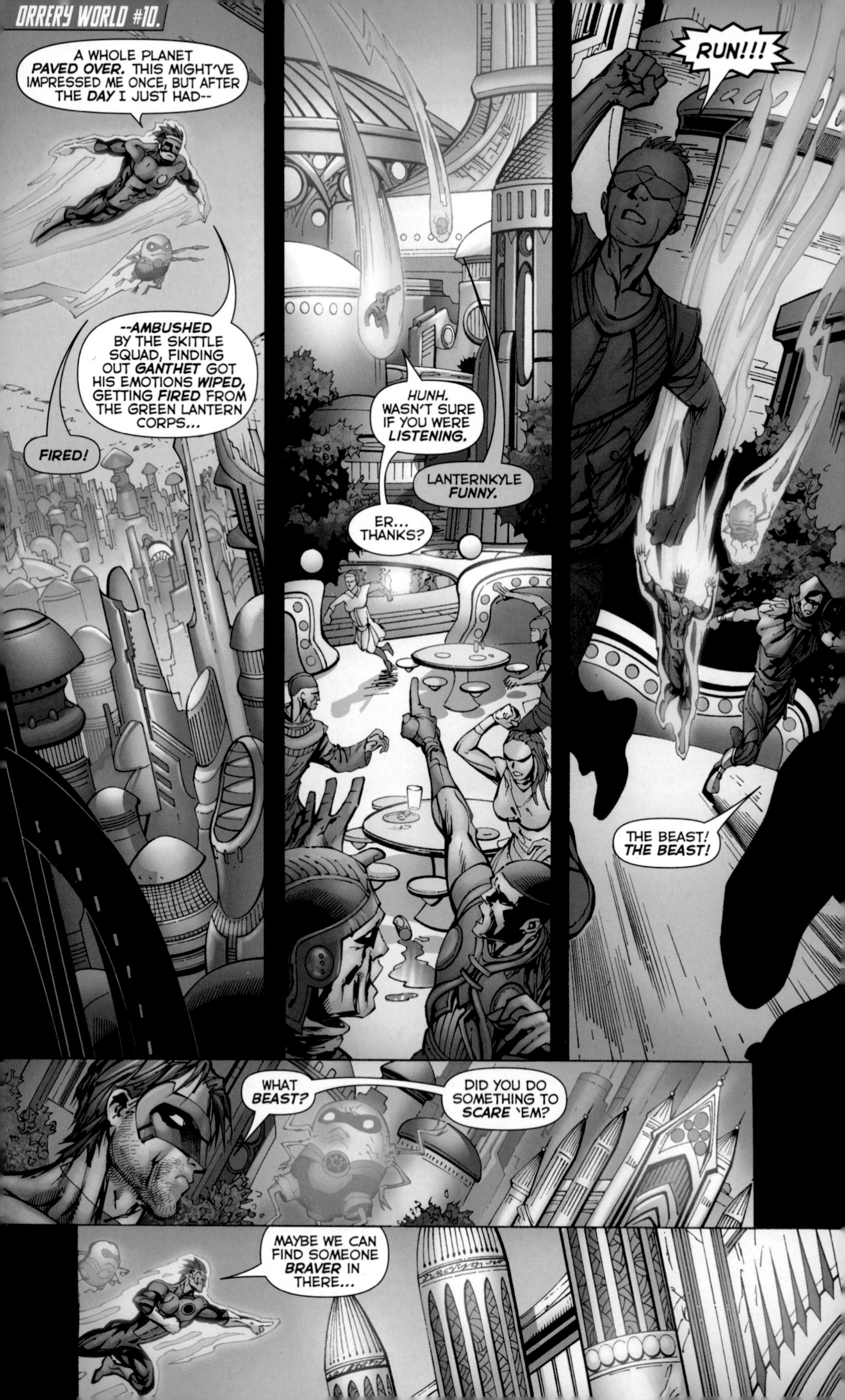
ORRERY WORLD #10.
A WHOLE PLANET PAVED OVER. THIS MIGHT'VE IMPRESSED ME ONCE, BUT AFTER THE DAY I JUST HAD--
--AMBUSHED BY THE SKITTLE SQUAD, FINDING OUT GANTHET GOT HIS EMOTIONS WIPED, GETTING FIRED FROM THE GREEN LANTERN CORPS...
FIRED!
HUNH. WASN'T SURE IF YOU WERE LISTENING.
LANTERNKYLE FUNNY.
ER... THANKS?
RUN!!!
THE BEAST! THE BEAST!
WHAT BEAST?
DID YOU DO SOMETHING TO SCARE 'EM?
MAYBE WE CAN FIND SOMEONE BRAVER IN THERE...

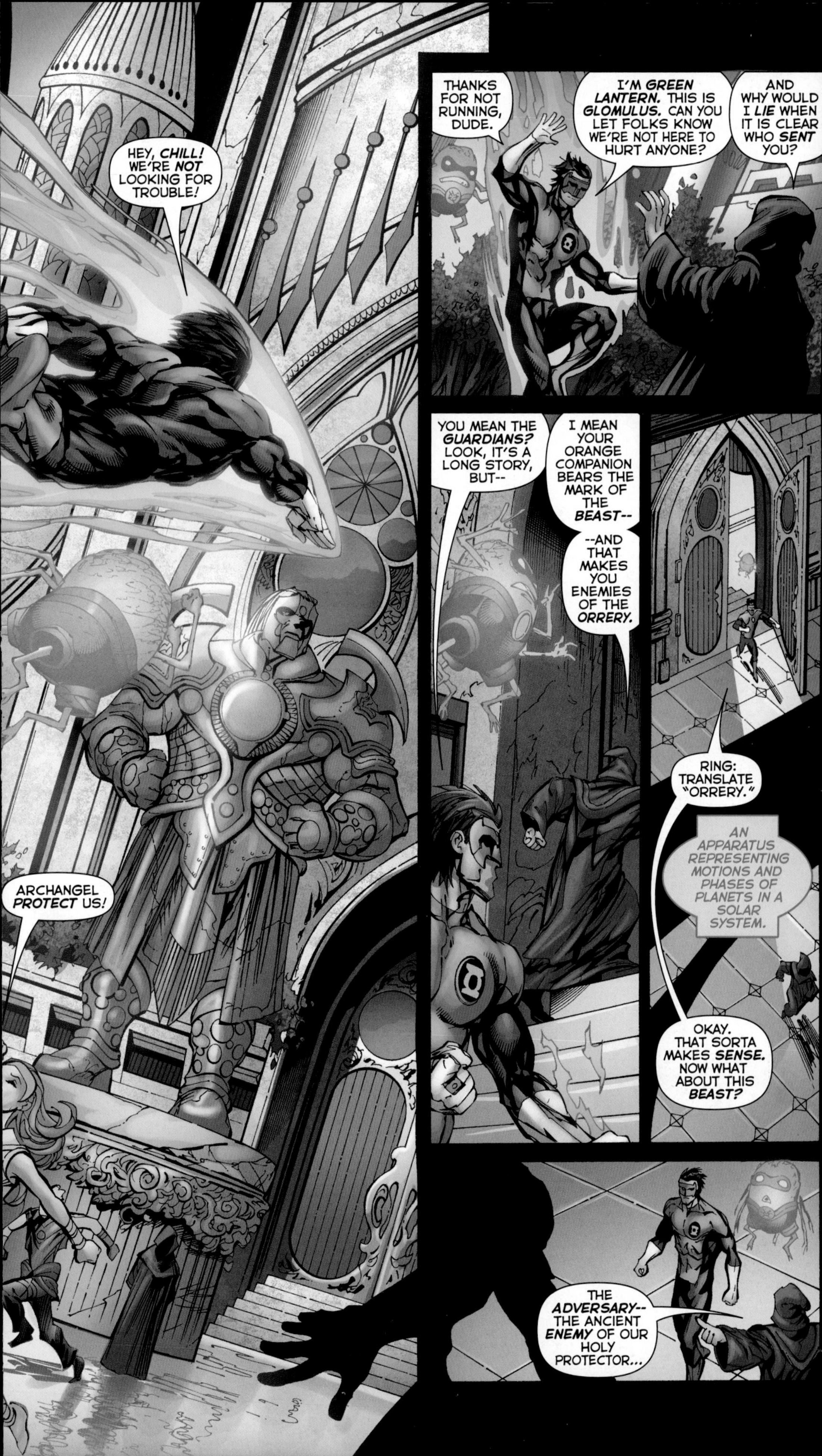

HEY, CHILL! WE'RE NOT LOOKING FOR TROUBLE!
ARCHANGEL PROTECT US!
THANKS FOR NOT RUNNING, DUDE.
I'M GREEN LANTERN. THIS IS GLOMULUS. CAN YOU LET FOLKS KNOW WE'RE NOT HERE TO HURT ANYONE?
AND WHY WOULD I LIE WHEN IT IS CLEAR WHO SENT YOU?
YOU MEAN THE GUARDIANS? LOOK, IT'S A LONG STORY, BUT--
I MEAN YOUR ORANGE COMPANION BEARS THE MARK OF THE BEAST--
--AND THAT MAKES YOU ENEMIES OF THE ORRERY.
RING: TRANSLATE "ORRERY."
AN APPARATUS REPRESENTING MOTIONS AND PHASES OF PLANETS IN A SOLAR SYSTEM.
OKAY. THAT SORTA MAKES SENSE. NOW WHAT ABOUT THIS BEAST?
THE ADVERSARY-- THE ANCIENT ENEMY OF OUR HOLY PROTECTOR...

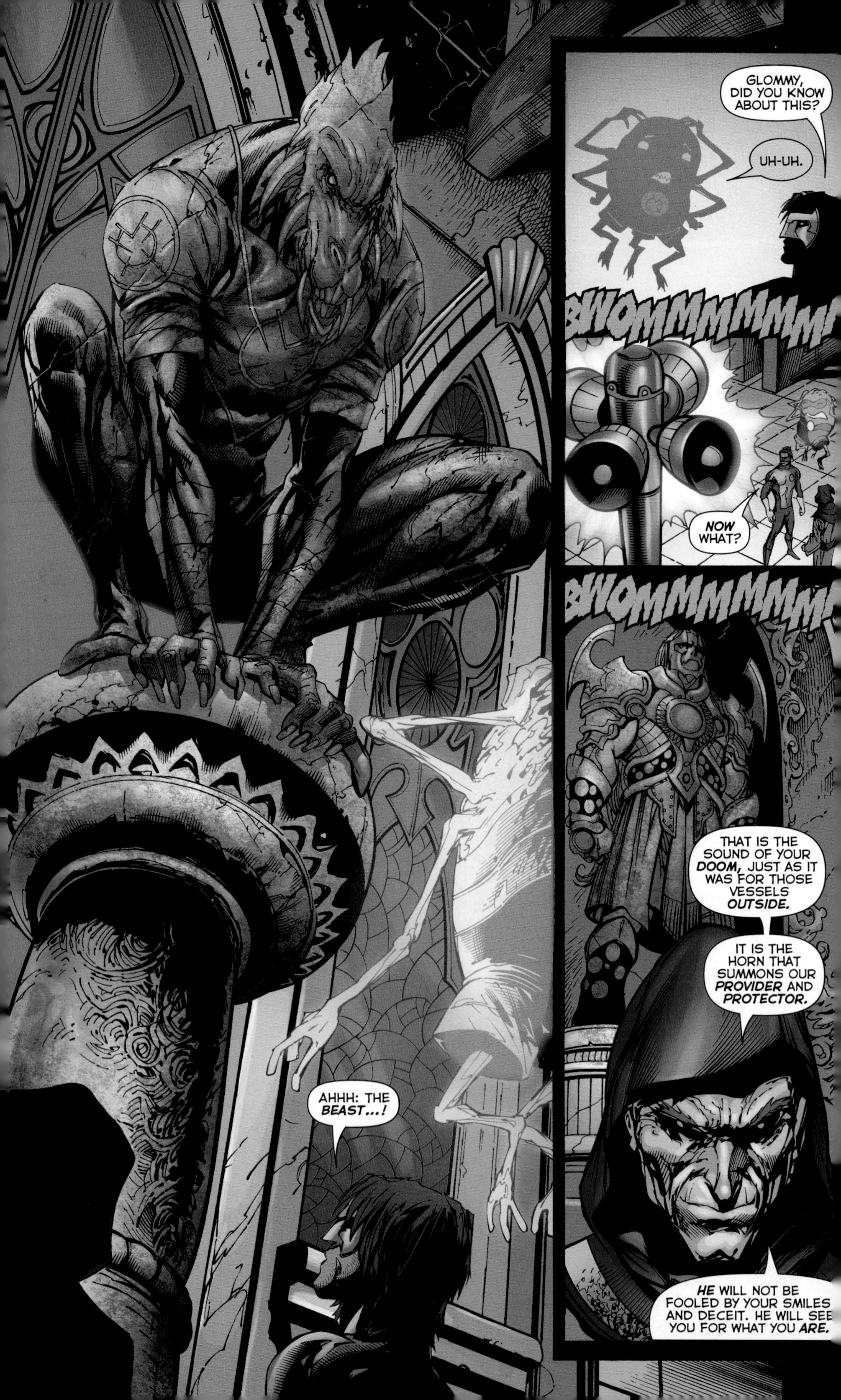
GLOMMY, DID YOU KNOW ABOUT THIS?
UH-UH.
BWOMMMMMMMM
NOW WHAT?
BWOMMMMMMMM
THAT IS THE SOUND OF YOUR DOOM, JUST AS IT WAS FOR THOSE VESSELS OUTSIDE.
IT IS THE HORN THAT SUMMONS OUR PROVIDER AND PROTECTOR.
HE WILL NOT BE FOOLED BY YOUR SMILES AND DECEIT. HE WILL SEE YOU FOR WHAT YOU ARE.
AHHH: THE BEAST...!

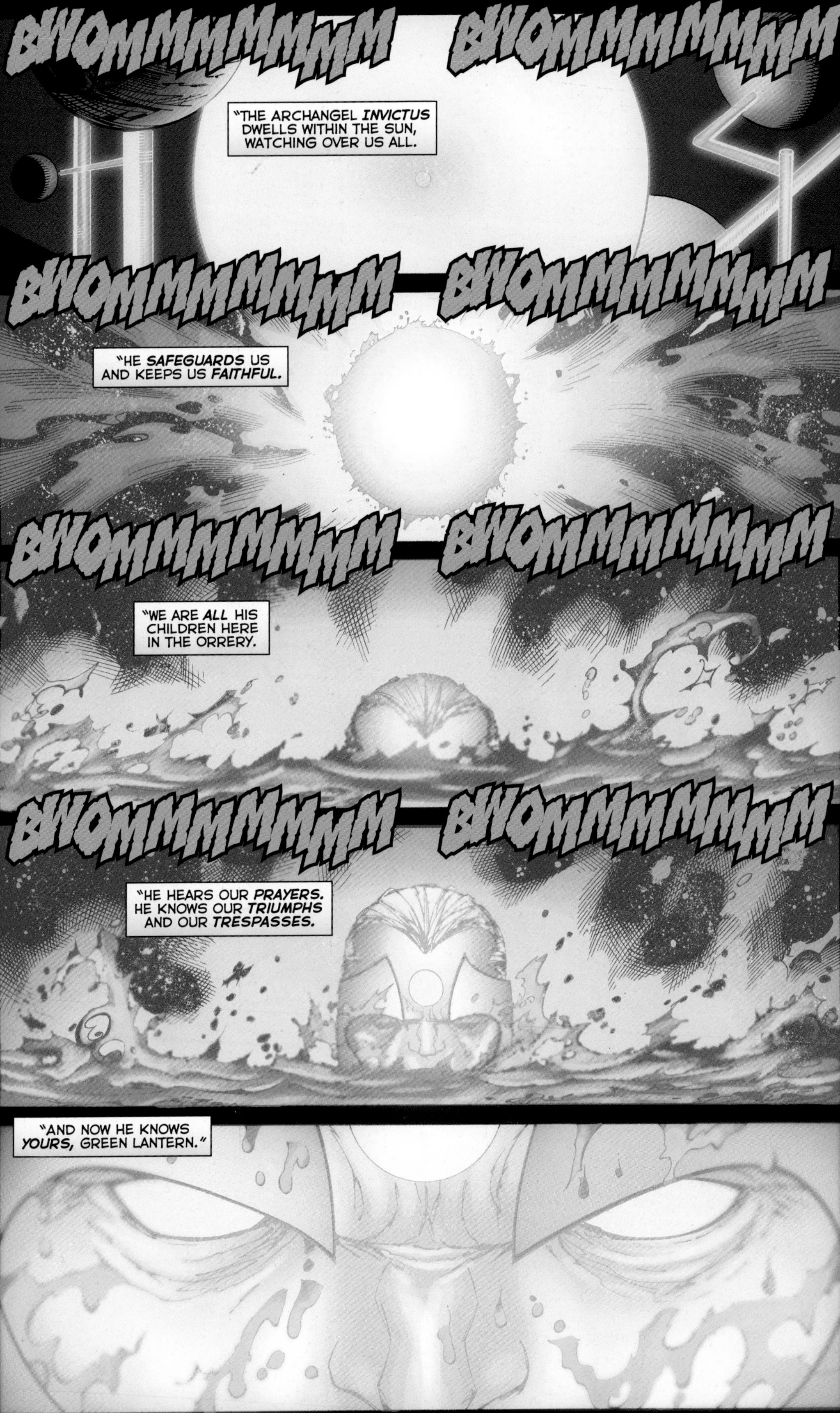
BWOMMMMMMMM BWOMMMMMMMMM
"THE ARCHANGEL *INVICTUS* DWELLS WITHIN THE SUN, WATCHING OVER US ALL.
BWOMMMMMMMM BWOMMMMMMMMM
"HE *SAFEGUARDS* US AND KEEPS US *FAITHFUL.*
BWOMMMMMMMM BWOMMMMMMMMM
"WE ARE *ALL* HIS CHILDREN HERE IN THE ORRERY.
BWOMMMMMMMM BWOMMMMMMMMM
"HE HEARS OUR *PRAYERS.* HE KNOWS OUR *TRIUMPHS* AND OUR *TRESPASSES.*
"AND NOW HE KNOWS *YOURS,* GREEN LANTERN."

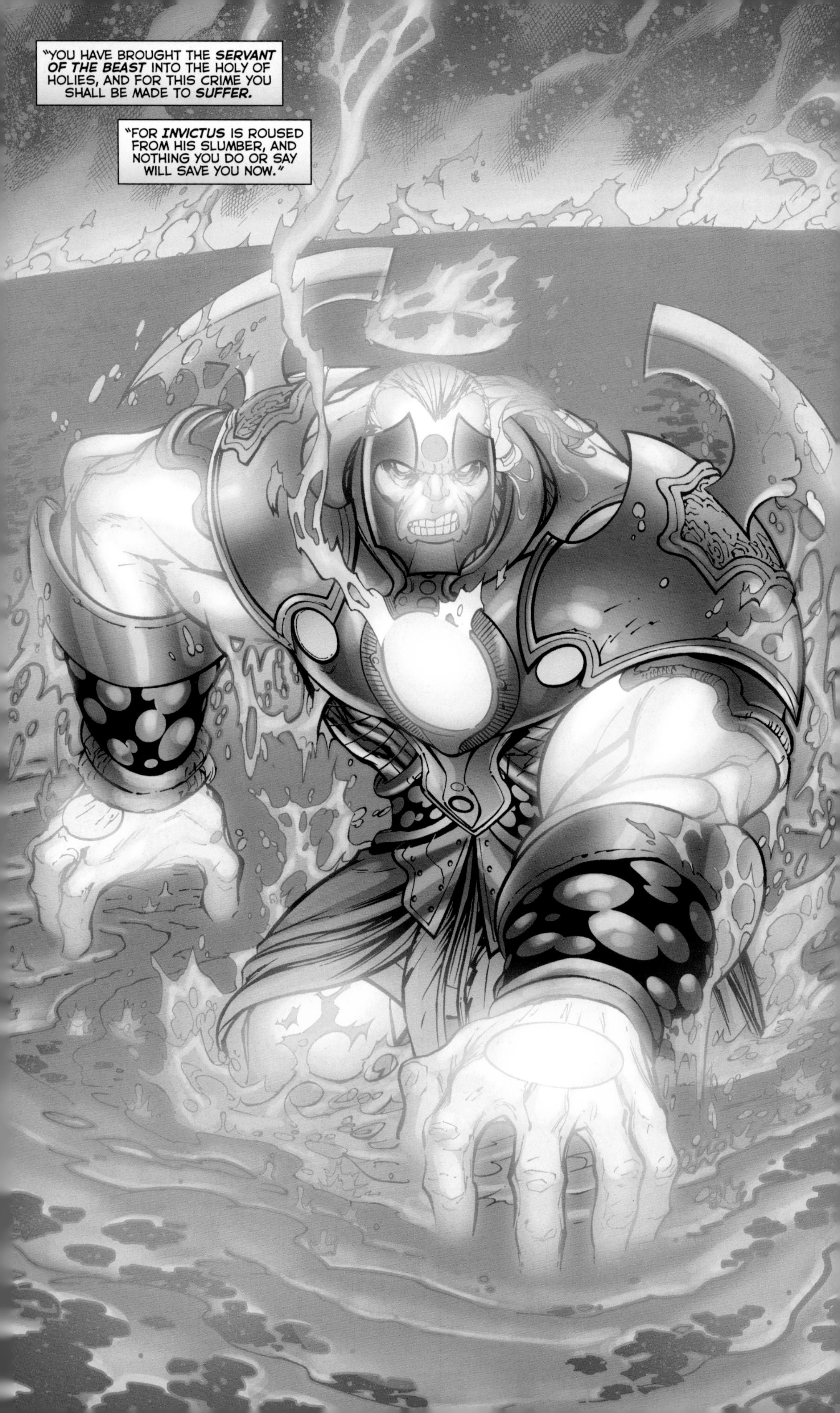
"YOU HAVE BROUGHT THE SERVANT OF THE BEAST INTO THE HOLY OF HOLIES, AND FOR THIS CRIME YOU SHALL BE MADE TO SUFFER.
"FOR INVICTUS IS ROUSED FROM HIS SLUMBER, AND NOTHING YOU DO OR SAY WILL SAVE YOU NOW."

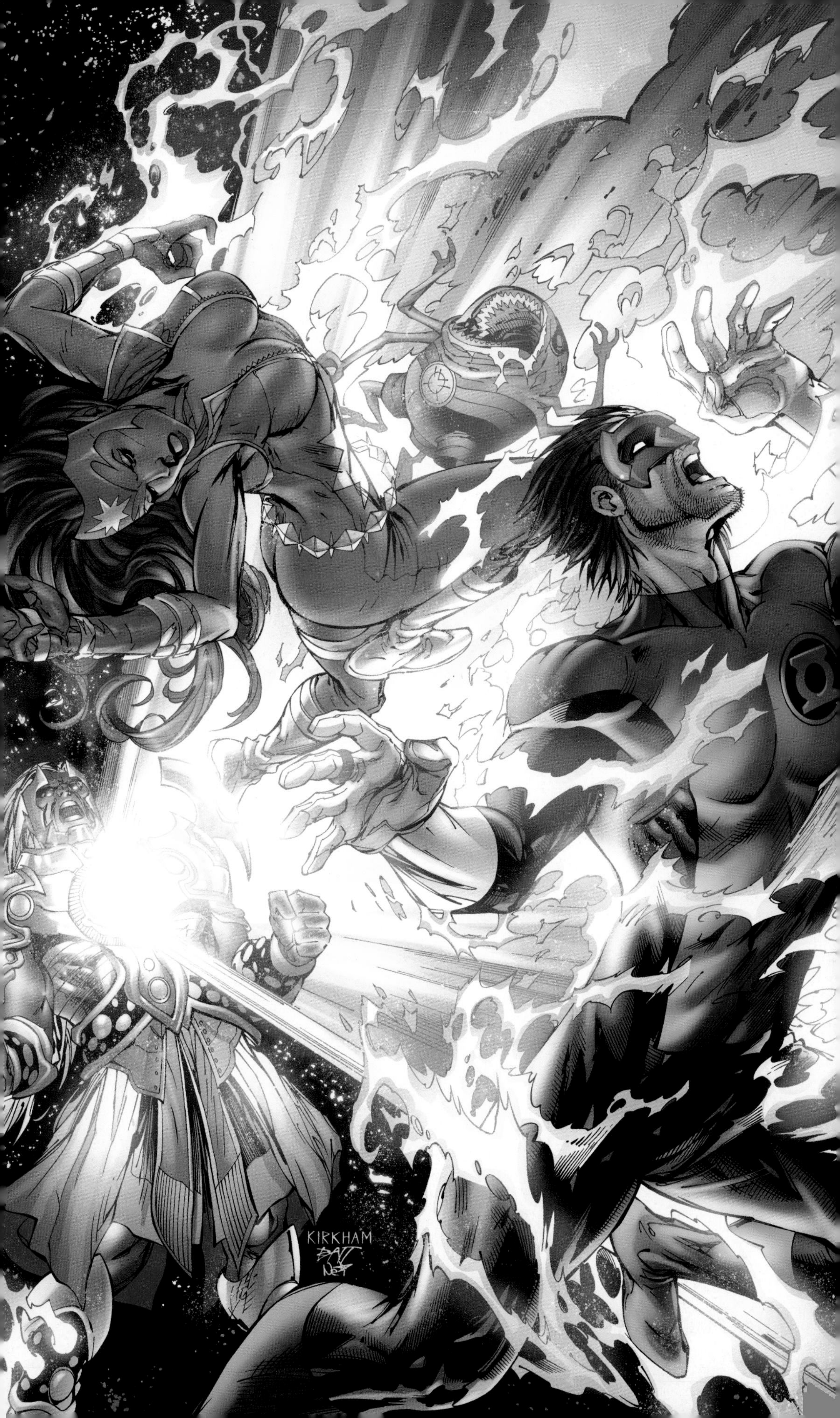
KIRKHAM

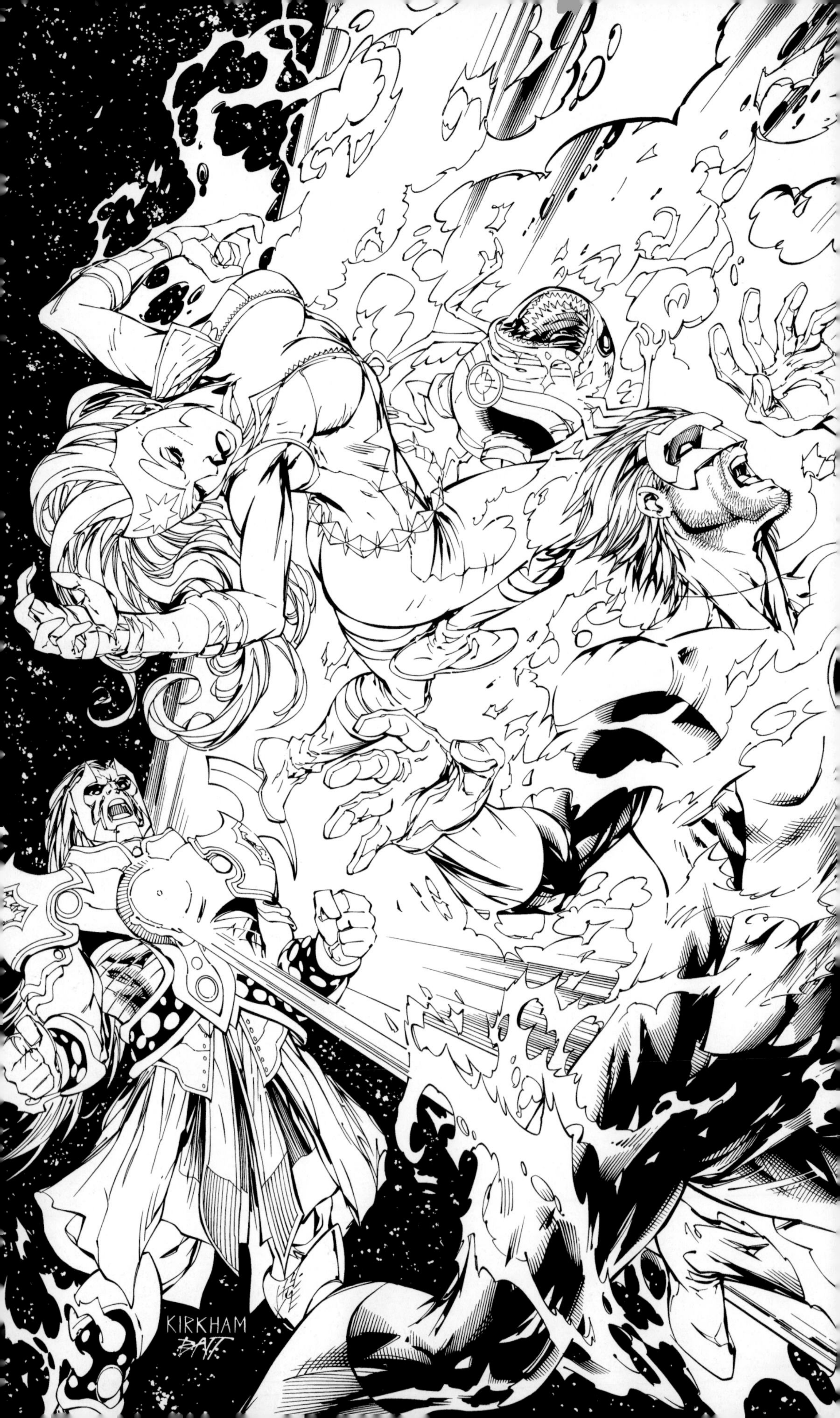

KIRKHAM
BATT

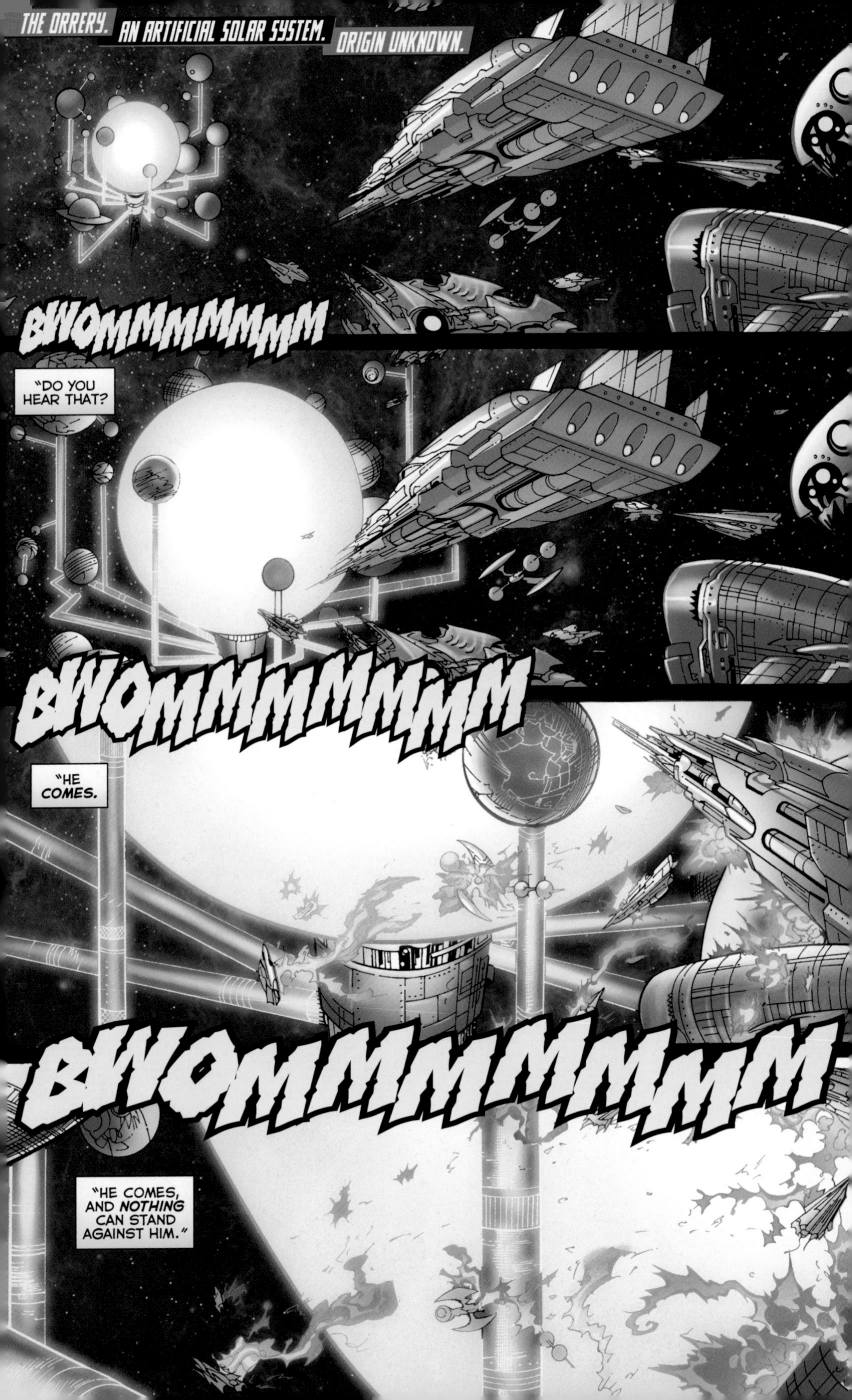
THE ORRERY.
AN ARTIFICIAL SOLAR SYSTEM.
ORIGIN UNKNOWN.
BWOMMMMMMM
"DO YOU HEAR THAT?
BWOMMMMMMMM
"HE COMES.
BWOMMMMMMMM
"HE COMES, AND NOTHING CAN STAND AGAINST HIM."

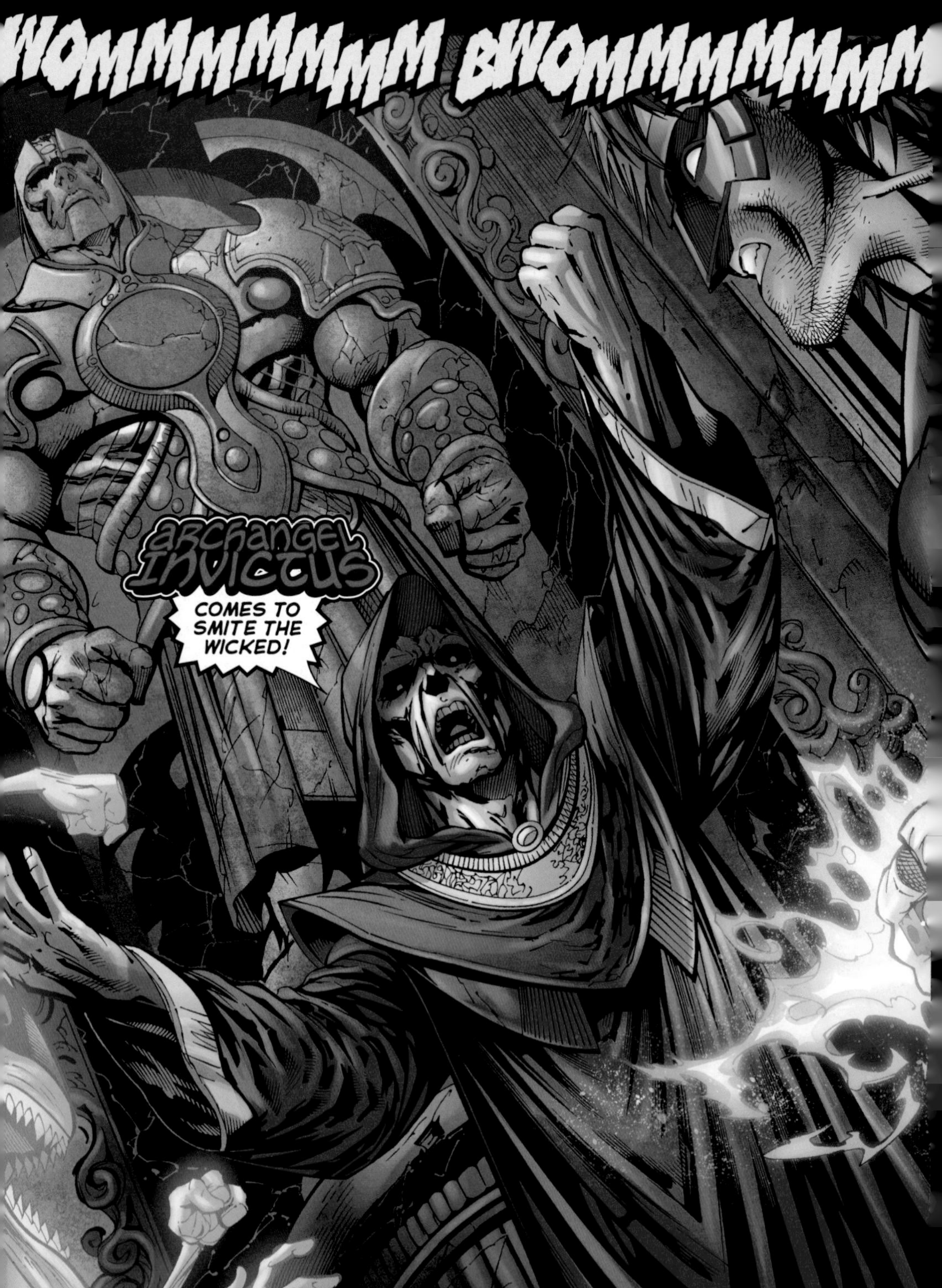

WOMMMMMMM BWOMMMMMMMM
ARCHANGEL INVICTUS
COMES TO SMITE THE WICKED!

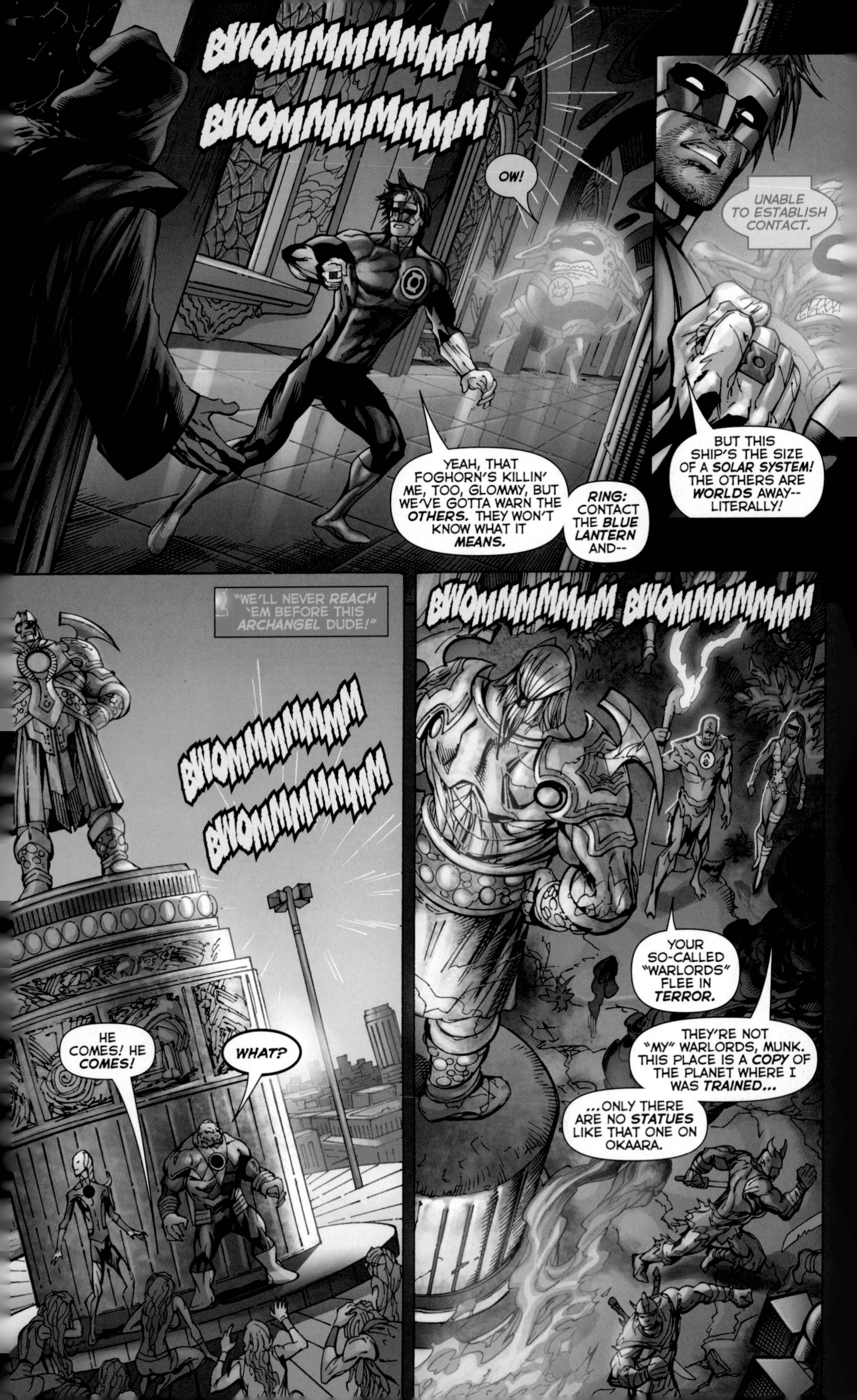
BWOMMMMMMM
BWOMMMMMMM
OW!
YEAH, THAT FOGHORN'S KILLIN' ME, TOO, GLOMMY, BUT WE'VE GOTTA WARN THE OTHERS. THEY WON'T KNOW WHAT IT MEANS.
RING: CONTACT THE BLUE LANTERN AND--
UNABLE TO ESTABLISH CONTACT.
BUT THIS SHIP'S THE SIZE OF A SOLAR SYSTEM! THE OTHERS ARE WORLDS AWAY--LITERALLY!
"WE'LL NEVER REACH 'EM BEFORE THIS ARCHANGEL DUDE!"
BWOMMMMMMM
BWOMMMMMMM
HE COMES! HE COMES!
WHAT?
BWOMMMMMMM BWOMMMMMMM
YOUR SO-CALLED "WARLORDS" FLEE IN TERROR.
THEY'RE NOT "MY" WARLORDS, MUNK. THIS PLACE IS A COPY OF THE PLANET WHERE I WAS TRAINED...
...ONLY THERE ARE NO STATUES LIKE THAT ONE ON OKAARA.

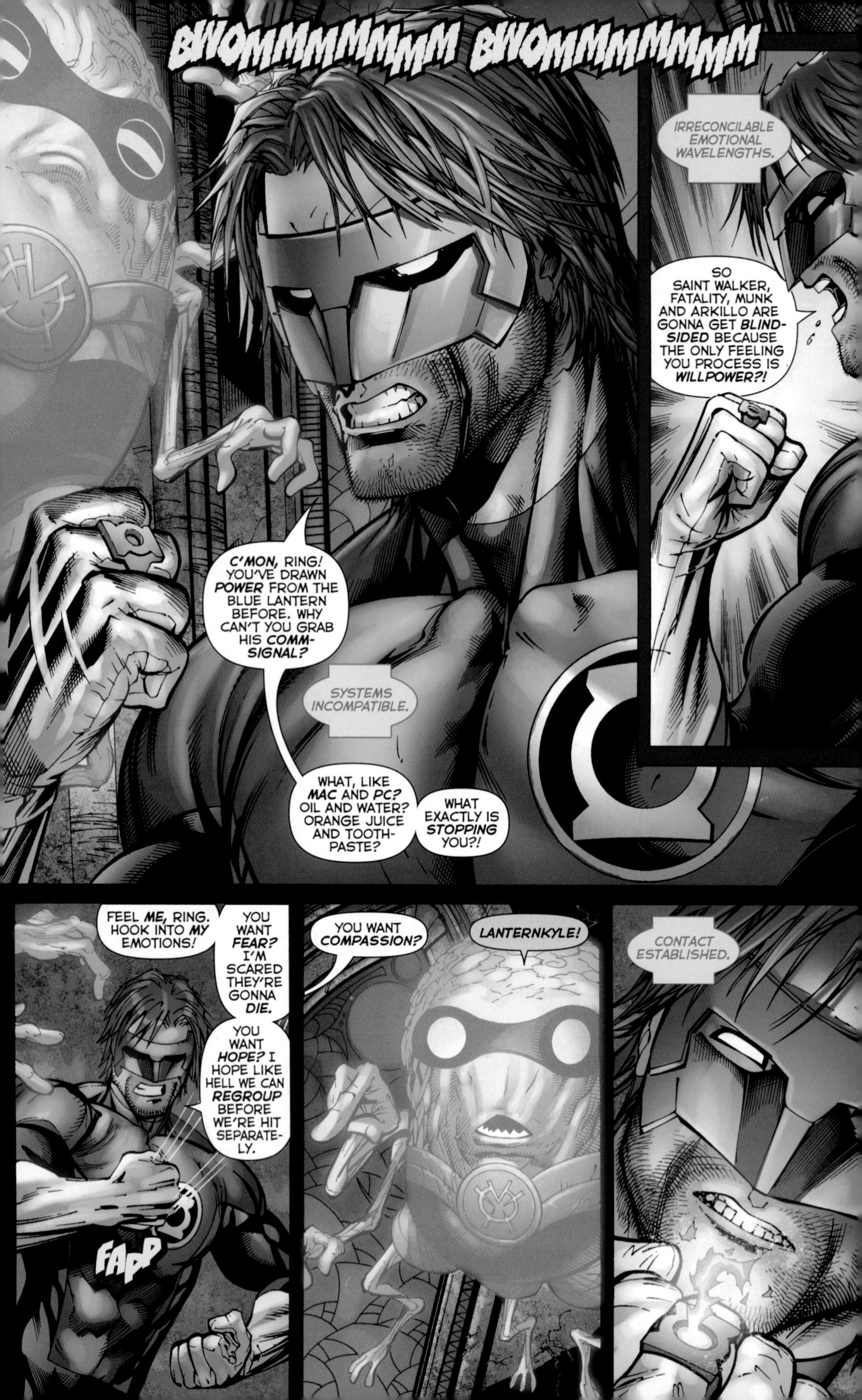
BWOMMMMMMM BWOMMMMMMM
IRRECONCILABLE EMOTIONAL WAVELENGTHS.
SO SAINT WALKER, FATALITY, MUNK AND ARKILLO ARE GONNA GET BLIND-SIDED BECAUSE THE ONLY FEELING YOU PROCESS IS WILLPOWER?!
C'MON, RING! YOU'VE DRAWN POWER FROM THE BLUE LANTERN BEFORE. WHY CAN'T YOU GRAB HIS COMM-SIGNAL?
SYSTEMS INCOMPATIBLE.
WHAT, LIKE MAC AND PC? OIL AND WATER? ORANGE JUICE AND TOOTH-PASTE?
WHAT EXACTLY IS STOPPING YOU?!
FEEL ME, RING. HOOK INTO MY EMOTIONS!
YOU WANT FEAR? I'M SCARED THEY'RE GONNA DIE.
YOU WANT HOPE? I HOPE LIKE HELL WE CAN REGROUP BEFORE WE'RE HIT SEPARATE-LY.
FAPP
YOU WANT COMPASSION?
LANTERNKYLE!
CONTACT ESTABLISHED.

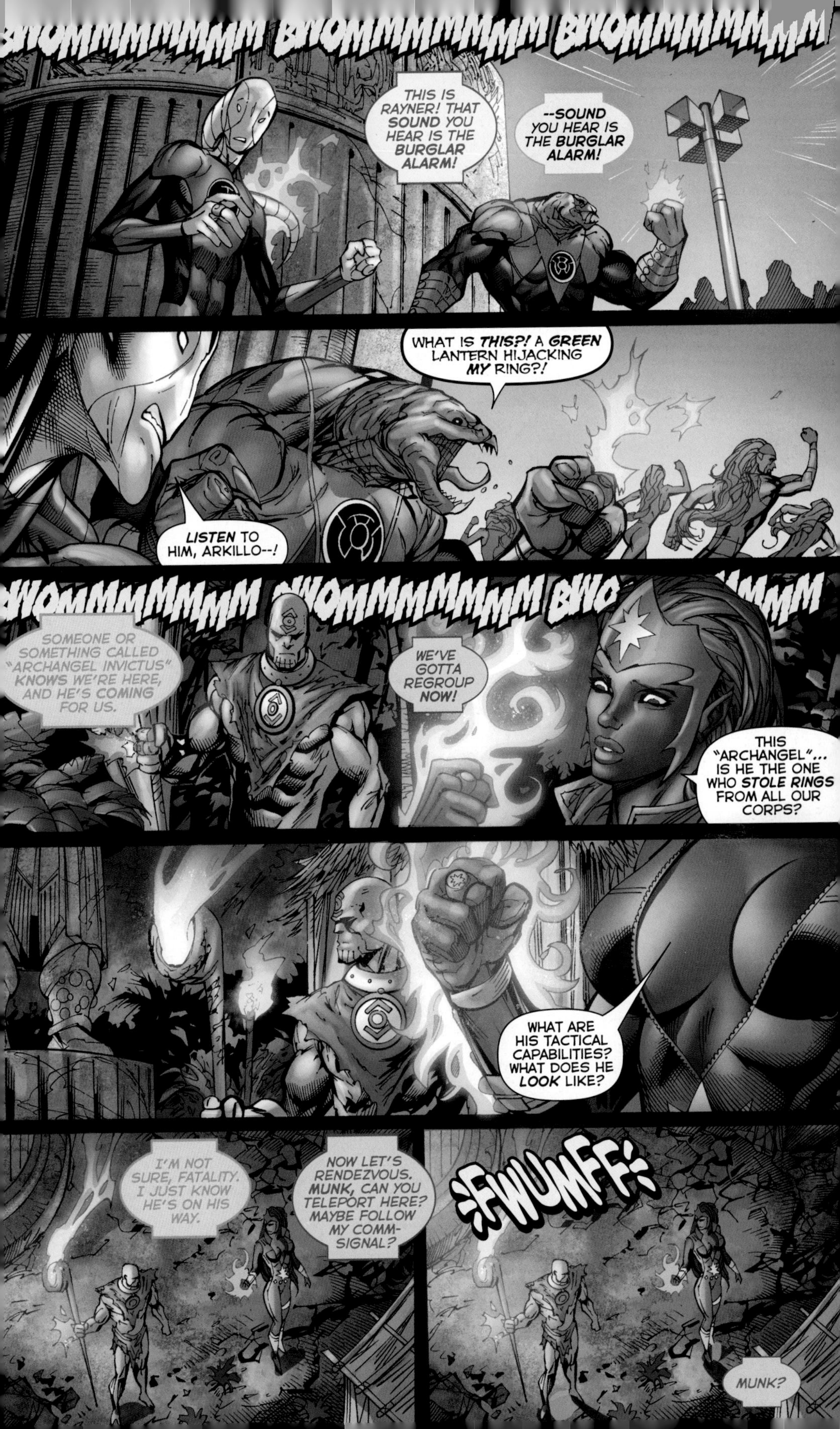

BWOMMMMMMMM BWOMMMMMMMM BWOMMMMMMMM
THIS IS RAYNER! THAT SOUND YOU HEAR IS THE BURGLAR ALARM!
--SOUND YOU HEAR IS THE BURGLAR ALARM!
WHAT IS THIS?! A GREEN LANTERN HIJACKING MY RING?!
LISTEN TO HIM, ARKILLO--!
BWOMMMMMMMM BWOMMMMMMMM
SOMEONE OR SOMETHING CALLED "ARCHANGEL INVICTUS" KNOWS WE'RE HERE, AND HE'S COMING FOR US.
WE'VE GOTTA REGROUP NOW!
THIS "ARCHANGEL"... IS HE THE ONE WHO STOLE RINGS FROM ALL OUR CORPS?
WHAT ARE HIS TACTICAL CAPABILITIES? WHAT DOES HE LOOK LIKE?
I'M NOT SURE, FATALITY. I JUST KNOW HE'S ON HIS WAY.
NOW LET'S RENDEZVOUS. MUNK, CAN YOU TELEPORT HERE? MAYBE FOLLOW MY COMM-SIGNAL?
FWUMFF
MUNK?

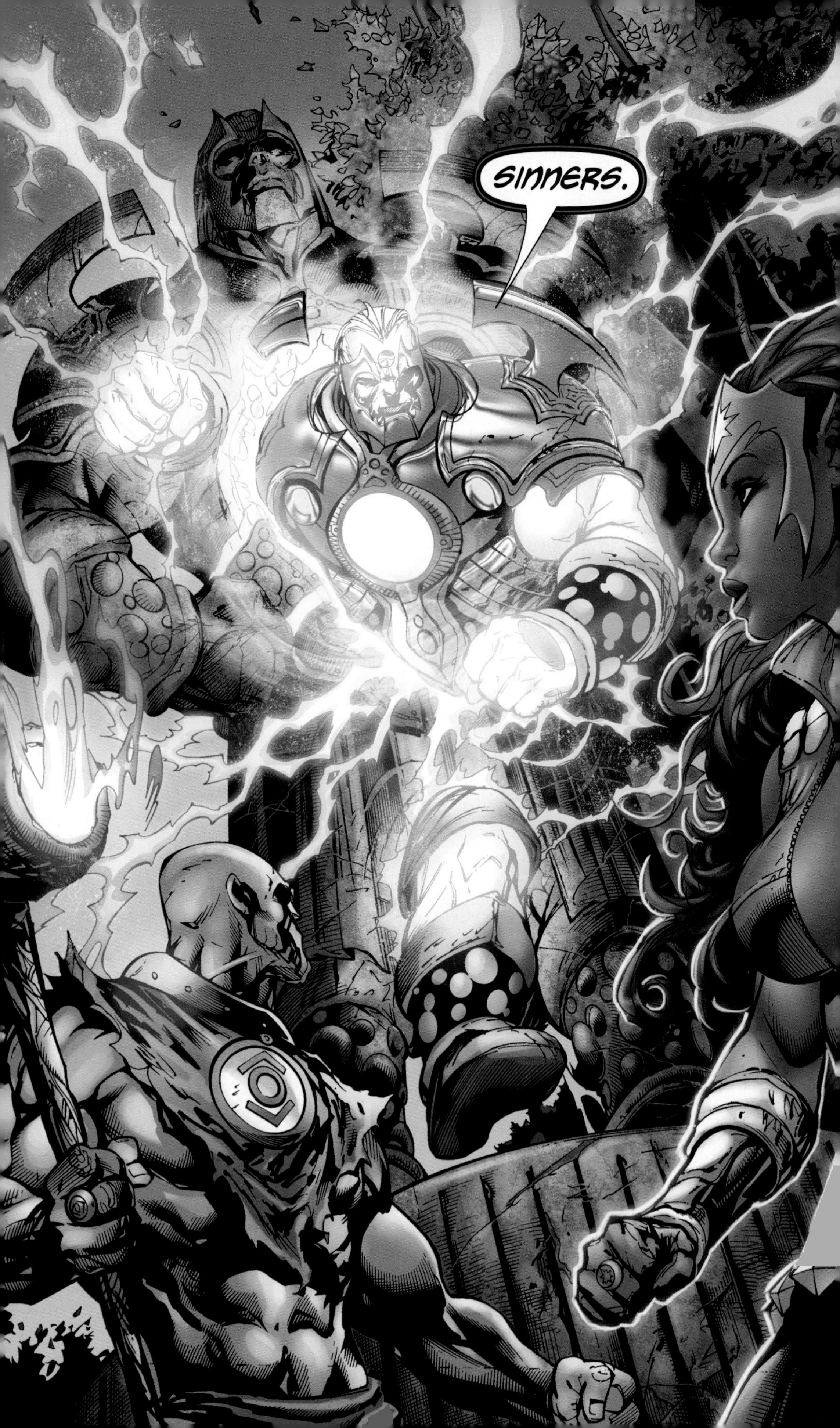
SINNERS.

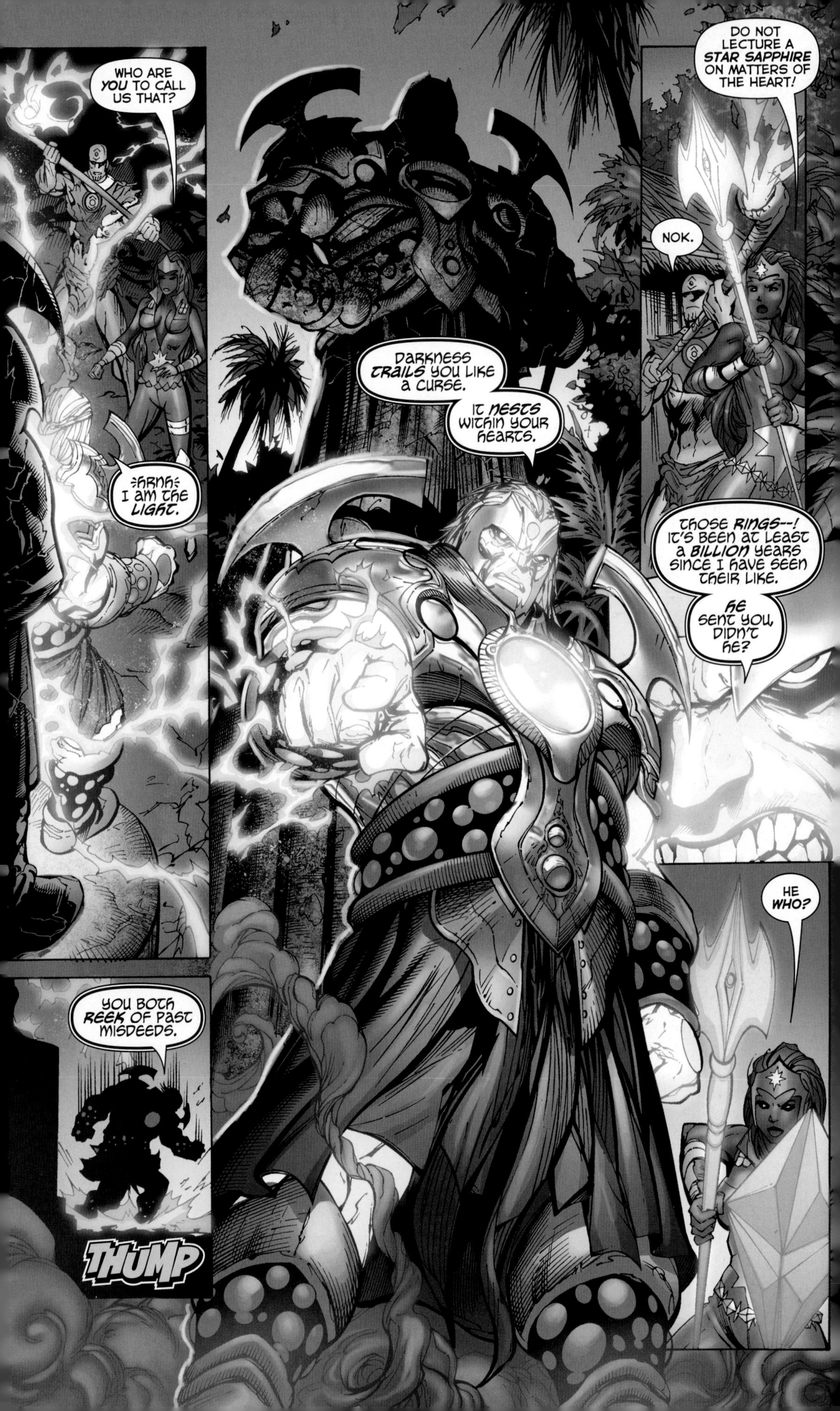
WHO ARE YOU TO CALL US THAT?
DO NOT LECTURE A STAR SAPPHIRE ON MATTERS OF THE HEART!
NOK.
DARKNESS TRAILS YOU LIKE A CURSE.
IT NESTS WITHIN YOUR HEARTS.
HRNH I AM THE LIGHT.
THOSE RINGS--! IT'S BEEN AT LEAST A BILLION YEARS SINCE I HAVE SEEN THEIR LIKE.
HE SENT YOU, DIDN'T HE?
HE WHO?
YOU BOTH REEK OF PAST MISDEEDS.
THUMP

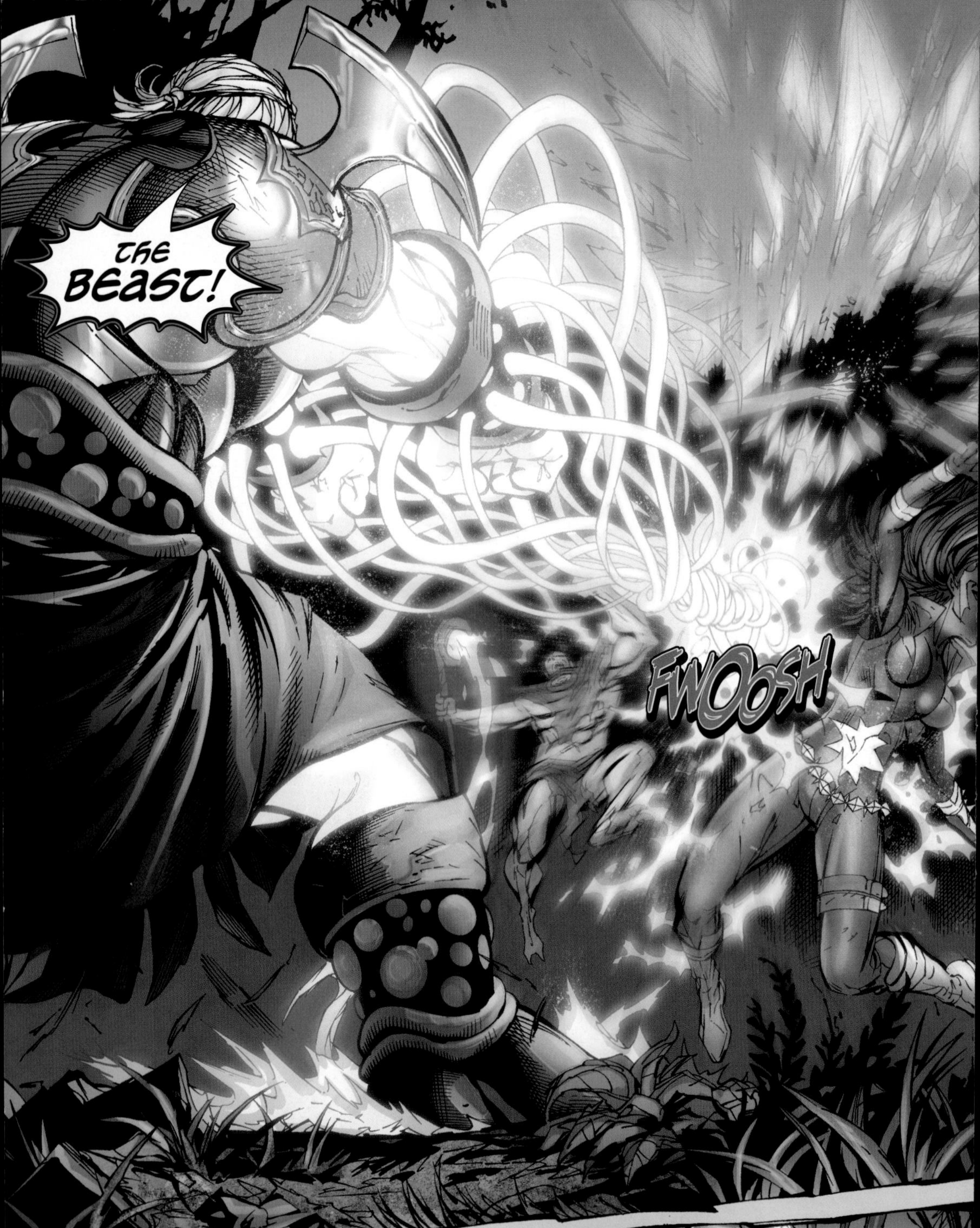
THE BEAST!
FWOOSH

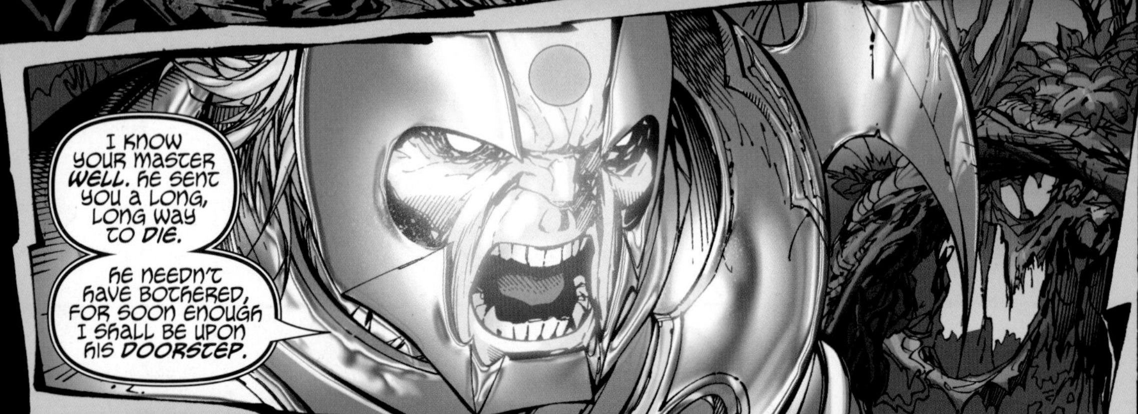
I KNOW YOUR MASTER WELL. HE SENT YOU A LONG, LONG WAY TO DIE.
HE NEEDN'T HAVE BOTHERED, FOR SOON ENOUGH I SHALL BE UPON HIS DOORSTEP.

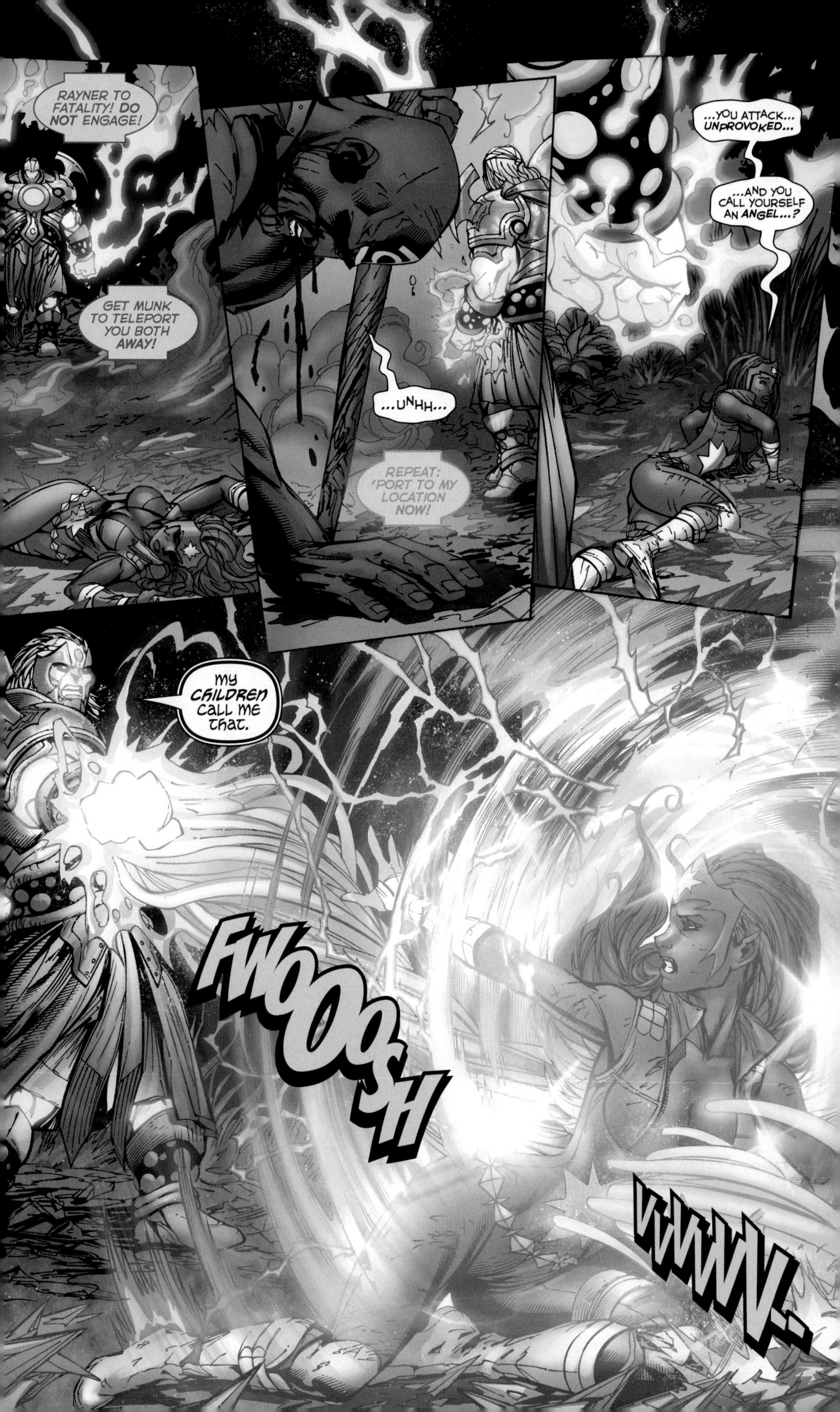
RAYNER TO FATALITY! DO NOT ENGAGE!
GET MUNK TO TELEPORT YOU BOTH AWAY!
...UNHH...
REPEAT: 'PORT TO MY LOCATION NOW!
...YOU ATTACK... UNPROVOKED...
...AND YOU CALL YOURSELF AN ANGEL...?
MY CHILDREN CALL ME THAT.
FWOOOSH
VVVVVV..

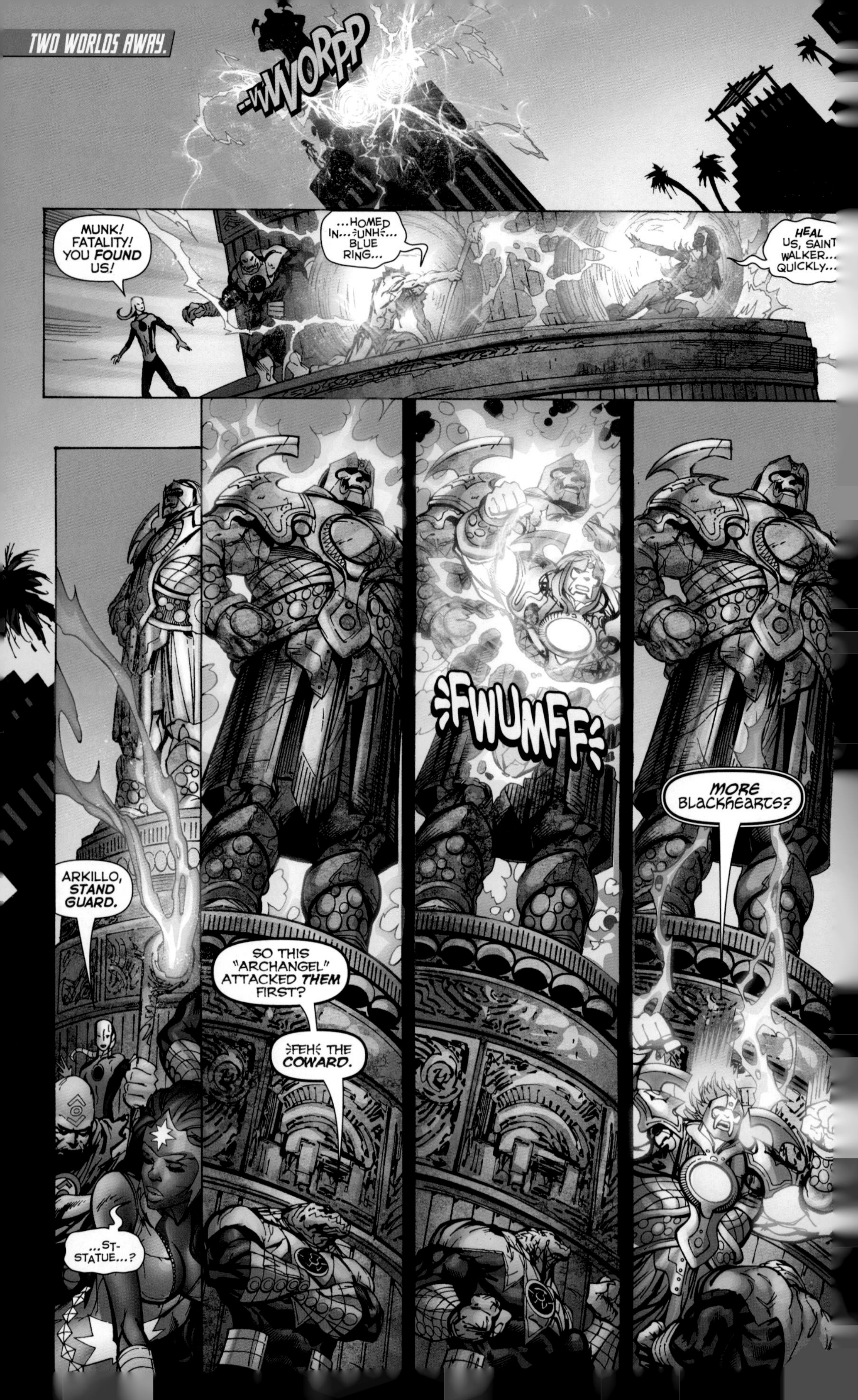
TWO WORLDS AWAY.
VVWORPP
MUNK! FATALITY! YOU FOUND US!
...HOMED IN... UNH... BLUE RING...
HEAL US, SAINT WALKER... QUICKLY...
ARKILLO, STAND GUARD.
...ST- STATUE...?
SO THIS "ARCHANGEL" ATTACKED THEM FIRST?
FEH THE COWARD.
FWUMFF
MORE BLACKHEARTS?

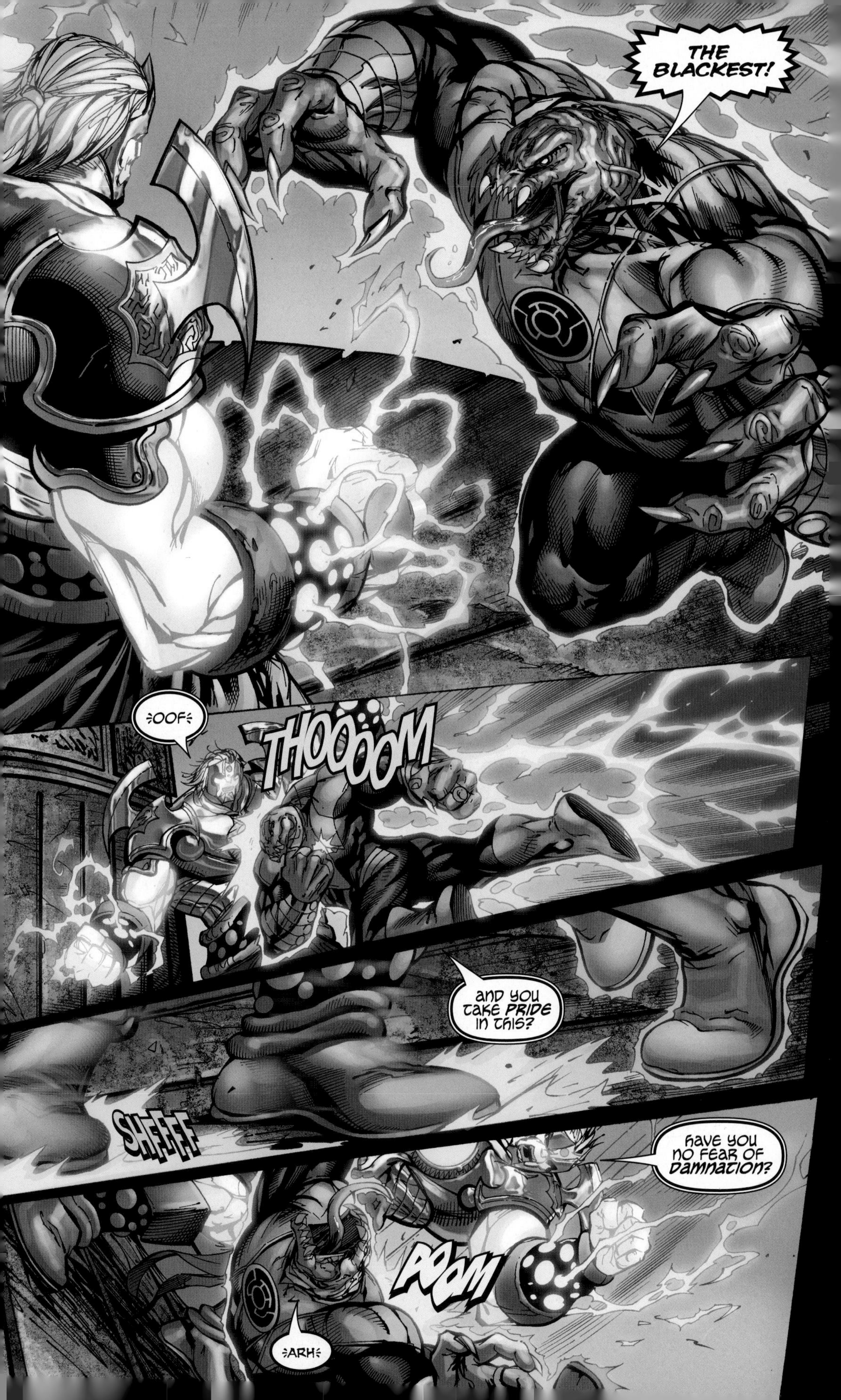
THE BLACKEST!
OOF
THOOOOM
and you take PRIDE in this?
SHFFFF
have you no fear of Damnation?
POOM
ARH

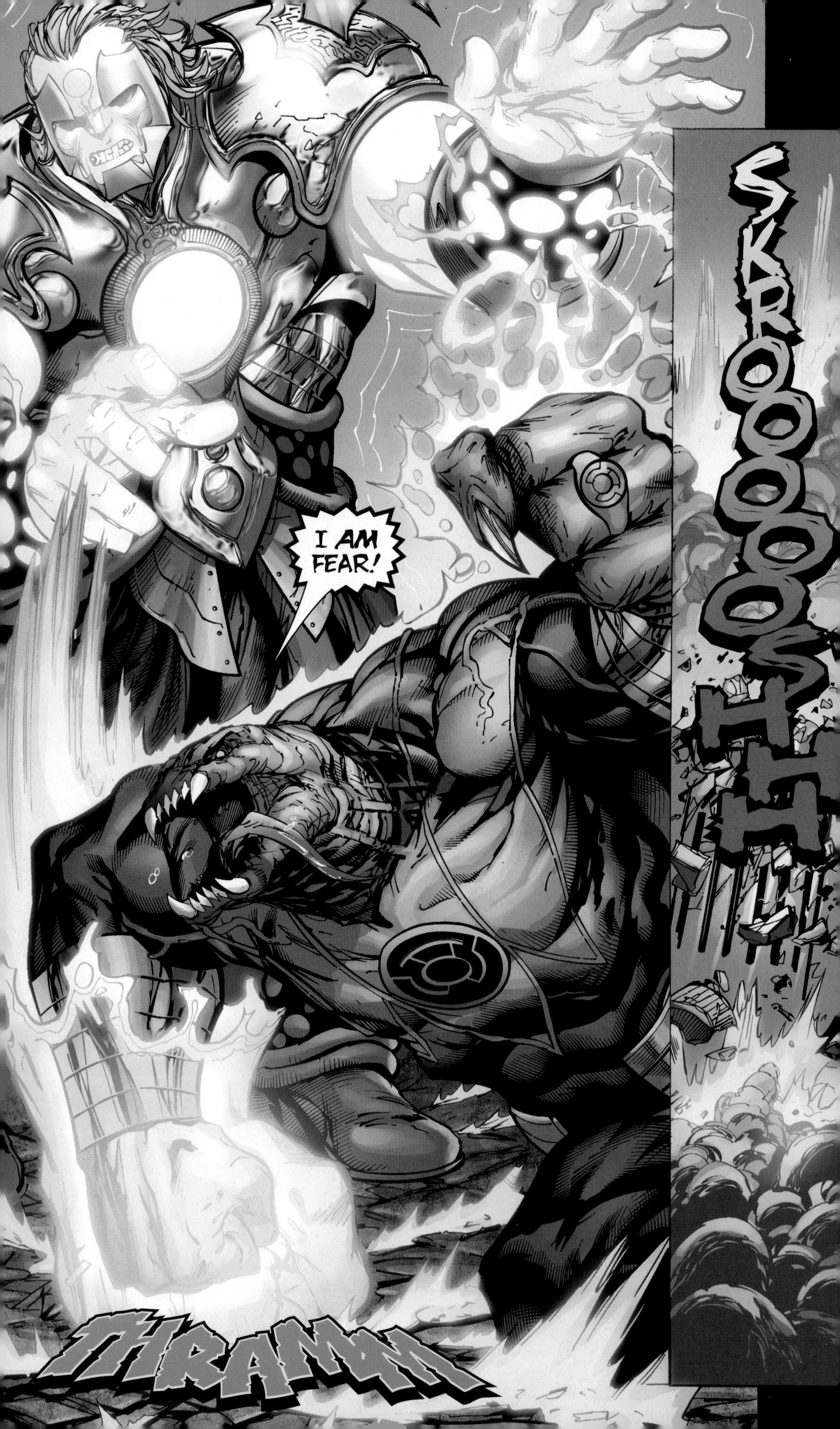
I AM FEAR!
SKROOOOOOSHHH
THRAMM

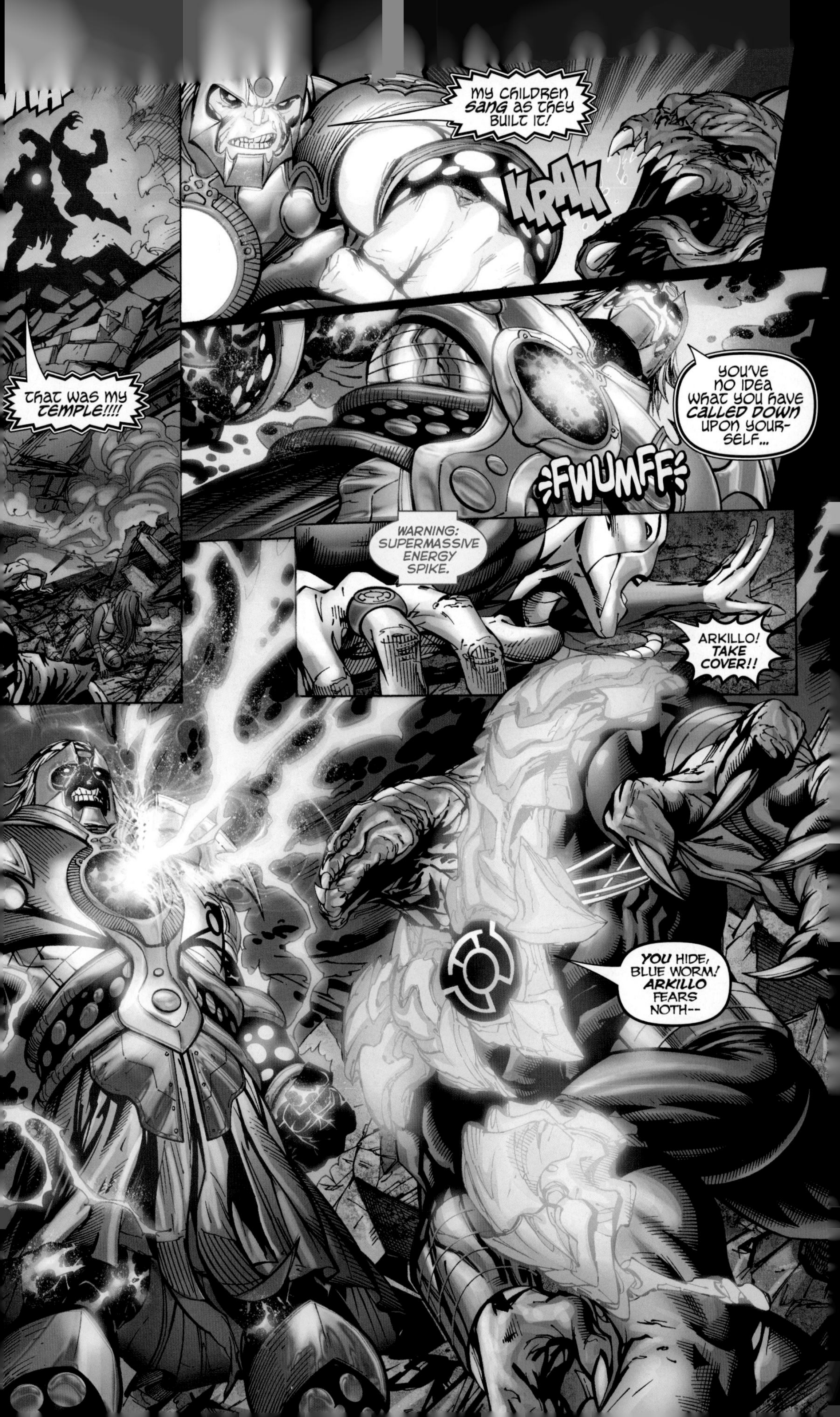

MY CHILDREN SANG AS THEY BUILT IT!
KRAK
THAT WAS MY TEMPLE!!!!
YOU'VE NO IDEA WHAT YOU HAVE CALLED DOWN UPON YOURSELF...
FWUMFF
WARNING: SUPERMASSIVE ENERGY SPIKE.
ARKILLO! TAKE COVER!!
YOU HIDE, BLUE WORM! ARKILLO FEARS NOTH--

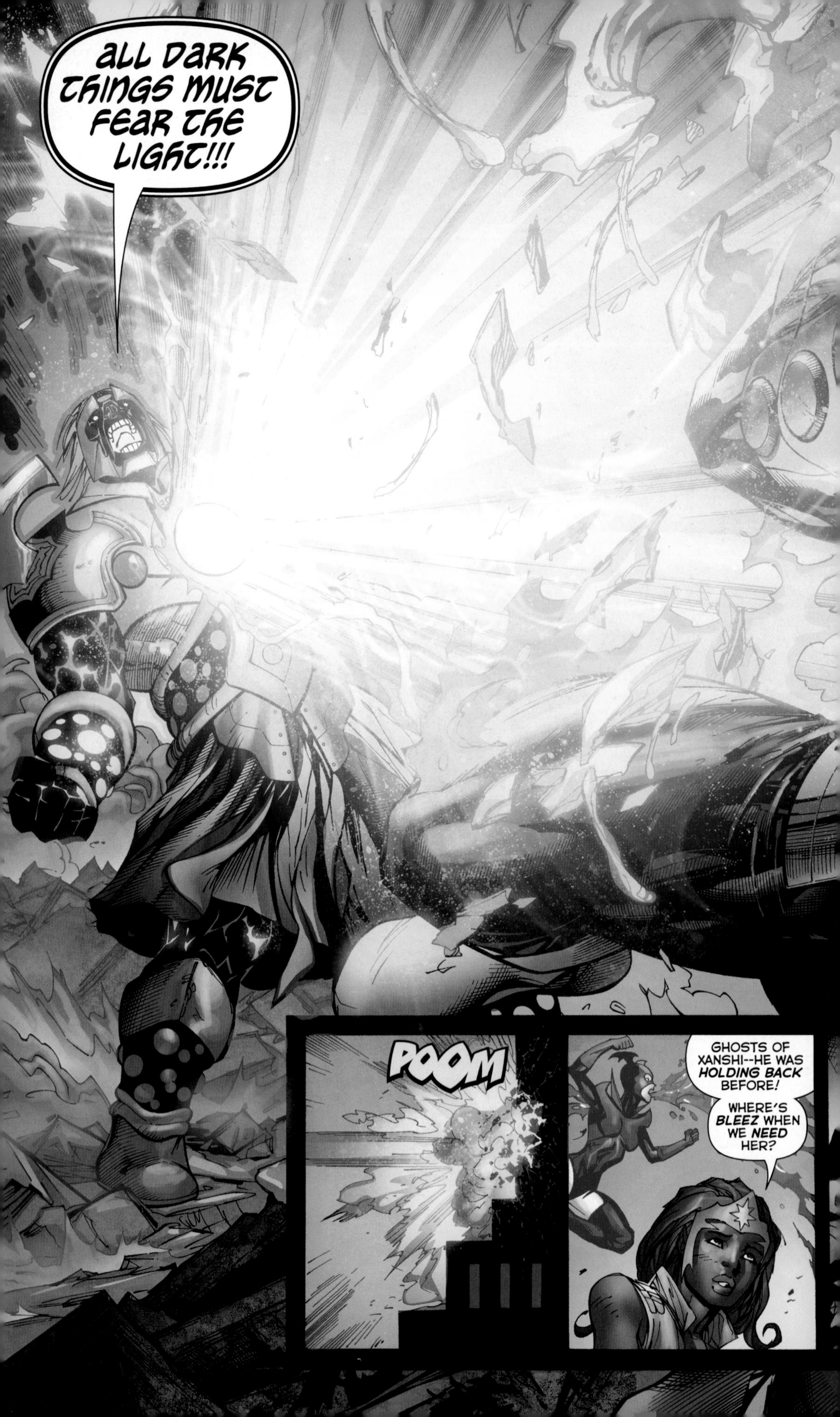
ALL DARK THINGS MUST FEAR THE LIGHT!!!
POOM
GHOSTS OF XANSHI--HE WAS HOLDING BACK BEFORE!
WHERE'S BLEEZ WHEN WE NEED HER?

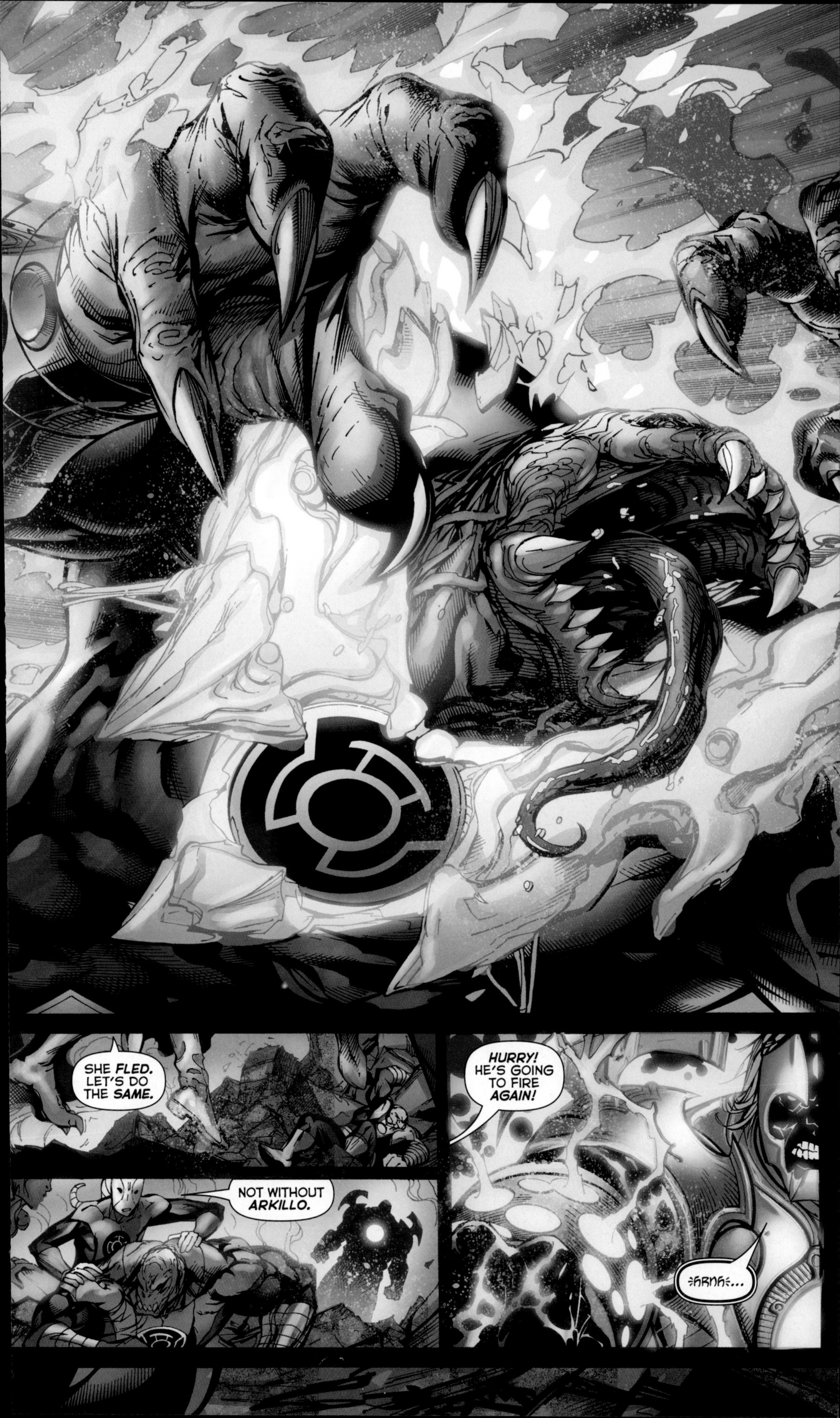
SHE FLED. LET'S DO THE SAME.
HURRY! HE'S GOING TO FIRE AGAIN!
NOT WITHOUT ARKILLO.
<HRNH>...

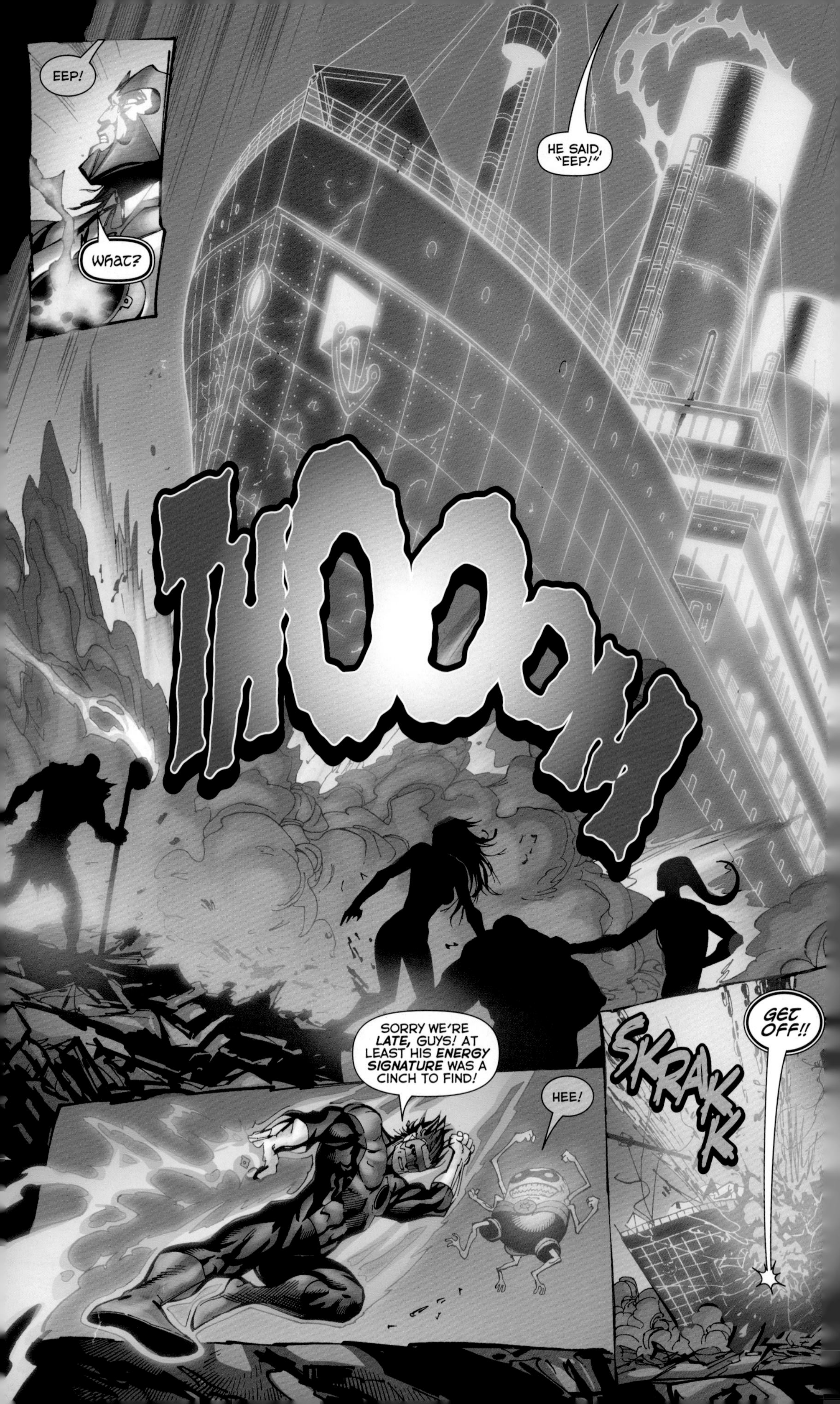

EEP!
WHAT?
HE SAID, "EEP!"
THOOOM
SORRY WE'RE LATE, GUYS! AT LEAST HIS ENERGY SIGNATURE WAS A CINCH TO FIND!
HEE!
SKRAKK
GET OFF!!

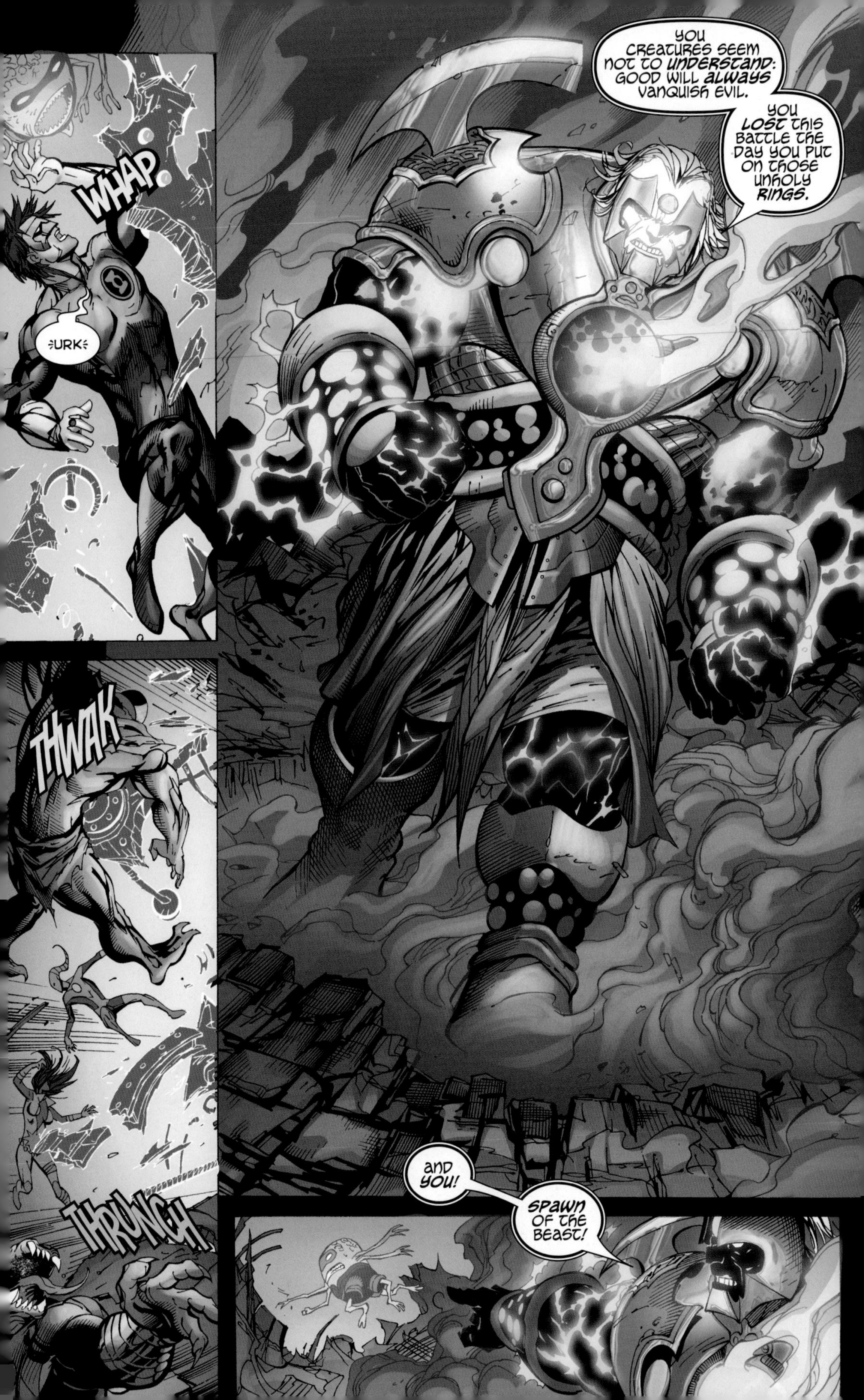
WHAP
URK
THWAK
THRUNCH
YOU CREATURES SEEM NOT TO UNDERSTAND: GOOD WILL ALWAYS VANQUISH EVIL.
YOU LOST THIS BATTLE THE DAY YOU PUT ON THOSE UNHOLY RINGS.
AND YOU!
SPAWN OF THE BEAST!

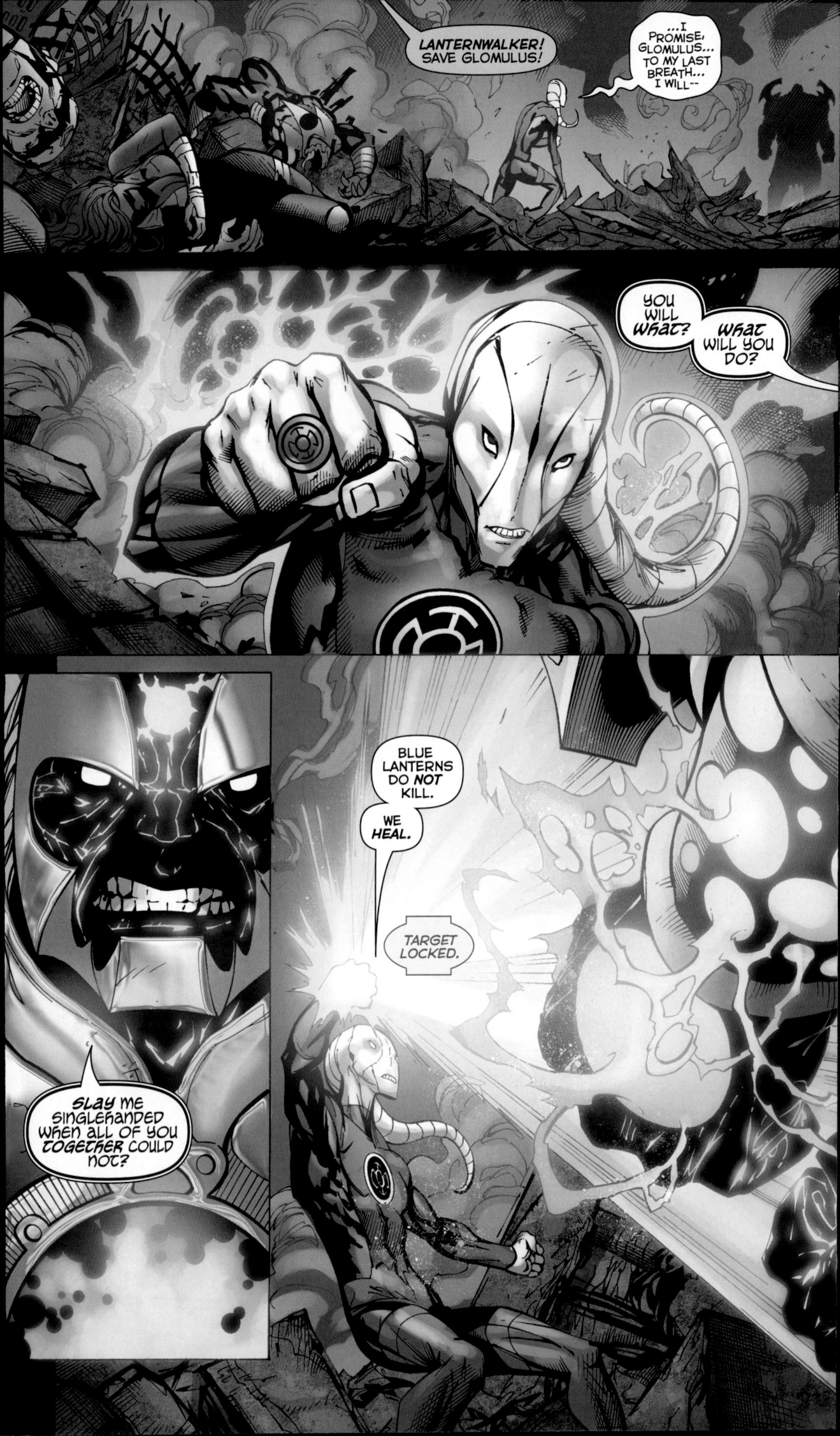
LANTERNWALKER! SAVE GLOMULUS!
...I PROMISE, GLOMULUS... TO MY LAST BREATH... I WILL--
YOU WILL WHAT?
WHAT WILL YOU DO?
SLAY ME SINGLEHANDED WHEN ALL OF YOU TOGETHER COULD NOT?
BLUE LANTERNS DO NOT KILL.
WE HEAL.
TARGET LOCKED.

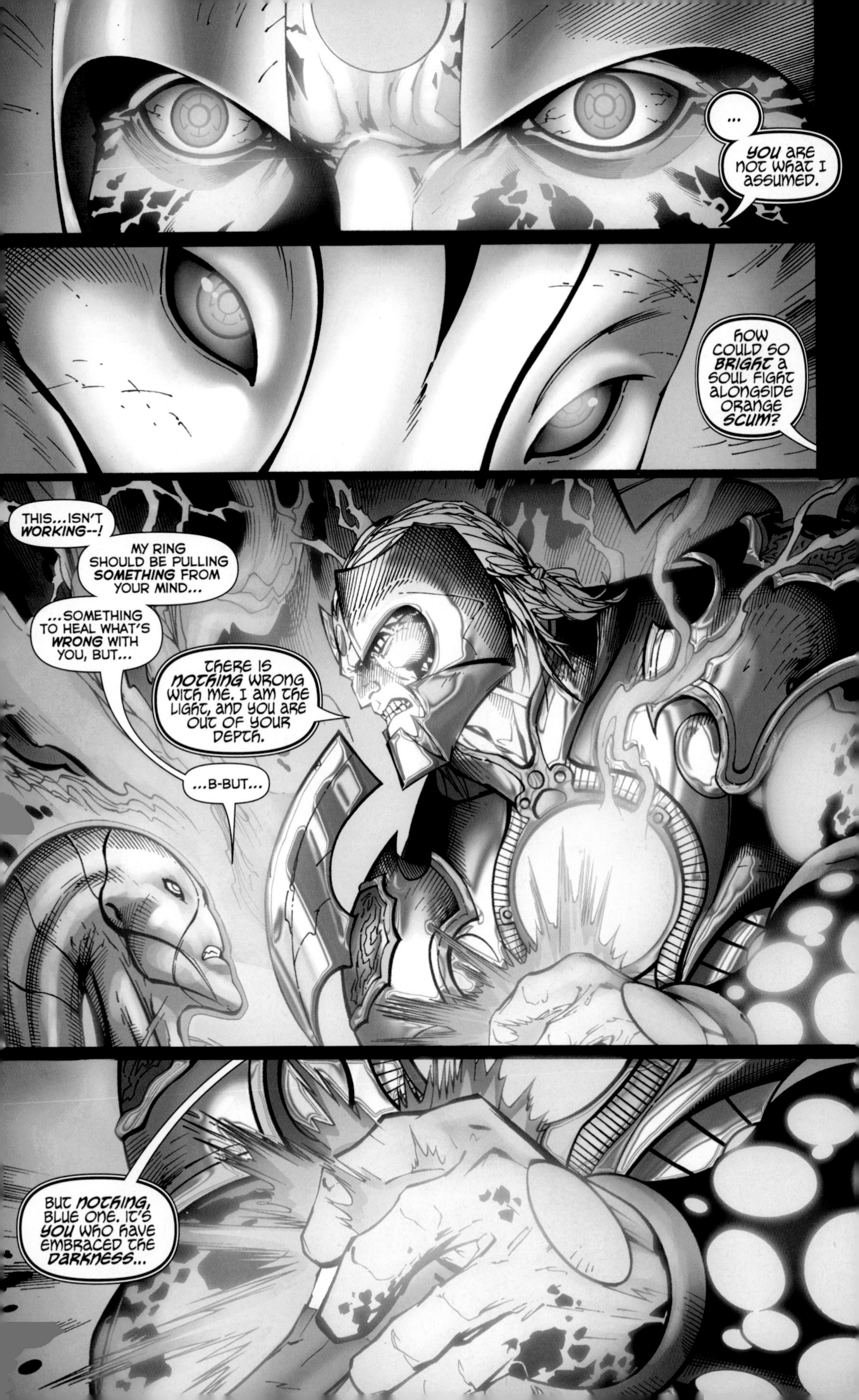
...
YOU ARE NOT WHAT I ASSUMED.
HOW COULD SO BRIGHT A SOUL FIGHT ALONGSIDE ORANGE SCUM?
THIS...ISN'T WORKING--!
MY RING SHOULD BE PULLING SOMETHING FROM YOUR MIND...
...SOMETHING TO HEAL WHAT'S WRONG WITH YOU, BUT...
THERE IS NOTHING WRONG WITH ME. I AM THE LIGHT, AND YOU ARE OUT OF YOUR DEPTH.
...B-BUT...
BUT NOTHING, BLUE ONE. IT'S YOU WHO HAVE EMBRACED THE DARKNESS...

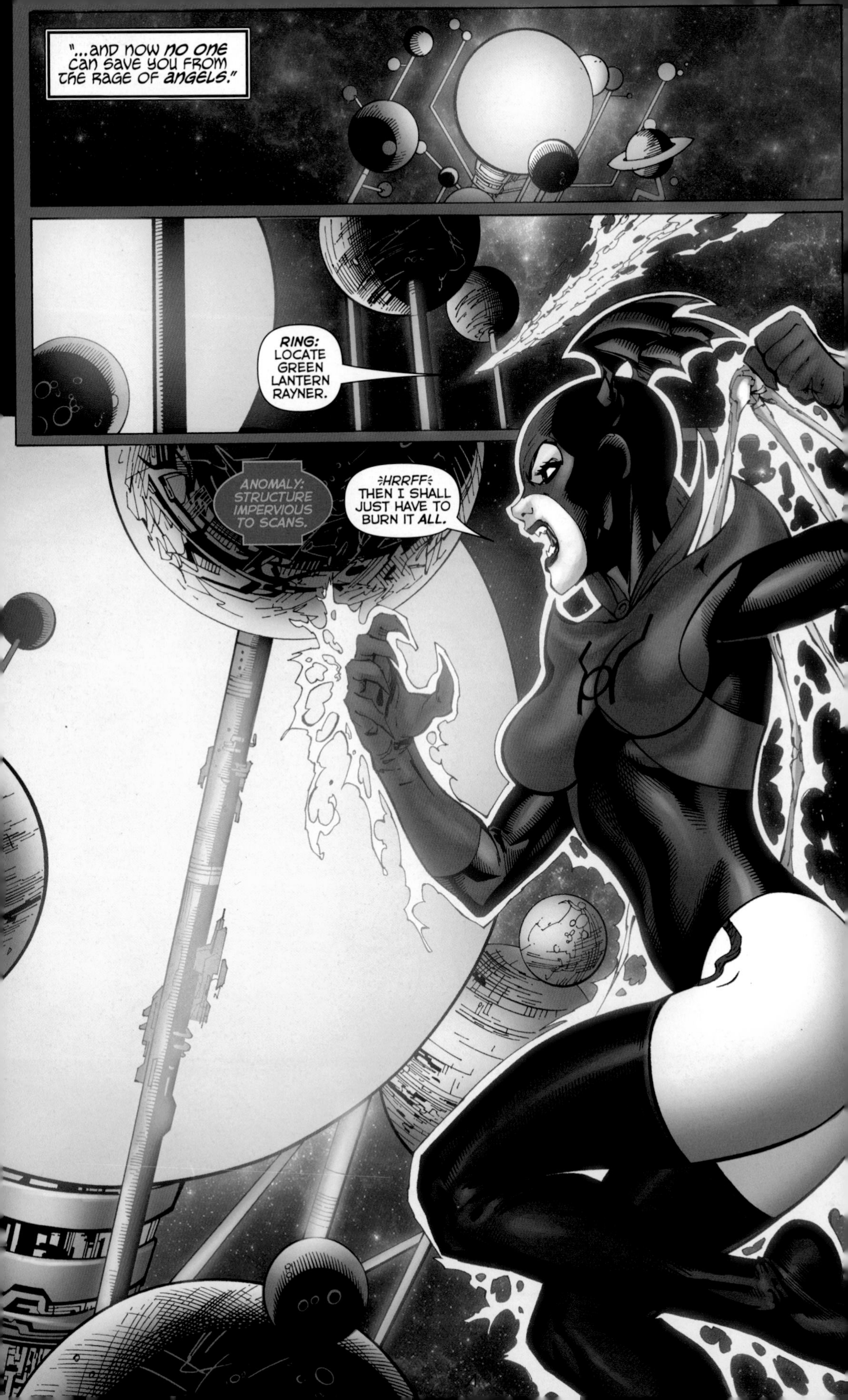
"...and now no one can save you from the rage of angels."
RING: LOCATE GREEN LANTERN RAYNER.
ANOMALY: STRUCTURE IMPERVIOUS TO SCANS.
HRRFF THEN I SHALL JUST HAVE TO BURN IT ALL.

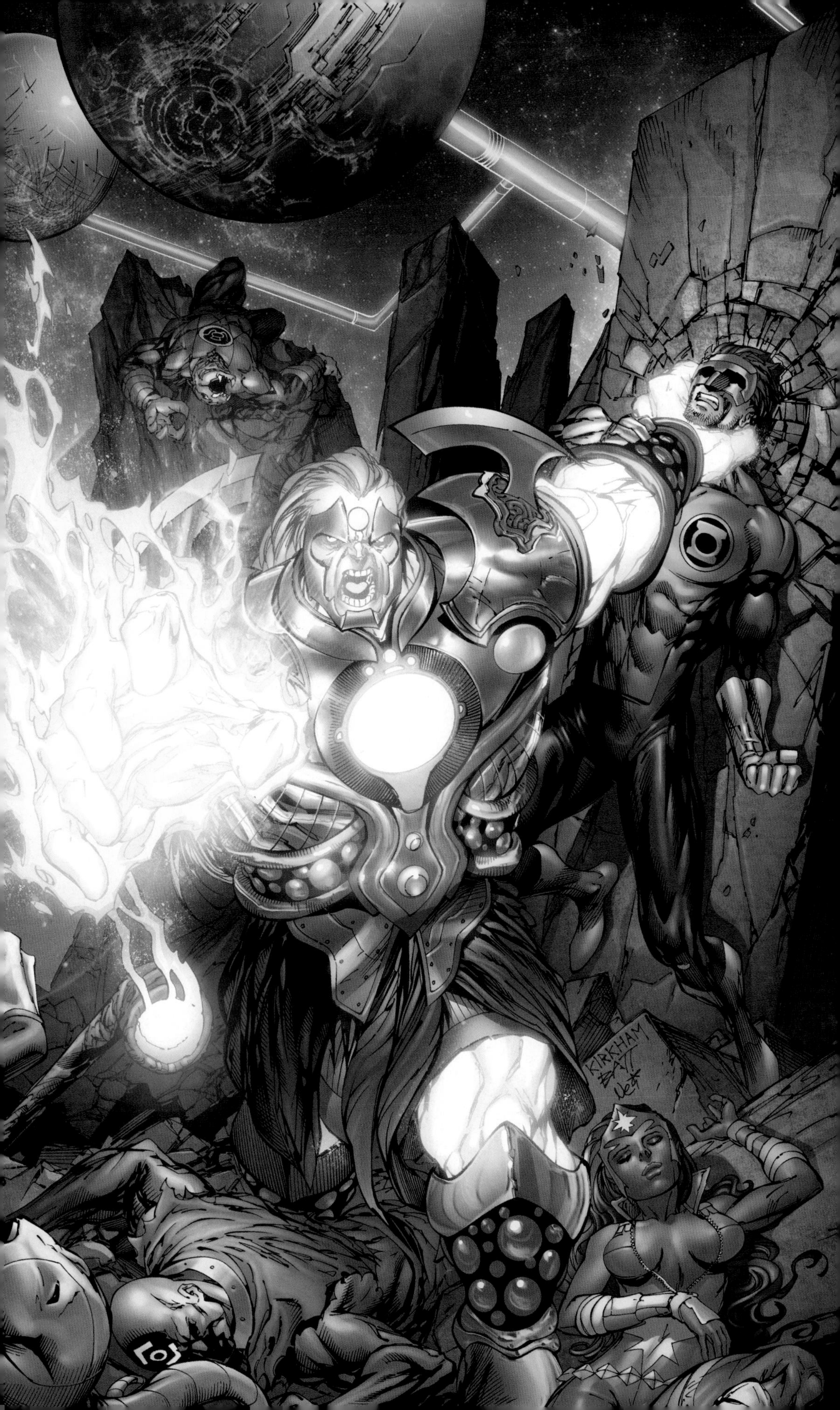
KIRKHAM

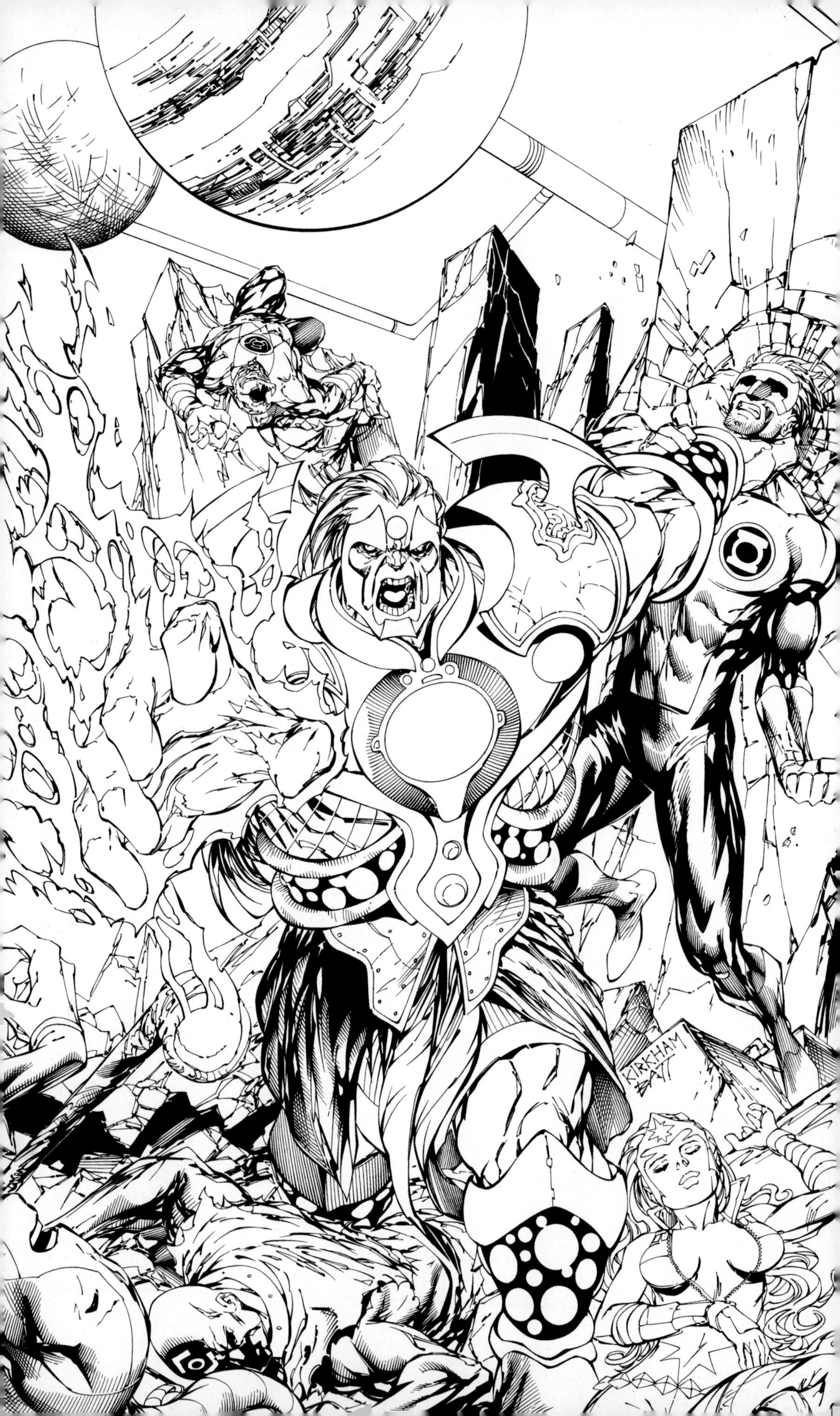
KIRKHAM
BAT!

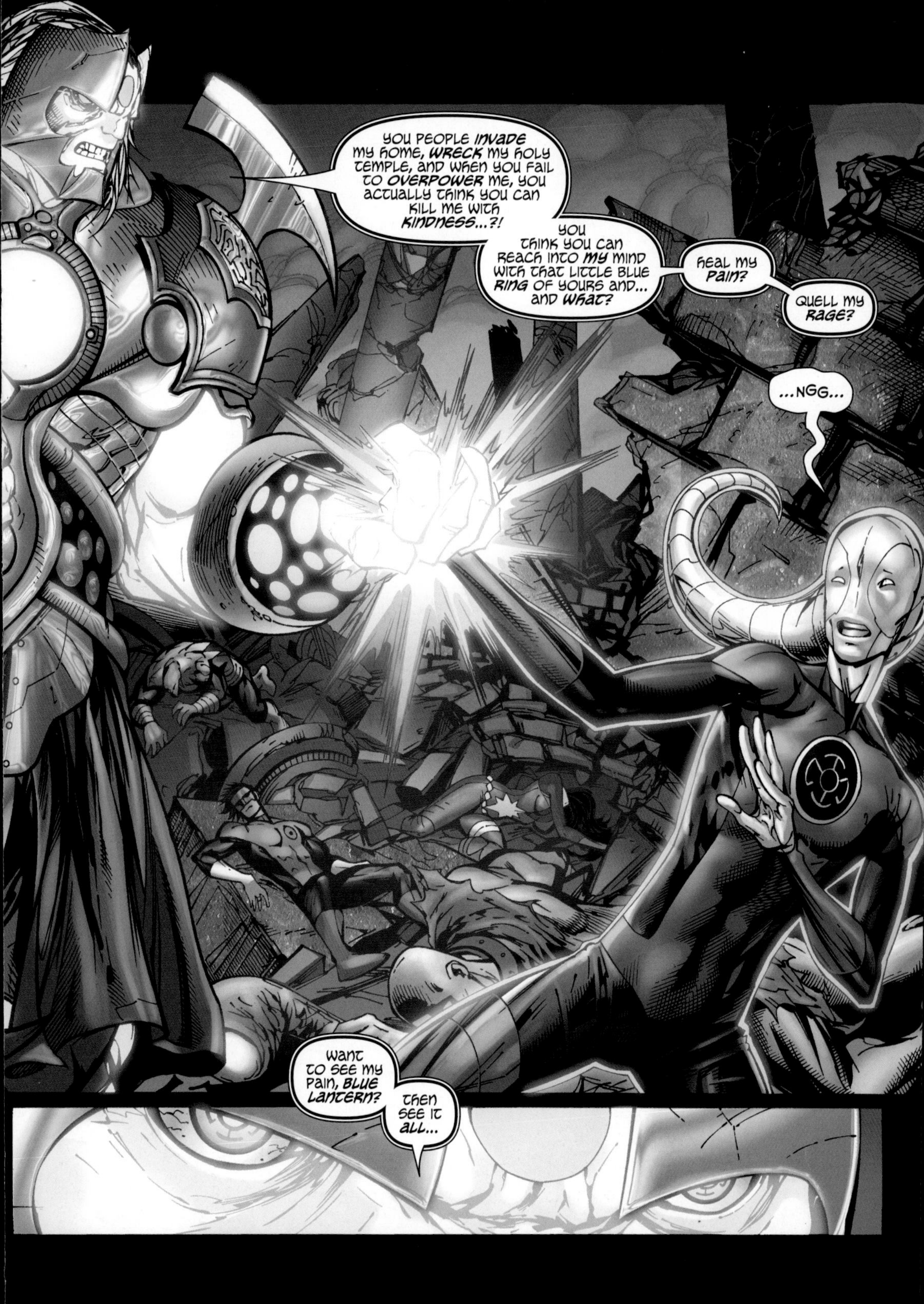
YOU PEOPLE INVADE MY HOME, WRECK MY HOLY TEMPLE, AND WHEN YOU FAIL TO OVERPOWER ME, YOU ACTUALLY THINK YOU CAN KILL ME WITH KINDNESS...?!
YOU THINK YOU CAN REACH INTO MY MIND WITH THAT LITTLE BLUE RING OF YOURS AND... AND WHAT?
HEAL MY PAIN?
QUELL MY RAGE?
...NGG...
WANT TO SEE MY PAIN, BLUE LANTERN?
THEN SEE IT ALL...

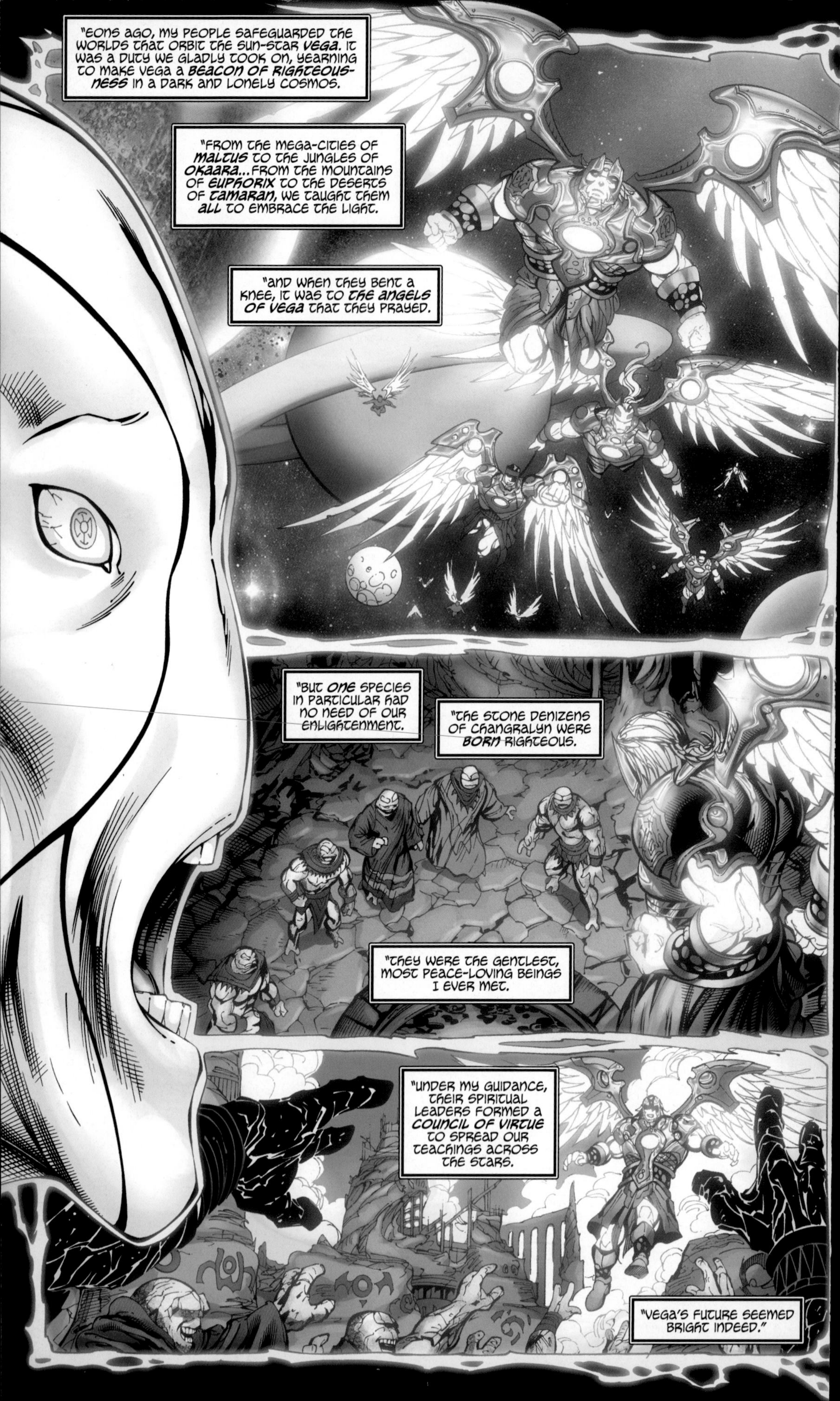
"EONS AGO, MY PEOPLE SAFEGUARDED THE WORLDS THAT ORBIT THE SUN-STAR VEGA. IT WAS A DUTY WE GLADLY TOOK ON, YEARNING TO MAKE VEGA A BEACON OF RIGHTEOUSNESS IN A DARK AND LONELY COSMOS.
"FROM THE MEGA-CITIES OF MALTUS TO THE JUNGLES OF OKAARA...FROM THE MOUNTAINS OF EUPHORIX TO THE DESERTS OF TAMARAN, WE TAUGHT THEM ALL TO EMBRACE THE LIGHT.
"AND WHEN THEY BENT A KNEE, IT WAS TO THE ANGELS OF VEGA THAT THEY PRAYED.
"BUT ONE SPECIES IN PARTICULAR HAD NO NEED OF OUR ENLIGHTENMENT.
"THE STONE DENIZENS OF CHANGRALYN WERE BORN RIGHTEOUS.
"THEY WERE THE GENTLEST, MOST PEACE-LOVING BEINGS I EVER MET.
"UNDER MY GUIDANCE, THEIR SPIRITUAL LEADERS FORMED A COUNCIL OF VIRTUE TO SPREAD OUR TEACHINGS ACROSS THE STARS.
"VEGA'S FUTURE SEEMED BRIGHT INDEED."

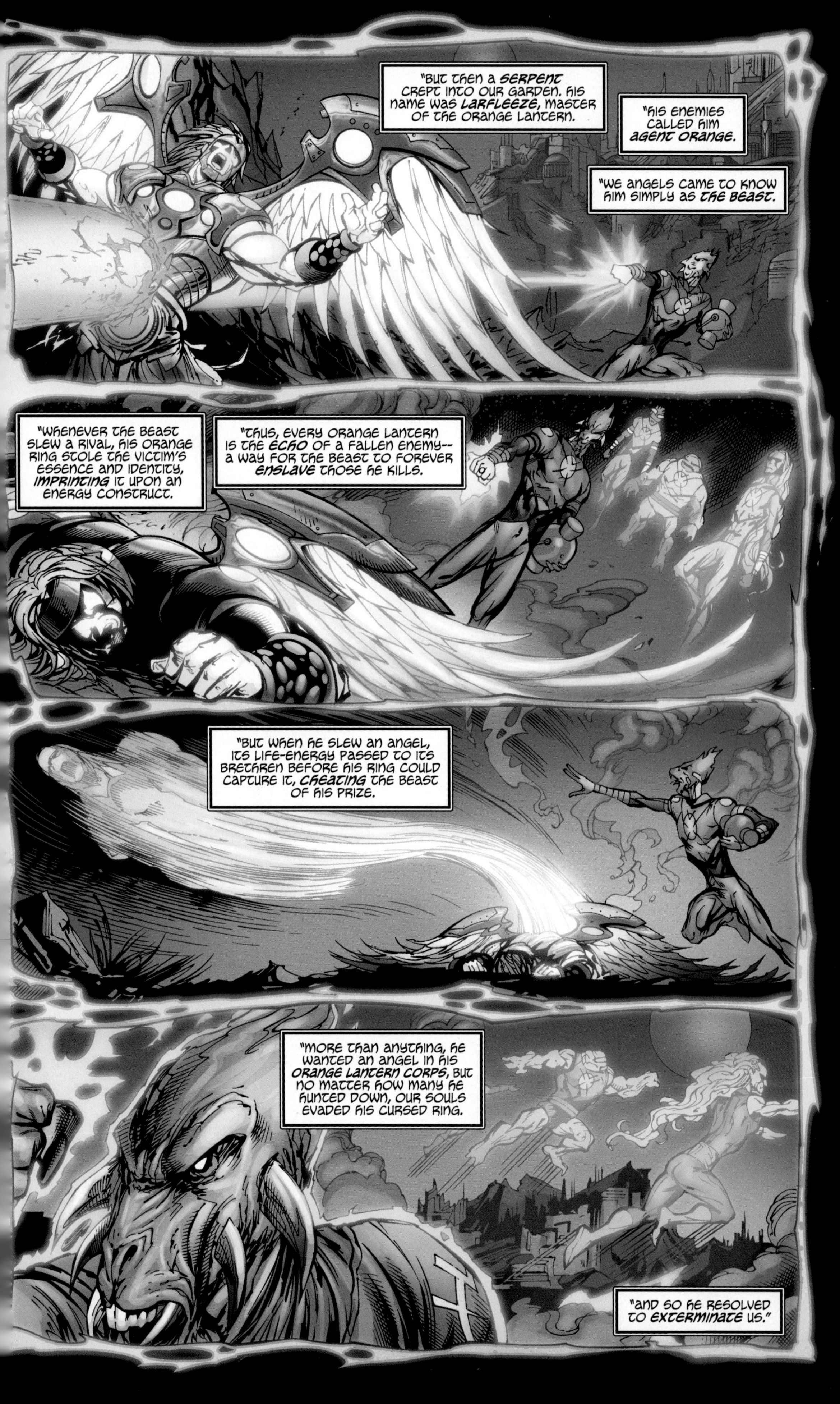
"BUT THEN A SERPENT CREPT INTO OUR GARDEN. HIS NAME WAS LARFLEEZE, MASTER OF THE ORANGE LANTERN.
"HIS ENEMIES CALLED HIM AGENT ORANGE.
"WE ANGELS CAME TO KNOW HIM SIMPLY AS THE BEAST.
"WHENEVER THE BEAST SLEW A RIVAL, HIS ORANGE RING STOLE THE VICTIM'S ESSENCE AND IDENTITY, IMPRINTING IT UPON AN ENERGY CONSTRUCT.
"THUS, EVERY ORANGE LANTERN IS THE ECHO OF A FALLEN ENEMY-- A WAY FOR THE BEAST TO FOREVER ENSLAVE THOSE HE KILLS.
"BUT WHEN HE SLEW AN ANGEL, ITS LIFE-ENERGY PASSED TO ITS BRETHREN BEFORE HIS RING COULD CAPTURE IT, CHEATING THE BEAST OF HIS PRIZE.
"MORE THAN ANYTHING, HE WANTED AN ANGEL IN HIS ORANGE LANTERN CORPS, BUT NO MATTER HOW MANY HE HUNTED DOWN, OUR SOULS EVADED HIS CURSED RING.
"AND SO HE RESOLVED TO EXTERMINATE US."

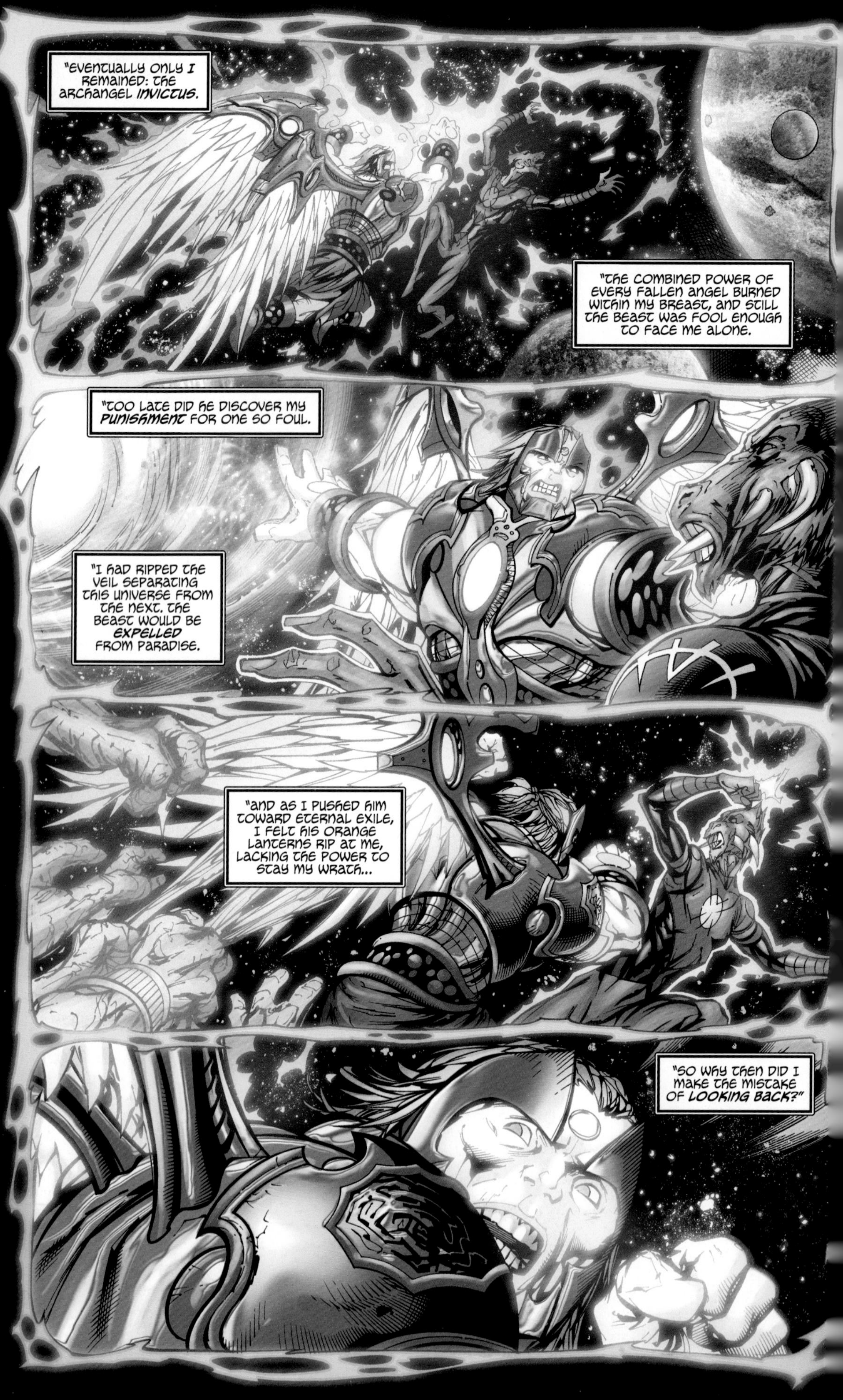
"EVENTUALLY ONLY I REMAINED: THE ARCHANGEL INVICTUS.
"THE COMBINED POWER OF EVERY FALLEN ANGEL BURNED WITHIN MY BREAST, AND STILL THE BEAST WAS FOOL ENOUGH TO FACE ME ALONE.
"TOO LATE DID HE DISCOVER MY PUNISHMENT FOR ONE SO FOUL.
"I HAD RIPPED THE VEIL SEPARATING THIS UNIVERSE FROM THE NEXT. THE BEAST WOULD BE EXPELLED FROM PARADISE.
"AND AS I PUSHED HIM TOWARD ETERNAL EXILE, I FELT HIS ORANGE LANTERNS RIP AT ME, LACKING THE POWER TO STAY MY WRATH...
"SO WHY THEN DID I MAKE THE MISTAKE OF LOOKING BACK?"

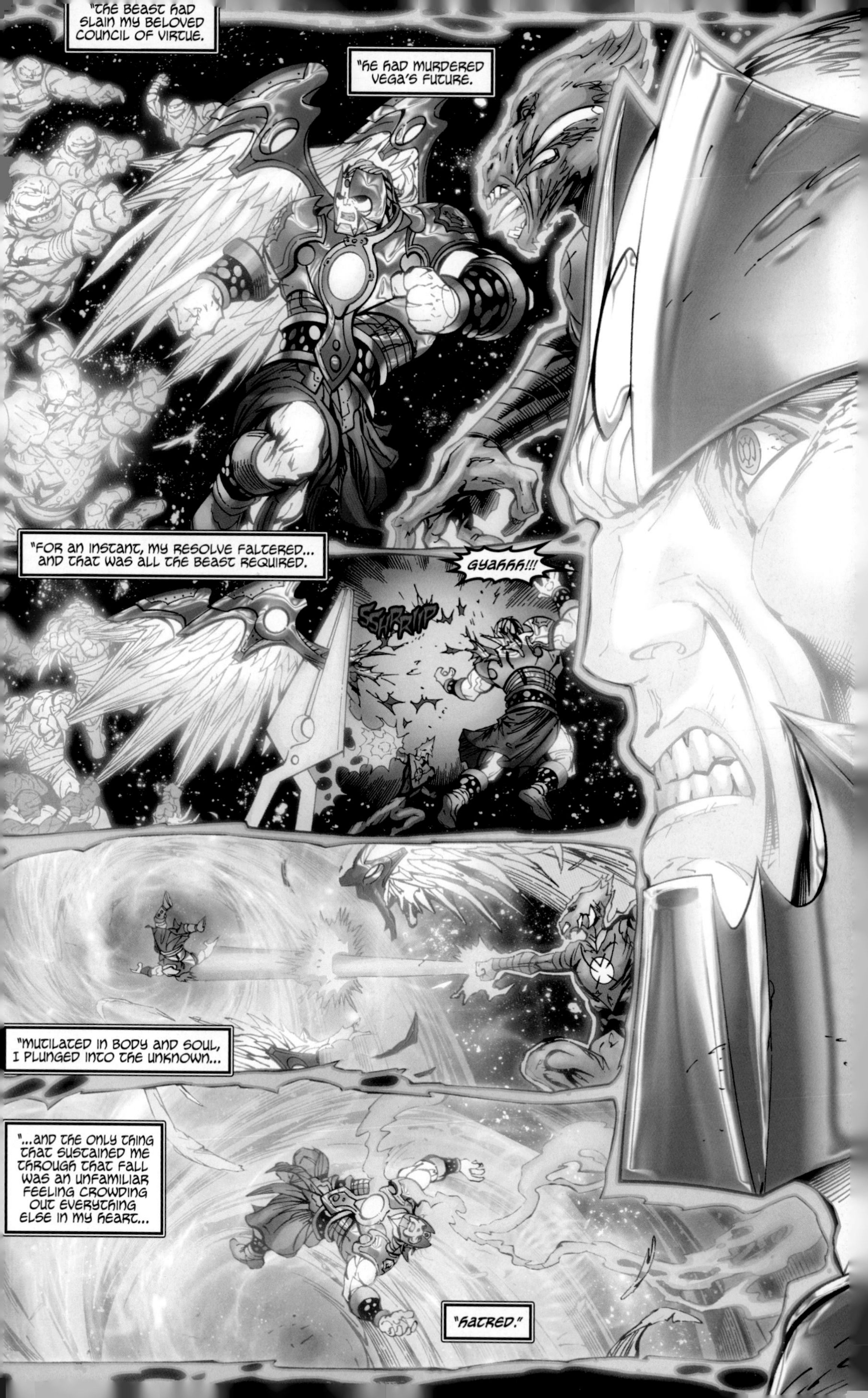
"THE BEAST HAD SLAIN MY BELOVED COUNCIL OF VIRTUE.
"HE HAD MURDERED VEGA'S FUTURE.
"FOR AN INSTANT, MY RESOLVE FALTERED... AND THAT WAS ALL THE BEAST REQUIRED.
GYAHHH!!!
SSHRRIIP
"MUTILATED IN BODY AND SOUL, I PLUNGED INTO THE UNKNOWN...
"...AND THE ONLY THING THAT SUSTAINED ME THROUGH THAT FALL WAS AN UNFAMILIAR FEELING CROWDING OUT EVERYTHING ELSE IN MY HEART...
"HATRED."

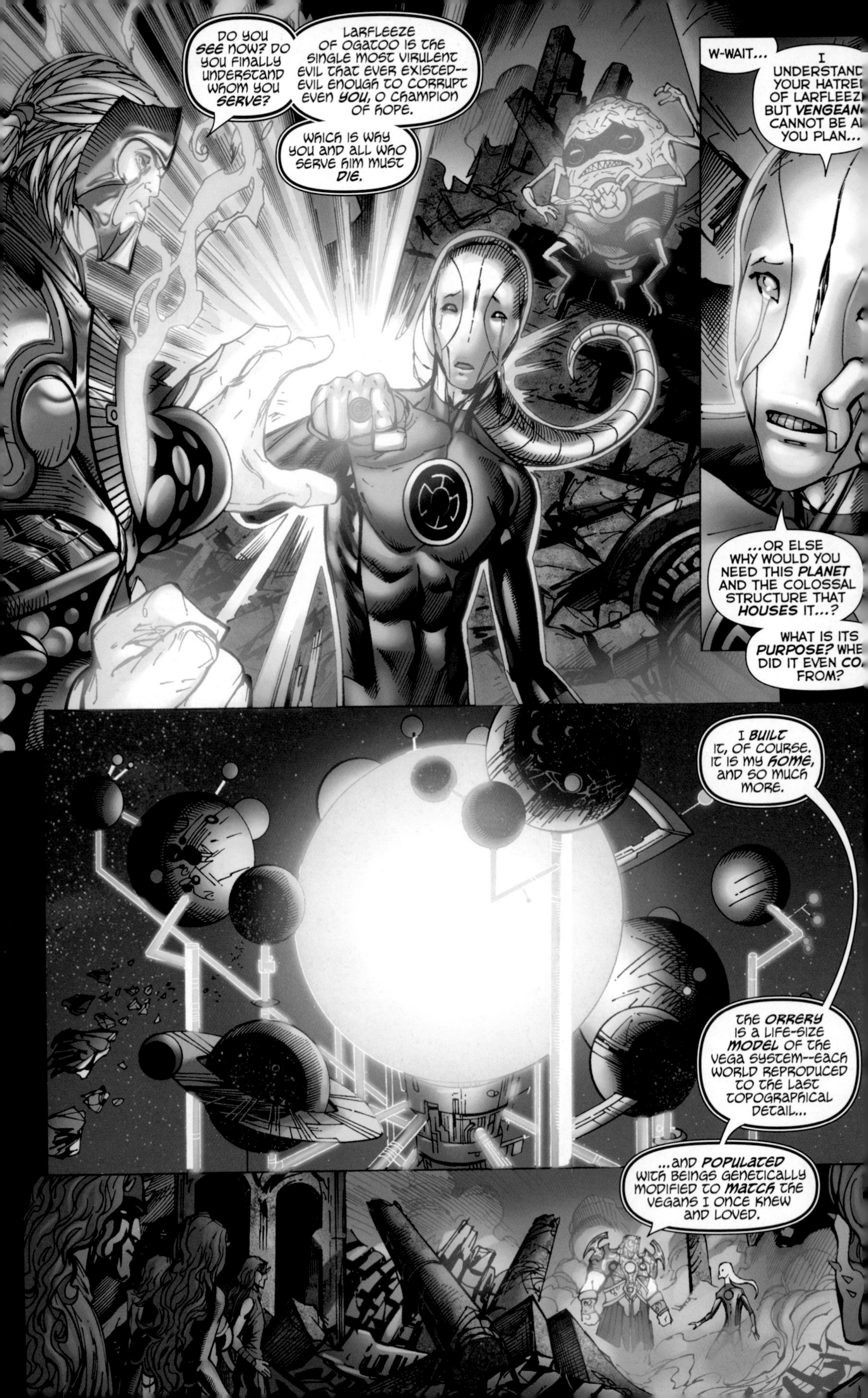
DO YOU SEE NOW? DO YOU FINALLY UNDERSTAND WHOM YOU SERVE?
LARFLEEZE OF OGATOO IS THE SINGLE MOST VIRULENT EVIL THAT EVER EXISTED--EVIL ENOUGH TO CORRUPT EVEN YOU, O CHAMPION OF HOPE.
WHICH IS WHY YOU AND ALL WHO SERVE HIM MUST DIE.
W-WAIT...
I UNDERSTAND YOUR HATRED OF LARFLEEZE BUT VENGEANCE CANNOT BE ALL YOU PLAN...
...OR ELSE WHY WOULD YOU NEED THIS PLANET AND THE COLOSSAL STRUCTURE THAT HOUSES IT...?
WHAT IS ITS PURPOSE? WHERE DID IT EVEN COME FROM?
I BUILT IT, OF COURSE. IT IS MY HOME, AND SO MUCH MORE.
THE ORRERY IS A LIFE-SIZE MODEL OF THE VEGA SYSTEM--EACH WORLD REPRODUCED TO THE LAST TOPOGRAPHICAL DETAIL...
...AND POPULATED WITH BEINGS GENETICALLY MODIFIED TO MATCH THE VEGANS I ONCE KNEW AND LOVED.

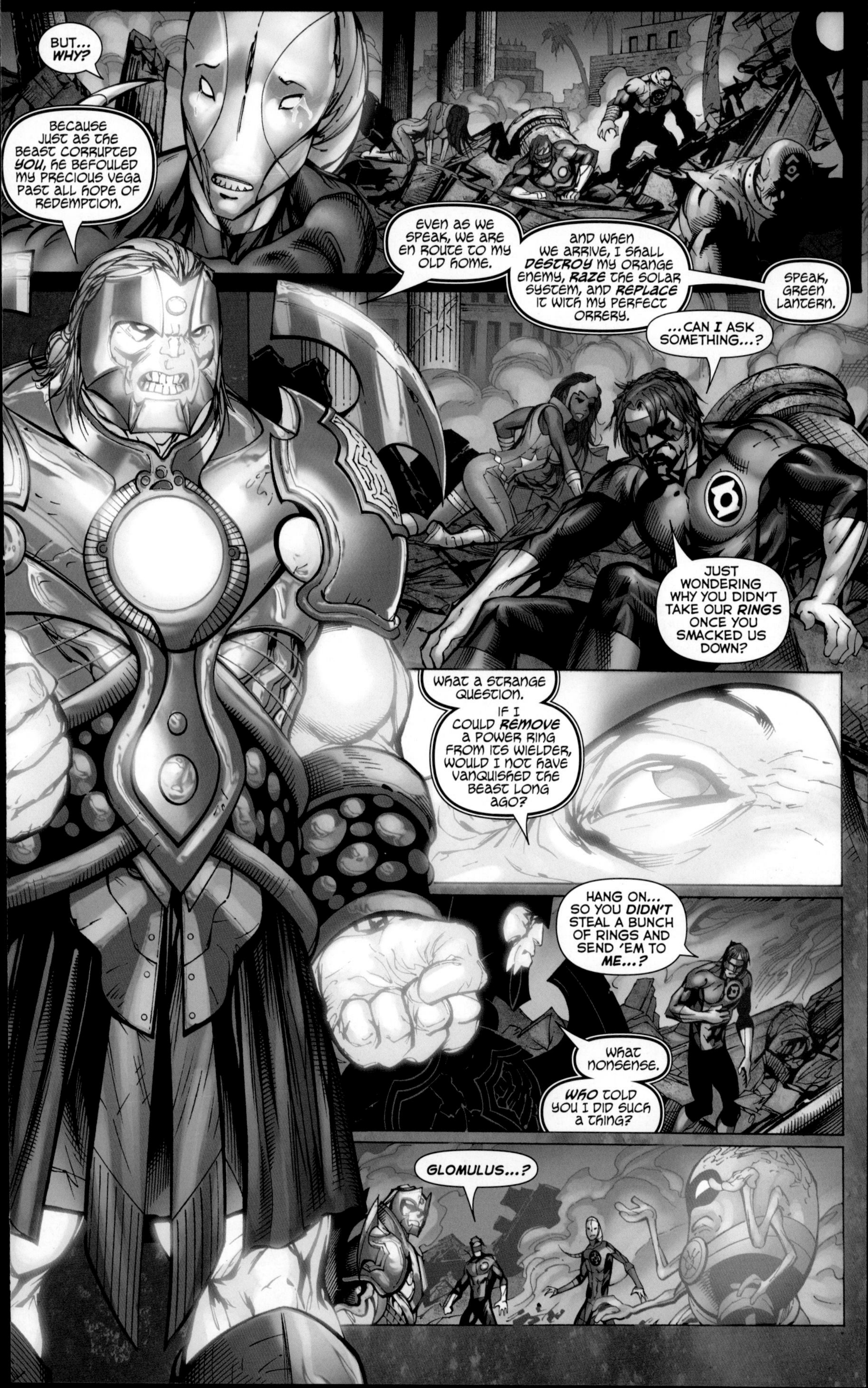

BUT... WHY?
BECAUSE JUST AS THE BEAST CORRUPTED YOU, HE BEFOULED MY PRECIOUS VEGA PAST ALL HOPE OF REDEMPTION.
EVEN AS WE SPEAK, WE ARE EN ROUTE TO MY OLD HOME.
AND WHEN WE ARRIVE, I SHALL DESTROY MY ORANGE ENEMY, RAZE THE SOLAR SYSTEM, AND REPLACE IT WITH MY PERFECT ORRERY.
SPEAK, GREEN LANTERN.
...CAN I ASK SOMETHING...?
JUST WONDERING WHY YOU DIDN'T TAKE OUR RINGS ONCE YOU SMACKED US DOWN?
WHAT A STRANGE QUESTION.
IF I COULD REMOVE A POWER RING FROM ITS WIELDER, WOULD I NOT HAVE VANQUISHED THE BEAST LONG AGO?
HANG ON... SO YOU DIDN'T STEAL A BUNCH OF RINGS AND SEND 'EM TO ME...?
WHAT NONSENSE.
WHO TOLD YOU I DID SUCH A THING?
GLOMULUS...?

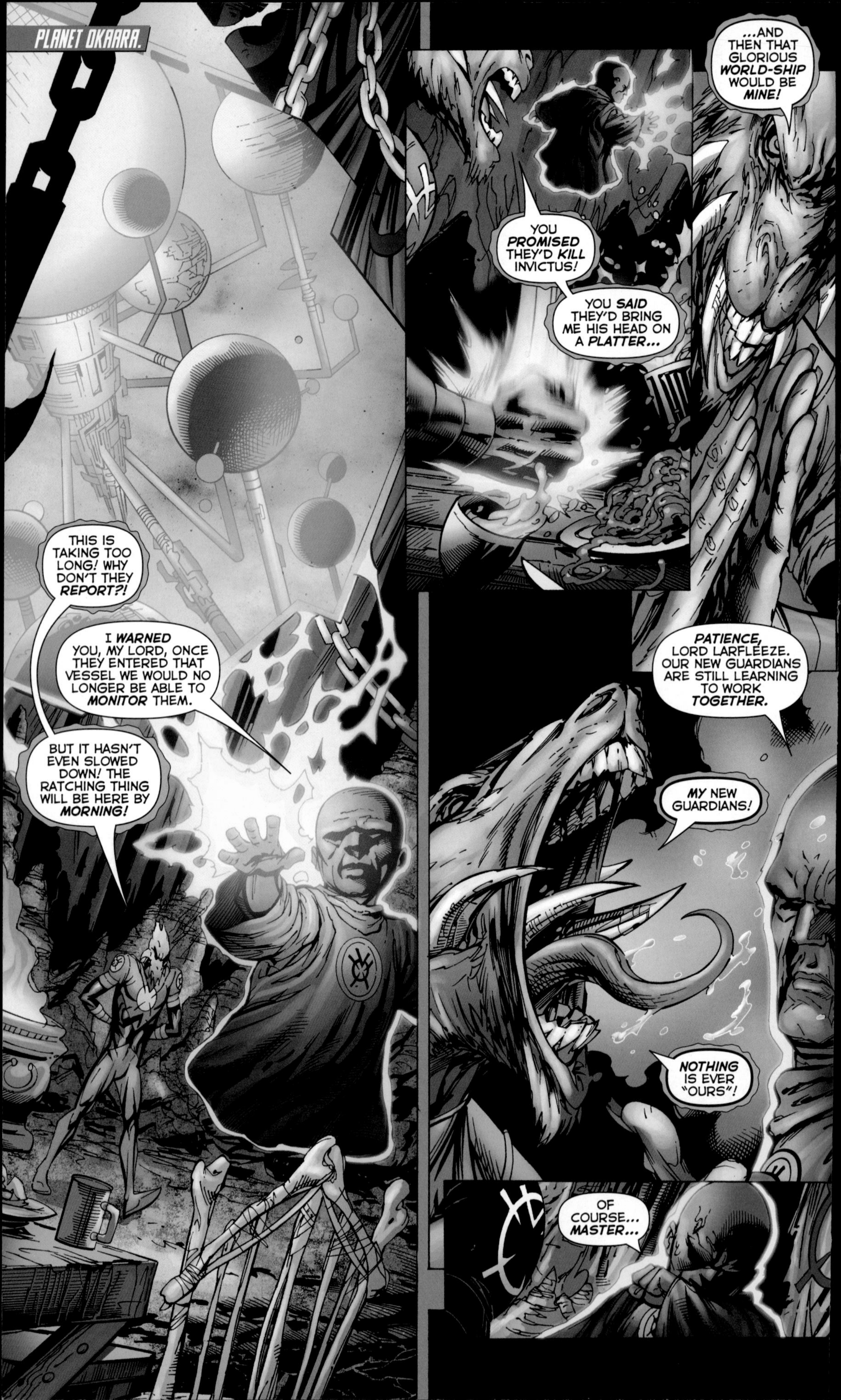
PLANET OKAARA.
THIS IS TAKING TOO LONG! WHY DON'T THEY REPORT?!
I WARNED YOU, MY LORD, ONCE THEY ENTERED THAT VESSEL WE WOULD NO LONGER BE ABLE TO MONITOR THEM.
BUT IT HASN'T EVEN SLOWED DOWN! THE RATCHING THING WILL BE HERE BY MORNING!
YOU PROMISED THEY'D KILL INVICTUS!
YOU SAID THEY'D BRING ME HIS HEAD ON A PLATTER...
...AND THEN THAT GLORIOUS WORLD-SHIP WOULD BE MINE!
PATIENCE, LORD LARFLEEZE. OUR NEW GUARDIANS ARE STILL LEARNING TO WORK TOGETHER.
MY NEW GUARDIANS!
NOTHING IS EVER "OURS"!
OF COURSE... MASTER...

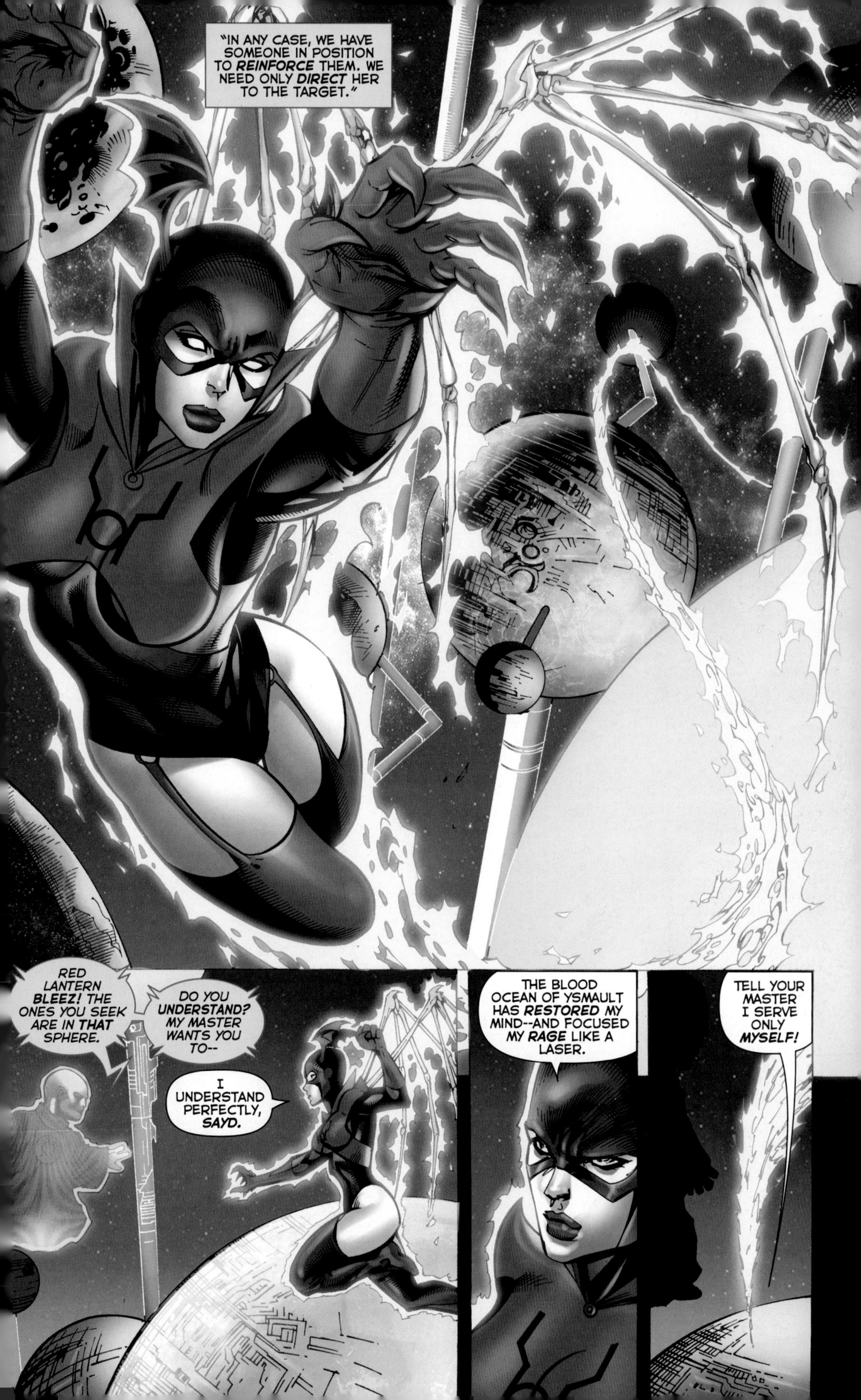
"IN ANY CASE, WE HAVE SOMEONE IN POSITION TO REINFORCE THEM. WE NEED ONLY DIRECT HER TO THE TARGET."
RED LANTERN BLEEZ! THE ONES YOU SEEK ARE IN THAT SPHERE.
DO YOU UNDERSTAND? MY MASTER WANTS YOU TO--
I UNDERSTAND PERFECTLY, SAYD.
THE BLOOD OCEAN OF YSMAULT HAS RESTORED MY MIND--AND FOCUSED MY RAGE LIKE A LASER.
TELL YOUR MASTER I SERVE ONLY MYSELF!

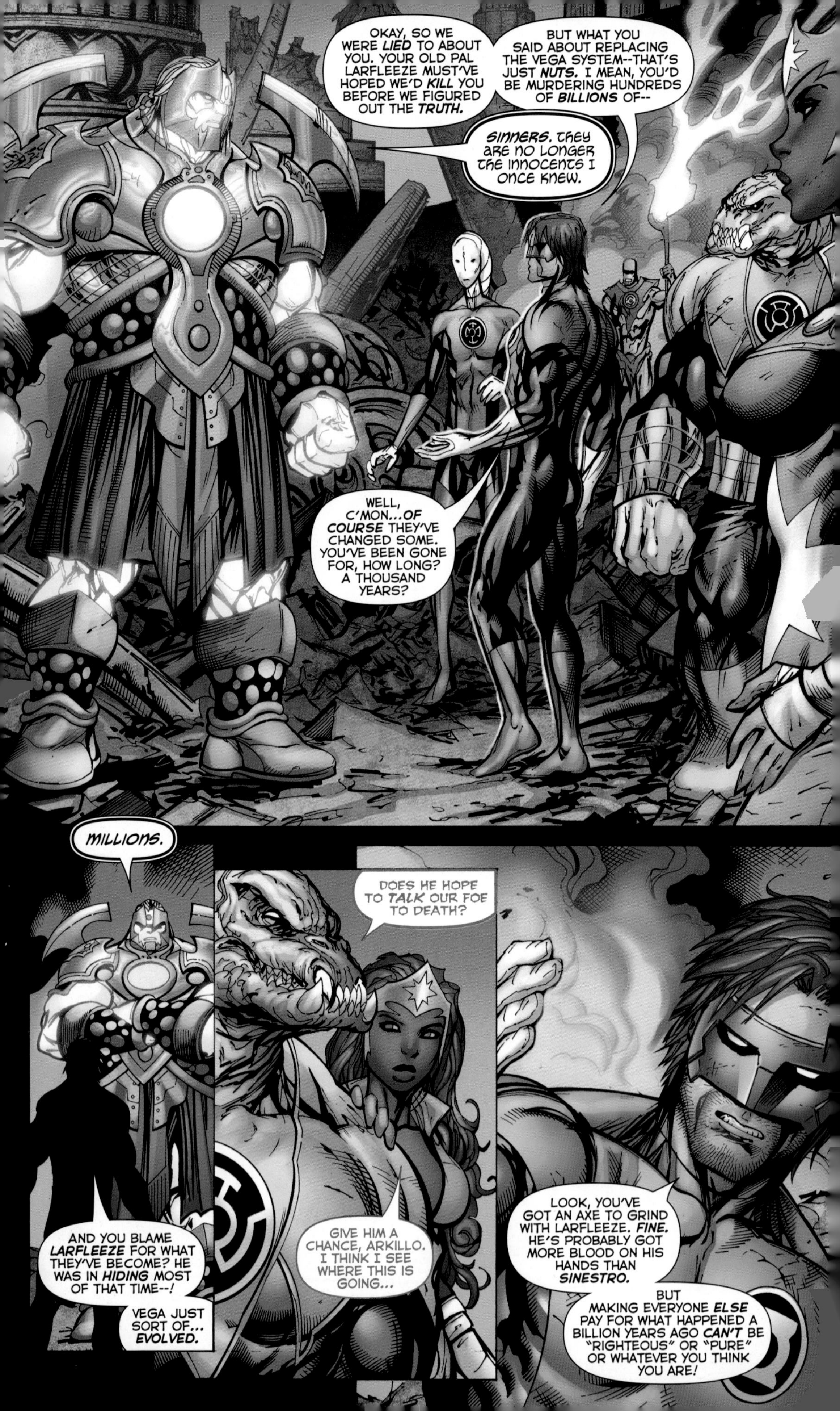
OKAY, SO WE WERE LIED TO ABOUT YOU. YOUR OLD PAL LARFLEEZE MUST'VE HOPED WE'D KILL YOU BEFORE WE FIGURED OUT THE TRUTH.
BUT WHAT YOU SAID ABOUT REPLACING THE VEGA SYSTEM--THAT'S JUST NUTS. I MEAN, YOU'D BE MURDERING HUNDREDS OF BILLIONS OF--
SINNERS. THEY ARE NO LONGER THE INNOCENTS I ONCE KNEW.
WELL, C'MON...OF COURSE THEY'VE CHANGED SOME. YOU'VE BEEN GONE FOR, HOW LONG? A THOUSAND YEARS?
MILLIONS.
AND YOU BLAME LARFLEEZE FOR WHAT THEY'VE BECOME? HE WAS IN HIDING MOST OF THAT TIME--!
VEGA JUST SORT OF... EVOLVED.
DOES HE HOPE TO TALK OUR FOE TO DEATH?
GIVE HIM A CHANCE, ARKILLO. I THINK I SEE WHERE THIS IS GOING...
LOOK, YOU'VE GOT AN AXE TO GRIND WITH LARFLEEZE. FINE. HE'S PROBABLY GOT MORE BLOOD ON HIS HANDS THAN SINESTRO.
BUT MAKING EVERYONE ELSE PAY FOR WHAT HAPPENED A BILLION YEARS AGO CAN'T BE "RIGHTEOUS" OR "PURE" OR WHATEVER YOU THINK YOU ARE!

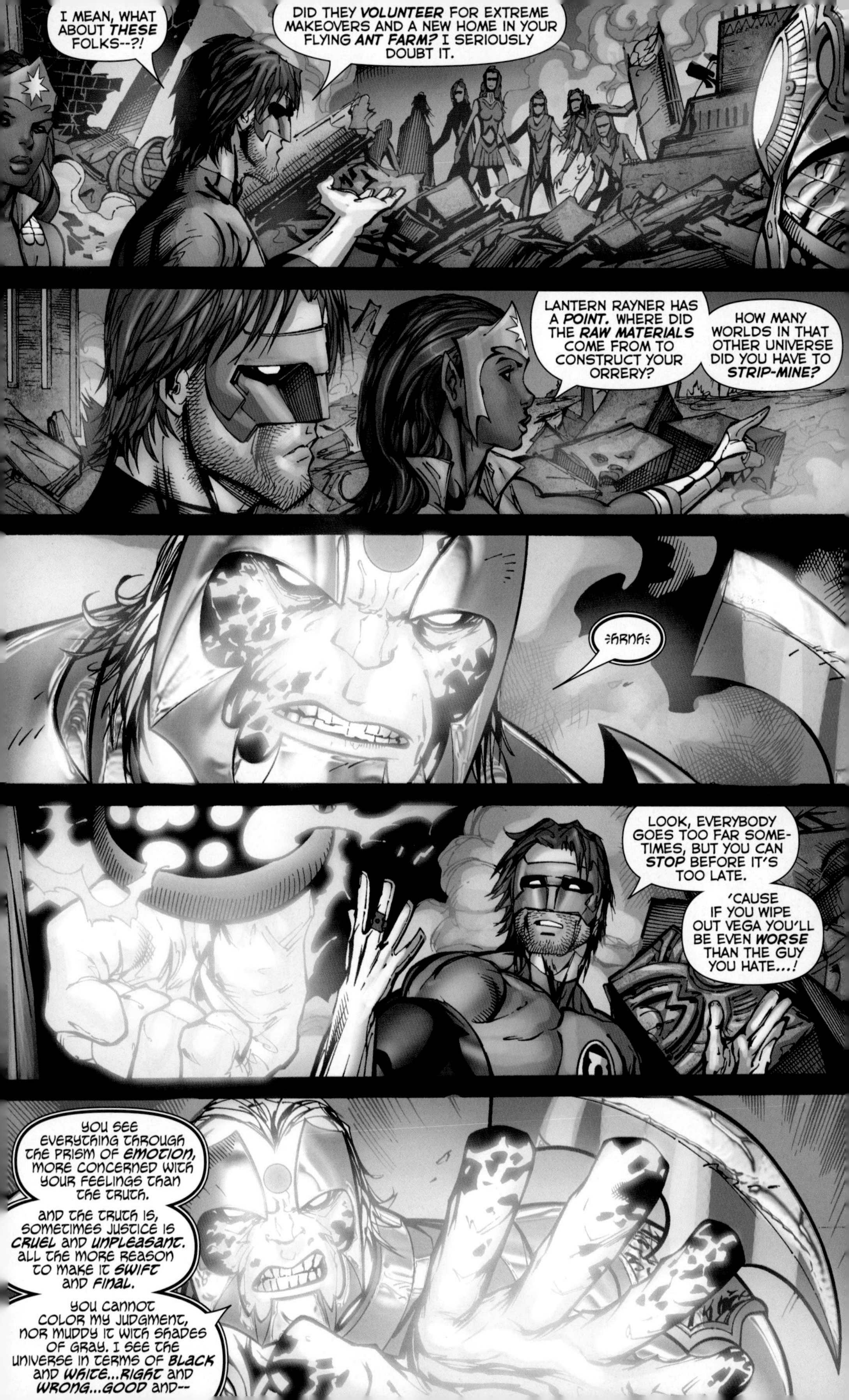
I MEAN, WHAT ABOUT THESE FOLKS--?!
DID THEY VOLUNTEER FOR EXTREME MAKEOVERS AND A NEW HOME IN YOUR FLYING ANT FARM? I SERIOUSLY DOUBT IT.
LANTERN RAYNER HAS A POINT. WHERE DID THE RAW MATERIALS COME FROM TO CONSTRUCT YOUR ORRERY?
HOW MANY WORLDS IN THAT OTHER UNIVERSE DID YOU HAVE TO STRIP-MINE?
HRNH
LOOK, EVERYBODY GOES TOO FAR SOMETIMES, BUT YOU CAN STOP BEFORE IT'S TOO LATE.
'CAUSE IF YOU WIPE OUT VEGA YOU'LL BE EVEN WORSE THAN THE GUY YOU HATE...!
YOU SEE EVERYTHING THROUGH THE PRISM OF EMOTION, MORE CONCERNED WITH YOUR FEELINGS THAN THE TRUTH.
AND THE TRUTH IS, SOMETIMES JUSTICE IS CRUEL AND UNPLEASANT. ALL THE MORE REASON TO MAKE IT SWIFT AND FINAL.
YOU CANNOT COLOR MY JUDGMENT, NOR MUDDY IT WITH SHADES OF GRAY. I SEE THE UNIVERSE IN TERMS OF BLACK AND WHITE...RIGHT AND WRONG...GOOD AND--

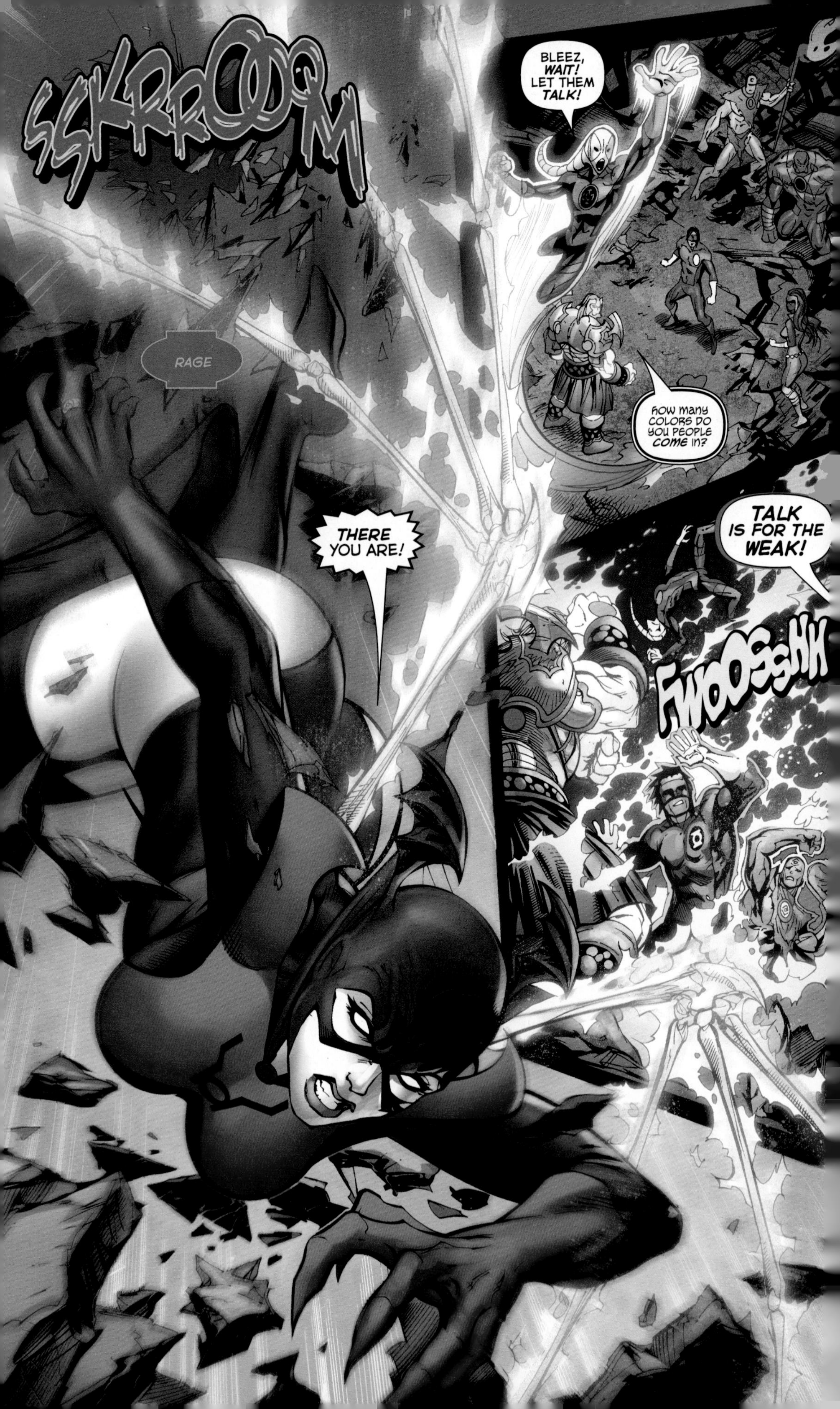
SSKRROOOM
BLEEZ, WAIT! LET THEM TALK!
RAGE
HOW MANY COLORS DO YOU PEOPLE COME IN?
THERE YOU ARE!
TALK IS FOR THE WEAK!
FWOOSSHK

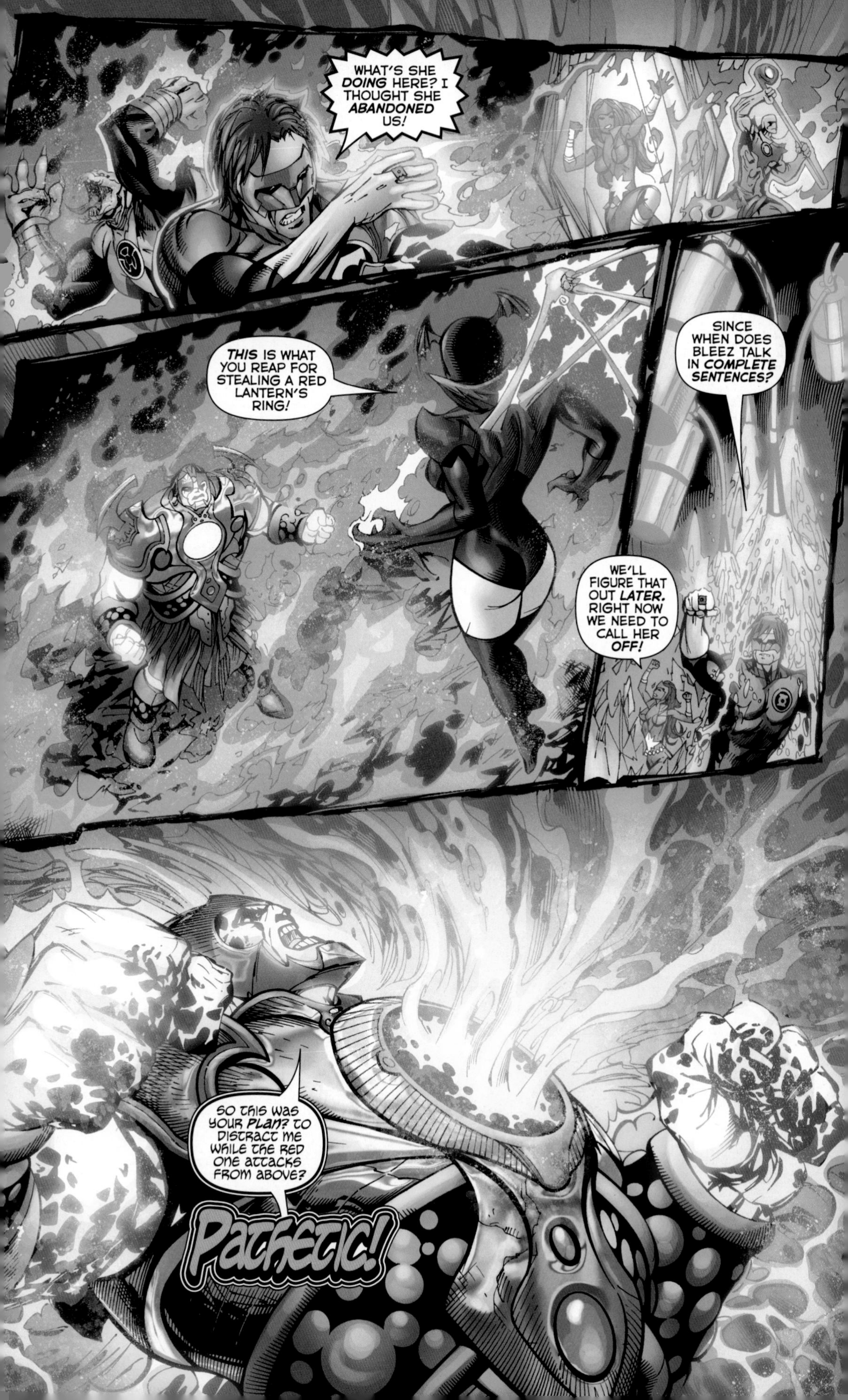

WHAT'S SHE DOING HERE? I THOUGHT SHE ABANDONED US!
THIS IS WHAT YOU REAP FOR STEALING A RED LANTERN'S RING!
SINCE WHEN DOES BLEEZ TALK IN COMPLETE SENTENCES?
WE'LL FIGURE THAT OUT LATER. RIGHT NOW WE NEED TO CALL HER OFF!
SO THIS WAS YOUR PLAN? TO DISTRACT ME WHILE THE RED ONE ATTACKS FROM ABOVE?
PATHETIC!

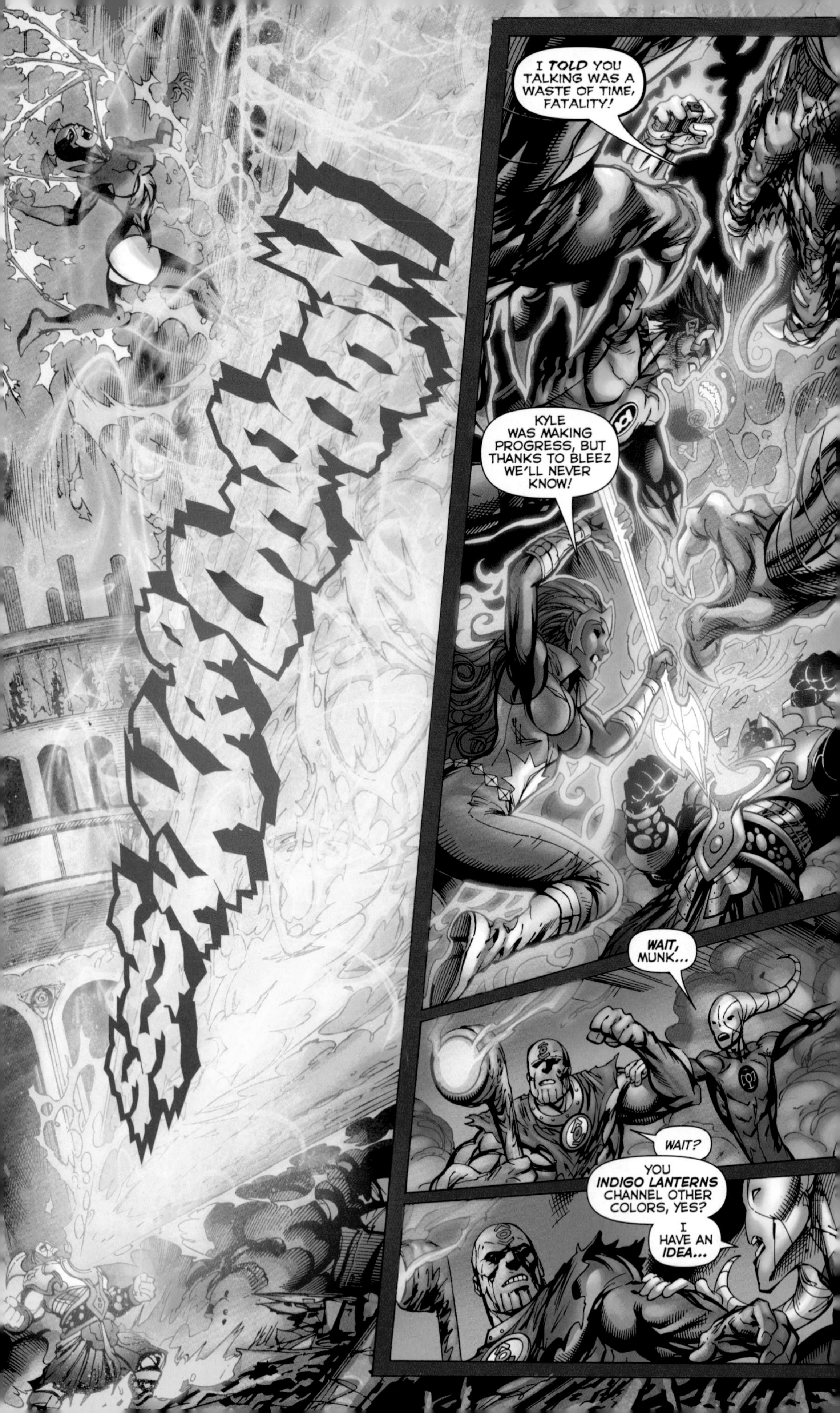

I TOLD YOU TALKING WAS A WASTE OF TIME, FATALITY!
KYLE WAS MAKING PROGRESS, BUT THANKS TO BLEEZ WE'LL NEVER KNOW!
WAIT, MUNK...
WAIT?
YOU INDIGO LANTERNS CHANNEL OTHER COLORS, YES?
I HAVE AN IDEA...

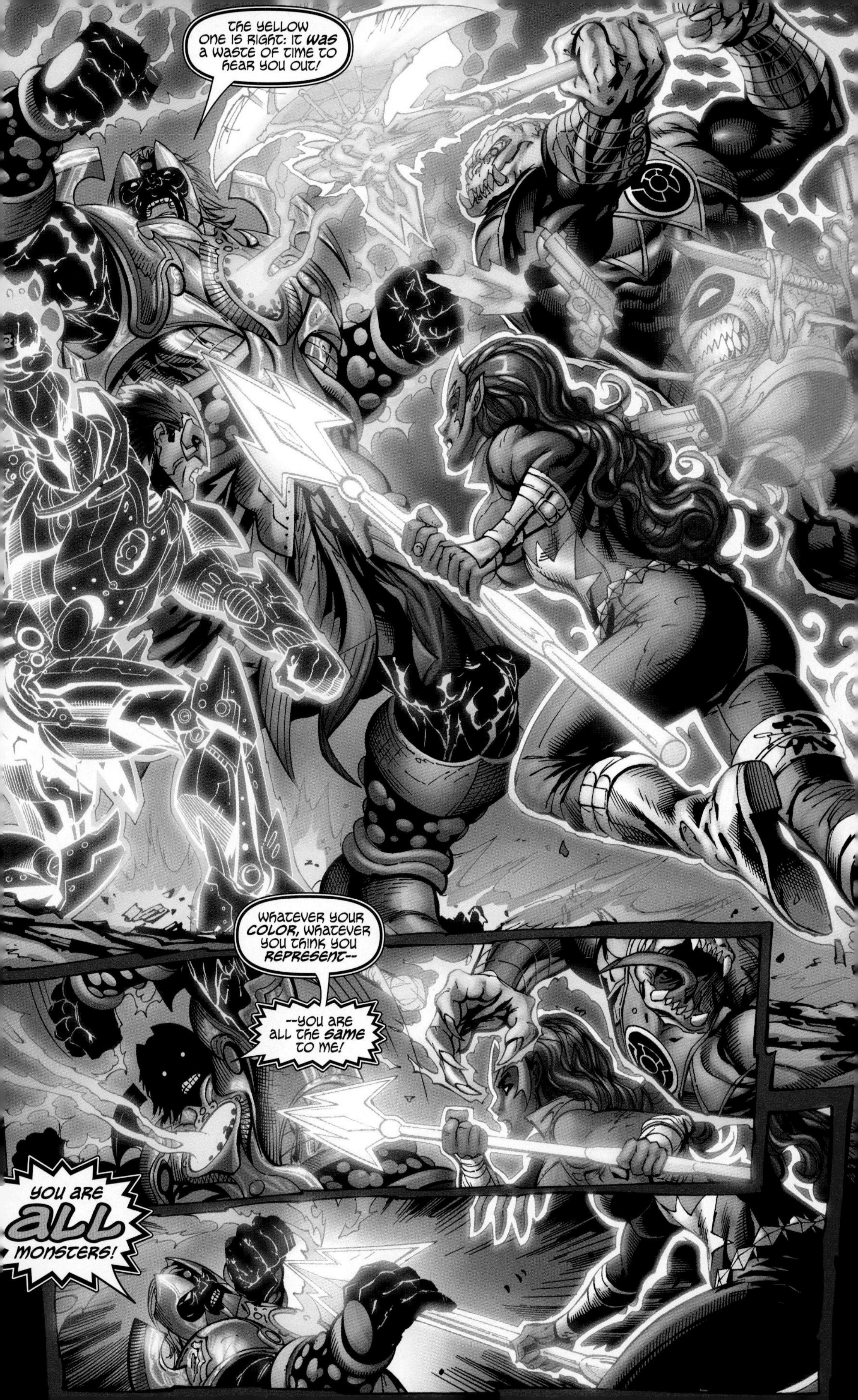
THE YELLOW ONE IS RIGHT: IT WAS A WASTE OF TIME TO HEAR YOU OUT!
WHATEVER YOUR COLOR, WHATEVER YOU THINK YOU REPRESENT--
--YOU ARE ALL THE SAME TO ME!
YOU ARE ALL MONSTERS!

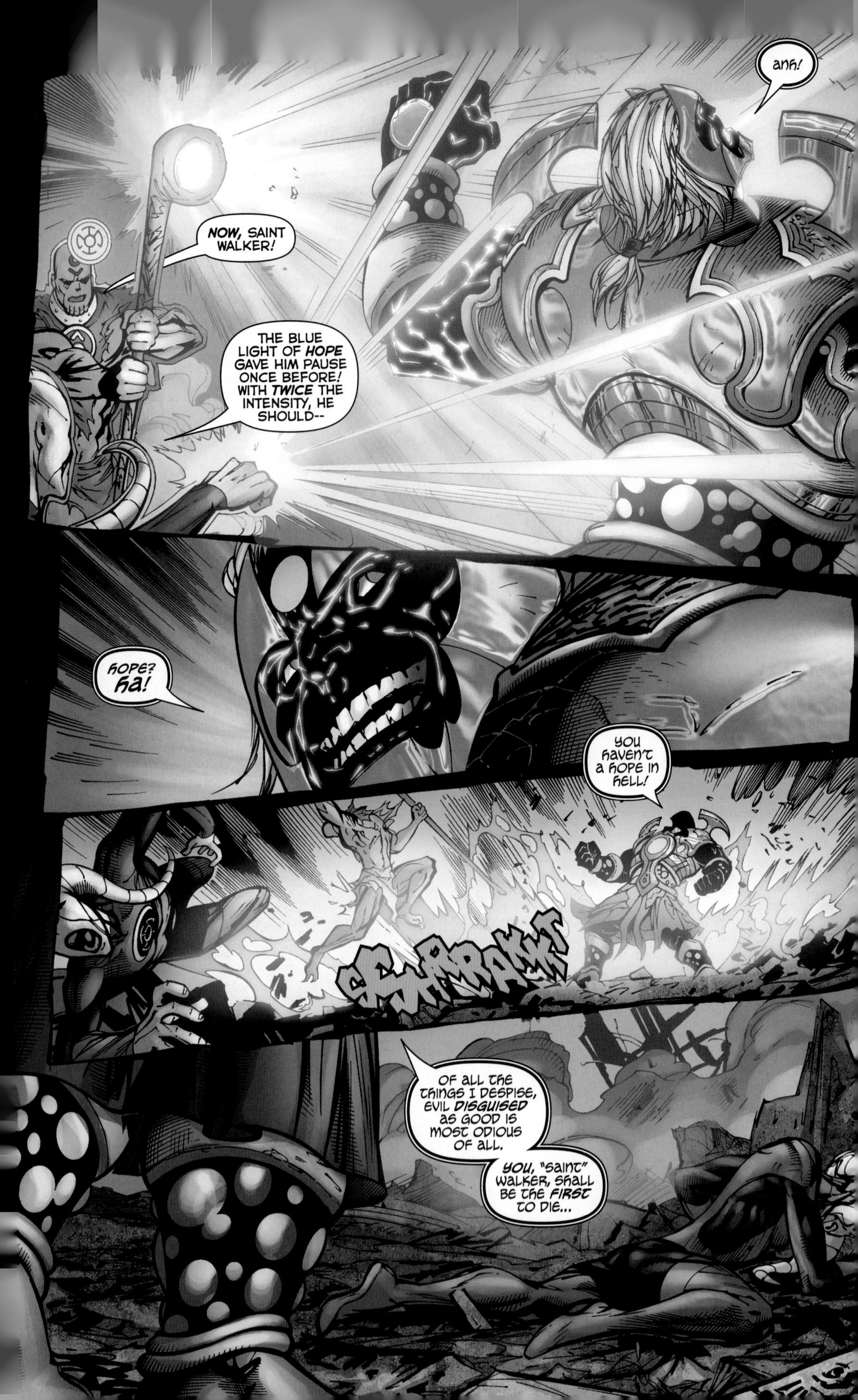
anh!
NOW, SAINT WALKER!
THE BLUE LIGHT OF HOPE GAVE HIM PAUSE ONCE BEFORE! WITH TWICE THE INTENSITY, HE SHOULD--
HOPE? HA!
YOU HAVEN'T A HOPE IN HELL!
SKRAKT
OF ALL THE THINGS I DESPISE, EVIL DISGUISED AS GOOD IS MOST ODIOUS OF ALL.
YOU, "SAINT" WALKER, SHALL BE THE FIRST TO DIE...

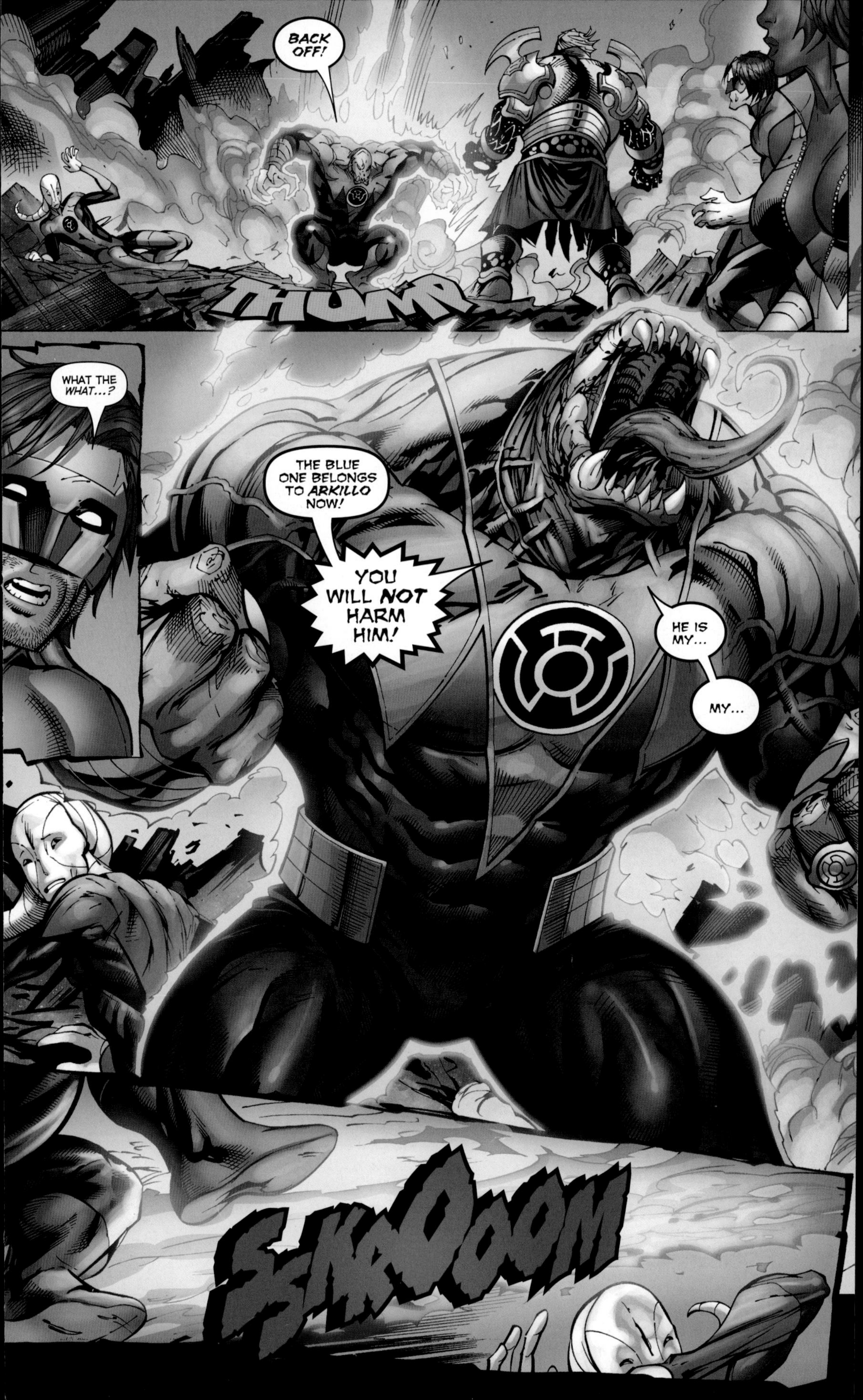
BACK OFF!
THUMP
WHAT THE WHAT...?
THE BLUE ONE BELONGS TO ARKILLO NOW!
YOU WILL NOT HARM HIM!
HE IS MY...
MY...
SHROOOM

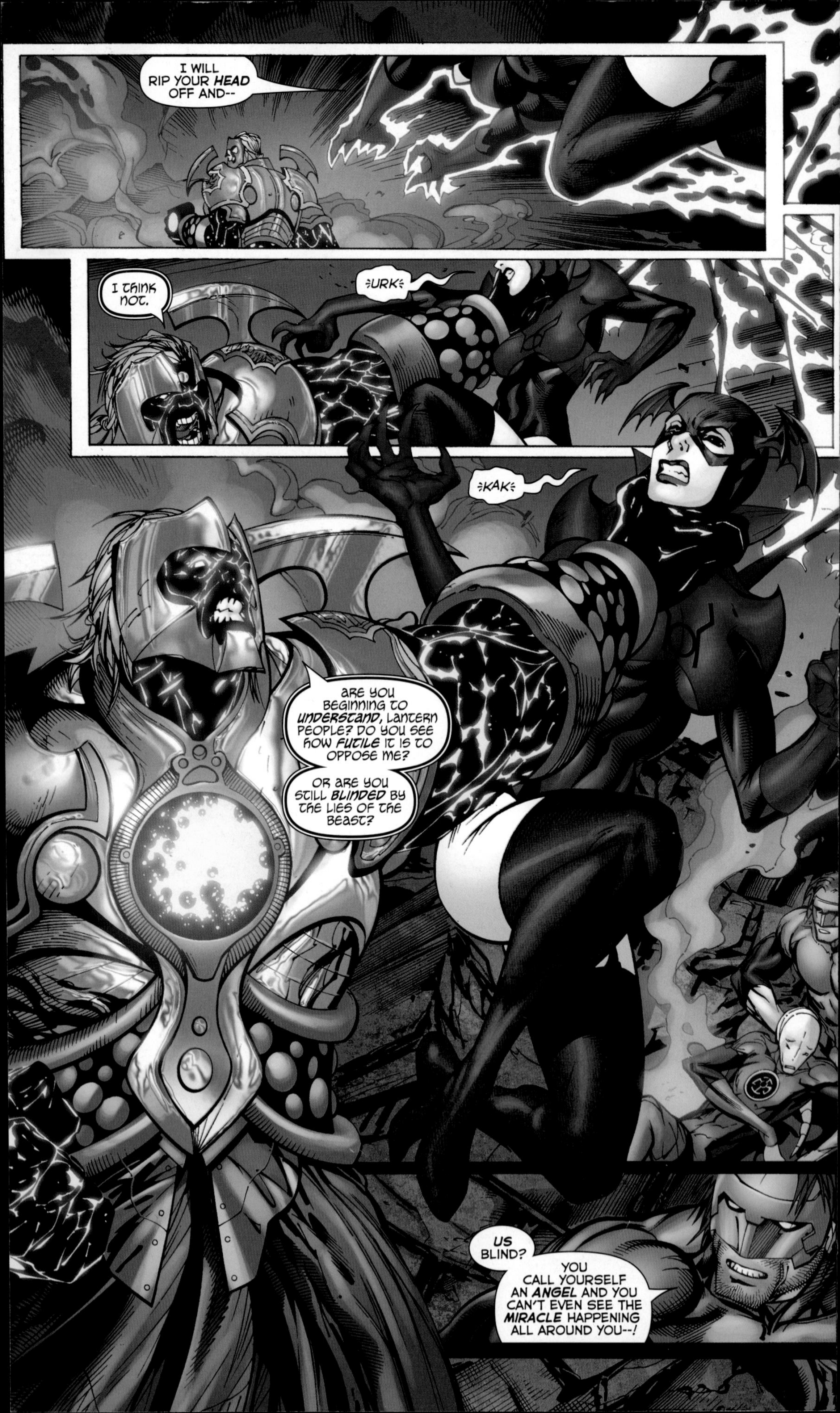
I WILL RIP YOUR HEAD OFF AND--
I THINK NOT.
URK
KAK
ARE YOU BEGINNING TO UNDERSTAND, LANTERN PEOPLE? DO YOU SEE HOW FUTILE IT IS TO OPPOSE ME?
OR ARE YOU STILL BLINDED BY THE LIES OF THE BEAST?
US BLIND?
YOU CALL YOURSELF AN ANGEL AND YOU CAN'T EVEN SEE THE MIRACLE HAPPENING ALL AROUND YOU--!

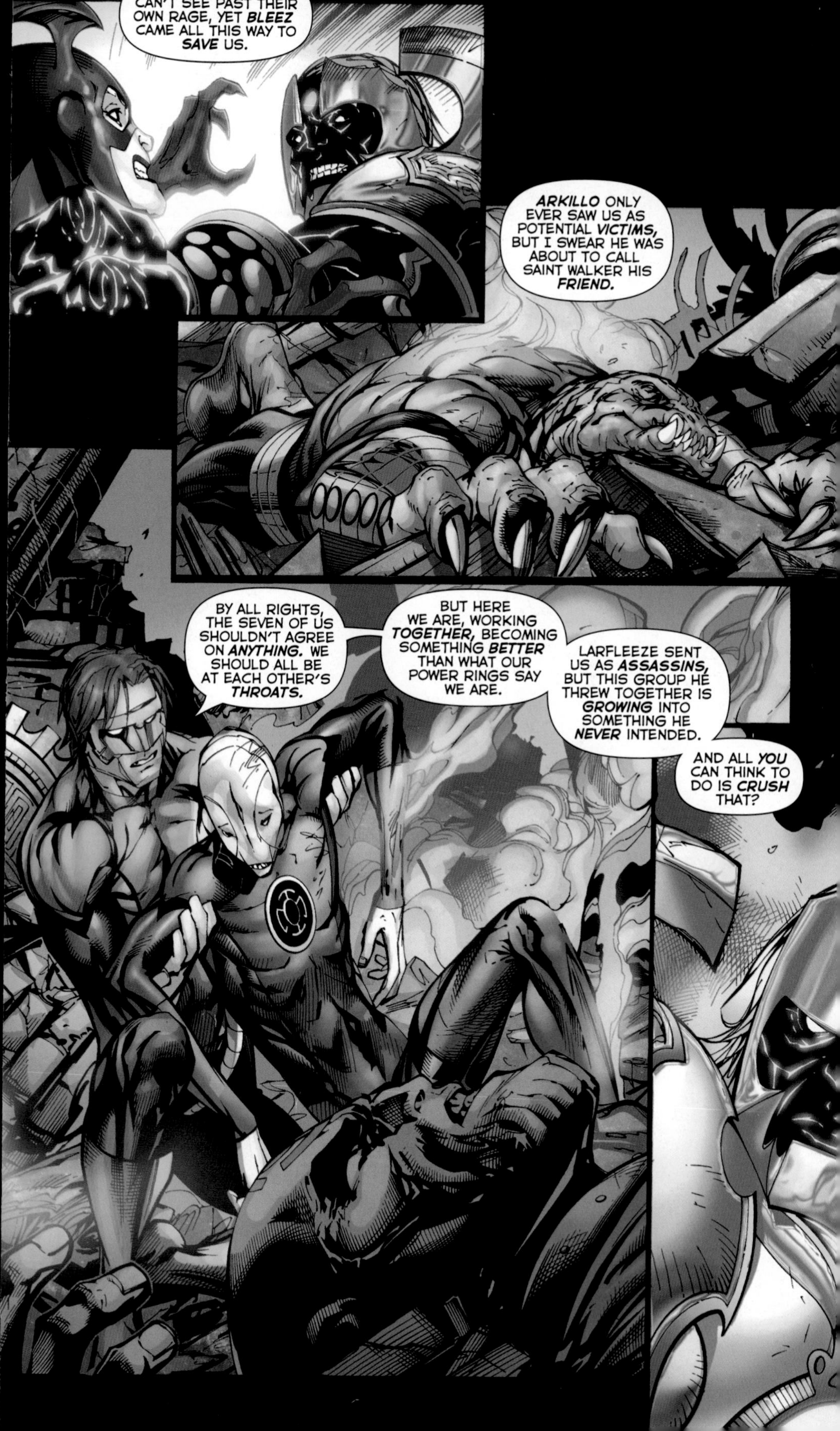
RED LANTERNS CAN'T SEE PAST THEIR OWN RAGE, YET BLEEZ CAME ALL THIS WAY TO SAVE US.
ARKILLO ONLY EVER SAW US AS POTENTIAL VICTIMS, BUT I SWEAR HE WAS ABOUT TO CALL SAINT WALKER HIS FRIEND.
BY ALL RIGHTS, THE SEVEN OF US SHOULDN'T AGREE ON ANYTHING. WE SHOULD ALL BE AT EACH OTHER'S THROATS.
BUT HERE WE ARE, WORKING TOGETHER, BECOMING SOMETHING BETTER THAN WHAT OUR POWER RINGS SAY WE ARE.
LARFLEEZE SENT US AS ASSASSINS, BUT THIS GROUP HE THREW TOGETHER IS GROWING INTO SOMETHING HE NEVER INTENDED.
AND ALL YOU CAN THINK TO DO IS CRUSH THAT?

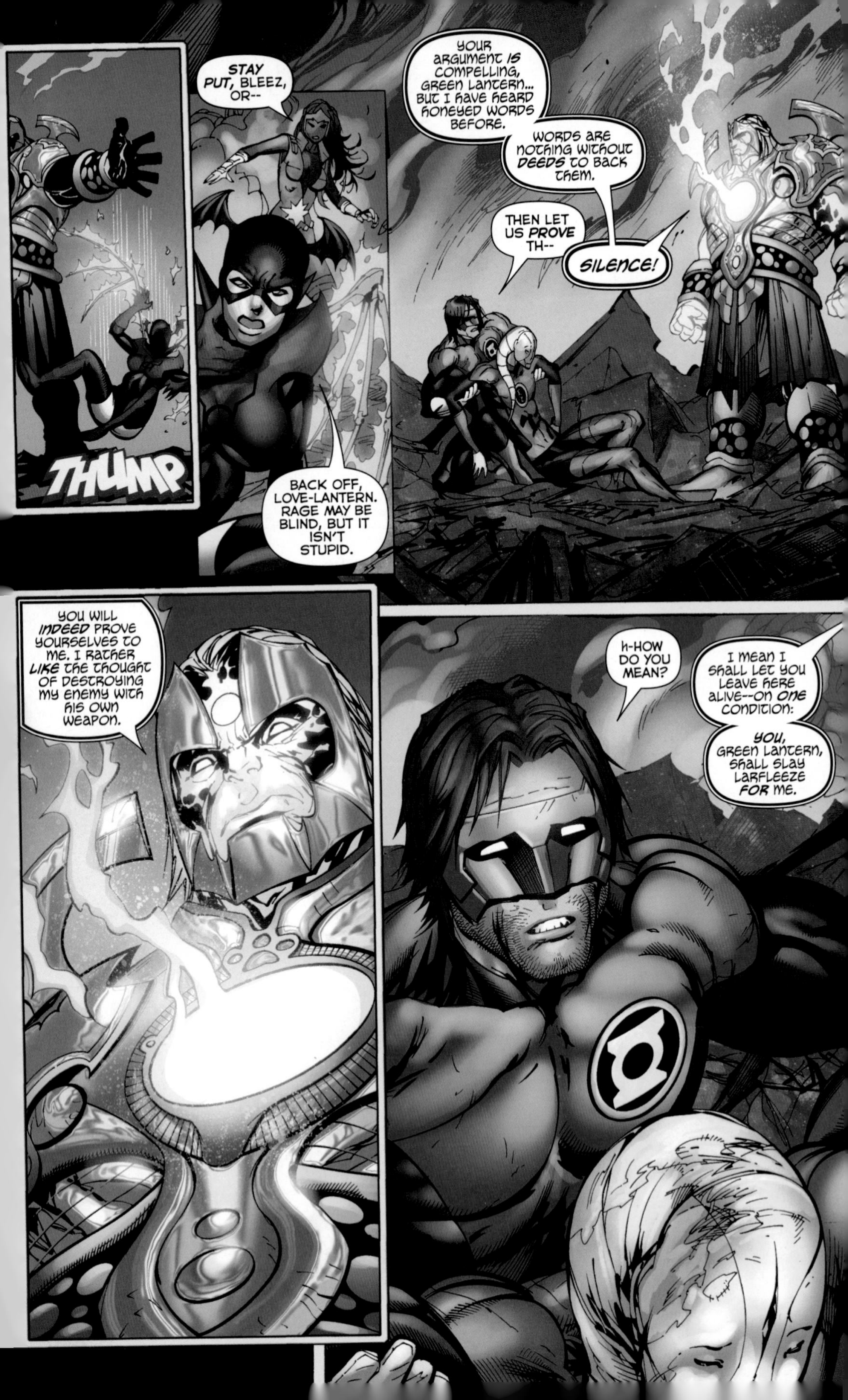
STAY PUT, BLEEZ, OR--
THUMP
BACK OFF, LOVE-LANTERN. RAGE MAY BE BLIND, BUT IT ISN'T STUPID.
YOUR ARGUMENT IS COMPELLING, GREEN LANTERN... BUT I HAVE HEARD HONEYED WORDS BEFORE.
WORDS ARE NOTHING WITHOUT DEEDS TO BACK THEM.
THEN LET US PROVE TH--
SILENCE!
YOU WILL INDEED PROVE YOURSELVES TO ME. I RATHER LIKE THE THOUGHT OF DESTROYING MY ENEMY WITH HIS OWN WEAPON.
H-HOW DO YOU MEAN?
I MEAN I SHALL LET YOU LEAVE HERE ALIVE--ON ONE CONDITION:
YOU, GREEN LANTERN, SHALL SLAY LARFLEEZE FOR ME.

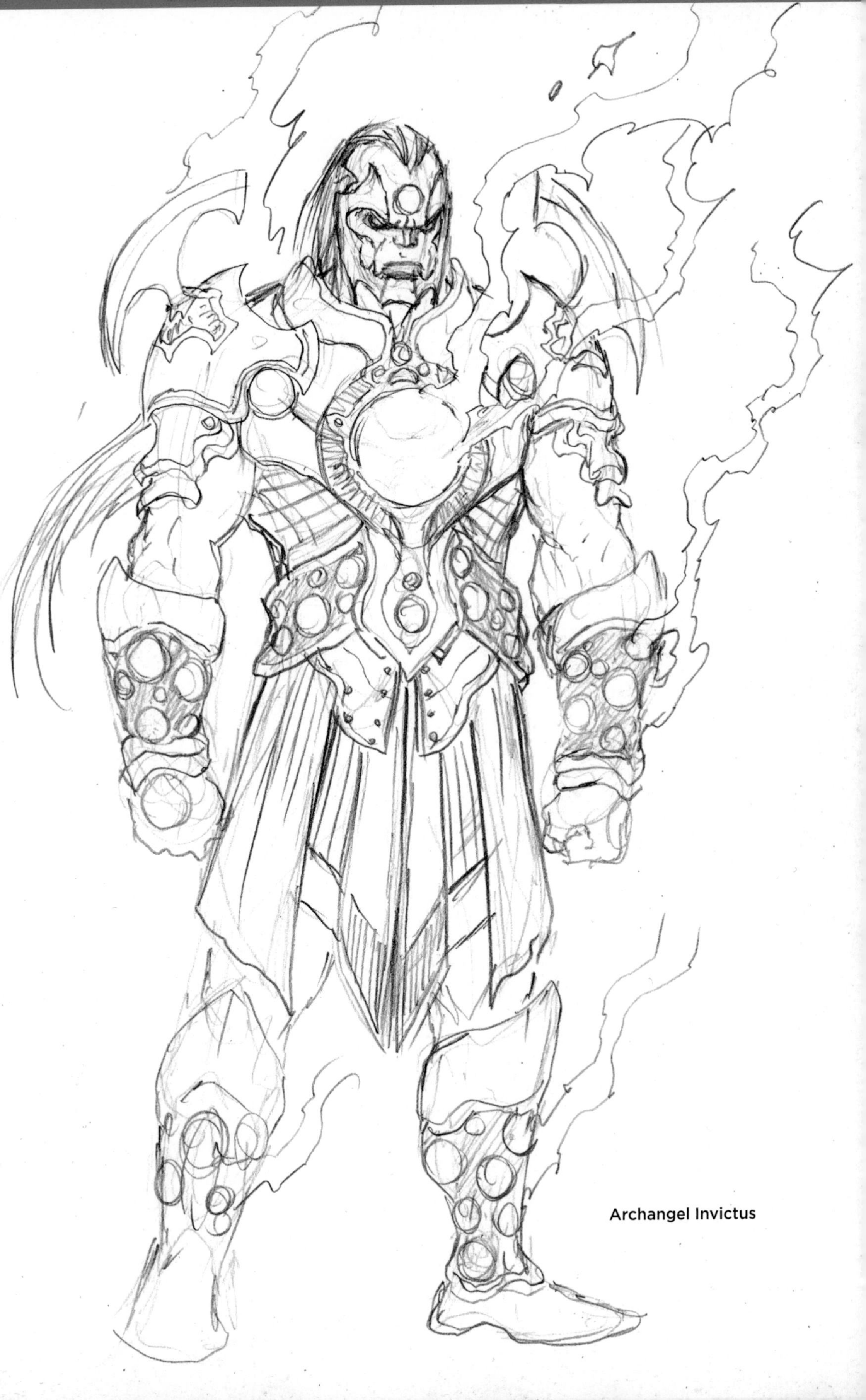

Archangel Invictus

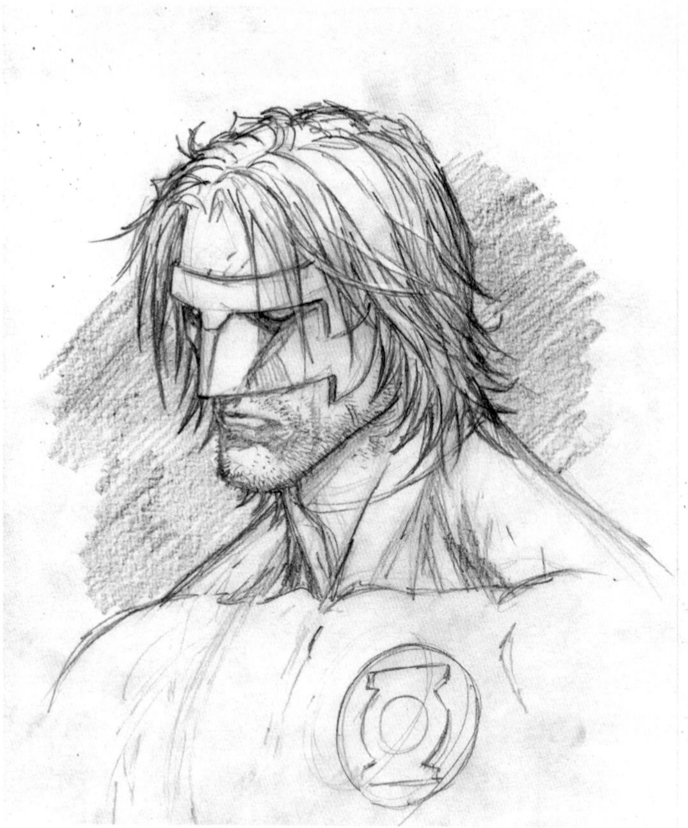

Kyle's new haircu

Fatality's redesign

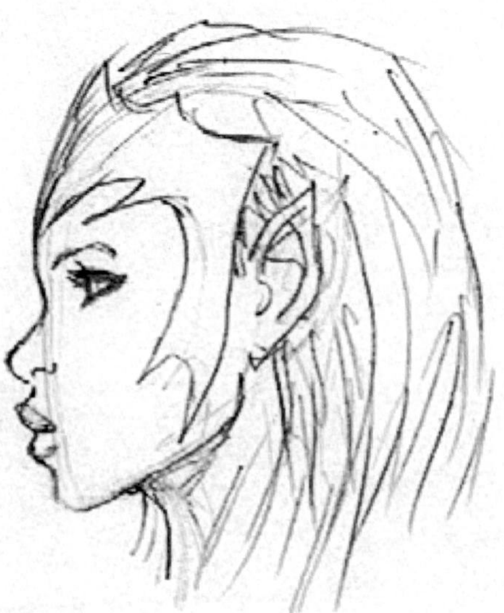

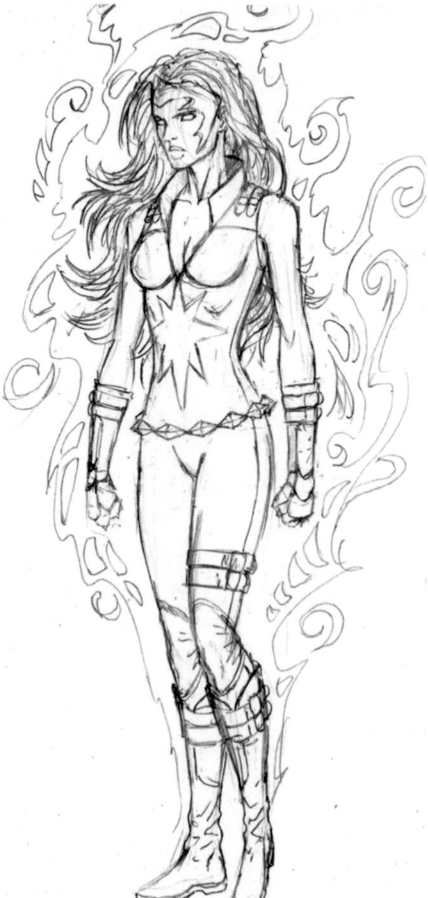

Bedard, Tony.
Green Lantern, new guardians.
Volume 1, The ring bearer